Zend Framework:
A Beginner's Guide

Vikram Vaswani

New York   Chicago   San Francisco
Lisbon   London   Madrid   Mexico City
Milan   New Delhi   San Juan
Seoul   Singapore   Sydney   Toronto

The *McGraw·Hill* Companies

Cataloging-in-Publication Data is on file with the Library of Congress

McGraw-Hill books are available at special quantity discounts to use as premiums and sales promotions, or for use in corporate training programs. To contact a representative, please e-mail us at bulksales@mcgraw-hill.com.

Zend Framework: A Beginner's Guide

1234567890 DOC DOC 109876543210

ISBN   978-0-07-163939-2
MHID   0-07-163939-X

Sponsoring Editor   Megg Morin
Editorial Supervisor   Patty Mon
Project Manager   Harleen Chopra, Glyph International
Acquisitions Coordinator   Joya Anthony
Technical Editor   Ryan Mauger
Copy Editor   Margaret Berson
Proofreader   Laura Bowman
Indexer   Ted Laux
Production Supervisor   Jean Bodeaux
Composition   Glyph International
Illustration   Glyph International
Art Director, Cover   Jeff Weeks
Cover Designer   Jeff Weeks

For Tonka, who keeps asking "Why?",
and Farah, who always knows the answer.

About the Author

Vikram Vaswani is the founder and CEO of Melonfire (**http://www.melonfire.com/**), a consultancy firm with special expertise in open-source tools and technologies. He has 12 years of experience working with PHP and MySQL as a Web application developer and product manager, and has created and deployed a variety of PHP applications for corporate intranets, high-traffic Internet Web sites, and mission-critical thin-client applications.

Vikram is also a passionate proponent of the open-source movement and is a regular contributor of articles and tutorials on PHP, MySQL, XML, and related tools to the community through his regular columns on the Zend Developer Zone and IBM DeveloperWorks. He is the author of Zend Technologies' well-regarded *PHP 101* series for PHP beginners, and his previous books include *MySQL: The Complete Reference* (**http://www.mysql-tcr.com/**), *How to Do Everything with PHP & MySQL* (**http://www.everythingphpmysql.com/**), *PHP Programming Solutions* (**http://www.php-programming-solutions.com/**), and *PHP: A Beginner's Guide* (**http://www.php-beginners-guide.com/**).

A Felix Scholar at the University of Oxford, England, Vikram combines his interest in Web application development with various other activities. When not dreaming up plans for world domination, he amuses himself by reading crime fiction, watching movies, playing squash, blogging, and keeping a wary eye out for Agent Smith. Read more about him and *Zend Framework: A Beginner's Guide* at **http://www.zf-beginners-guide.com**.

About the Technical Editor

Ryan Mauger is the Lead Developer for Lupimedia (**http://www.lupimedia.com/**), a multimedia design agency in Somerset, England that specializes in bespoke content management systems for design-oriented Web sites. Ryan is a keen Zend Framework supporter and contributor, and can often be found answering questions and guiding people on IRC (#channel). When not evangelizing the Zend Framework, Ryan is a proud father, and enjoys escaping to the lakes for a spot of fly fishing. Read more about him and his work at **http://www.rmauger.co.uk/**.

Contents

v

Foreword

The PHP ecosystem has changed dramatically in the past six years. Prior to PHP 5's advent, we PHP developers were primarily creating our projects on an ad-hoc basis, each project differing from its predecessor; if we paid attention, each project improved on the previous—but there was no guarantee. While tools and practices existed for managing code quality and standards, they were still maturing, and not in widespread use. The idea of using PHP as the basis for a stable, enterprise-worthy application was widely scoffed as a result—despite the fact that it was powering some of the most trafficked sites on the Web.

With the advent of PHP 5, we started seeing more of a focus on solid programming practices. With a revised and reworked object model, we now had a solid foundation on which to build our re-usable objects. Tools such as PHPUnit capitalized on the object model to simplify and enable solid testing practices. These in turn led to an increased look at where code quality fit in the PHP application life cycle.

It is from this ecosystem that PHP frameworks began to arise. While several began in PHP 4, the idea took off in PHP 5, and a handful of frameworks started taking over the landscape. These frameworks aim to provide best practices to their users, and repeatable, reusable structure for the applications they build.

Among these is Zend Framework. Zend Framework's mission, from its Web site, is simply this: Extending the art and spirit of PHP, Zend Framework is based on simplicity, object-oriented best practices, corporate-friendly licensing, and a rigorously tested agile codebase. Zend Framework is focused on building more secure, reliable, and modern Web 2.0 applications and Web services, and consuming widely available APIs.

In this book, you'll learn how Zend Framework approaches these goals, from an author who is both well-versed in the subject as well as a capable and clear technical writer. You'll get both thorough and understandable explanations as well as complete examples—and hopefully come away from reading with an appetite to develop your own applications using what has become the de facto standard in the industry: Zend Framework.

—Matthew Weier O'Phinney, Project Lead, Zend Framework

Acknowledgments

The Zend Framework is a complex piece of software, and writing a book about it is *not*—as I found out over the last eight months—a particularly simple task. Fortunately, I was aided in this process by a diverse and dynamic group of people, all of whom played an important part in getting this book into your hands.

First and foremost, a gigantic thank you to my wife, who supported me through the entire process and made sure I had a comfortable and stress-free working environment. I'm pretty sure this book would never have made it out into the world without her help. Thanks, babe!

The editorial and marketing team at McGraw-Hill deserves an honorable mention here as well. This is my sixth book with them and, as usual, they have been an absolute pleasure to work with. Acquisitions coordinator Joya Anthony, editorial supervisor Patty Mon, and executive editors Jane Brownlow and Megg Morin all guided this manuscript through the development process and played a huge role in turning it from pixels on a page to the polished and professional product you hold in your hands. I would like to thank them for their expertise, dedication, and efforts on my behalf.

I'd also like to single out Ryan Mauger, the technical editor for this book, for special praise. Ryan reviewed every line of code and applied his extensive knowledge of the Zend Framework to make the sure that the final product was both technically sound and reflective of current best practices. I'd like to thank him for his help and advice throughout the book-writing process. If you're ever in the market for a PHP expert, you can't do better than him!

Finally, for making the entire book-writing process more enjoyable than it usually is, thanks to: Patrick Quinlan, Ian Fleming, Bryan Adams, the Stones, Peter O'Donnell, *MAD Magazine,* Scott Adams, Gary Larson, VH1, Britney Spears, George Michael, Kylie Minogue, *Buffy the Vampire Slayer,* Farah Malegam, Stephen King, Shakira, Anahita Marker, John le Carre, The Saturdays, Barry White, Gwen Stefani, Ping Pong, Robert Crais, Robert B. Parker, Baz Luhrmann, Stefy, Anna Kournikova, John Connolly, Wasabi, Omega, Pidgin, Cal Evans, Ling's Pavilion, Tonka and his evil twin Bonka, Richelle Mead, Din Tai Fung, HBO, Mark Twain, Tim Burton, Harish Kamath, Madonna, John Sandford, *Dollhouse,* Iron Man, the London Tube, Dido, Google.com, *The Matrix,* Lee Child, Michael Connelly, Celio, Antonio Prohias, Quentin Tarantino, Alfred Hitchcock, Woody Allen, Kinokuniya, Percy Jackson, Jennifer Hudson, Mambo's and Tito's, Easyjet, Humphrey Bogart, Thai Pavilion, Wikipedia, Amazon.com, U2, Ubuntu, The Three Stooges, Pacha, Oscar Wilde, Hugh Grant, Alex Rider, Punch, Kelly Clarkson, Scott Turow, Slackware Linux, Calvin and Hobbes, Yo! Sushi, Blizzard Entertainment, Alfred Kropp, Otto, Pablo Picasso, Popeye and Olive Oyl, Dennis Lehane, Trattoria, Dire Straits, Bruce Springsteen, David Mitchell, *The West Wing,* Wagamama, Santana, Rod Stewart, and all my friends, at home and elsewhere.

Introduction

The Zend Framework is indeed, in the words of the immortal Ernest Hemingway, a "moveable feast." Conceived and implemented as a robust, feature-rich component library for PHP developers, it allows you to quickly and efficiently perform a variety of common application development tasks, including creating and validating form input, processing XML, generating dynamic menus, paginating data, working with Web services, and much, much more!

Perhaps the most important contribution of the Zend Framework, however, is that it has advanced the art of PHP development by introducing PHP developers to a more standardized and structured approach to PHP programming. This structured approach results in cleaner, more maintainable and more secure applications, and it's one of the key reasons that more and more developers are switching away from the older "ad-hoc" style of programming to the newer, framework-based approach.

For many novice PHP developers, though, the Zend Framework is a scary leap into the unknown. The Model-View-Controller pattern, the loosely coupled architecture, and the large number of available components often serve to befuddle developers who are used to "regular" procedural programming and find framework-based development too complex to understand.

That's where this book comes in. If you're one of the many millions of users who've heard about the Zend Framework and wondered what it could do for you, this is the book for you. It takes a close look at some of the Zend Framework's most important features—such as Model-View-Controller implementation, routing, input validation, internationalization, and caching—and shows you how to use them in a practical context. It also walks you through the process of building a complete Web application with the Zend Framework, starting with the basics and then adding in more complex features such as data pagination and sorting, user authentication, exception handling, localization, and Web services. In short, it gives you the knowledge you need to supercharge your PHP development by leveraging the power of the Zend Framework.

Who Should Read This Book

As you might have guessed from the title, *Zend Framework: A Beginner's Guide* is intended for users who are new to the Zend Framework. It assumes that you know the basics of PHP programming (including the new object model in PHP 5.x) and have some familiarity with HTML, CSS, SQL, XML, and JavaScript programming. If you're completely new to PHP, this is probably not the first book you should read—instead, consider working your way through the introductory PHP tutorials at **http://www.melonfire.com/community/columns/trog/** or purchasing a beginner guide such as *How to Do Everything with PHP & MySQL* (**http://www .everythingphpmysql.com/**) or *PHP: A Beginner's Guide* (**http://www.php-beginners-guide .com/**) and then returning to this book.

In order to work with the example application in this book, you will need a functioning PHP 5.x installation, ideally with an Apache 2.2.x Web server and a MySQL 5.x database server. You'll also need (obviously!) the latest version of the Zend Framework. Details on how to obtain and configure a PHP development environment are available in the Appendix of this book, while Chapter 1 covers the Zend Framework installation process in detail.

What This Book Covers

Since *Zend Framework: A Beginner's Guide* is aimed at users new to the Zend Framework, the first half of the book starts out by explaining basic concepts and solving fairly easy problems. Once you've gained familiarity with the basics of Zend Framework development, the second half of the book brings up more complex problems, such as internationalization and performance optimization, and illustrates possible solutions. This also means that you should read the chapters in order, since each chapter develops knowledge that you will need in subsequent chapters.

Here's a quick overview of what each chapter covers:

- **Chapter 1, "Introducing the Zend Framework,"** introduces the Zend Framework, explaining the benefits of framework-based development and walking you through the process of creating a new Zend Framework project.

- **Chapter 2, "Working with Models, Views, Controllers, and Routes"** discusses the basics of the Model-View-Controller (MVC) pattern and introduces you to important concepts like routing, global layouts, and modules.

- **Chapter 3, "Working with Forms,"** introduces the Zend_Form component, explaining how to programmatically create and validate Web forms, protect forms from attack, and control form error messages.

- **Chapter 4, "Working with Models,"** discusses the role of models in a Zend Framework application and introduces the Doctrine ORM toolkit and the Zend Framework bootstrapper.

- **Chapter 5, "Handling CRUD Operations,"** discusses how to integrate Doctrine models with Zend Framework controllers to implement the four common CRUD operations, add authentication to an application, and build a simple login/logout system.

- **Chapter 6, "Indexing, Searching, and Formatting Data,"** discusses data indexing and searching, and also demonstrates how to add support for multiple output types to a Zend Framework application.

- **Chapter 7, "Paging, Sorting, and Uploading Data,"** discusses how to paginate and sort database query results; filter and process file uploads; and read and write configuration files in INI and XML formats.

- **Chapter 8, "Logging and Debugging Exceptions,"** explains how the Zend Framework handles application-level exceptions and demonstrates how to add exception logging and filtering to a Zend Framework application.

- **Chapter 9, "Understanding Application Localization,"** discusses the various tools available in the Zend Framework to build a localized, multilingual application that can be easily "ported" to different countries and regions.

- **Chapter 10, "Working with News Feeds and Web Services,"** discusses how to use the Zend Framework to generate and read Atom or RSS news feeds; access third-party Web services using SOAP or REST; and allow developers to access your application using REST.

- **Chapter 11, "Working with User Interface Elements,"** discusses how to improve site navigation with menus, breadcrumbs, and sitemaps, and also explains the Zend Framework's Dojo integration with examples of an AJAX-enabled autocomplete form field and a pop-up calendar widget.

- **Chapter 12, "Optimizing Performance,"** discusses various techniques for measuring and improving Web application performance, including benchmarking, stress testing, code profiling, caching, and query optimization.

- **Appendix, "Installing and Configuring Required Software,"** guides you through the process of installing and configuring an Apache/PHP/MySQL development environment on Windows and Linux.

Conventions

This book uses different types of formatting to highlight special advice. Here's a list:

NOTE
Additional insight or information on the topic

TIP
A technique or trick to help you do things better

CAUTION
Something to watch out for

Ask the Expert

Q: A frequently asked question, …

A: … and its answer

In the code listings in this book, text highlighted in bold is a command to be entered at the prompt. For example, in the following listing

```
mysql> INSERT INTO movies (mtitle, myear) VALUES ('Rear Window', 1954);
Query OK, 1 row affected (0.06 sec)
```

the line in bold is a query that you would type in at the command prompt. You can use this as a guide to try out the commands in the book.

Companion Web Site

You can find the code for the example application discussed in this book at its companion Web site, **http://www.zf-beginners-guide.com/**. Code archives are organized by chapter, and may be directly downloaded and used in your Zend Framework development environment.

Chapter 1

Introducing the Zend Framework

Key Skills & Concepts

- Learn the benefits of framework-based development
- Understand the history and unique advances of the Zend Framework
- Understand the structure of a Zend Framework application
- Install and start using the Zend Framework

It's no exaggeration to say that PHP is today one of the most popular programming languages in the world, and the toolkit of choice for millions of Web application developers across the planet. According to recent statistics, the language is in use on more than 22 million Web sites and a third of the world's Web servers—no small feat, especially when you consider that PHP is developed and maintained entirely by a worldwide community of volunteers with no commercial backing whatsoever!

The reasons for PHP's popularity are not hard to understand. It's scalable, easily available, and plays well with third-party software. It uses clear, simple syntax and delights in non-obfuscated code, making it easy to learn and use and encouraging rapid application development. And it has a massive advantage over commercial programming toolkits, because it's available free of charge for a variety of platforms and architectures, including UNIX, Microsoft Windows, and Mac OS, under an open-source license.

Developers too report high levels of satisfaction with PHP. In an August 2009 study of ten scripting languages by Evans Data Corporation, PHP developers had the highest user satisfaction levels (followed closely by Ruby and Python users). In particular, PHP ranked highest for cross-platform compatibility, availability and quality of tools, and performance, and second highest for maintainability and readability, extensibility, ease of use, and security.

For organizations and independent developers, all these facts add up to just one thing: Using PHP saves both money and time. Building applications with PHP costs less, because the language can be used for a variety of purposes without payment of licensing fees or investment in expensive hardware or software. And using PHP also reduces development time without sacrificing quality, because of the easy availability of ready-made, robust, and community-tested widgets and extensions that developers can use to painlessly add new functions to the language.

Now, although it might not seem apparent at first glance, PHP's much-vaunted ease of use is both good and bad. It's good because unlike, say, C++ or Java, PHP programs are relatively easy to read and understand, and this encourages novice programmers to experiment with the language and pick up the basics without requiring intensive study. It's bad because PHP's corresponding lack of "strictness" can lull those same programmers into a false sense of security and encourage them to write applications for public consumption without awareness of the necessary standards for code quality, security, and reusability.

With this in mind, there's been a concerted and visible effort in the PHP community over the last few years to move from ad-hoc "anything goes" programming to a more standardized, framework-oriented approach. Not only does this approach make it easier to get up and running when building a PHP application from scratch, but it produces cleaner, more consistent, and more secure application code. This chapter, and the remainder of this book, introduces you to one such framework, the Zend Framework, which provides a flexible and scalable approach to building PHP applications for serious developers.

Overview

In the words of its official Web site (**http://framework.zend.com/**), the Zend Framework is "an open source framework for developing web applications and services with PHP 5 […] based on simplicity, object-oriented best practices, corporate friendly licensing, and a rigorously tested agile codebase." It provides a comprehensive set of tools to build and deploy PHP-based Web applications, with built-in APIs for common functions like security, input validation, data caching, database and XML operations, and internationalization.

Unlike many other frameworks, the Zend Framework uses a "loosely coupled" architecture. Simply put, this means that although the framework itself consists of numerous components, these components are largely independent and have minimal links to each other. This loosely coupled architecture helps in producing lightweight applications, because developers can choose to use only the specific components they need for the task at hand. So, for example, developers looking to add authentication or caching to their application can directly make use of the Zend_Auth or Zend_Cache components, without needing the rest of the framework.

The Zend Framework also provides a complete implementation of the Model-View-Controller (MVC) pattern, which allows application business logic to be separated from the user interface and data models. This pattern is recommended for applications of medium to large complexity and is commonly used for Web application development, as it encourages code reusability and produces a more manageable code structure. Zend Framework's implementation of the MVC pattern is discussed in detail in Chapter 2.

The Zend Framework is created and maintained by Zend Technologies, a commercial software vendor whose founders, Andi Gutmans and Zeev Suraski, were also responsible for the first major rewrite of the PHP parser, released as PHP 3.0 in 1997. The first version of the Zend Framework, v1.0, was released in July 2007 and contained 35 core components, including components for caching, authentication, configuration management, database access, RSS and Atom feed generation, and localization.

Since then, the framework has been through numerous iterations with the most recent release, v1.10, now containing more than 65 components that support (among other things) Adobe's Action Message Format (AMF), Google's GData APIs, and Amazon's EC2 and SQS Web services. Fortunately, the increase in the number of components has been accompanied by a corresponding increase in documentation—the manual for Zend Framework v1.9 (circa 2009) weighs in at 3.7MB, as compared to the 780KB manual that shipped with Zend Framework v1.0 in 2007.

Although Zend Technologies operates commercially in a number of different markets, it makes the Zend Framework available to the public as an open-source project under the BSD License, thereby allowing it to be freely used in proprietary commercial products without the payment of a license fee. This "business-friendly" licensing policy has made the Zend Framework popular with both corporate and individual users. Startups, Fortune 500 companies, independent developers, and PHP hobbyists are all fans of the project—as of this writing, the Zend Framework has been downloaded more than 10 million times and there are more than 400 open-source projects that are either based on, or extend, the Zend Framework.

A vibrant, enthusiastic developer community can be found swapping bug patches and tips on the mailing list and wiki, with additional support coming from the online manual and reference guide. The community is also encouraged to "give back" to the framework by submitting new components—there are currently over 500 independent contributors to the project—so long as the contributions meet Zend's requirements for documentation and unit testing.

Features

You might be wondering why using the Zend Framework is a better idea than simply rolling your own code, the way you're used to right now. Well, here are some reasons.

Standards Compliance and Best Practices

Unlike some other programming languages, PHP doesn't enforce a common coding standard. As a result, the manner in which PHP applications are written differs significantly from developer to developer, making it hard to ensure project-wide consistency. PHP's relative lack of "strictness" can also produce code that fails to adhere to best practices, rendering it vulnerable to attack.

The Zend Framework, on the other hand, incorporates current thinking on best practices, provides a standard filesystem layout, and provides built-in support for common application development tasks such as input validation and sanitization. Therefore, using it as the basis for a PHP project automatically produces higher-quality code and an application that's more forward-leaning on security issues. Additionally, because the Zend Framework is well-documented, developers joining the project team at a later date will have a much shorter learning curve and can begin contributing to the project faster.

Reusability

The Zend Framework is completely object-oriented and makes full use of the new object model in PHP 5.x. This object-oriented programming (OOP) architecture encourages code reusability, allowing developers to significantly reduce the time spent writing duplicate code. This fact is particularly important in the context of Web applications, which often need to expose multiple interfaces to their data. Suppose, for example, that you wish to build an XML interface to your application's existing search engine functionality. With the Zend Framework, this is as simple as defining a new view that takes care of reformatting controller output in XML. It's not necessary to rewrite any of the existing controller logic, and the entire process is transparent and easy to accomplish.

Internationalization

As a project that is intended for use in Web application development, it would be unusual indeed if the Zend Framework did not include comprehensive support for application internationalization and localization. The Zend_Locale component allows for application-level control over the user's locale, while the Zend_Translate component makes it possible to support multilingual applications that include Latin, Chinese, and European character sets. Other useful components include Zend_Date and Zend_Currency, for localized date/time and currency formatting.

Open Source

The Zend Framework is an open-source project. Although the project is sponsored by Zend Technologies, much of the development is handled by a worldwide team of volunteers who take care of fixing bugs and adding new features. Zend Technologies provides direction to the project, as well as a group of "master engineers" who make decisions on what gets included in the final product. As noted earlier, the framework may be used without payment of licensing fees or investments in expensive hardware or software. This reduces software development costs without affecting either flexibility or reliability. The open-source nature of the code further means that any developer, anywhere, can inspect the code tree, spot errors, and suggest possible fixes; this produces a stable, robust product wherein bugs, once discovered, are rapidly resolved—often within a few hours of discovery!

Community Support

Looking for a way to integrate Flickr photostreams or Google Maps data into your application? Try the Zend_Service_Flickr or Zend_Gdata components. Need to communicate with a Flash application using Adobe Action Message Format (AMF)? Reach for the Zend_Amf component. Need to quickly integrate an RSS feed into your application? Zend_Feed has everything you need.

As these examples illustrate, one of the nice things about a community-supported project like the Zend Framework is the access it offers to the creativity and imagination of hundreds of developers across the world. The Zend Framework is composed of a large number of independent components that developers can use to painlessly add new functionality to their PHP project. Using these components is usually a more time- and cost-efficient alternative to rolling your own code.

Unique Advantages

Now, one might well argue that the features listed above apply to all PHP frameworks, not just the Zend Framework. However, the Zend Framework does possess some unique features that give it an edge over the competition.

Loose Coupling

Unlike many other frameworks, where the individual pieces of the framework are closely linked with each other, the components of the Zend Framework can be easily separated and used on an "as needed" basis. So, while the Zend Framework certainly includes everything you need to build a modern, MVC-compliant Web application, it doesn't force you to do so—you're just as welcome to pull out any of the individual library components and integrate them into your non-MVC application. This *loose coupling* helps reduce the footprint of your application and preserves flexibility for future changes.

Rapid Release Cycle

The Zend Framework team follows an aggressive release schedule, with an average of between one and three releases each month. In addition to these stable releases, there are also previews and release candidates, which serve to give the community a heads-up on what to expect while the final release is being prepared. These frequent releases serve not only to keep the project moving forward, but to ensure that bugs are picked up and resolved as quickly as possible. Developers can also access "bleeding edge" code from the project's public Subversion repository.

Unit Testing Policy

Given that the Zend Framework is a loosely coupled set of components that are subject to ongoing development, unit testing assumes particular importance to ensure that components continue working correctly and the code base remains stable throughout multiple release cycles. The Zend Framework has a strict unit testing policy, which dictates that components can only be added to the framework if they are accompanied by a reasonably complete and working collection of unit tests (written under the PHPUnit testing framework). This policy ensures that backward compatibility is maintained between releases and regressions are readily visible.

Code-Generation Tools

Zend Framework includes a "tooling" feature that allows developers to get a new Zend Framework project up and running with minimal effort. This feature, implemented as a command-line script built on top of the Zend_Tool component, takes care of creating the base filesystem layout for a new project and populating it with an initial set of controllers, views, and actions. Developers can use this tooling script as a convenient shortcut to quickly create new project objects as development progresses.

Market Credibility

The Zend Framework is sponsored by Zend Technologies, one of the best-known software companies in the PHP space. The company produces a number of commercial products for enterprise use and has a long track record of creating successful and innovative products for PHP developers, such as Zend Server, a PHP Web application server for business-critical applications, and Zend Studio, an integrated IDE for PHP application development. Zend Technologies' customers include IBM, McAfee, FOX Interactive Media, Lockheed Martin, SalesForce.com, NASA, and Bell Canada; as such, its support of the Zend Framework ensures immediate credibility in the marketplace and serves as a useful tool when convincing clients and/or senior managers to take the leap into framework-based development.

Third-Party Application Interoperability

Zend Technologies' market position as one of the leading vendors of enterprise PHP solutions has allowed it to garner broad industry support for the Zend Framework. Zend Framework includes native support for many third-party tools and technologies, including Adobe Action Message Format (AMF), the Google Data APIs, the Dojo Toolkit, Microsoft CardSpace, and Web services from Amazon, Yahoo!, Twitter, Flickr, Technorati, and Del.icio.us.

That's not all. One of PHP's strengths has historically been its support for a wide range of different databases, file formats, and protocols. The Zend Framework provides a common API for accessing MySQL, PostgreSQL, Oracle, and Microsoft SQL Server databases (among others) via its Zend_Db components, and also includes components for sending and receiving email using the SMTP, IMAP, and POP3 protocols; building Web services using the SOAP and REST protocols; encoding and decoding JSON data; parsing feeds in Atom and RSS formats; and creating and manipulating PDF documents.

Commercial Support Options

The Zend Framework is "free"—users can download and use it at no cost under the terms of the BSD License, but by the same token, users are expected to support themselves via community tools such as mailing lists and wikis. For companies and individuals looking for a greater level of support, Zend Technologies offers commercial support and training packages, consultancy services from Zend engineers, and proprietary PHP development and deployment tools that can help speed and optimize Zend Framework development. For many business organizations, this ability to access technical support, albeit at a fee, is a key reason for selecting the Zend Framework as their application toolkit of choice. There's also the Zend Framework Certification program, which provides a measure of an individual developer's Zend Framework skills, and is recognized throughout the industry as an indicator of his or her Zend Framework competence.

Extensive Documentation

The Zend Framework comes with extensive documentation for the 60+ components included with the core distribution. This documentation includes a programmer's reference guide containing more than 1000 pages; a "quick start" guide for experienced developers; detailed API documents; video tutorials; webinars; and podcasts by well-known Zend engineers. This wide range of learning materials can significantly reduce the learning curve for both novice and experienced programmers and it is, in fact, one of the key areas where Zend Framework surpasses competing PHP frameworks.

Application Environment

All Zend Framework applications are also PHP applications and can run in any PHP-capable environment. This environment typically consists of at least the following three components:

- A base operating system, usually either Linux or Microsoft Windows

- A Web server, usually Apache on Linux or Internet Information Services on Microsoft Windows, to intercept HTTP requests and either serve them directly or pass them on to the PHP interpreter for execution

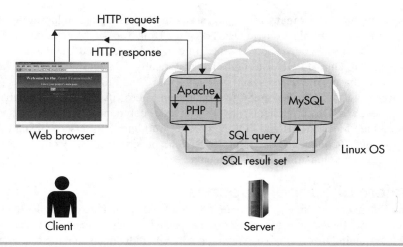

Figure 1-1 The components of a typical PHP application environment

- A PHP interpreter to parse and execute PHP code, and return the results to the Web server

  There's also often a fourth *optional but very useful* component:

- A database engine, such as MySQL or PostgreSQL, that holds application data, accepts connections from the PHP layer, and modifies or retrieves data from the database

  Figure 1-1 illustrates the interaction between these components.

  It's worth noting that the Linux/Apache/PHP/MySQL combination is extremely popular with developers, and is colloquially referred to as the "LAMP stack." The LAMP stack is popular because all its components are open-source projects and, as such, can be downloaded from the Internet at no charge. As a general principle, there are also no fees or charges associated with using these components for either personal or commercial purposes, or for developing and distributing applications that use them. If you do intend to write commercial applications, however, it's a good idea to review the licensing terms that are associated with each of these components; typically, you will find these on the component's Web site as well as in the product archive.

Installing the Zend Framework

Now that you know a little bit about the Zend Framework, let's dive right into actually building applications in it. As a necessary first step, you must first ensure that you have a working Apache/PHP/MySQL development environment. The appendix of this book has detailed instructions for obtaining these components, for installing them, and for testing your development environment to ensure that it's working correctly, so flip ahead and come back here once you're ready.

All done? The next step is to download and install the Zend Framework to your development environment. Visit the official Zend Framework Web site at **http://framework**

.zend.com/ and get a copy of the most recent release of the software. Zend Technologies makes two versions of the package available: a "minimal" version, which contains just the standard libraries and command-line tools, and a "full" version, which contains additional documentation, examples, unit tests, and third-party toolkits. The full version is recommended.

Once you've downloaded the code archive, extract its contents to a temporary area on the file system.

```
shell> cd /tmp
shell> tar -xzvf ZendFramework-XX.tar.gz
```

You should end up with a directory structure that looks something like Figure 1-2.

Of all these directories, the two you'll need immediately are the *library/* and *bin/* directories. The *library/* directory contains all the Zend Framework components, while the *bin/* directory contains command-line tools that are helpful in initializing a new project and adding objects to it. These two directories need to be manipulated as follows:

- The contents of the *library/* directory should be moved to a location in your PHP "include path" list. On UNIX/Linux systems, good possible locations for this are */usr/local/lib/php* or */usr/local/share/php*. On Windows, consider using your PHP or PEAR installation directory, such as *C:\Program Files\PHP* or *C:\Program Files\PHP\PEAR*. Note that in case the target directory is not already part of your PHP "include path" list, you must add it before proceeding.

- The contents of the *bin/* directory should be moved to a location in your system's executable path. If the directory containing your PHP binary—typically */usr/local/bin* on UNIX/Linux or *C:\PHP* on Windows—is already part of your system's executable path, then that is usually the ideal location to use. Alternatively, move the contents of the *bin/* directory to any other location you find convenient, always remembering to add that location to your system's executable path list.

NOTE

The *bin/* directory contains three scripts: *zf.sh*, the command-line interface for UNIX/Linux; *zf.bat*, the command-line interface for Windows; and *zf.php*, the main "worker" script. On UNIX/Linux, you will need to make the *zf.sh* script executable with the `chmod` command; you may also wish to rename or alias it to make it easier to access.

Figure 1-2   The contents of a Zend Framework release archive

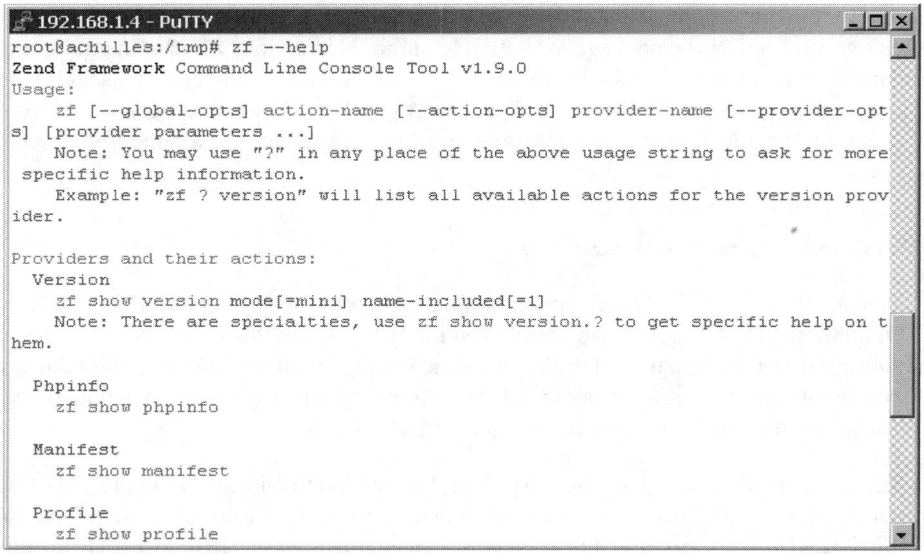

```
192.168.1.4 - PuTTY                                                    _ □ ×
root@achilles:/tmp# zf --help
Zend Framework Command Line Console Tool v1.9.0
Usage:
    zf [--global-opts] action-name [--action-opts] provider-name [--provider-opt
s] [provider parameters ...]
    Note: You may use "?" in any place of the above usage string to ask for more
 specific help information.
    Example: "zf ? version" will list all available actions for the version prov
ider.

Providers and their actions:
  Version
    zf show version mode[=mini] name-included[=1]
    Note: There are specialties, use zf show version.? to get specific help on t
hem.

  Phpinfo
    zf show phpinfo

  Manifest
    zf show manifest

  Profile
    zf show profile
```

Figure 1-3 The output of the `zf --help` command

Here are examples of commands you can use to perform these tasks:

```
shell> cd ZendFramework-XX
shell> mv library/* /usr/local/lib/php/
shell> mv bin/* /usr/local/bin/
shell> chmod +x  /usr/local/bin/zf.sh
shell> ln -s /usr/local/bin/zf.sh /usr/local/bin/zf
```

You should now be able to access the *zf* command-line script from your shell prompt, on both Linux and Windows. Try this by issuing the following command at your shell prompt:

```
shell> zf —help
```

If all is working as it should, you should be presented with a list of options. Figure 1-3 illustrates the output on Linux.

Try This 1-1 Starting a New Project

Once you've got the Zend Framework installed and the *zf* command-line script working, you're ready to start creating applications with it. The following steps discuss how to accomplish this task.

Understand Application Requirements

Before diving into the code, it's worthwhile spending a few minutes understanding the example application you'll be building in the first half of this book. The application is the Web site of a fictional store that specializes in the sale of rare postal stamps to hobbyists and professional philatelists. Unlike other hobbyist stores, though, this one has an interesting twist: It functions as an online stamp sourcing agency, allowing individual collectors to upload pictures and descriptions of stamps they may have for sale into a central database, and letting buyers search this stamp database by country, year, and keyword. In the event of a match, the store will purchase the stamp from the seller and resell it to the buyer…at a hefty commission, naturally!

Designated site moderators would have direct access to the uploaded listings, and would manually approve suitable ones for display in search results. Moderators would also have access to a simple content management system for news and press releases; this information would be accessible both via the Web site and as an RSS feed. And just to make things interesting, the stamp database would also be available via a SOAP interface, to facilitate integration with third-party applications.

Sounds funky? It is. And it even has a cool name: the Stamp Query and Research Engine or, as its friends like to call it, SQUARE.

The SQUARE example application is conceived such that it covers common requirements encountered in day-to-day application development: static pages, input forms, image upload, login-protected administration panel, data paging and sorting, multiple output types, and keyword search. Implementing these features requires one to understand the nitty-gritties of form processing, input validation, session management, authentication and security, CRUD database operations, Web service APIs, and integration with third-party libraries. As such, it should be a good starting point to begin understanding application development with the Zend Framework.

Create the Application Directory

Let's get started. Change to the Web server's document root directory (typically */usr/local/ apache/htdocs* on UNIX/Linux or *C:\Program Files\Apache\htdocs* on Windows) and create a new subdirectory for the application. For reasons that have been explained in the preceding section, name this directory *square/*.

```
shell> cd /usr/local/apache/htdocs
shell> mkdir square
```

This directory will be referenced throughout this book as *$APP_DIR*.

Create the Application Skeleton

The next step is to initialize the application and create the basic files and directories needed for a skeletal Zend Framework application. The *zf* command-line script can do this for you automatically—simply change to *$APP_DIR* and run the following command (see Figure 1-4):

```
shell> cd /usr/local/apache/htdocs/square
shell> zf create project.
```

(continued)

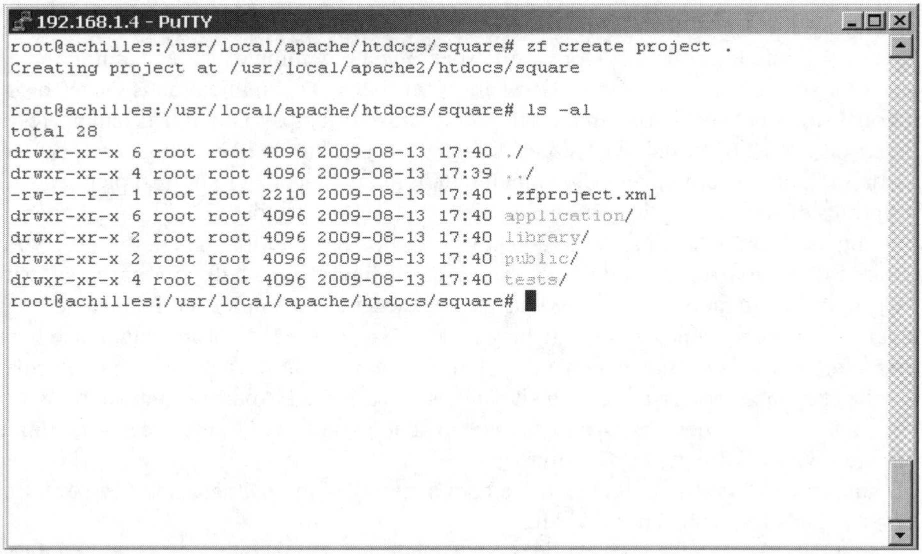

192.168.1.4 - PuTTY
root@achilles:/usr/local/apache/htdocs/square# zf create project .
Creating project at /usr/local/apache2/htdocs/square
root@achilles:/usr/local/apache/htdocs/square# ls -al
total 28
drwxr-xr-x 6 root root 4096 2009-08-13 17:40 ./
drwxr-xr-x 4 root root 4096 2009-08-13 17:39 ../
-rw-r--r-- 1 root root 2210 2009-08-13 17:40 .zfproject.xml
drwxr-xr-x 6 root root 4096 2009-08-13 17:40 application/
drwxr-xr-x 2 root root 4096 2009-08-13 17:40 library/
drwxr-xr-x 2 root root 4096 2009-08-13 17:40 public/
drwxr-xr-x 4 root root 4096 2009-08-13 17:40 tests/
root@achilles:/usr/local/apache/htdocs/square#

Figure 1-4 The output of the `zf create project` command

The script will now create an empty application container and populate it with an initial set of files. Once the process is complete, you'll see a number of new subdirectories in the application directory, as shown in Figure 1-5.

This is the default directory structure for Zend Framework applications. Each directory serves a different purpose, as discussed in the following list:

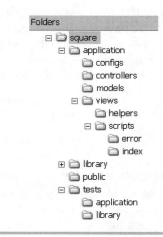

- *$APP_DIR/application/* is the main application directory, which contains all the application code, including controllers, views, and models.
- *$APP_DIR/library/* holds third-party libraries and classes used by the application. If you decide to bundle the Zend Framework with your application (see the next section), this is where you'll put it.
- *$APP_DIR/public/* holds publicly accessible content, such as image and media files, CSS style sheets, JavaScript code, and other static resources.
- *$APP_DIR/tests/* holds unit tests for the application.

Folders
square
application
configs
controllers
models
views
helpers
scripts
error
index
library
public
tests
application
library

Figure 1-5 The default directory structure for a new Zend Framework application

Add Zend Framework Libraries

At this point, you have an important decision to make. You must decide whether to include the Zend Framework libraries with your application, or leave it up to users to download and install these libraries themselves. There are pros and cons to each option, as follows:

● Requiring users to download the Zend Framework libraries themselves ensures that they always have access to the latest code (and bug fixes). However, the process can be intimidating for novice users, and if the newer libraries are not backward-compatible with the original versions used, unusual and hard-to-track bugs could appear.

● Bundling the Zend Framework libraries with the application ensures that users can begin using the application out of the box, with no version incompatibilities. However, it also "locks in" users to a particular version of the Zend Framework, possibly making it harder to upgrade to newer versions with additional features or necessary bug fixes.

For purposes of this book, I'll assume that the Zend Framework libraries will be bundled with the application. Therefore, copy the contents of the Zend Framework *library/* directory to *$APP_DIR/library/*, as you did earlier in the chapter, using the following command. The default application settings are to automatically look in this location for libraries to be included.

```
shell> cp -R /usr/local/lib/php/Zend library/
```

Define Virtual Host Settings

To make it easier to access the application, it's a good idea to define a new virtual Web host and point it to the application's public directory. This is an optional but recommended step, as it helps simulate a "live" environment and presents application resources (URLs) as they would appear to users in a public environment.

Assuming you're using the Apache Web server, you can set up a named virtual host for the application by editing the Apache configuration file (*httpd.conf* or *httpd-vhosts.conf*) and adding the following lines to it:

```
NameVirtualHost *:80
<VirtualHost *:80>
    DocumentRoot "/usr/local/apache/htdocs/square/public"
    ServerName square.localhost
</VirtualHost>
```

These lines define a new virtual host, **http://square.localhost/**, whose document root corresponds to the *$APP_DIR/public/* directory. Restart the Web server to activate these new settings. Note that if you're on a network, it might be necessary to update your network's local DNS server to let it know about the new host as well.

(continued)

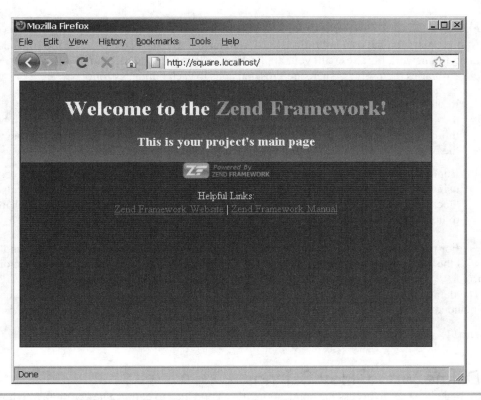

Figure 1-6 The default application index page

Once these steps are complete, pop open your Web browser and browse to the virtual host that you just set up, by entering the URL **http://square.localhost/**. If you see a Zend Framework welcome page, like the one shown in Figure 1-6, pat yourself on the back, because you just got a complete (albeit extremely simple) Zend Framework application up and running!

Using the Command-Line Tool

As illustrated in the previous section, the *zf* command-line script allows you to perform a number of different operations. For example, drop to your command prompt and issue the following command:

```
shell> zf show version
```

Ask the Expert

Q: Can I use the Zend Framework in a shared hosting environment, where I'm likely to have limited or no control over global PHP configuration directives like the PHP "include path"?

A: Yes, absolutely. There are a couple of ways to accomplish this:

- If you're simply concerned about using Zend Framework classes in your application, all you need to do is copy the *library/Zend* directory to your home area, and then use the `ini_set()` function to dynamically add this location to your PHP include path in your application scripts.

- If you'd like to use the *zf* command-line script, you should also copy the *bin/* directory to your home area (at the same level as the *library/* directory). You should then be able to invoke the *zf* command-line script as usual, by prepending the complete filesystem path to the script name. This will work because, if the Zend Framework cannot be found in the PHP include path, the *zf* command-line script will also look for a *library/Zend* directory one level above it in the current directory hierarchy and use it if available. Alternatively, you can explicitly tell the *zf* command-line script where to find your Zend Framework installation, by setting the `ZEND_TOOL_INCLUDE_PATH_PREPEND` environment variable to the appropriate location.

This command displays the version number of the currently installed Zend Framework release. Figure 1-7 and Figure 1-8 illustrate the output on Linux and Windows, respectively.

You can also try the following command to retrieve complete `phpinfo()` information:

```
shell> zf show phpinfo
```

The *zf* command-line tool also provides a quick and easy way to view the current "profile" of your application. This profile contains a hierarchical list of the current contents of your application, with descriptions of the files within it, and it's a great way to get a fast bird's-eye view of the application without manually drilling down into each directory.

Figure 1-7   The output of the `zf show version` command on Linux

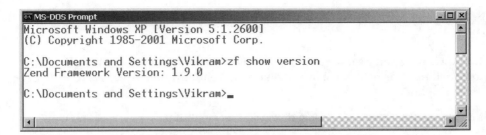

Figure 1-8 The output of the zf show version command on Windows

Try it out by changing directories to *$APP_DIR* and executing the following command:

```
shell> zf show profile
```

Figure 1-9 illustrates the output on Linux.

```
192.168.1.4 - PuTTY
root@achilles:/usr/local/apache/htdocs/square# zf show profile
ProjectDirectory
    ProjectProfileFile
    ApplicationDirectory
        ConfigsDirectory
            ApplicationConfigFile
        ControllersDirectory
            ControllerFile
                ActionMethod
            ControllerFile
        ModelsDirectory
        ViewsDirectory
            ViewScriptsDirectory
                ViewControllerScriptsDirectory
                    ViewScriptFile
                ViewControllerScriptsDirectory
                    ViewScriptFile
            ViewHelpersDirectory
        BootstrapFile
    LibraryDirectory
    PublicDirectory
        PublicIndexFile
        HtaccessFile
    TestsDirectory
        TestPHPUnitConfigFile
        TestApplicationDirectory
            TestApplicationBootstrapFile
        TestLibraryDirectory
            TestLibraryBootstrapFile
```

Figure 1-9 An example project profile

Summary

This chapter provided a gentle introduction to the world of Zend Framework development, introducing you to the project and illustrating some of its unique features and advantages vis-à-vis competing alternatives. It also guided you through the process of installing the Zend Framework and using the command-line tool to start a new project. These basic skills will serve you well as you move to the next chapter, which discusses core application development concepts and gets you started with building a framework-based Web application.

If you'd like to learn more about the topics discussed in this chapter, you'll find the following links useful:

- The official Zend Framework Web site, at
  http://framework.zend.com/

- The Zend Framework community wiki, at
  http://framework.zend.com/wiki/

- Zend Framework usage statistics, at
  http://framework.zend.com/about/numbers

- Zend Framework case studies, at
  http://framework.zend.com/about/casestudies

- Zend Framework components, at
  http://framework.zend.com/about/components

- The Zend Framework CLI tool, at
  http://framework.zend.com/manual/en/zend.tool.framework.clitool.html

- The Zend Framework filesystem layout, at
  http://framework.zend.com/wiki/display/ZFDEV/Choosing+Your+Application%27s+Directory+Layout

- The Zend Framework development roadmap, at
  http://framework.zend.com/roadmap

Chapter 2

Working with Models, Views, Controllers, and Routes

Key Skills & Concepts

- Understand the basics of the Model-View-Controller pattern

- Find out how URL requests are handled in a Zend Framework application

- Gain the benefits of a modular directory layout

- Define and apply a global template to application views

- Create custom routes for application resources

- Learn to serve static content pages

T he preceding chapter gave you a gentle introduction to the Zend Framework, by guiding you through the process of installing the framework and starting a new project. You now need to start fleshing out the application skeleton with code that makes it functional. This chapter will help you to do so, by introducing you to the fundamental design principles of a Zend Framework application and then applying this knowledge to the task of building a real-world application. So without further ado, let's jump straight in!

Understanding Basic Concepts

When you are developing a PHP application, the typical approach is to embed PHP code into one or more HTML documents using special delimiters. This makes it easy to construct dynamic Web pages containing programming constructs like variables and function calls; simply alter the values of the variables embedded within the HTML code, and the content displayed on the page changes appropriately.

As every application developer knows, however, this convenience comes at a price. The approach described in the previous paragraph produces PHP scripts that are so closely interwoven with HTML code that maintaining them is a nightmare. Since the same physical file usually contains both HTML interface elements and PHP code, developers and interface designers must coordinate with each other to make changes. The most common example of this is when interface designers need to alter the look and feel of a Web application—typically, the changes they make to the HTML code must be monitored by a developer to ensure the integrity of the embedded business logic.

This type of arrangement is easily recognized by its most visible symptom: a bunch of harried developers and designers clustered around a single computer arguing with each other as they take turns at the keyboard. Needless to say, in addition to producing frayed tempers and suboptimal code, this approach also usually requires more time and money than is strictly necessary for the task at hand. And that's where the Zend Framework can help.

Zend Framework applications are built according to a widely accepted set of principles which encourage code reusability, maintainability, and scalability. One of the linchpins of this approach is the Model-View-Controller (MVC) design pattern, which allows application business logic to be separated from the user interface and data models, such that they can be manipulated independent of each other. The MVC pattern also encourages efficient organization and separation of an application's responsibilities, and allows different components to be tested independently.

The following sections explain the key components of the MVC pattern, with specific notes on the Zend Framework's implementation where relevant.

Models

Every application is driven by data, whether it's something as simple as a username and password or as complex as a multicurrency shopping cart. In the MVC pattern, this "data layer" is represented by one or more *models*, which provide functions to retrieve, save, delete, and otherwise manipulate application data. This data layer is output-agnostic: it is completely concerned with the data itself, and completely unconcerned with how that data is presented to the user. As such, it provides a logically independent interface to manipulate application data.

To illustrate, consider a simple Web application that allows users to post classified advertisements for used cars. Under the MVC pattern, this application's data—the car listings—would be represented by a Listing model, which would expose methods for manipulating the underlying data. This model would not be concerned with the visual display of the listings; rather, its focus would be on the functions needed to access and manipulate individual listings and their attributes in the data store.

Here's an example of what one such model might look like:

```php
<?php
class ListingModel
{
  public function __construct()
  {
    // constructor
  }

  public function read($id)
  {
    // code to retrieve a single listing using its ID
  }

  public function find($criteria)
  {
    // code to retrieve listings matching given criteria
  }

  public function save()
  {
```

```
    // code to insert or update a listing
  }

  public function delete()
  {
    // code to delete a listing
  }
}
?>
```

When application data is stored in a database, such as MySQL, SQLite, or PostgreSQL, models may make use of an underlying database abstraction layer to handle the tasks of managing database connections and executing SQL queries. The Zend Framework includes a database abstraction layer, Zend_Db, which provides a common interface to many different database systems, and models in the Zend Framework are typically expressed using the Data Mapper pattern. It's also quite easy to integrate third-party models, such as those created with Object-Relational Mapping (ORM) tools such as Doctrine and Propel, into a Zend Framework application.

Views

If models are concerned solely with accessing and manipulating the application's raw data, *views* are concerned solely with how this data is presented to the user. Views can simply be thought of as the "user interface layer," responsible for displaying data but not capable of directly accessing or manipulating it. Views can also receive input from the user, but their responsibility is again limited to the appearance and behavior of the input form; they are not concerned with processing, sanitizing, or validating the input data.

In the context of the classifieds application discussed earlier, views would be responsible for displaying current listings and for generating forms into which new listings could be entered. So, for example, there might be a view to display all the latest listings in a particular category, and a view to input new listings. In all of these cases, the controller and/or the model would handle the tasks of retrieving and processing data, while the view would take care of massaging this data into an acceptable format for display and then rendering it to the user.

Here's an example of a view intended to display the most recent listings:

```
<!DOCTYPE html PUBLIC "-//W3C//DTD XHTML 1.0 Strict//EN"
"http://www.w3.org/TR/xhtml1/DTD/xhtml1-strict.dtd">
<html xmlns="http://www.w3.org/1999/xhtml" xml:lang="en" lang="en">
  <head>
    <meta http-equiv="Content-Type" content="text/html;
charset=utf-8"/>
    <base href="/" />
  </head>
  <body>
    <div id="header">
      <div id="logo">
```

```
        <img src="/images/logo.gif" />
      </div>
    </div>

    <div id="content">
      <h1>Recent listings</h1>
      <?php foreach ($this->listings as $l): ?>
        <div class="listing">
          <h3 class="listing_title">
            <a href="/listing/view/<?php echo $l->id; ?>">
              <?php echo $l->title; ?>
            </a>
          </h3>
          <span class="listing_content">
            <?php echo $l->content; ?>
          </span>
        </div>
      <?php endforeach; ?>
    </div>

  </body>
</html>
```

As this example illustrates, views are typically expressed as PHP scripts containing the HTML code or markup necessary to correctly render and display output to the user. These scripts can also contain variable placeholders for dynamic data; values for these placeholders are set by the corresponding controller and interpolated into the view when it is rendered. Under the Zend Framework, view scripts are rendered by the Zend_View component, which also provides ancillary functions for output escaping and a set of "helpers" for common view tasks such as navigation, metatag creation, and link generation. It's also quite easy to integrate third-party template engines, such as Smarty or Savant, into a Zend Framework application by extending the Zend_View_Interface abstract class.

Controllers

Controllers are the link between models and views. They make changes to application data using models, and then call views to display the results to the user. A controller may be linked to multiple views, and it may call a different view depending on the result that is to be shown at any given time. Controllers can thus be thought of as the "processing layer," responsible for responding to user actions, triggering changes in application state, and displaying the new state to the user.

In the context of the application discussed earlier, controllers would be responsible for reading and validating request parameters, saving and retrieving listings using model functions, and selecting appropriate views to display listing details. So, for example, a controller would intercept a request for the most recent listings, query the ListingModel model for a list of recent entries, select an appropriate view, interpolate the entries into the view, and render the view. Similarly, if the user chose to add a new listing, the controller would select and render an input view, validate and sanitize the user's input, insert the sanitized input into the data store using the ListingModel model, and then select and render another view to display whether or not the operation was successful.

Here's an example of a controller that brings together the model and view illustrated previously:

```php
<?php
class ListingController
{
  function indexAction()
  {
    // code to initialize model
    // and retrieve data
    $listing = new ListingModel();
    $matches = $listing->find(
      array(
        'date'    => '-10 days',
        'status'  => 'published'
        )
    );

    // code to initialize view
    // and populate with data returned from model
    $view = new ListingView();
    $view->listings = $matches;
    echo $view->render('recent.php');
  }
}
?>
```

As this example illustrates, a controller serves as an intermediary, invoking model methods to perform operations on application data, and using views to display the results of those operations to the user. Under the Zend Framework, controllers are created as children of the Zend_Controller_Action class, and contain methods, also called *actions*, which hold the processing code necessary to interact with models and views. There's also an über-controller, the *front controller*, which is responsible for intercepting user requests and invoking appropriate controller and action methods to satisfy them (more on this in the next section).

In addition to the three key components described above, the Zend Framework also introduces some additional ideas to streamline application development. These are described in the following sections.

Modules

By default, all models, controllers, actions, and views live in the—what else?—"default" module. However, you may often wish to group models, views, and controllers together into self-contained "boxes" based on the different functional areas of your Web application.

Modules provide a way to accomplish this. So, for example, if your application includes functions for search, user profile management, and news, you could create separate "search," "profile," and "news" modules, and place the corresponding models, views, and controllers for each in these modules.

Modules provide a convenient way to organize application code, or a way to build third-party application components that can easily be plugged in to an existing installation. The Zend Framework's default router is fully module-aware, allowing you to begin using modules in your application without any custom programming, and each module (except the "default" module) also has its own namespace to prevent object and variable collisions.

Routes

Routes provide the link between user requests and actions. When a user makes a request for an application URL, the front controller intercepts that request and decides, based on the URL pattern, which controller and action should be invoked to fulfill the request. This process of *routing* requests to controllers is a key part of the application execution flow, and is capable of extensive configuration. Routes make use of regular expressions for pattern matching, and can be expressed using either XML or INI file syntax.

By default, the Zend Framework includes some standard routes that are suitable for applications of small to medium complexity. These standard routes assume that application URLs are of the form */module/controller/action*, and divert user requests accordingly. So, for example, a request for **http://application/auto/listing/index** would be automatically mapped to `ListingController::indexAction` in the "auto" module. Notice that controller and action names follow a specific case and naming convention.

NOTE
The Zend Framework's routing subsystem automatically applies default values to routes that don't conform to the */module/controller/action* format. A detailed discussion of these default values, and their impact on how request URLs are mapped to controllers and actions, can be found in the section entitled "Understanding Component Interaction."

In case the standard routes described in the previous paragraph are too limiting or inflexible for the demands of your application, the Zend Framework also supports custom, user-defined routes. These routes support (among other things) optional and mandatory parameters, default values, and multiple chained routes, and they allow you to micromanage your application's routing so that application URLs need not directly reflect your internal classification of controllers, actions, and modules.

Layouts

In the classical sense, a layout is a definition of how a collection of elements is arranged. In the context of a Zend Framework application, *layouts* can be thought of as interface templates, providing a way to "decorate" application content using one or more standard application-wide interfaces. Layouts provide a way to abstract common interface elements, such as page headers and footers or site-wide navigation widgets, into separate files that can be edited and maintained independent of individual views.

It's quite common for an application to have more than one layout. For example, you might wish to present one interface to users and another to administrators, or you might wish to allow users to customize their experience of the application by selecting from a set of predefined interface themes. Layouts make these, and other templating options, reasonably easy to implement.

NOTE
You'll begin working with modules, custom routes, and layouts later in this chapter.

Understanding Component Interaction

If you think of a Zend Framework application like a circus (and the analogy is often more than a little apt), then the front controller is the ringmaster, whipping the acts into shape and making sure the audience is satisfied. This section examines its role in more detail, illustrating it in the context of the steps that go into intercepting and satisfying a request for an application resource.

Figure 2-1 illustrates the flow of a request through a typical Zend Framework application.

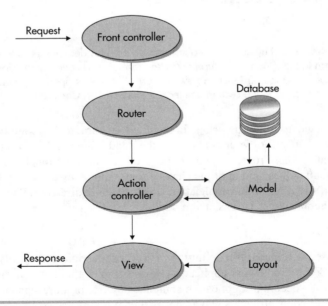

Figure 2-1 Interaction between models, views, and controllers

As the controller tasked with intercepting client requests and directing them to the appropriate target for response, the front controller has a key role to play in the overall flow of a request through the application.

1. When a request arrives, the Web server's *.htaccess* file automatically rewrites it into a standard format and passes it on to the *index.php* script. This script sets up the application environment, reads the application configuration file, and creates an instance of the front controller.

2. The front controller examines the request and determines the key components of the URL. It then attempts to route the request to an appropriate controller and action. To perform this routing, the front controller will check both default and custom routes, and make use of pattern-matching techniques to select an appropriate target for the request.

3. If a match is found, the front controller transfers control to the corresponding controller and action. Once invoked, the action makes changes to the application state using one or more models. It also selects the view to be displayed and sets any required view properties. Once the action has completed, the selected view renders its output, wrapping it in a layout as needed. This output is then transmitted back to the requesting client.

4. In the event that none of the application's defined routes match the request, an exception is thrown and the error controller and action are invoked. Based on the parameters of the exception, the error action renders a view containing a failure notice. This output is then transmitted back to the requesting client.

NOTE

Any uncaught exceptions generated during the request-handling process will invoke the error controller and corresponding action. This will produce a view containing a failure notice, which is transmitted back to the requesting client.

As noted earlier, the routing subsystem automatically maps URLs in the format */module/controller/action* to the corresponding module, controller, and action. So, for example, to access the `ListingController::saveAction` in the "auto" module, you'd need to request the URL **http://application/auto/listing/save**. Similarly, to access the `NewsController::editAction` in the "content" module, you'd need to request the URL **http://application/content/news/edit**.

If the routing subsystem receives a request that doesn't conform to the */module/controller/ action* format, it automatically applies default settings, as follows:

- For requests without a module name, the routing subsystem automatically assumes the module to be the "default" module.

- For requests without a controller name, the routing subsystem automatically assumes the controller to be the `IndexController` of the selected module.

- For requests without an action name, the routing subsystem automatically assumes the controller to be the `indexAction` of the selected controller.

To better understand how these default settings play out in practice, consider the following examples:

- The `ContactController::sendAction` in the "default" module can be accessed at both **http://application/default/contact/send** and **http://application/contact/send**.

- The `PostController::indexAction` in the "default" module can be accessed at both **http://application/default/post/index** and **http://application/post/**.

- The `NewsController::indexAction` in the "content" module can be accessed at both **http://application/content/news/index** and **http://application/content/news**.

Looking Behind the Default Index Page

With all this background information at hand, let's go back to the code generated by the *zf* command-line tool in Chapter 1 and take a closer look at how the default Zend Framework welcome page is generated. We'll begin at the beginning, with the initial request for **http://square.localhost/**. This request produces the default application index page shown in Figure 2-2.

What goes into making this happen? Well, consider that when you request the URL **http://square.localhost/**, the default routes described in the previous section come into play, and this URL is automatically rewritten to **http://square.localhost/default/index/index**. The Zend Framework's routing subsystem then redirects this request to the "default" module's `IndexController` and `indexAction()` method.

This controller and action is automatically created by the *zf* command-line tool, and by convention is stored at *$APP_DIR/application/controllers/IndexController.php*. Here's what it looks like:

```php
<?php
class IndexController extends Zend_Controller_Action
{
    public function init()
    {
        /* Initialize action controller here */
    }

    public function indexAction()
    {
        // action body
    }
}
```

Here, the `indexAction()` method is a simple stub without any executable code. Once it completes executing, it automatically selects its default view for rendering. By convention,

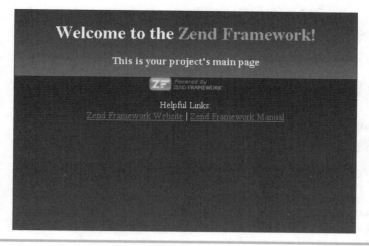

Figure 2-2   The default application index page

this view is named after the controller and action and can be found in the corresponding view scripts directory, which in this case would be *$APP_DIR/application/views/scripts/index/index .phtml*. Open this file and you'll see the HTML markup that generates the output shown in Figure 2-2:

```
<style>
    a:link,
    a:visited
    {
        color: #0398CA;
    }

    span#zf-name
    {
        color: #91BE3F;
    }

    div#welcome
    {
        color: #FFFFFF;
        background-image: url(
          http://framework.zend.com/images/bkg_header.jpg);
        width:  600px;
        height: 400px;
        border: 2px solid #444444;
        overflow: hidden;
        text-align: center;
    }
```

```
    div#more-information
    {
        background-image: url(
          http://framework.zend.com/images/bkg_body-bottom.gif);
        height: 100%;
    }
</style>
<div id="welcome">
    <h1>Welcome to the <span id="zf-name">Zend Framework!</span></h1>

    <h3>This is your project's main page</h3>

    <div id="more-information">
        <p><img src=
          "http://framework.zend.com/images/PoweredBy_ZF_4LightBG.png"
/>
        </p>
        <p>
            Helpful Links: <br />
            <a href="http://framework.zend.com/">Zend Framework
Website</a> |
            <a href="http://framework.zend.com/manual/en/">
            Zend Framework Manual</a>
        </p>
    </div>
</div>
```

From this markup, it should be clear that so long as you name and place your controllers, actions, and views correctly, there isn't really very much work for you to do. The framework will automatically locate and execute files for you, using its default routes, without requiring any manual intervention. As you proceed through this chapter and the remainder of this book, you'll learn a little more about how these standard Zend Framework conventions can be used to your advantage, by reducing the amount of manual coding required in getting an application up and running.

Understanding the Modular Directory Layout

In the previous chapter, you saw how the *zf* command-line tool creates a directory structure for your new Zend Framework application. In its initial form, this structure only contains the directories needed to get a basic test application up and running. As you flesh out your application with new features, you'll also need to expand this basic structure and create additional directories to hold different types of data.

To better understand this, consider Figure 2-3, which illustrates the full directory structure for a Zend Framework application.

Each of the directories shown in Figure 2-3 has a specific purpose, as listed in Table 2-1. The *$APP_DIR/application/modules/* directory bears special mention. This directory

Directory	Description
$APP_DIR/application	Main application directory
$APP_DIR/application/controllers	Global controllers
$APP_DIR/application/views	Global views
$APP_DIR/application/models	Global models
$APP_DIR/application/configs	Global configuration data
$APP_DIR/application/layouts	Global layouts
$APP_DIR/application/modules	Modules
$APP_DIR/library	Third-party libraries and classes
$APP_DIR/public	Main publicly accessible directory
$APP_DIR/public/css	CSS style sheets
$APP_DIR/public/js	JavaScript program code
$APP_DIR/public/images	Application images
$APP_DIR/tests	Unit tests
$APP_DIR/temp	Temporary data

Table 2-1   The Key Directories in a Zend Framework Application

is intended to store application modules, with each module represented as a subdirectory under *$APP_DIR/application/modules/*. The internal structure of each module directory mirrors that of the global *$APP_DIR/application/* directory, as shown in Figure 2-4.

This directory structure thus makes a distinction between global application controllers, views, and models, which are stored under the *$APP_DIR/application/* hierarchy, and module-specific controllers, views, and models, which are stored under the *$APP_DIR/application/modules/* hierarchy.

From a development perspective, the choice of which location to use for your application's code is an entirely subjective one. There is no one "correct" approach, and so you can choose to store your code in the global directories, in per-module directories, or in a hybrid combination of both, depending on what approach you find

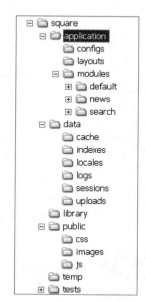

Figure 2-3   The recommended directory structure for a Zend Framework application

appropriate to your application's requirements and structure.

That said, the SQUARE example application described in these chapters makes extensive use of modules, and this book recommends the use of modules in general for Zend Framework application development, for the following reasons:

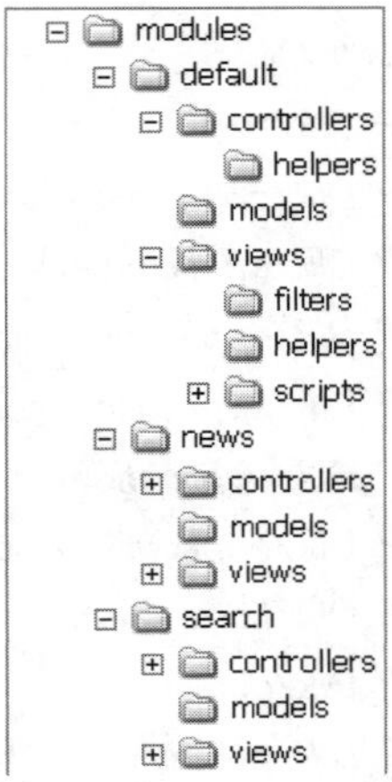

- Organizing code into modules produces a structured code tree, because all the controllers, views, and models related to a particular function or set of functions are stored within the same directory tree. A module-based directory layout also makes the areas of logical separation within an application immediately visible, with no additional documentation necessary, and is more maintainable in the long run.

- Organizing code into modules encourages the creation of more robust and extensible software. Modules can be structured as independent packages with their own controllers, views, and models. Modules can thus be thought of as reusable components that can be plugged in to an existing application to quickly give it new functionality.

Figure 2-4 The recommended directory structure for a Zend Framework application module

When you are using modules with the Zend Framework's default routes, it's necessary to include the module name in your URL request, in the format */module/controller/action*. If the routing subsystem receives a request that doesn't contain a module name, it automatically looks in what it considers the "default" module—the global application directory, *$APP_DIR/application/*.

This behavior can create confusion and no small degree of inconsistency in application URLs when the application also contains additional modules in the *$APP_DIR/application/modules/* hierarchy. Therefore, when following a modular directory structure, it's a good idea to explicitly create a directory for the "default" module, at *$APP_DIR/application/modules/default*, and move controllers, views, and models that were previously stored in the *$APP_DIR/application/** hierarchy to the *$APP_DIR/application/modules/default/** hierarchy.

Try This 2-1 Using a Modular Directory Layout

As discussed in the previous section, a modular directory layout enforces consistency and produces a more manageable code tree. The following steps discuss how to adopt this layout for the example application created in Chapter 1, as a prelude to beginning application development.

Creating the Default Module

The first step is to create the *$APP_DIR/application/modules/* directory, and then create a set of subdirectories within that for the default module and its controllers and views. The *zf* command-line tool does not create these directories, and so it is necessary to perform this task manually.

```
shell> cd /usr/local/apache/htdocs/square/application
shell> mkdir modules
shell> mkdir modules/default
```

Next, move the existing models, controllers, and views from *$APP_DIR/application/** to *$APP_DIR/application/modules/default/**:

```
shell> mv controllers modules/default/
shell> mv views modules/default/
shell> mv models modules/default/
```

Updating the Application Configuration File

The next step is to update the global application configuration file, located at *$APP_DIR/application/configs/application.ini*, with the location of the modules directory. This tells the Zend Framework's routing subsystem how to resolve module-specific entities.

To perform this update, open the application configuration file in a text editor and add the following lines to the [production] section:

```
resources.frontController.moduleDirectory = APPLICATION_PATH "/
modules"
resources.modules = ""
```

Once you've completed the preceding steps, try accessing the application index page using the URLs **http://square.localhost/** and **http://square.localhost/default/index/index**. If all has gone well, you should see the default application index page in both cases, as shown in Figure 2-2.

TIP

Regardless of whether or not you organize your application into modules, remember that you can always redirect URL requests to specific modules, controllers, and actions through the use of custom routes.

Understanding Master Layouts and Custom Routes

At this point, you know enough about the inner workings of a Zend Framework application to actually begin writing some code of your own. The following sections get you started, by guiding you through the process of creating a custom welcome page, setting up a master layout for the application, and building a custom route to it.

Ask the Expert

Q: **How is it that the URLs** http://square.localhost/ **and** http://square.localhost/default/index/index **produce the same output page?**

A: The Zend Framework's routing subsystem automatically applies certain default settings to routes that don't conform to the standard /module/controller/action format. Simply put, in the absence of a module name, it assumes the "default" module, and in the absence of a controller and action name, it assumes the `indexAction()` method of the `IndexController` of the selected module. As a result of these default substitutions, the request http://square.localhost/ is automatically rewritten to http://square.localhost/default/index/index, and directed to the "default" module's `IndexController::indexAction` for completion.

Q: **How do naming conventions for controllers, actions, and views work in the Zend Framework?**

A: The Zend Framework uses "camel-casing" for controller and action names. Controller names are specified using upper camel-case and are suffixed with the word `Controller` (examples: `IndexController`, `StaticContentController`, `FunkyChickenController`), while action names are specified using lower camel-case and suffixed with the word `Action` (examples: `indexAction`, `displayPostAction`, `redButtonAction`). For modules other than the "default" module, controller names must be additionally prefixed with the module name (examples: `News_IndexController`, `Catalog_EntryController`).

View scripts take their name from the corresponding controller and action. Typically, the view script is stored in a directory corresponding to the controller name (without the `Controller` suffix), in a file whose name corresponds to the action name (without the `Action` suffix). Therefore, the view script for the `clickAction` in the `ExampleController` would be located at */views/scripts/example/click.phtml*.

Multiple words in the controller or action name are represented by hyphens or periods in the corresponding view script file path. Therefore, the view script for the `displayItemAction` in the `ShoppingCartController` would be located at */views/scripts/shopping-cart/display-item.phtml*.

To prevent name collisions, the Zend Framework also allows the use of custom namespaces, which can be prefixed to object or class names. These namespaces can be registered with the Zend Framework autoloader, to have the corresponding definitions automatically loaded on demand, as needed. You'll see an example of this in Chapter 3.

Updating the Application Index Page

Now, while the default welcome page created by the *zf* command-line tool is certainly pretty, it's not really what you want application users to see in a live environment. So, how about updating it with a custom welcome message and some descriptive information about the application?

You already know that the application index page is served by the "default" module's `IndexController::indexAction`. Under a modular layout, the view corresponding to this controller and action is located at *$APP_DIR/application/modules/default/views/scripts/index/index.phtml*. Open this file in a text editor, and replace its contents with the following markup:

```
<h2>Welcome!</h2>
<p>Welcome to SQUARE, our cutting-edge Web search application for rare
stamps.</p>
<p>We have a wide collection of stamps in our catalog for your
browsing pleasure, and we also list <strong>hundreds of thousands of
stamps</strong> from individual collectors across the country. If
you find something you like, drop us a line and we'll do our best to
obtain it for you. Needless to say, all stamps purchased through us
come with a certificate of authenticity, and <strong>our unique 60-day
money-back guarantee</strong>.</p>
<p>The SQUARE application is designed to be as user-friendly as
possible. Use the links in the menu above to navigate and begin
searching.</p>
```

Save the changes, and revisit the application index page at **http://square.localhost/**. You should see a revised index page, as shown in Figure 2-5.

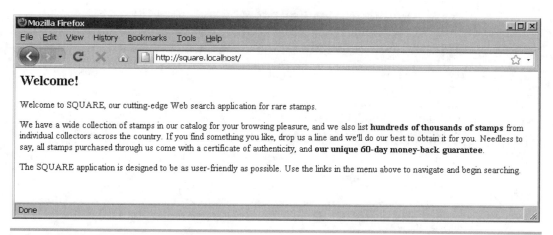

Figure 2-5   The updated application index page

Setting a Master Layout

The application index page now displays relevant content, but it's still a long way from being easy on the eyes. So, the next step is to give it some visual pizzazz by adding some images and navigation to it. These elements will be common to all the pages of the application, so, although you can add them to each individual view of your application, they're better suited for placement in a master layout, which can then be wrapped around each view. Using a layout is not only less time-consuming, but because the layout is stored in a single file that's accessed from multiple views, it's also easier to make changes as the application evolves.

To set a master layout for the application, perform the following steps.

Creating the Layout Template File

The first step is to create the *$APP_DIR/application/layouts/* directory, which is the default location for layout files under the Zend Framework's recommended directory layout.

```
shell> cd /usr/local/apache/htdocs/square/application
shell> mkdir layouts
```

Within this directory, create a new text file containing the following markup:

```
<!DOCTYPE html PUBLIC "-//W3C//DTD XHTML 1.0 Strict//EN"
"http://www.w3.org/TR/xhtml1/DTD/xhtml1-strict.dtd">
<html xmlns="http://www.w3.org/1999/xhtml" xml:lang="en" lang="en">
  <head>
    <meta http-equiv="Content-Type" content="text/html;
charset=utf-8"/>
    <base href="/" />
    <link rel="stylesheet" type="text/css" href="/css/master.css" />
  </head>
  <body>
    <div id="header">
      <div id="logo">
        <img src="/images/logo.gif" />
      </div>

      <div id="menu">
        <a href="#">HOME</a>
        <a href="#">SERVICES</a>
        <a href="#">CONTACT</a>
      </div>
    </div>

    <div id="content">
      <?php echo $this->layout()->content ?>
    </div>

    <div id="footer">
      <p>
```

```
      Created with <a href="http://framework.zend.com/">
      Zend Framework</a>. Licensed under
      <a href="http://www.creativecommons.org/">Creative Commons</a>.
      </p>
   </div>
  </body>
</html>
```

Save this file as *$APP_DIR/application/layouts/master.phtml.*

You'll notice that the master layout also makes use of two additional assets—a CSS stylesheet and a logo image. These files need to be located in the application's public area, so that they can be retrieved over HTTP by connecting clients. Accordingly, also create the *$APP_DIR/public/css/* and *$APP_DIR/public/images/* directories and copy over the necessary assets to these locations. You'll find these assets in the code archive for this chapter, which can be downloaded from this book's companion Web site at **http://www.zf-beginners-guide.com/.**

Updating the Application Configuration File
The next step is to update the global application configuration file, located at *$APP_DIR/ application/configs/application.ini,* with the location of the layouts directory and the name of the default layout to use when rendering application views. Open the file in a text editor, and add the following directives to the [production] section:

```
resources.layout.layoutPath = APPLICATION_PATH "/layouts"
resources.layout.layout = master
```

And now, when you revisit the application index page, you should see your new layout in all its glory, as shown in Figure 2-6.

Using a Custom Route
Custom routes make it possible to map application URLs to specific modules, controllers, and actions, and are particularly useful when the Zend Framework's default routes turn out to be inadequate or limiting.

To illustrate, let's say that you'd like the application URL /home to redirect users to the application index page. To create a custom route that maps this URL to the "default" module's `IndexController::indexAction`, simply update the application configuration file at *$APP_DIR/application/configs/application.ini* and add the following route entry to the [production] section:

```
resources.router.routes.home.route = /home
resources.router.routes.home.defaults.module = default
resources.router.routes.home.defaults.controller = index
resources.router.routes.home.defaults.action = index
```

A route entry typically contains `route`, `module`, `controller`, and `action` attributes. The `route` attribute specifies the URL pattern that the route should match, while the `module`, `controller`, and `action` attributes indicate which module, controller, and action should be used to fulfill the request. Each route also has a unique name (in this case, home), which serves as a shortcut for automatic URL generation inside views.

After saving your changes, try visiting the URL **http://square.localhost/home** in your Web browser. If all is well, you should be presented with the application index page, as shown in Figure 2-6.

TIP

Route names are useful because you can use them with the url() view helper to automatically generate URLs inside views. For example, a call to $view->url(array(), 'home') inside a view script would automatically generate the URL string /home.

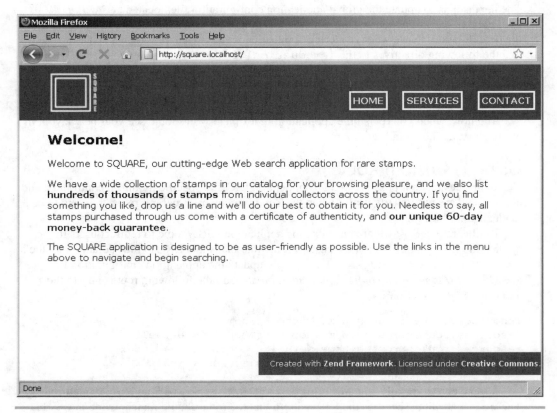

Figure 2-6 The application index page, wrapped in a custom layout

Ask the Expert

Q: Why are layouts stored at the global level and not the module level?

A: With Web applications, it's quite common for views in different modules to share the same common layout. Therefore, the Zend Framework's default directory layout suggests placing layouts at the global, or application, level under *$APP_DIR/application/layouts/*, rather than under the *$APP_DIR/application/modules/* hierarchy.

That said, if your application is structured such that each module uses a different layout, you could relocate your layout files to the module level, and write a custom plug-in that dynamically changes the layout based on the module being accessed. You'll find a more detailed discussion of how to do this in the links at the end of this chapter.

Try This 2-2   Serving Static Content

In previous sections, your activities have been limited to modifying the application's existing controllers and views. However, as development progresses, you'll find it necessary to begin creating new controllers, actions, and views to encapsulate additional functionality. This shouldn't be any cause for alarm, though, because there's a standard process you can follow whenever you need to add new functionality to a Zend Framework application.

These steps are illustrated in the following sections, which will guide you through the process of adding a new `StaticContentController` and associated views that will be responsible for serving up static content pages such as "About Us" and "Services" pages.

Defining Custom Routes

The first step is to define a base route for static content pages. For simplicity, we'll assume that all static content page URLs will be of the form */content/xx*, where *xx* is a variable indicating the name of the content page. To set up a custom route to handle such URLs, add the following route definition to the application configuration file at *$APP_DIR/application/configs/application.ini*:

```
resources.router.routes.static-content.route = /content/:page
resources.router.routes.static-content.defaults.module = default
resources.router.routes.static-content.defaults.controller =
static-content
resources.router.routes.static-content.defaults.action = display
```

This route is a little more complex than the one you saw earlier, because it contains a variable placeholder. The Zend Framework supports the use of variable placeholders, indicated by a preceding colon, in route patterns, and will automatically convert that segment of the request

(continued)

URL into a variable that can be accessed from within a controller. This means that if, for example, a client requested the URL */content/hello-world*, the routing subsystem would automatically capture the URL segment "hello-world" and store it in a request variable named *page*.

Defining the Controller

Why do we need to capture the final segment of the URL and store it as a request variable? That question is answered in the next paragraph, but, until we get there, let's create the "default" module's `StaticContentController`, which, by convention, should be located at *$APP_DIR/application/modules/default/controllers/StaticContentController.php*. Create this file and fill it with the following code:

```php
<?php
class StaticContentController extends Zend_Controller_Action
{
    public function init()
    {
    }


    // display static views
    public function displayAction()
    {
      $page = $this->getRequest()->getParam('page');
      if (file_exists($this->view->getScriptPath(null) .
      "/" . $this->getRequest()->getControllerName() .
      "/$page." . $this->viewSuffix)) {
        $this->render($page);
      } else {
        throw new Zend_Controller_Action_Exception('Page not found',
404);
      }
    }

}
```

   This controller exposes a single action, `displayAction()`, which is responsible for reading the `page` variable set up by the routing subsystem using the request object's `getParam()` method. It then attempts to find a view script matching the value of this variable. If a matching view script is found, it is rendered and sent to the client. So, for example, if the URL requested by the client was */content/hello-world*, the call to `$request->getParam('page')` would return the value "hello-world," and the action would therefore attempt to render a view named *$APP_DIR/application/modules/default/ views/scripts/static-content/hello-world.phtml*.

   If no matching view can be found, a 404 exception is raised and propagated forward to the default exception handler, which formats it into a readable error page and displays it to the client.

Ask the Expert

Q: Why do none of the class definitions in this chapter include a closing PHP tag?

A: According to the Zend Framework coding standard, files that contain only PHP code should not include the closing tag ?>, as it can lead to header problems with the HTTP response if the text editor you're using automatically adds a new line to the end of your files. For more information on the Zend Framework coding standard, refer to the links at the end of this chapter.

Defining the View

The next (and final) step is to create views corresponding to the controllers and actions created in the previous step. In most cases, the view name will be based on the controller and action name. However, in this particular case, the action is a generic display action that receives the view name as a variable from the URL request. So, to define a static "Services" page accessible at the URL */content/services*, create a file at *$APP_DIR/application/modules/default/views/ scripts/static-content/services.phtml* and fill it with some content, as in the following example:

```
<h2>Services</h2>
<p>We provide a number of services, including procurement, valuation
and mail-order sales. Please contact us to find out more.</p>
<p>Lorem ipsum dolor sit amet, consectetur adipisicing elit, sed
do eiusmod tempor incididunt ut labore et dolore magna aliqua. Ut
enim ad minim veniam, quis nostrud exercitation ullamco laboris
nisi ut aliquip ex ea commodo consequat. Duis aute irure dolor in
reprehenderit in voluptate velit esse cillum dolore eu fugiat nulla
pariatur. Excepteur sint occaecat cupidatat non proident, sunt in
culpa qui officia deserunt mollit anim id est laborum.</p>
<p>Lorem ipsum dolor sit amet, consectetur adipisicing elit, sed
do eiusmod tempor incididunt ut labore et dolore magna aliqua. Ut
enim ad minim veniam, quis nostrud exercitation ullamco laboris
nisi ut aliquip ex ea commodo consequat. Duis aute irure dolor in
reprehenderit in voluptate velit esse cillum dolore eu fugiat nulla
pariatur. Excepteur sint occaecat cupidatat non proident, sunt in
culpa qui officia deserunt mollit anim id est laborum.</p>
```

Similarly, to define an "About Us" page accessible at the URL */content/about-us*, create a file named *$APP_DIR/application/modules/default/views/scripts/static-content/about-us.phtml* and fill it with some content, as in the following example:

```
<h2>About Us</h2>
<p>We have been in the business of stamp procurement and sales since
1927, and are internationally known for our expertise and industry-wide
```

network. We encourage you to find out more about us using the links
above.</p>
<p>Lorem ipsum dolor sit amet, consectetur adipisicing elit, sed
do eiusmod tempor incididunt ut labore et dolore magna aliqua. Ut
enim ad minim veniam, quis nostrud exercitation ullamco laboris
nisi ut aliquip ex ea commodo consequat. Duis aute irure dolor in
reprehenderit in voluptate velit esse cillum dolore eu fugiat nulla
pariatur. Excepteur sint occaecat cupidatat non proident, sunt in
culpa qui officia deserunt mollit anim id est laborum.</p>
<p>Lorem ipsum dolor sit amet, consectetur adipisicing elit, sed
do eiusmod tempor incididunt ut labore et dolore magna aliqua. Ut
enim ad minim veniam, quis nostrud exercitation ullamco laboris
nisi ut aliquip ex ea commodo consequat. Duis aute irure dolor in
reprehenderit in voluptate velit esse cillum dolore eu fugiat nulla
pariatur. Excepteur sint occaecat cupidatat non proident, sunt in
culpa qui officia deserunt mollit anim id est laborum.</p>

If you now try visiting the URL **http://square.localhost/content/about-us** or **http://
square.localhost/content/services** through your Web browser, you should see the static pages
above. Figure 2-7 illustrates a sample of the result.

Updating the Master Layout

As a final step, you can update the navigation links in the application's main menu to reflect
the new static content pages using the url() helper method. To do this, update the master
layout, at *$APP_DIR/application/layouts/master.phtml*, with the changes highlighted in bold:

```
<!DOCTYPE html PUBLIC "-//W3C//DTD XHTML 1.0 Strict//EN" "http://www.
w3.org/TR/xhtml1/DTD/xhtml1-strict.dtd">
<html xmlns="http://www.w3.org/1999/xhtml" xml:lang="en" lang="en">
  <head>
    <meta http-equiv="Content-Type" content="text/html;
charset=utf-8"/>
    <base href="/" />
    <link rel="stylesheet" type="text/css" href="/css/master.css" />
  </head>
  <body>
    <div id="header">
      <div id="logo">
        <img src="/images/logo.gif" />
      </div>

      <div id="menu">
        <a href="<?php echo $this->url(array(), 'home'); ?>">HOME</a>
        <a href="<?php echo $this->url(array('page' => 'services'),
          'static-content'); ?>">SERVICES</a>
        <a href="#">CONTACT</a>
      </div>
    </div>
```

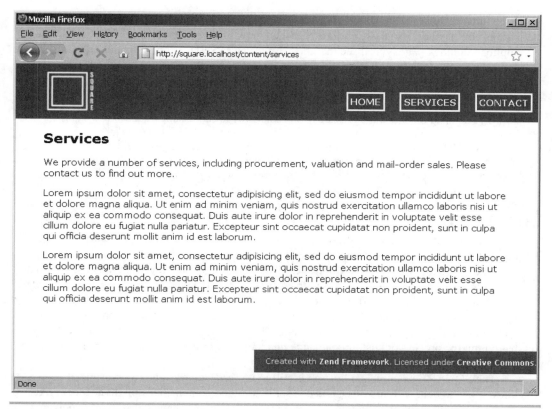

Figure 2-7   A static content page

```
    <div id="content">
      <?php echo $this->layout()->content ?>
    </div>

    <div id="footer">
      <p>Created with <a href="http://framework.zend.com/">
      Zend Framework</a>. Licensed under
      <a href="http://www.creativecommons.org/">Creative Commons</a>.
      </p>
    </div>
  </body>
</html>
```

Here, the `url()` helper method is used to automatically generate URLs for the */home* and */content/services* routes. This helper accepts two parameters—an array of variable-value pairs to be interpolated into the URL string, and the name of the route—and then generates URL strings corresponding to these parameters when the view is rendered. And if you revisit the application index page, you'll see that the "Home" and "Services" main menu links are now active and, when clicked, display the correct content.

NOTE
It's worth pointing out that there is actually an easier way to serve static pages in a Zend Framework application: You can simply place them in the *$APP_DIR/public/* directory as HTML files, and link to them manually. However, these pages would not be able to use any of the Zend Framework's built-in features, such as global layouts, routes, caching, or security, and, as such, this approach is not usually recommended.

Summary
Now that you are at the end of this chapter, you should have a much deeper understanding of what goes into making a Zend Framework application tick. This chapter began with an introduction to the Model-View-Controller design pattern, explaining what models, views, and controllers are and how they interact with each other to produce a logically separated, layered application. It also introduced some additional important concepts, such as modules, routes, layouts, and the front controller, and explained the basics of how user requests are routed and handled in an application context. Finally, it applied all this theory to the real world, by beginning the process of customizing and enhancing the simple test application created at the end of the previous chapter.

The SQUARE example application is still in its early stages: It has a customized layout, knows how to deal with modules, and can serve up static content. This might not seem like much, but implementing even this very basic functionality will have helped you understand the main principles of MVC-based development with the Zend Framework and created a solid foundation for the more advanced material in subsequent chapters.

To learn more about the topics discussed in this chapter, consider visiting the following links:

- Wikipedia's discussion of Model-View-Controller architecture, at
  http://en.wikipedia.org/wiki/Model-view-controller

- The basics of the Zend Framework's MVC implementation, at
  http://framework.zend.com/docs/quickstart

- The Zend Framework router, at
  http://framework.zend.com/manual/en/zend.controller.router.html

- The Zend Framework front controller, at
  http://framework.zend.com/manual/en/zend.controller.front.html

- The Zend Framework layout engine, at
  http://framework.zend.com/manual/en/zend.layout.html

- A discussion of building a modular application with the Zend Framework (Jeroen Keppens), at
  http://blog.keppens.biz/2009/06/create-modular-application-with-zend.html

- A discussion of using per-module layouts in the Zend Framework wiki and forums, at
  http://framework.zend.com/wiki/display/ZFPROP/Zend_Layout and **http://www
  .zfforums.com/zend-framework-components-13/model-view-controller-mvc-21/
  modules-layouts-2645.html**

- The Zend Framework directory layout, at
  **http://framework.zend.com/wiki/display/ZFPROP/Zend+Framework+Default+
  Project+Structure+-+Wil+Sinclair**

- The Zend Framework coding standard, at
  http://framework.zend.com/manual/en/coding-standard.html

Chapter 3

Working with Forms

Key Skills & Concepts

- Learn to programmatically create forms and form elements
- Understand how to filter and validate user input
- Protect your forms from Cross-Site Request Forgery (CSRF) attacks and spambots
- Control the appearance of form elements and error messages
- Create a working contact form

In the previous chapter, you learned how the Zend Framework implements the Model-View-Controller pattern, and you looked underneath the hood of the example application to see how it works. You also started to flesh out the example application by adopting a modular directory structure, adding a master layout, and creating custom controllers, views, and routes for static content.

Now, while you can certainly use the Zend Framework to serve up static content, doing so is a lot like using a bulldozer to knock over a tower of plastic blocks. There's nothing stopping you from doing it, but it's not really what the bulldozer was intended for, and you're liable to face hard questions about why there's a bulldozer in your living room in the first place! The Zend Framework is similar, in that it's intended to provide robust, elegant, and extensible solutions to complex Web application development tasks. The more complex the task, the better suited it is to the power and flexibility of the framework...and the more fun you'll have knocking it down!

In this chapter, you'll learn how the Zend Framework can simplify one of the most common application development tasks: creating Web forms and processing user input. You'll also apply this knowledge to add some interactivity to the SQUARE example application, by creating a contact form. So without further ado, let's jump right in!

Understanding Form Basics

To demonstrate how the Zend Framework can help you with forms, a brief yet illustrative example will suffice. If you're like most PHP developers, chances are that you've written a form-processing script like the following one at some point in your career:

```
<!DOCTYPE html PUBLIC "-//W3C//DTD XHTML 1.0 Strict//EN"
"http://www.w3.org/TR/xhtml1/DTD/xhtml1-strict.dtd">
<html xmlns="http://www.w3.org/1999/xhtml" xml:lang="en" lang="en">
  <head>
  </head>
```

```php
<body>
  <h2>Create Item</h2>
<?php
if (!isset($_POST['submit'])) {
// no POST submission, display form
?>
  <form method="post" action="/item/create">
    <table>
      <tr>
        <td>Item name:</td>
        <td><input type="text" name="name" size="30" /></td>
      </tr>

      <tr>
        <td>Item quantity:</td>
        <td><input type="text" name="qty" size="3" /></td>
      </tr>

      <tr>
        <td colspan="2">
          <input type="submit" name="submit" value="Submit" />
        </td>
      </tr>
    </table>
  </form>
<?php
} else {
  // POST submission, validate input
  if (trim($_POST['name']) == '') {
    die('ERROR: Missing value - Item name');
  }
  if (trim($_POST['qty']) == '') {
    die('ERROR: Missing value - Item quantity');
  }
  if ($_POST['qty'] <= 0) {
    die('ERROR: Invalid value - Item quantity');
  }

  // process input
  // eg: save to database
  // attempt a connection
  try {
    $pdo = new PDO('mysql:dbname=test;host=localhost', 'user',
'pass');

    // create and execute INSERT query
    $name = $pdo->quote($_POST['name']);
    $qty = $pdo->quote($_POST['qty']);
```

```
    $sql = "INSERT INTO shoppinglist (name, qty) VALUES ($name,
$qty)";
    $pdo->exec($sql) or die("ERROR: " . implode(":", $pdo-
>errorInfo())));

    // close connection
    unset($pdo);

    // display success message
    echo 'Thank you for your submission';
  } catch (Exception $e) {
    die("ERROR: " . $e->getMessage());
  }
}
?>
</body>
</html>
```

There's nothing very clever or complicated here. This script is divided into two parts, split by a conditional test that inspects the $_POST variable to determine if the form has been submitted. The first half displays an input form containing two fields and a submit button; the second half validates the input to ensure that it is in the correct format and then proceeds to escape it and insert it into a database.

Figure 3-1 illustrates what the form looks like.

Now, while the script and general approach that you've just seen work in practice, there's no denying that it has a couple of problems:

● The same script file contains both HTML interface elements and PHP business logic. As discussed in the previous chapter, this is both messy to look at and hard to maintain. It's also hard to enforce consistency between forms, since the code required to produce each form is customized to a very high degree.

● Every time you add a new field to the form in the first half of the script, you need to add a corresponding set of validation tests and error messages to the second half of the script. This is annoying, and often repetitive; witness that the first two tests in the previous example do essentially the same thing.

Create Item

Item name: Hammer
Item quantity: 2
Submit

● There's no way to reuse validation tests from one form in other forms (unless you had the foresight to package them into classes or functions from the get-go). As a result, you often end up writing the same code time and time again, especially when working with forms that perform related or similar operations.

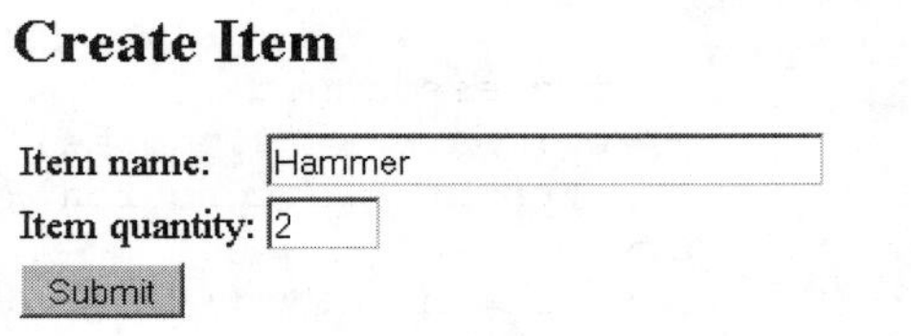

Figure 3-1   A form created using standard HTML markup

The Zend Framework comes with a set of components, collectively referred to as Zend_ Form, which addresses these problems. To illustrate, consider the following example, which uses Zend_Form to produce a result equivalent to the previous script:

```php
<?php
class Form_Item_Create extends Zend_Form
{
  public function init()
  {
    // initialize form
    $this->setAction('/item/create')
         ->setMethod('post');

    // create text input for name
    $name = new Zend_Form_Element_Text('name');
    $name->setLabel('Item name:')
         ->setOptions(array('size' => '35'))
         ->setRequired(true)
         ->addValidator('NotEmpty', true)
         ->addValidator('Alpha', true)
         ->addFilter('HTMLEntities')
         ->addFilter('StringTrim');

    // create text input for quantity
    $qty = new Zend_Form_Element_Text('qty');
    $qty->setLabel('Item quantity:');
    $qty->setOptions(array('size' => '4'))
         ->setRequired(true)
         ->addValidator('NotEmpty', true)
         ->addValidator('Int', true)
         ->addFilter('HTMLEntities')
         ->addFilter('StringTrim');

    // create submit button
    $submit = new Zend_Form_Element_Submit('submit');
    $submit->setLabel('Submit')
         ->setOptions(array('class' => 'submit'));

    // attach elements to form
    $this->addElement($name)
         ->addElement($qty)
         ->addElement($submit);

  }
}

class ExampleController extends Zend_Controller_Action
{
```

```
public function formAction()
{
  $form = new Form_Item_Create;
  $this->view->form = $form;
  if ($this->getRequest()->isPost()) {
    if ($form->isValid($this->getRequest()->getPost())) {
      $values = $form->getValues();
      $pdo = new PDO('mysql:dbname=test;host=localhost', 'user',
'pass');
      $sql = sprintf("INSERT INTO shoppinglist (name, qty)
            VALUES ('%s', '%d')", $values['name'], $values['qty']);
      $pdo->exec($sql);
      $this->_helper->getHelper('FlashMessenger')
          ->addMessage('Thank you for your submission');
      $this->_redirect('/index/success');
    }
  }
}
```

Figure 3-2 illustrates what the form looks like.

You'll immediately notice three things about the code that creates the form in Figure 3-2:

- There isn't a single line of HTML code in the script. Form and form elements are represented as PHP objects, and they are configured using object methods. This ensures consistency and produces a standards-compliant Web form.

- Predefined validators and filters are available for common input validation and sanitization tasks. This reduces the amount of work involved, produces more maintainable code, and avoids repetition. Validators can also be combined or extended to support custom requirements.

- Validators are specified at the same time as form fields. This allows the form to "know" what each field can support and to easily identify the source of input errors. A single field can also be associated with multiple validators for more stringent input validation.

It should be clear from these points that Zend_Form provides a convenient, maintainable, and extensible solution for input form creation and data validation. The remainder of this chapter will explore Zend_Form in detail, illustrating it in a practical context.

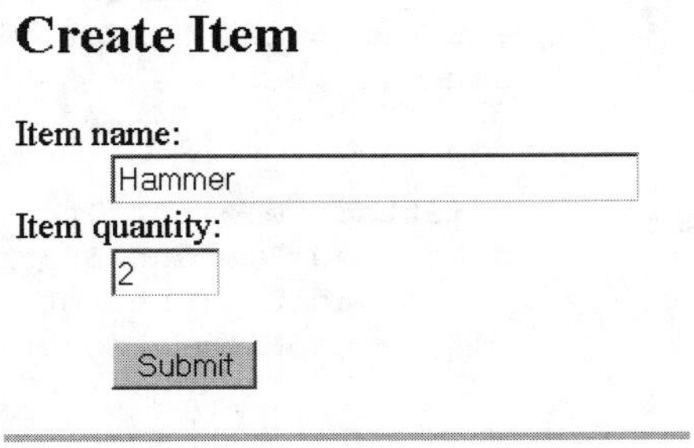

Create Item

Item name:

Hammer

Item quantity:

2

Submit

Figure 3-2 A form created using the Zend_Form component

Creating Forms and Form Elements

From the previous section, you know that Zend_Form offers an object-oriented API for generating forms and validating user input. Under the Zend_Form approach, *forms* are represented as instances of, or objects inheriting from, the Zend_Form base class. This base class exposes a number of methods to control the operation of the form, including the `setAction()` method to set the form's action URL and the `setMethod()` method to set the submission method. There's also a catch-all `setAttribs()` method, which allows you to set other form attributes. Here's an example of using these methods:

```php
<?php
class Form_Example extends Zend_Form
{
  public function init()
  {
    // initialize form
    $this->setAction('/my/action')
         ->setAttribs(array(
            'class' => 'form',
            'id'    => 'example'
         ))
         ->setMethod('post');
  }
}
```

Form elements are added by instantiating objects of the corresponding Zend_Form_Element_* class, setting element properties via class methods, and then attaching them to the form with the `addElement()` method. Here's an example of adding a text input and a submit button to a form:

```php
<?php
class Form_Example extends Zend_Form
{
  public function init()
  {
    // initialize form
    $this->setAction('/my/action')
         ->setAttribs(array(
            'class' => 'form',
            'id'    => 'example'
         ))
         ->setMethod('post');

    // create text input for title
    $title = new Zend_Form_Element_Text('title');
    $title->setLabel('Title:')
          ->setOptions(array(
```

```
                  'size' => '35'
            ));

    // create submit button
    $submit = new Zend_Form_Element_Submit('submit', array(
      'label' => 'Submit',
      'class' => 'submit'
    ));

    // attach elements to form
    $this->addElement($title)
        ->addElement($submit);
  }
}
```

Element objects can be configured either by passing values to the object constructor or by using named object methods. In the previous example, the object constructor for the text input element was passed the element name in the constructor, and the `setLabel()` and `setOptions()` methods were then used to set the element label and display properties, respectively. On the other hand, the submit button was configured directly in the object constructor, which was passed an array of options as the second argument.

TIP
You can also attach descriptions to form fields with the `setDescription()` method.

If you prefer, you can also create form elements using the `createElement()` method, by passing the element type to the method as its first argument. Here's an example, which is equivalent to the previous one:

```php
<?php
class Form_Example extends Zend_Form
{
  public function init()
  {
    // initialize form
    $this->setAction('/my/action')
        ->setAttribs(array(
            'class' => 'form',
            'id'    => 'example'
          ))
        ->setMethod('post');

    // create text input for title
    $title = $this->createElement('text', 'title', array(
      'label' => 'Title:',
      'size'  => 35,
    ));
```

```
    // create submit button
    $submit = $this->createElement('submit', 'submit', array(
      'label' => 'Submit',
      'class' => 'submit'
    ));


    // attach elements to form
    $this->addElement($title)
         ->addElement($submit);

  }
}
```

TIP

In many of the code listings in this chapter, you'll see examples of *method chaining*, wherein one method appears to invoke another. This is an example of the Zend Framework's "fluent interface," which provides a convenient shortcut to configure form objects with minimal additional coding. The end result is also significantly more readable. You can read more about fluent interfaces in the links at the end of this chapter.

Working with Form Elements

By default, the Zend Framework ships with definitions for 16 form elements, ranging from simple text input elements to more complex multiple selection lists, and it's useful to learn more about them. Table 3-1 gives a list of these 16 elements, together with their corresponding class names.

   The following sections examine these in more detail.

Text and Hidden Fields

Text input fields, password input fields, and larger text input areas are represented by the Zend_Form_Element_Text, Zend_Form_Element_Password, and Zend_Form_Element_Textarea classes, respectively, while hidden form fields are represented by the Zend_Form_Element_Hidden class. The following example demonstrates these elements in action:

```php
<?php
class Form_Example extends Zend_Form
{
  public function init()
  {
    // initialize form
    $this->setAction('/sandbox/example/form')
         ->setMethod('post');

    // create text input for name
```

Element Class	Description
Zend_Form_Element_Text	Text input field
Zend_Form_Element_Hidden	Hidden field
Zend_Form_Element_Password	Password field
Zend_Form_Element_Radio	Radio button
Zend_Form_Element_Checkbox	Check box
Zend_Form_Element_MultiCheckbox	Group of related check boxes
Zend_Form_Element_Select	Selection list (single)
Zend_Form_Element_MultiSelect	Selection list (multiple)
Zend_Form_Element_Textarea	Text input field
Zend_Form_Element_File	File input field
Zend_Form_Element_Image	Image
Zend_Form_Element_Button	Button
Zend_Form_Element_Hash	Unique string (for session identification)
Zend_Form_Element_Captcha	CAPTCHA (for spam filtering)
Zend_Form_Element_Reset	Reset button
Zend_Form_Element_Submit	Submit button

Table 3-1   Form Element Classes Included with the Zend Framework

```
$name = new Zend_Form_Element_Text('name');
$name->setLabel('First name:')
    ->setOptions(array('id' => 'fname'));

// create password input
$pass = new Zend_Form_Element_Password('pass');
$pass->setLabel('Password:')
    ->setOptions(array('id' => 'upass'));

// create hidden input
$uid = new Zend_Form_Element_Hidden('uid');
$uid->setValue('49');

// create text area for comments
$comment = new Zend_Form_Element_Textarea('comment');
$comment->setLabel('Comment:')
        ->setOptions(array(
            'id'   => 'comment',
```

```
                    'rows' => '10',
                    'cols' => '30',
               ));

       // attach elements to form
       $this->addElement($name)
            ->addElement($pass)
            ->addElement($uid)
            ->addElement($comment);
     }
}
```

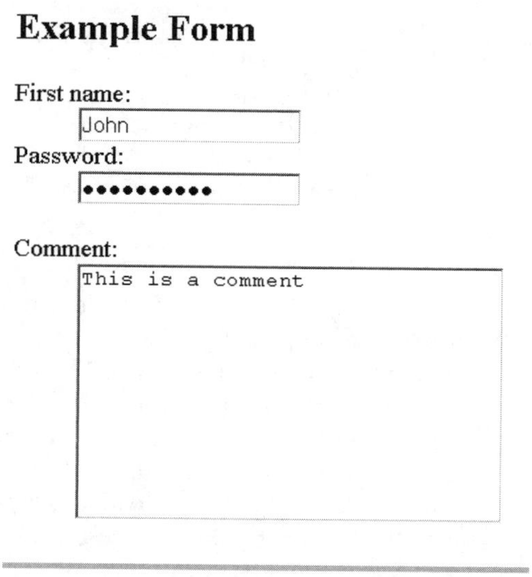

Figure 3-3 illustrates the result.

Radio Buttons and Checkboxes

Radio buttons are represented by the Zend_
Form_Element_Radio class, while check
boxes are represented by the Zend_Form_
Element_Checkbox class. Here's an example
of these two classes in action:

Example Form

First name:
John

Password:
••••••••••

Comment:
This is a comment

Figure 3-3 A form with text and hidden input elements

```
<?php
class Form_Example extends Zend_Form
{
  public function init()
  {
    // initialize form
    $this->setAction('/sandbox/example/form')
         ->setMethod('post');

    // create text input for name
    $name = new Zend_Form_Element_Text('name');
    $name->setLabel('Name:')
         ->setOptions(array('id' => 'fname'));

    // create radio buttons for type
    $type = new Zend_Form_Element_Radio('type');
    $type->setLabel('Membership type:')
         ->setMultiOptions(array(
            'silver'   => 'Silver',
            'gold'     => 'Gold',
            'platinum' => 'Platinum'
          ))
         ->setOptions(array('id' => 'mtype'));

    // create checkbox for newsletter subscription
    $subscribe = new Zend_Form_Element_Checkbox('subscribe');
    $subscribe->setLabel('Subscribe to newsletter')
```

```
            ->setCheckedValue('yes')
            ->setUncheckedValue('no');

    // attach elements to form
    $this->addElement($name)
        ->addElement($type)
        ->addElement($subscribe);
  }
}
```

The `setMultiOptions()` method of the Zend_Form_Element_Radio object accepts an array, and uses it to set the list of available radio button options. The keys of the array represent the form values that will be submitted, while the corresponding values represent the human-readable labels for each option. Similarly, the `setCheckedValue()` and `setUncheckedValue()` methods of the Zend_Form_Element_Checkbox object allow you to customize the value for the element's checked and unchecked states. By default, these values are set to 1 and 0, respectively.

Figure 3-4 illustrates the result.

If you'd like the user to select from a set of options, the Zend_Form_Element_MultiCheckbox class is often a better bet than the Zend_Form_Element_Checkbox class, because it exposes a `setMultiOptions()` method that allows for multiple items to be selected. The resulting collection is then formatted and submitted as an array. Here's an example of it in action:

Figure 3-4 A form with radio buttons and check boxes

```php
<?php
class Form_Example extends Zend_Form
{
  public function init()
  {
    // initialize form
    $this->setAction('/sandbox/example/form')
        ->setMethod('post');

    // create text input for name
    $name = new Zend_Form_Element_Text('name');
    $name->setLabel('Name:')
        ->setOptions(array('id' => 'fname'));

    // create radio buttons for type
    $type = new Zend_Form_Element_Radio('type');
    $type->setLabel('Pizza crust:')
```

```
        ->setMultiOptions(array(
           'thin'    => 'Thin',
           'thick'   => 'Thick'
        ))
        ->setOptions(array('id' => 'type'));

    // create checkbox for toppings
    $toppings = new Zend_Form_Element_MultiCheckbox('toppings');
    $toppings->setLabel('Pizza toppings:')
             ->setMultiOptions(array(
                'bacon'     => 'Bacon',
                'olives'    => 'Olives',
                'tomatoes'  => 'Tomatoes',
                'pepperoni' => 'Pepperoni',
                'ham'       => 'Ham',
                'peppers'   => 'Red peppers',
                'xcheese'   => 'Extra cheese',
             ));

    // attach elements to form
    $this->addElement($name)
         ->addElement($type)
         ->addElement($toppings);
    }
}
```

Figure 3-5 illustrates what the result looks like.

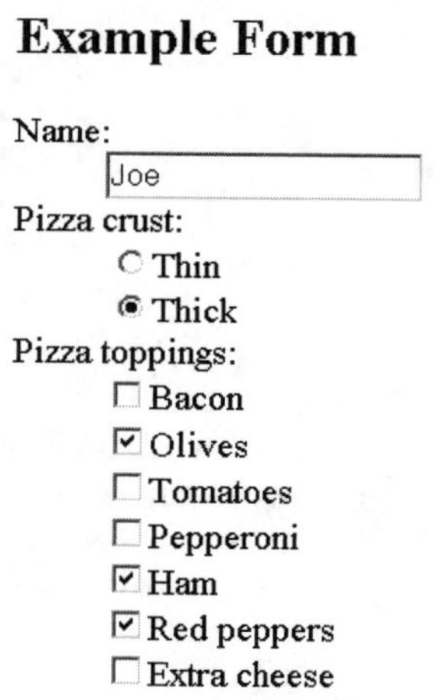

Selection Lists

Single- and multiple-selection lists are supported through the Zend_Form_Element_Select and Zend_Form_Element_MultiSelect classes. Like the Zend_Form_Element_MultiCheckbox class, they too expose a setMultiOptions() method that can be used to set up the list of available options. The following example demonstrates both these element types in action:

```
<?php
class Form_Example extends Zend_Form
{
  public function init()
  {
    // initialize form
    $this->setAction('/sandbox/example/form')
         ->setMethod('post');
```

Example Form

Name:

  Joe

Pizza crust:

  ○ Thin
  ● Thick

Pizza toppings:

  ☐ Bacon
  ☑ Olives
  ☐ Tomatoes
  ☐ Pepperoni
  ☑ Ham
  ☑ Red peppers
  ☐ Extra cheese

Figure 3-5 A form with radio buttons and multiple check boxes

```php
    // create text input for name
    $name = new Zend_Form_Element_Text('name');
    $name->setLabel('Name:')
        ->setOptions(array('id' => 'fname'));

    // create selection list for source country
    $from = new Zend_Form_Element_Select('from');
    $from->setLabel('Travelling from:')
        ->setMultiOptions(array(
            'IN'  => 'India',
            'US'  => 'United States',
            'DE'  => 'Germany',
            'FR'  => 'France',
            'UK'  => 'United Kingdom'
        ));

    // create multi-select list for destination countries
    $to = new Zend_Form_Element_MultiSelect('to');
    $to->setLabel('Travelling to:')
        ->setMultiOptions(array(
            'IT'  => 'Italy',
            'SG'  => 'Singapore',
            'TR'  => 'Turkey',
            'DK'  => 'Denmark',
            'ES'  => 'Spain',
            'PT'  => 'Portugal',
            'RU'  => 'Russia',
            'PL'  => 'Poland'
        ));

    // attach elements to form
    $this->addElement($name)
        ->addElement($from)
        ->addElement($to);
    }
}
```

Figure 3-6 illustrates the result.

File Upload Fields

If you're looking to upload one or more files through a form, you'll need the Zend_Form_Element_File class, which provides a browseable file input box. Here's an example of it in use:

```php
<?php
class Form_Example extends Zend_Form
{
```

Example Form

Name:
[Joe]
Travelling from:
[India ▼]
Travelling to:
Italy
Singapore
Turkey
Denmark
Spain
Portugal
Russia
Poland

Figure 3-6 A form with selection lists

```
public function init()
{
  // initialize form
  $this->setAction('/sandbox/example/form')
       ->setEnctype('multipart/form-data')
       ->setMethod('post');

  // create file input for photo upload
  $photo = new Zend_Form_Element_File('photo');
  $photo->setLabel('Photo:')
        ->setDestination('/tmp/upload');

  // attach elements to form
  $this->addElement($photo);
}
}
```

CAUTION

Remember that you must set the form encoding type to `'multipart/form-data'` for form uploads to be correctly handled. This can be done using the `setEnctype()` method of the form object.

Figure 3-7 illustrates what it looks like.

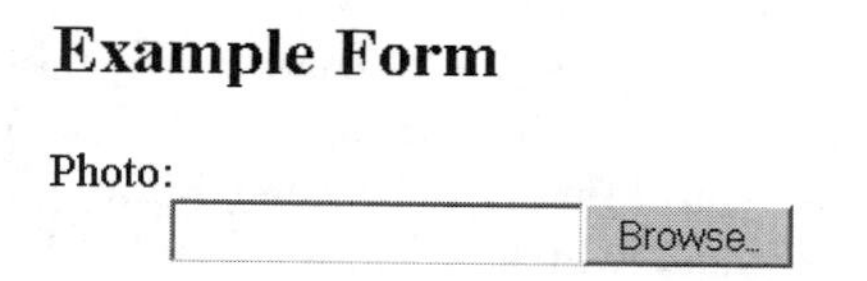

Example Form

Photo:

Figure 3-7   A form with file input fields

TIP

If you're trying to upload multiple related files, there's a convenient `setMultiFile()` method that generates a sequence of file input fields and saves you the hassle of instantiating multiple Zend_Form_Element_File objects. You'll see an example of this in the next chapter.

Buttons

Every form needs a submit button, and some also need a reset button. These two critical form elements are represented by the Zend_Form_Element_Submit and Zend_Form_Element_Reset classes, respectively, and they're illustrated in the next listing:

```
<?php
class Form_Example extends Zend_Form
{
  public function init()
  {
    // initialize form
    $this->setAction('/sandbox/example/form')
         ->setMethod('post');

    // create text input for title
```

```
$title = new Zend_Form_Element_Text('title');
$title->setLabel('Title:')
      ->setOptions(array('size' => '35'));

// create submit button
$submit = new Zend_Form_Element_Submit('submit');
$submit->setLabel('Submit');

// create reset button
$reset = new Zend_Form_Element_Reset('reset');
$reset->setLabel('Cancel');

// attach elements to form
$this->addElement($title)
     ->addElement($submit)
     ->addElement($reset);
  }
}
```

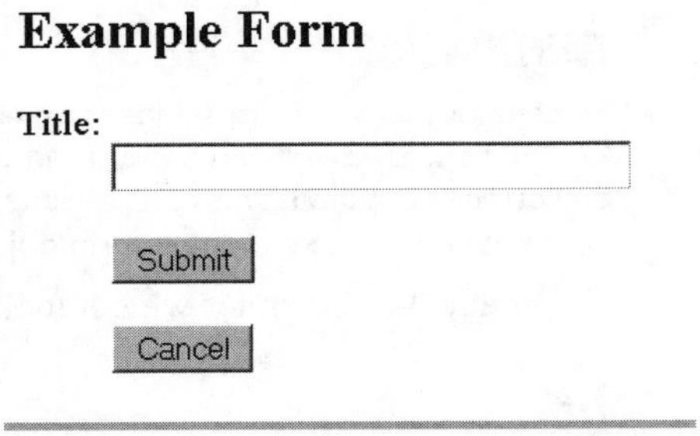

Figure 3-8 illustrates the resulting output.

If you're after a more generic form button, you'll find it in the Zend_Form_Element_Button class, which provides a simple, clickable form button that is useful for many different purposes. Image buttons can be generated with the Zend_Form_Element_Image class; use the setImage() method to specify the source image for the button. Here's an example of one such image button:

Example Form

Title:

[   ]

[Submit]

[Cancel]

Figure 3-8 A form with submit and reset buttons

```
<?php
class Form_Example extends Zend_Form
{
  public function init()
  {
    // initialize form
    $this->setAction('/sandbox/example/form')
         ->setMethod('post');

    // create text input for title
    $title = new Zend_Form_Element_Text('title');
    $title->setLabel('Title:')
          ->setOptions(array('size' => '35'));

    // create image submit button
    $submit = new Zend_Form_Element_Image('submit');
    $submit->setImage('/images/submit.jpg');
```

```
      // attach elements to form
      $this->addElement($title)
            ->addElement($submit);
   }
}
```

Figure 3-9 illustrates the resulting output.

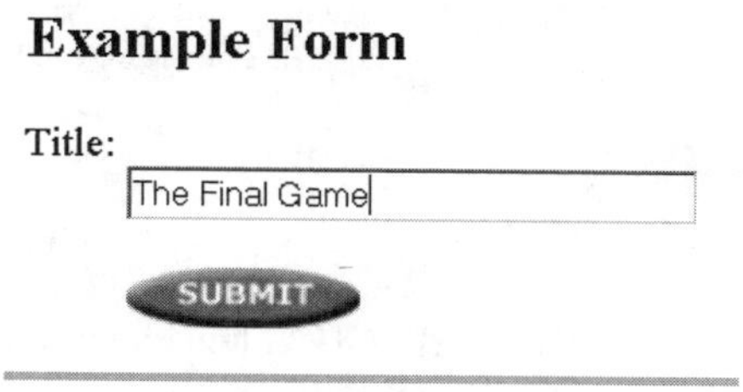

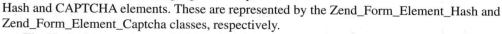

Example Form

Title:

The Final Game

SUBMIT

Figure 3-9 A form with an image button

Hash and CAPTCHA Fields

The Zend Framework includes two "special" form elements to assist in maintaining input security: the Hash and CAPTCHA elements. These are represented by the Zend_Form_Element_Hash and Zend_Form_Element_Captcha classes, respectively.

The Hash element uses a salt value to generate a unique key for the form and store it in the session. When the form is submitted, the hash value submitted with the form is automatically compared to the value stored in the session. If a match is found, the form submission is assumed to be genuine. If there is a mismatch, it's a reasonable supposition that the form has been hijacked and is being used in a Cross-Site Request Forgery (CSRF) attack.

Here's an example of using this element:

```
<?php
class Form_Example extends Zend_Form
{
  public function init()
  {
    // initialize form
    $this->setAction('/sandbox/example/form')
         ->setMethod('post');

    // create text input for number
    $cc = new Zend_Form_Element_Text('ccnum');
    $cc->setLabel('Credit card number:')
       ->setOptions(array('size' => '16'));

    // create text input for amount
    $amount = new Zend_Form_Element_Text('amount');
    $amount->setLabel('Payment amount:')
           ->setOptions(array('size' => '4'));

    // create hash
    $hash = new Zend_Form_Element_Hash('hash');
    $hash->setSalt('hf823hflw03j');

    // create submit button
    $submit = new Zend_Form_Element_Submit('submit');
    $submit->setLabel('Submit');

    // attach elements to form
```

```
    $this->addElement($cc)
        ->addElement($amount)
        ->addElement($hash)
        ->addElement($submit);
  }
}
```

The CAPTCHA element automatically generates a CAPTCHA verification input, which is a useful tool to filter out automated form submissions. More and more Web sites are using CAPTCHAs to reduce the number of false registrations and/or spam messages received through online forms. Although manually generating and verifying a CAPTCHA is a tedious process, the Zend_Form_Element_Captcha makes it as simple as adding a few lines of code to your form. Here's an example:

```php
<?php
class Form_Example extends Zend_Form
{
  public function init()
  {
    // initialize form
    $this->setAction('/sandbox/example/form')
        ->setMethod('post');

    // create text input for user name
    $name = new Zend_Form_Element_Text('username');
    $name->setLabel('Username:')
        ->setOptions(array('size' => '16'));
```

Ask the Expert

Q: What is a CSRF attack, and how do I protect against it?

A: Typically, when a user visits a protected Web site and validates his/her access credentials, a user session is generated and the access credentials are revalidated from the session data store on each request. A CSRF attack involves hijacking a validated user session and using the implicit trust relationship that already exists between the user and the host application to invisibly transmit unauthorized requests through input sources such as Web forms. By generating a unique hash value for each Web form and validating this value when the form is submitted, a developer is able to make it harder to perform this type of attack. Using a hash value also provides (limited) protection from automated spam mailers ("spambots"), and is more user-friendly than a CAPTCHA.

```php
    // create password input
    $pass = new Zend_Form_Element_Password('password');
    $pass->setLabel('Password:')
        ->setOptions(array('size' => '16'));

    // create captcha
    $captcha = new Zend_Form_Element_Captcha('captcha', array(
        'captcha'  => array(
            'captcha'   => 'Figlet',
            'wordLen'   => 5,
            'timeout'   => 300,
            )
        ));
    $captcha->setLabel('Verification:');

    // create submit button
    $submit = new Zend_Form_Element_Submit('submit');
    $submit->setLabel('Sign Up');

    // attach elements to form
    $this->addElement($name)
        ->addElement($pass)
        ->addElement($captcha)
        ->addElement($submit);
  }
}
```

Figure 3-10 illustrates what the result might look like.

NOTE
A number of predefined CAPTCHA adapters are included with the Zend Framework, including adapters for simple string-transposition operations ("Dumb") and for visual CAPTCHAS ("Image" and "Figlet"). You'll see another example of an image CAPTCHA a little further along in this chapter.

Setting Required and Default Values
You can mark a specific input element as required by calling its `setRequired()` method with a true argument. Here's an example:

```php
<?php
class Form_Example extends Zend_Form
{

  public function init()
  {
    // initialize form
    $this->setAction('/sandbox/example/form')
        ->setMethod('post');
```

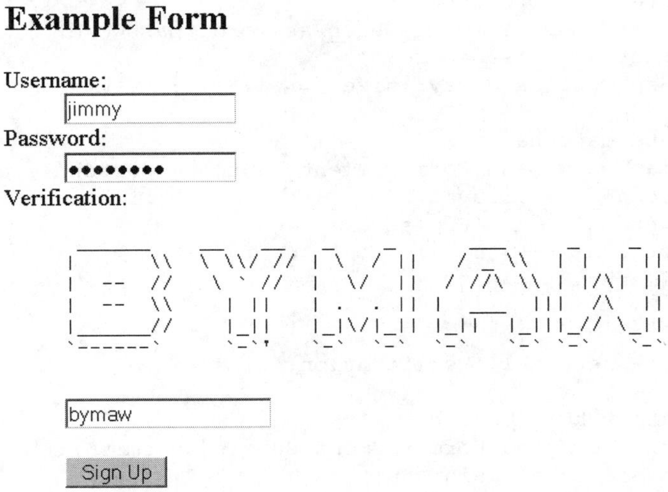

Example Form

Username:

    jimmy

Password:

    ••••••••

Verification:

```
 |‾‾‾‾\\    \\ \\//  |‾|\\/||  /‾‾\\ \\ |\/| |‾||
 |  -- //    \\'//  | |/ || / //\ \\ | \| ||
 |  -- \\    | ||  | .| || |  __  ||| /\ ||
 |_____//   |_|| |_|\/|_|| |_|'  |_||\_||//\_||
  `------'     `-`'  `-`'`-' `-`  `-`' `-`' `-`'
```

    bymaw

    [Sign Up]

Figure 3-10 A form containing a CAPTCHA

```
// create text input for name
$name = new Zend_Form_Element_Text('name');
$name->setLabel('Name:')
     ->setOptions(array('size' => '35'))
     ->setRequired(true);
```

Ask the Expert

Q: **What is a CAPTCHA?**

A: A CAPTCHA, or Completely Automated Public Turing test to tell Computers and Humans Apart, is a common challenge-response test used to identify whether the entity at the other end of a connection is a human being or a computer. On the Web, the typical form of a CAPTCHA is a distorted sequence of random alphanumeric characters, operating on the principle that a computer would be unable to see past the distortion, but a human, with greater powers of perception, would be able to correctly identify the sequence. Such CAPTCHAs are typically attached to input forms on the Web (for example, user registration forms), and they must be solved correctly before the input will be processed by the host application. CAPTCHAs need not always be visual; audio CAPTCHAs are also possible, and are most appropriate for visually handicapped users.

```
// create text input for email address
$email = new Zend_Form_Element_Text('email');
$email->setLabel('Email address:');
$email->setOptions(array('size' => '50'))
      ->setRequired(true);

// create submit button
$submit = new Zend_Form_Element_Submit('submit',
    array('class' => 'submit')
);
$submit->setLabel('Sign Up');

// attach elements to form
$this->addElement($name)
     ->addElement($email)
     ->addElement($submit);
    }
}
```

When you use the `setRequired()` method on an input field, Zend_Form automatically attaches a NotEmpty validator to that field. As a result, if the field is empty when the form is submitted, an error message will appear. Figure 3-11 illustrates the result.

TIP
You can tell Zend_Form not to attach a NotEmpty validator to required elements by explicitly calling the element's `setAutoInsertNotEmptyValidator()` method with a false argument. Validators are discussed in detail in the next section.

You can attach default values to input elements by calling the element object's `setValue()` method with the default value or by calling the form object's `setDefaults()` method with an array of default values. For text input fields, this can be any string value; for

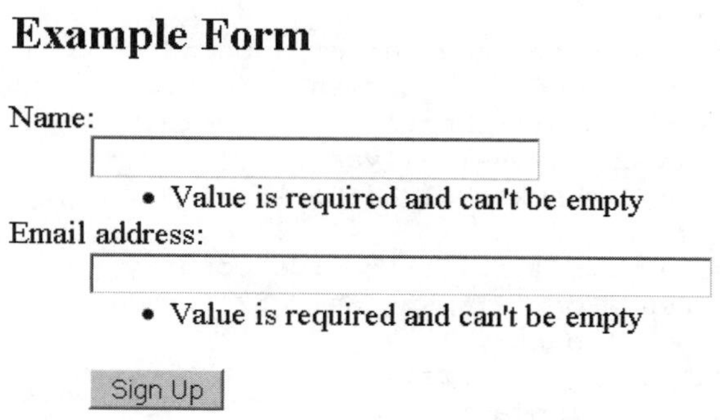

Example Form

Name:
[   ]
    • Value is required and can't be empty
Email address:
[   ]
    • Value is required and can't be empty

[Sign Up]

Figure 3-11   The result of submitting a form without required input values

radio buttons and selection lists, it should be the index of the selected item. Here's an example, which demonstrates both of these methods:

```php
<?php
class Form_Example extends Zend_Form
{
  public function init()
  {
    // initialize form
    $this->setAction('/sandbox/example/form')
         ->setMethod('post');

    // create text input for name
    $name = new Zend_Form_Element_Text('name');
    $name->setLabel('Name:')
         ->setOptions(array('size' => '35'))
         ->setRequired(true)
         ->setValue('Enter your name');

    // create text input for email address
    $email = new Zend_Form_Element_Text('email');
    $email->setLabel('Email address:');
    $email->setOptions(array('size' => '50'))
          ->setRequired(true)
          ->setValue('Enter your email address');

    // create radio buttons for type
    $type = new Zend_Form_Element_Radio('type');
    $type->setLabel('Membership type:')
         ->setMultiOptions(array(
            'silver'   => 'Silver',
            'gold'     => 'Gold',
            'platinum' => 'Platinum'
         ));

    // create checkbox for newsletter subscription
    $subscribe = new Zend_Form_Element_Checkbox('subscribe');
    $subscribe->setLabel('Subscribe to newsletter')
              ->setCheckedValue('yes')
              ->setUncheckedValue('no');

    // create selection list for source country
    $from = new Zend_Form_Element_Select('from');
    $from->setLabel('Country:')
         ->setMultiOptions(array(
            'IN' => 'India',
            'US' => 'United States',
            'DE' => 'Germany',
            'FR' => 'France',
```

```
              'UK'  => 'United Kingdom'
          ));

    // create submit button
    $submit = new Zend_Form_Element_Submit(
      'submit', array('class' => 'submit'));
    $submit->setLabel('Sign Up');

    // attach elements to form
    $this->addElement($name)
         ->addElement($email)
         ->addElement($type)
         ->addElement($from)
         ->addElement($subscribe)
         ->addElement($submit);

    // set default values
    $this->setDefaults(array(
      'type' => 'platinum',
      'subscribe' => 'yes',
      'from' => 'FR',
    ));
  }
}
```

Figure 3-12 illustrates what the result looks like.

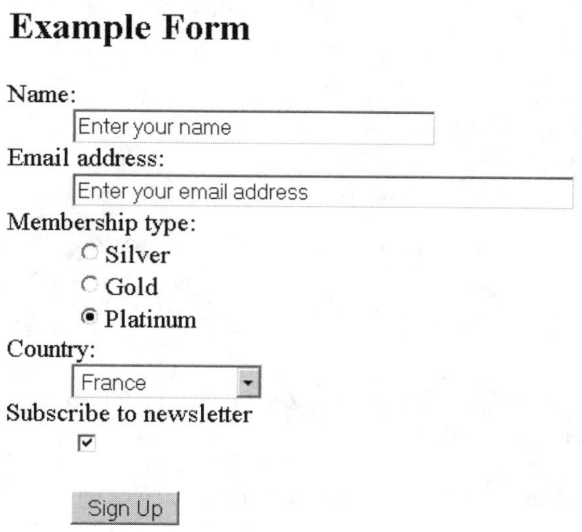

Figure 3-12   A form rendered with default values

Filtering and Validating Form Input

As a Web application developer, there's one unhappy fact that you'll have to learn to live with: There are always going to be people out there who get their chuckles from finding loopholes in your code and exploiting these loopholes for malicious purposes. Therefore, one of the most important things a developer can do to secure an application is to properly filter and validate all the input passing through it.

The following sections discuss the filtering and validation tools available in the Zend Framework, together with examples of how they can be used with Web forms to make your application more secure.

Using Input Filters

Most of the time, input exploits consist of sending your application cleverly disguised values that "trick" it into doing something it really, really shouldn't. A common example of this type of exploit is the SQL injection attack, wherein an attacker remotely manipulates your database with an SQL query embedded inside form input. Therefore, one of the most important things a developer must do before using any input supplied by the user is to "sanitize" it by removing any special characters or symbols from it.

PHP comes with various functions to assist developers in the task of sanitizing input. For example, the addslashes() function escapes special characters (like quotes and backslashes) in input so that it can be safely entered into a database, while the strip_tags() function strips all the HTML and PHP tags out of a string, returning only the ASCII content. There's also the htmlentities() function, which is commonly used to replace special characters like ", &, <, and > with their corresponding HTML entity values, rendering them harmless.

Here's an example of sanitizing form input with the htmlentities() function:

```php
<?php
// define array of sanitized data
$sanitized = array();

// strip tags from POST input
if (isset($_POST['name']) && !empty($_POST['name'])) {
  $sanitized['name'] = htmlentities($_POST['name']);
}

// processing code //
?>
```

When it comes to filtering user input, the Zend Framework does a lot of the heavy lifting for you. The Zend_Filter component provides a comprehensive set of *input filters*, which can either be attached to form elements with the addFilter() method or used on a stand-alone basis for ad-hoc input sanitization. Here's an example of using the HTMLEntities filter on a text input field:

```php
<?php
class Form_Example extends Zend_Form
```

```
{
  public function init()
  {
    // initialize form
    $this->setAction('/sandbox/example/form')
         ->setMethod('post');

    // create text input for user name
    // filter special characters
    $name = new Zend_Form_Element_Text('name');
    $name->setLabel('Username:')
         ->setOptions(array('size' => '16'))
         ->addFilter('HtmlEntities');

    // create submit button
    $submit = new Zend_Form_Element_Submit('submit');
    $submit->setLabel('Sign Up');

    // attach elements to form
    $this->addElement($name)
         ->addElement($submit);
  }
}
```

You can also pass the addFilter() method an instance of the Zend_Filter_* class, as shown in the following equivalent script:

```
<?php
class Form_Example extends Zend_Form
{
  public function init()
  {
    // initialize form
    $this->setAction('/sandbox/example/form')
         ->setMethod('post');

    // create text input for user name
    // filter special characters
    $name = new Zend_Form_Element_Text('name');
    $name->setLabel('Username:')
         ->setOptions(array('size' => '16'))
         ->addFilter(new Zend_Filter_HtmlEntities());

    // create submit button
    $submit = new Zend_Form_Element_Submit('submit');
    $submit->setLabel('Sign Up');

    // attach elements to form
```

```
    $this->addElement($name)
        ->addElement($submit);
  }
}
```

Some filters support additional options, which can be passed to the addFilter() method as an array or, if you're using a class instance, as arguments to the object constructor. Consider the next example, which uses the Alpha filter to strip out all non-alphabetic characters from user input. An additional option, passed to the addFilter() method as a second argument, retains whitespace (which is stripped by default).

```php
<?php
class Form_Example extends Zend_Form
{
  public function init()
  {
    // initialize form
    $this->setAction('/sandbox/example/form')
        ->setMethod('post');

    // create text input for name
    // allow alphabetic characters and whitespace
    $name = new Zend_Form_Element_Text('name');
    $name->setLabel('Name:')
        ->setOptions(array('size' => '4'))
        ->setRequired(true)
        ->addFilter('Alpha', array('allowWhiteSpace' => true))
        ->addFilter('HtmlEntities');

    // create submit button
    $submit = new Zend_Form_Element_Submit('submit');
    $submit->setLabel('Sign Up');

    // attach elements to form
    $this->addElement($name)
        ->addElement($submit);
  }
}
```

Table 3-2 gives a list of some important filters that ship with the Zend Framework, together with a brief description of each. You'll see many of these filters in use in this and subsequent chapters.

TIP
You can attach multiple filters to a form element in one of two ways: by calling the addFilter() method multiple times, with a different filter name on each invocation, or by using the addFilters() method and passing it an array containing a list of filter names.

Filter Name	Description
Alnum	Removes non-alphanumeric characters from argument
Alpha	Removes non-alphabetic characters from argument
Digits	Removes non-numeric characters from argument
Int	Returns integer value of argument
Dir	Returns directory name component of argument
BaseName	Returns filename component of argument
RealPath	Returns absolute filesystem path for argument
StringToLower	Converts argument to a lowercase string
StringToUpper	Converts argument to an uppercase string
StringTrim	Removes leading and trailing whitespace from argument
StripNewlines	Removes line break characters from argument
HtmlEntities	Converts special characters in argument to their HTML entity equivalents
StripTags	Removes HTML and PHP code from argument
Encrypt	Returns encrypted version of argument
Decrypt	Returns decrypted version of argument
NormalizedToLocalized	Returns argument in standard form
LocalizedToNormalized	Returns argument in localized form
Callback	Calls user-defined filter with argument
LowerCase	Converts contents of uploaded file to lowercase
UpperCase	Converts contents of uploaded file to uppercase
Rename	Renames uploaded file

Table 3-2 Input Filters Included with the Zend Framework

Using Input Validators

Filtering input is only part of the puzzle. It's also extremely important to validate user input to ensure that it is in the correct format before using it for calculations or saving it to the application's data store. Improperly validated application input can not only cause significant data corruption and loss, but it can also be embarrassing in the extreme to the proud application developer.

In order to illustrate the importance of input validation, consider a simple example: an online mortgage calculator that allows a user to enter the desired loan amount, finance term, and interest rate. Now, let's assume that the application doesn't include any input validation. And let's also suppose that the user decides to enter the string `'ten'`, instead of the number 10, into the term field.

It shouldn't be too hard to guess what happens next. The application will perform a few internal calculations that will end in it attempt to divide the total amount payable by the specified term. Since the term in this case is a string, PHP will cast it to the number 0, producing a division-by-zero error. The resulting slew of ugly error messages is likely to leave even the most blasé developer red-faced; more importantly, if the invalid input is also saved to the database as is, the error will recur every time the calculation is repeated on the record. Multiply this by even a few hundred records containing similar errors, scattered throughout the database, and you'll quickly see how the lack of appropriate input validation can significantly damage an application.

PHP comes with various functions to assist developers in the task of validating input. For example, the `is_numeric()` function tests if a value is numeric, while the `ctype_alpha()` and `ctype_alnum()` functions can be used to test for alphabetic and alphanumeric strings. There's also the `filter_var()` function, while can be used to test the validity of email addresses and URLs, and the `preg_match()` function, which allows for pattern validation using regular expressions. Here's an example of some of these functions in action:

```php
<?php
// define array of valid data
$valid = array();

// check if age is a number
if (is_numeric(trim($_POST['age']))) {
  $valid['age'] = trim($_POST['age']);
} else {
  die ('ERROR: Age is not a number.');
}

// check for valid first name
if (isset($_POST['firstname']) && ctype_alpha($_POST['firstname'])) {
  $valid['firstname'] = trim($_POST['firstname']);
} else {
  die ('ERROR: First name not present or invalid.');
}

// check for valid email address
if (isset($_POST['email'])
  && filter_var($_POST['email'], FILTER_VALIDATE_EMAIL)) {
  $valid['email'] = trim($_POST['email']);
} else {
  die ('ERROR: Email address not present or invalid.');
}

// processing code here //
?>
```

As with filters, the Zend Framework ships with a large number of predefined *input validators*, collectively referred to as Zend_Validate, which can either be attached to form elements with the `addValidator()` method or used ad hoc. Validator-specific options can be passed as the third argument to the addFilter() method as an associative array of key-value pairs, as shown in the following example:

```php
<?php
class Form_Example extends Zend_Form
{
  public function init()
  {
    // initialize form
    $this->setAction('/sandbox/example/form')
         ->setMethod('post');

    // create text input for age
    // should contain only integer values between 1 and 100
    $age = new Zend_Form_Element_Text('age');
    $age->setLabel('Age:')
        ->setOptions(array('size' => '4'))
        ->setRequired(true)
        ->addValidator('Int')
        ->addValidator('Between', false, array(1,100));

    // create text input for name
    // should contain only alphabetic characters and whitespace
    $name = new Zend_Form_Element_Text('name');
    $name->setLabel('First name:')
         ->setOptions(array('size' => '16'))
         ->setRequired(true)
         ->addValidator('Alpha', false, array('allowWhiteSpace' =>
true));

    // create text input for email address
    // should contain a valid email address
    $email = new Zend_Form_Element_Text('email');
    $email->setLabel('Email address:')
          ->setOptions(array('size' => '16'))
          ->setRequired(true)
          ->addValidator('EmailAddress');

    // create submit button
    $submit = new Zend_Form_Element_Submit('submit');
    $submit->setLabel('Sign Up');

    // attach elements to form
    $this->addElement($age)
         ->addElement($name)
         ->addElement($email)
         ->addElement($submit);
  }
}
```

As with filters, validators can also be specified as instances of the corresponding Zend_ Validate_* class, with validator options passed as arguments to the object constructor. The next example, which is equivalent to the previous one, illustrates this approach:

```php
<?php
class Form_Example extends Zend_Form
{
  public function init()
  {
    // initialize form
    $this->setAction('/sandbox/example/form')
         ->setMethod('post');

    // create text input for age
    // should contain only integer values between 1 and 100
    $age = new Zend_Form_Element_Text('age');
    $age->setLabel('Age:')
        ->setOptions(array('size' => '4'))
        ->setRequired(true)
        ->addValidator(new Zend_Validate_Int())
        ->addValidator(new Zend_Validate_Between(1,100));

    // create text input for name
    // should contain only alphabetic characters and whitespace
    $name = new Zend_Form_Element_Text('name');
    $name->setLabel('First name:')
         ->setOptions(array('size' => '16'))
         ->setRequired(true)
         ->addValidator(new Zend_Validate_Alpha(true));

    // create text input for email address
    // should contain a valid email address
    $email = new Zend_Form_Element_Text('email');
    $email->setLabel('Email address:')
          ->setOptions(array('size' => '16'))
          ->setRequired(true)
          ->addValidator(new Zend_Validate_EmailAddress());

    // create submit button
    $submit = new Zend_Form_Element_Submit('submit');
    $submit->setLabel('Sign Up');

    // attach elements to form
    $this->addElement($age)
         ->addElement($name)
         ->addElement($email)
         ->addElement($submit);
  }
}
```

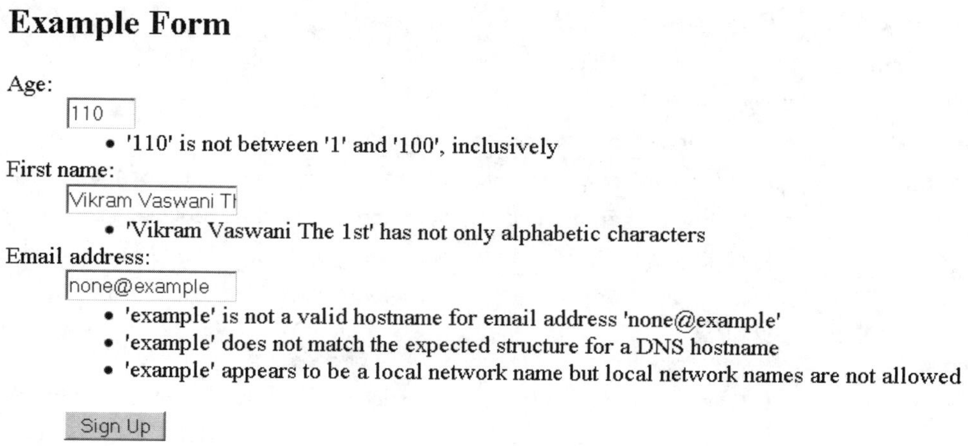

Example Form

Age:

[110]

- '110' is not between '1' and '100', inclusively

First name:

[Vikram Vaswani Th]

- 'Vikram Vaswani The 1st' has not only alphabetic characters

Email address:

[none@example]

- 'example' is not a valid hostname for email address 'none@example'
- 'example' does not match the expected structure for a DNS hostname
- 'example' appears to be a local network name but local network names are not allowed

[Sign Up]

Figure 3-13   The result of submitting a form with invalid input values

Figure 3-13 illustrates the result of attempting to submit invalid values through such a form.

Table 3-3 provides a list of some important validators available in the Zend Framework, together with a brief description of each. You'll see many of these validators in use further along in this chapter, as well as in subsequent chapters.

Validator Name	Description
NotEmpty	Returns false if argument is empty
StringLength	Returns false if argument does not conform to specified minimum/maximum length
InArray	Returns false if argument is not in specified array
Identical	Returns false if argument does not match specified value
Alnum	Returns false if argument does not contain only alphanumeric characters
Alpha	Returns false if argument does not contain only alphabetic characters
Int	Returns false if argument is not an integer
Float	Returns false if argument is not a floating-point number
Hex	Returns false if argument is not a hexadecimal value
Digits	Returns false if argument does not contain only numbers
Between	Returns false if argument is not in a specified numeric range

Table 3-3   Input Validators Included with the Zend Framework

Validator Name	Description
GreaterThan	Returns false if argument is not greater than a specified value
LessThan	Returns false if argument is not less than a specified value
Date	Returns false if argument is not a valid date
EmailAddress	Returns false if argument does not conform to standard email address conventions
Hostname	Returns false if argument does not conform to standard host name conventions
Ip	Returns false if argument does not conform to standard IP address conventions
Regex	Returns false if argument does not conform to specified regular expression pattern
Barcode	Returns false if argument is not a valid bar code
Ccnum	Returns false if argument does not conform to the Luhn algorithm for standard credit card number conventions
Iban	Returns false if argument is not a valid IBAN number
Exists	Returns false if argument is not a valid file
Count	Returns false if number of uploaded files is outside the range specified in argument
Size	Returns false if uploaded file size is outside the range specified in argument
FilesSize	Returns false if uploaded file size total is outside the range specified in argument
Extension	Returns false if uploaded file extension does not match those specified in argument
MimeType	Returns false if uploaded file MIME type does not match those specified in argument
IsCompressed	Returns false if uploaded file is not a compressed archive file
IsImage	Returns false if uploaded file is not an image file
ImageSize	Returns false if uploaded image dimensions are outside the range specified in argument
Crc32, Md5, Sha1, Hash	Returns false if uploaded file content does not match the hash value specified in argument (supports crc32, md5, and sha1 hash algorithms)
ExcludeExtension	Returns false if uploaded file extension matches those specified in argument
ExcludeMimeType	Returns false if uploaded file MIME type matches those specified in argument
WordCount	Returns false if number of words in uploaded file is outside the range specified in argument
Db_RecordExists	Returns false if a particular record does not exist in the database and table specified in argument
Db_NoRecordExists	Returns false if a particular record exists in the database and table specified in argument

Table 3-3 Input Validators Included with the Zend Framework (*continued*)

Ask the Expert

Q: I'm already validating form input using JavaScript. Why do I also need to validate it using PHP?

A: It's common practice to use client-side scripting languages like JavaScript or VBScript for client-side input validation. However, this type of client-side validation is not foolproof—if a user turns off JavaScript in the client, all your client-side code will become nonfunctional. That's why it's a good idea to couple client-side validation (which is faster) with server-side validation (which is more secure).

Using Validator and Filter Chains

One of the most interesting things about the Zend_Filter and Zend_Validate components is their support for *chaining* or *stacking*. Essentially, this means that it is possible to attach multiple filters and validators to a single input element, and have them automatically run, in sequence, once the form is submitted. The following example illustrates this by setting up a chain of four filters:

```php
<?php
    // create text input for name
    // filter tags, entities and whitespace
    $name = new Zend_Form_Element_Text('name');
    $name->setLabel('First name:')
        ->setOptions(array('size' => '16'))
        ->setRequired(true)
        ->addFilter('StripTags')
        ->addFilter('HTMLEntities')
        ->addFilter('StringTrim')
        ->addFilter('StringToLower');
?>
```

In this example, the first filter strips HTML and PHP tags from the input, the second encodes entities, the third trims leading and trailing whitespace, and the fourth transforms the result to lowercase. These filters are executed on the input value in their order of appearance in the chain.

Validator chains work in a similar manner and come with an additional property. A validator chain can be configured such that a failure in any one validator terminates the entire chain with an error message. This behavior is controlled by the second argument to the addValidator() method which, when set to true, breaks the chain if there is a failure in the corresponding validator. Consider the next example, which illustrates this:

```php
<?php
    // create text input for age
```

```
      // should contain only integer values between 1 and 100
      $age = new Zend_Form_Element_Text('age');
      $age->setLabel('Age:')
          ->setOptions(array('size' => '4'))
          ->setRequired(true)
          ->addValidator('NotEmpty', true)
          ->addValidator('Int', true)
          ->addValidator('Between', true, array(1,100));
?>
```

In this example, a failure in any one of the validators breaks the chain, and the remaining validators will not be processed. So, for example, if the input is not an integer value, the validation chain will terminate with the error message generated by the Int validator, and the Between validator will not be executed. Contrast this with the next listing:

```
<?php
      // create text input for age
      // should contain only integer values between 1 and 100
      $age = new Zend_Form_Element_Text('age');
      $age->setLabel('Age:')
          ->setOptions(array('size' => '4'))
          ->setRequired(true)
          ->addValidator('NotEmpty', false)
          ->addValidator('Int', false)
          ->addValidator('Between', false, array(1,100));
?>
```

In this version, even if one of the validators fails, the remaining validators will still be run, and error messages generated by any subsequent failures will be added to the message stack. This is illustrated in Figures 3-14 and 3-15, which compare and contrast the difference in behavior of these two listings.

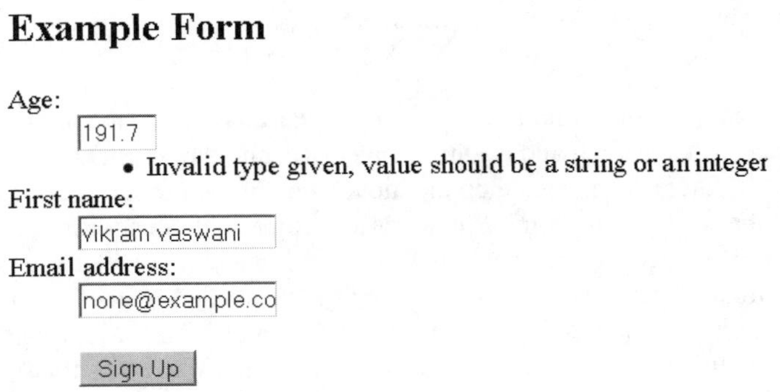

Example Form

Age:

191.7

- Invalid type given, value should be a string or an integer

First name:

vikram vaswani

Email address:

none@example.co

Sign Up

Figure 3-14 A validator chain, broken on the first failure

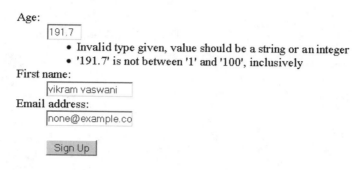

Example Form

Age:

191.7

- Invalid type given, value should be a string or an integer
- '191.7' is not between '1' and '100', inclusively

First name:

vikram vaswani

Email address:

none@example.co

Sign Up

Figure 3-15 A validator chain, processed without any break

TIP

In case the predefined filters and validators that ship with the Zend Framework don't meet your needs, remember that you can always write your own. The Zend Framework manual has examples of how to do this.

Retrieving and Processing Form Input

Within a controller script, you can use a number of Zend_Form methods to retrieve and process form input after submission:

- The `isValid()` method checks if the submitted input is valid. This method accepts an array of input values and returns Boolean true or false depending on whether these values match the validation rules set up with the various `addValidator()` calls.

- If the input is invalid, the `getMessages()` method returns a list of the error messages generated during the validation process. This list can be processed and displayed when the form is re-rendered to give the user a hint about what went wrong.

- If the input is valid, the `getValues()` method can be used to retrieve the valid, filtered values for further processing. Input values are returned as elements of an associative array, where the array key represents the element name and the array value represents the corresponding input value. There's also a `getUnfilteredValues()` method, which returns the original, unfiltered input as entered by the user.

TIP

The `isValid()` method automatically verifies CAPTCHA and hash values, with no additional programming required on your part.

The next listing illustrates how these methods are typically used in the context of a controller script:

```php
<?php
class ExampleController extends Zend_Controller_Action
{
  public function formAction()
  {
    $form = new Form_Example;
    $this->view->form = $form;

    // check the request
    // run the validators
    if ($this->getRequest()->isPost()) {
      if ($form->isValid($this->getRequest()->getPost())) {
        // valid data: get the filtered and valid values
        // do something, save to database or write to file
        // display a success view
        $values = $form->getValues();
        $this->_redirect('/form/success');
      } else {
        // invalid data: get the error message array
        // for manual processing (if needed)
        // redisplay the form with errors
        $this->view->messages = $form->getMessages();
      }
    }
  }
}
?>
```

Try This 3-1   Creating a Contact Form

With all this background information at hand, let's now look at how it plays out in the context of a practical application. The following section applies everything you've learned so far to create an email inquiry form for the SQUARE application. This form will invite the user to enter a message and, on submission, will format the input into an email message and send it to the site administrators for follow-up.

Defining the Form

To begin, let's consider the requirements of the input form. They aren't very complicated—all that's really needed are three fields for the user to enter his or her name, email address, and message. These values should be validated, particularly the email address, to ensure authenticity and thereby make it possible for administrators to respond to email inquiries. To filter out automated submissions and reduce the incidence of spam, it would also be nice to include a visual CAPTCHA—something that's quite easy to do with Zend_Form, as illustrated earlier. Here's an example of what the resulting form definition would look like:

```php
<?php
class Square_Form_Contact extends Zend_Form
{
  public function init()
  {
    // initialize form
    $this->setAction('/contact/index')
         ->setMethod('post');

    // create text input for name
    $name = new Zend_Form_Element_Text('name');
    $name->setLabel('Name:')
         ->setOptions(array('size' => '35'))
         ->setRequired(true)
         ->addValidator('NotEmpty', true)
         ->addValidator('Alpha', true)
         ->addFilter('HTMLEntities')
         ->addFilter('StringTrim');

    // create text input for email address
    $email = new Zend_Form_Element_Text('email');
    $email->setLabel('Email address:');
    $email->setOptions(array('size' => '50'))
          ->setRequired(true)
          ->addValidator('NotEmpty', true)
          ->addValidator('EmailAddress', true)
          ->addFilter('HTMLEntities')
          ->addFilter('StringToLower')
          ->addFilter('StringTrim');

    // create text input for message body
    $message = new Zend_Form_Element_Textarea('message');
    $message->setLabel('Message:')
            ->setOptions(array('rows' => '8','cols' => '40'))
            ->setRequired(true)
            ->addValidator('NotEmpty', true)
            ->addFilter('HTMLEntities')
            ->addFilter('StringTrim');

    // create captcha
    $captcha = new Zend_Form_Element_Captcha('captcha', array(
      'captcha' => array(
        'captcha' => 'Image',
```

(continued)

```
            'wordLen' => 6,
            'timeout' => 300,
            'width'   => 300,
            'height'  => 100,
            'imgUrl'  => '/captcha',
            'imgDir'  => APPLICATION_PATH . '/../public/captcha',
            'font'    => APPLICATION_PATH .
                         '/../public/fonts/LiberationSansRegular.ttf',
        )
    ));
    $captcha->setLabel('Verification code:');

    // create submit button
    $submit = new Zend_Form_Element_Submit('submit');
    $submit->setLabel('Send Message')
           ->setOptions(array('class' => 'submit'));

    // attach elements to form
    $this->addElement($name)
         ->addElement($email)
         ->addElement($message)
         ->addElement($captcha)
         ->addElement($submit);
    }
}
```

You should already be familiar with most of the preceding code. The form contains two text input elements for the user's name and email address, one text area for the message body, and a CAPTCHA element for verification. Alpha and NotEmpty validators are attached to the name and message body fields, while an EmailAddress validator is used to check the submitted email address. All fields are filtered using the HTMLEntities validator, and the email address is additionally converted to lowercase with the StringToLower validator.

The options passed to the Zend_Form_Element_Captcha instance are also worth looking into. Unlike the example shown in an earlier section, this definition generates a more complex CAPTCHA by dynamically overlaying a random sequence of characters on a distressed background. This type of CAPTCHA is commonly used in Web forms to stymie automated bot submissions, many of which include optical character recognition (OCR) algorithms that can "read" characters overlaid on a clear background. The options passed to the object instance include the dimensions of the CAPTCHA image, the disk location to store the generated CAPTCHA, the number of characters in the CAPTCHA, and the font file to use for the text overlay.

CAUTION
If you're using copyrighted fonts that cannot be redistributed, you should move the $APP_DIR/public/fonts/ directory to a location outside the server document root, such as $APP_DIR/application/fonts/, to ensure that the fonts are not publicly accessible through a Web browser. If you're doing this, remember to update the application code to reflect the new path as well.

You'll notice that the previous example makes use of a custom font, and it stores generated CAPTCHAs in a specified directory. Accordingly, also create the *$APP_DIR/public/captcha/* and *$APP_DIR/public/fonts/* directories and copy over the necessary assets to these locations. You'll find these assets in the code archive for this chapter, which can be downloaded from this book's companion Web site at **http://www.zf-beginners-guide.com/**.

NOTE

The font used for the CAPTCHA in this example is the Liberation Sans font, part of a collection of fonts released to the community under the GNU General Public License by RedHat Inc. in 2007. Users are free to use, modify, copy, and redistribute these fonts under the terms of the GNU GPL.

Using a Custom Namespace

The definition in the previous section uses a custom namespace, "Square," which is prefixed to the class name. This is a recommended practice for any custom objects or libraries that you may create for the application, as it helps avoid name collisions between your definitions and others that may exist in the application space. An added benefit is that if you register your custom namespace with the Zend Framework's autoloader and then locate your definitions correctly in the application directory structure, the Zend Framework will automatically find and load them as needed at run time.

With this in mind, save the class definition from the preceding code to *$APP_DIR/library/Square/Form/Contact.php*, and then add the following directive to the application configuration file, at *$APP_DIR/application/configs/application.ini*, to register the "Square" namespace with the autoloader:

```
autoloaderNamespaces[] = "Square_"
```

CAUTION

If your classes use an underscore to separate the namespace from the rest of the class name, you must include this underscore when registering the namespace with the Zend Framework autoloader.

Defining a Custom Route

This is also a good time to add a custom route for the new form. While you've got the application configuration file open in your text editor, add the following route definition to it:

```
resources.router.routes.contact.route = /contact
resources.router.routes.contact.defaults.module = default
resources.router.routes.contact.defaults.controller = contact
resources.router.routes.contact.defaults.action = index
```

(continued)

Based on the material discussed in Chapter 2, this should be quite familiar to you—it sets up a route such that requests for the application URL */contact* are handled by the "default" module's `ContactController::indexAction`.

Defining Controllers and Views

The next step is to define the aforesaid `ContactController::indexAction..` By convention, this controller should be located at *$APP_DIR/application/modules/default/controllers/ContactController.php*, and should look something like this:

```php
<?php
class ContactController extends Zend_Controller_Action
{

  public function init()
  {
    $this->view->doctype('XHTML1_STRICT');
  }

  public function indexAction()
  {
    $form = new Square_Form_Contact();
    $this->view->form = $form;
    if ($this->getRequest()->isPost()) {
      if ($form->isValid($this->getRequest()->getPost())) {
        $values = $form->getValues();
        $mail = new Zend_Mail();
        $mail->setBodyText($values['message']);
        $mail->setFrom($values['email'], $values['name']);
        $mail->addTo('info@square.example.com');
        $mail->setSubject('Contact form submission');
        $mail->send();
        $this->_helper->getHelper('FlashMessenger')
          ->addMessage('Thank you. Your message was successfully
sent.');
        $this->_redirect('/contact/success');
      }
    }
  }

  public function successAction()
  {
    if ($this->_helper->getHelper('FlashMessenger')->getMessages()) {
      $this->view->messages =
        $this->_helper->getHelper('FlashMessenger')->getMessages();
    } else {
```

```
        $this->_redirect('/');
    }
  }
}
```

Most of the heavy lifting here is done by the `indexAction()` method, which creates an object of the Square_Form_Contact class discussed earlier and attaches it to the view. When the form is submitted, the object's `isValid()` method is used to validate the input submitted by the user. If the input is found to be valid, an instance of the Zend_Mail component is created, and object methods are used to format the input into an email message and send it to a specified email address. Once the message has been sent, control is transferred to the `successAction()` method, which renders a success view.

That's what happens if all goes well...but there's many a slip 'twixt the cup and the lip, so it's useful to understand what happens if things go wrong. If the input is found to be invalid, the `isValid()` method will return false and the form will be redisplayed, with error messages indicating the source of the error(s). Zend_Form will also automatically populate the form with the original input values to ensure that the user doesn't need to re-enter all the requested data. On the other hand, if the input is valid but an error occurs in the process of email generation and transmission, Zend_Mail will throw a PHP exception, which will be caught and handled by the application's default error handler.

NOTE

In order for the Zend_Mail object's `send()` method to work correctly, a mail delivery agent (such as *sendmail*) must be available and correctly configured in your *php.ini* configuration file. If this is not the case, message transmission will fail and the `send()` method will throw an exception at the point of failure.

This controller also introduces a new tool, the FlashMessenger helper, which is a useful little "helper" to simplify the display of status messages to the user. Messages can be added to the FlashMessenger object via its `addMessage()` method; these messages are then stored in the session until retrieved with a call to the `getMessages()` method, at which point they are removed from the session. This makes the FlashMessenger a convenient place to temporarily store messages between the time an operation ends and the time the subsequent view completes rendering, and you'll see it being used frequently throughout this book.

CAUTION

You'll notice that the controller's `init()` method sets the view's document type to XHTML 1.0 Strict. This is because, by default, Zend_Form doesn't produce well-formed XHTML markup. Setting the document type in this manner forces it to do so.

Obviously, you also need a couple of views, one for the input form and one for the success message. Here's the input view, which by convention should be located at *$APP_DIR/application/modules/default/views/scripts/contact/index.phtml*:

```
<h2>Contact</h2>
<?php echo $this->form; ?>
```

(continued)

And here's the success view, which by convention should be stored at *$APP_DIR/ application/modules/default/views/scripts/contact/success.phtml*:

```
<h2>Success</h2>
<?php echo implode($this->messages); ?>
```

Updating the Master Layout

All that's left now is to update the navigation links in the application's main menu to reflect the new inquiry form using the url() helper method. To do this, update the master layout, at *$APP_DIR/application/layouts/master.phtml*, with the changes highlighted in bold:

```
<!DOCTYPE html PUBLIC "-//W3C//DTD XHTML 1.0 Strict//EN"
"http://www.w3.org/TR/xhtml1/DTD/xhtml1-strict.dtd">
<html xmlns="http://www.w3.org/1999/xhtml" xml:lang="en" lang="en">
  <head>
    <meta http-equiv="Content-Type" content="text/html;
charset=utf-8"/>
    <base href="/" />
    <link rel="stylesheet" type="text/css" href="/css/master.css" />
  </head>
  <body>
    <div id="header">
      <div id="logo">
        <img src="/images/logo.gif" />
      </div>

      <div id="menu">
        <a href="<?php echo $this->url(array(), 'home'); ?>">HOME</a>
        <a href="<?php echo $this->url(array('page' => 'services'),
          'static-content'); ?>">SERVICES</a>
        <a href="<?php echo $this->url(array(), 'contact');
?>">CONTACT</a>
      </div>
    </div>

    <div id="content">
      <?php echo $this->layout()->content ?>
    </div>

    <div id="footer">
      <p>Created with <a href="http://framework.zend.com/">
      Zend Framework</a>. Licensed under
      <a href="http://www.creativecommons.org/">Creative Commons
      </a>.</p>
    </div>
  </body>
</html>
```

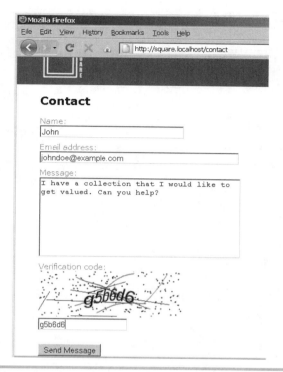

Figure 3-16   The SQUARE contact form

If you now try visiting the URL **http://square.localhost/contact** through your Web browser, you should see a form like the one in Figure 3-16.

Enter values into the form fields and submit it; if all goes well, you should see a success message like the one in Figure 3-17.

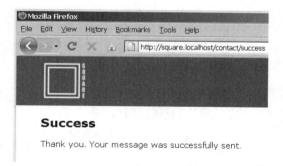

Figure 3-17   The result of successfully submitting the SQUARE contact form

(continued)

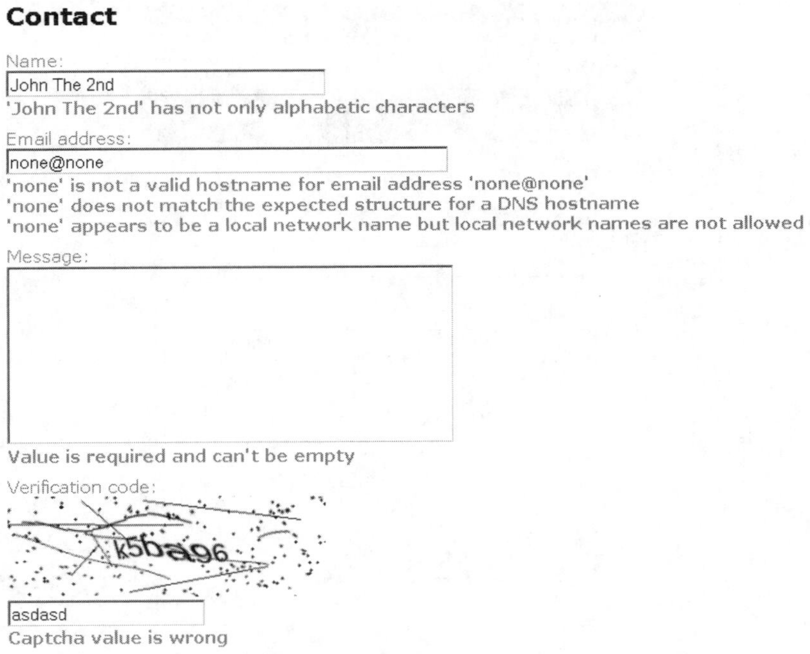

Contact

Name:

| John The 2nd |

'John The 2nd' has not only alphabetic characters

Email address:

| none@none |

'none' is not a valid hostname for email address 'none@none'
'none' does not match the expected structure for a DNS hostname
'none' appears to be a local network name but local network names are not allowed

Message:

Value is required and can't be empty

Verification code:

| asdasd |

Captcha value is wrong

Figure 3-18 The result of submitting the SQUARE contact form with invalid input values

You can also try submitting the form with invalid values. The built-in validators will catch your invalid input and redisplay the form with error messages, as shown in Figure 3-18.

NOTE

Remember to update the recipient email address in the `ContactController::indexAction` to reflect your own email address, or else the email messages generated by the Zend_Mail component will never be received by you.

Customizing Form Appearance

You should now have a reasonably good idea about what goes into building a form with the Zend Framework, as well as some insight into the tools available to help you secure your application against invalid and malicious input. This section takes a quick look at some of the tools available to help you improve the appearance and behavior of your forms, with a view to making them clearer and more informative.

Using Custom Error Messages

Each input validator comes with a set of default error messages appropriate to the type of data being validated. More often than not, these default error messages provide enough information for users to locate and correct the errors in their input. However, cases may arise when these default messages need to be modified to be more descriptive and user-friendly.

This is not very difficult to do, because each validator can be configured to display custom error messages via the 'messages' key of the options array passed to the addValidator() method. Consider the following example, which illustrates this:

```php
<?php
class Form_Example extends Zend_Form
{
  public function init()
  {
    // initialize form
    $this->setAction('/sandbox/example/form')
        ->setMethod('post');

    // create text input for name
    $name = new Zend_Form_Element_Text('name');
    $name->setLabel('Name:')
        ->setOptions(array('size' => '35'))
        ->setRequired(true)
        ->addValidator('Alpha', false, array(
            'messages' => array(
              Zend_Validate_Alpha::INVALID
                => "ERROR: Invalid name",
              Zend_Validate_Alpha::NOT_ALPHA
                => "ERROR: Name cannot contain non-alpha characters",
              Zend_Validate_Alpha::STRING_EMPTY
                => "ERROR: Name cannot be empty"
          )
        ))
        ->addFilter('StringTrim');
    $validator = $name->getValidator('Alpha');

    // create text input for email address
    $email = new Zend_Form_Element_Text('email');
    $email->setLabel('Email address:');
    $email->setOptions(array('size' => '50'))
        ->setRequired(true)
        ->addValidator('EmailAddress', true, array(
            'messages' => array(
              Zend_Validate_EmailAddress::INVALID
                => "ERROR: Invalid email address",
              Zend_Validate_EmailAddress::INVALID_FORMAT
                => "ERROR: Invalid email address",
```

```
                    Zend_Validate_EmailAddress::INVALID_HOSTNAME
                       => "ERROR: Invalid hostname format",
                    Zend_Validate_EmailAddress::INVALID_LOCAL_PART
                       => "ERROR: Invalid username format",
                    Zend_Validate_EmailAddress::LENGTH_EXCEEDED
                       => "ERROR: Email address too long"
               )
            ))
         ->addFilter('StringTrim');

      // create submit button
      $submit = new Zend_Form_Element_Submit('submit');
      $submit->setLabel('Sign Up');

      // attach elements to form
      $this->addElement($name)
           ->addElement($email)
           ->addElement($submit);
   }
}
```

In this example, the default error messages for each invalid case are overridden by the custom messages specified in the `'messages'` key of the array passed to the `addValidator()` method. The constants on the left side of the message array can be obtained by inspecting the corresponding validator's source code. These new messages will then be generated, added to the error stack, and displayed in the form whenever the corresponding element fails validation. An example of the output is shown in Figure 3-19.

TIP
You can also pass custom error messages to a validator via its `setMessages()` method.

Example Form

Name:

> me?

> • ERROR: Name cannot contain non-alpha characters

Email address:

> user1user2user3user4user5user6user7user8user9us

> • ERROR: Email address too long

> Sign Up

Figure 3-19   A form with custom error messages

Using Display Groups

It's usually a good idea to group together form elements that have some tenuous or not-so-tenuous connection to each other. This is a more usable and readable approach than a collection of unordered elements clumped together without any clear categorization. With Zend_Form, this is accomplished through the use of *display groups*.

Display groups are added to a form with the form object's addDisplayGroup() method, which accepts two arguments: an array containing the names of the elements in the group, and a name for the group. The elements in question should have already been added to the form with the addElement() method. The setLegend() method can then be used to specify a name for the display group. At render time, these display groups and legends are represented by the <fieldset> and <legend> elements, respectively.

Here's an illustrative example:

```php
<?php
class Form_Example extends Zend_Form
{
  public function init()
  {
    // initialize form
    $this->setAction('/sandbox/example/form')
         ->setMethod('post');

    // create text input for name
    $name = new Zend_Form_Element_Text('name');
    $name->setLabel('Name:')
         ->setOptions(array('size' => '35'))
         ->setRequired(true)
         ->addFilter('StringTrim');

    // create text input for email address
    $email = new Zend_Form_Element_Text('email');
    $email->setLabel('Email address:');
    $email->setOptions(array('size' => '50'))
          ->setRequired(true)
          ->addValidator('EmailAddress', true)
          ->addFilter('StringTrim');

    // create text input for tel number
    $tel = new Zend_Form_Element_Text('tel');
    $tel->setLabel('Telephone number:');
    $tel->setOptions(array('size' => '50'))
        ->setRequired(true);

    // create submit button
    $submit = new Zend_Form_Element_Submit('submit');
    $submit->setLabel('Sign Up');
```

```
    // attach elements to form
    $this->addElement($name)
        ->addElement($email)
        ->addElement($tel);

    // add display group
    $this->addDisplayGroup(
        array('name', 'email', 'tel', 'address'),
        'contact'
    );
    $this->getDisplayGroup('contact')
        ->setLegend('Contact Information');

    $this->addElement($submit);
  }
}
```

Figure 3-20 illustrates what the result looks like.

Using Decorators

When rendering a form, Zend_Form automatically wraps each form element in a set of HTML code blocks that control the location and appearance of the element. These blocks of HTML markup are referred to as *decorators* and, in addition to providing a ready hook for CSS-based manipulation, they can be customized on a per-element basis to radically alter how form elements are rendered.

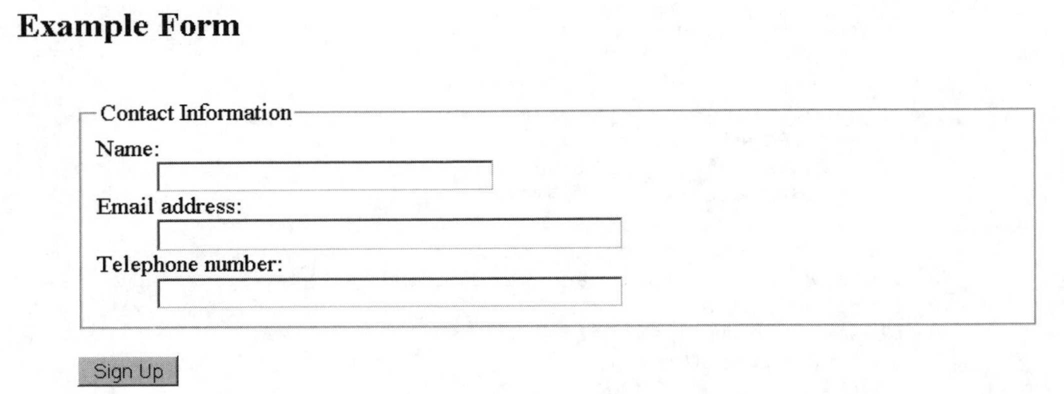

Example Form

┌─ Contact Information ──┐
│ Name: │
│ ┌──────────────────────────────────┐   │
│ └──────────────────────────────────┘   │
│ Email address: │
│ ┌──┐   │
│ └──┘   │
│ Telephone number: │
│ ┌──┐   │
│ └──┘   │
└──┘

[Sign Up]

Figure 3-20 A form with display groups

Decorator Name	Description
Form	Controls the markup around the form
FormElements	Controls the markup around form fields
HtmlTag	Controls the markup around form fields
ViewHelper	Controls the view helper
Errors	Controls the markup around validation errors (per field)
FormErrors	Controls the markup around validation errors (summary)
Description	Controls the markup around field descriptions
Label	Controls the markup around field labels
Fieldset	Controls the markup around fieldsets

Table 3-4   Commonly Used Form Decorators

Like filters and validators, the Zend Framework ships with a number of default decorators. Table 3-4 lists the ones you're most likely to encounter.

The default Zend_Form decorators use the following markup:

- Form labels are wrapped in `<dt>...</dt>` elements.

- Input fields are wrapped in `<dd>...</dd>` elements.

- Validation errors are rendered as list items and wrapped in `<ul>...</ul>` elements.

Figure 3-21 illustrates the HTML source code of one such form, while Figure 3-22 illustrates the rendered result.

```html
<html>
  <head>
  </head>
  <body>
    <h2>Example Form</h2>
    <form enctype="application/x-www-form-urlencoded" action="/sandbox/example/form" method="post"><dl class="z
<dt id="name-label"><label for="name" class="required">Name:</label></dt>
<dd id="name-element">
<input type="text" name="name" id="name" value="" size="35" />
<ul class="errors"><li>Value is required and can't be empty</li></ul></dd>
<dt id="email-label"><label for="email" class="required">Email address:</label></dt>
<dd id="email-element">
<input type="text" name="email" id="email" value="" size="50" />
<ul class="errors"><li>Value is required and can't be empty</li></ul></dd>
<dt id="subscribe-label"><label for="subscribe" class="optional">Subscribe to newsletter:</label></dt>
<dd id="subscribe-element">
<input type="hidden" name="subscribe" value="no" /><input type="checkbox" name="subscribe" id="subscribe" value
<dt id="submit-label"> </dt><dd id="submit-element">
<input type="submit" name="submit" id="submit" value="Sign Up" class="submit" /></dd></dl></form>   </body>
</html>
```

Figure 3-21   The source code of a form using default decorators

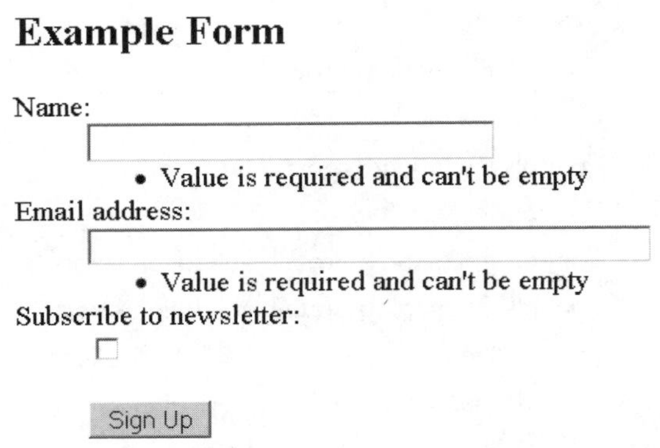

Example Form

Name:

• Value is required and can't be empty

Email address:

• Value is required and can't be empty

Subscribe to newsletter:

☐

Sign Up

Figure 3-22   The rendered version of a form in Figure 3-21

Often, this arrangement is not suitable for your application's user interface. To alter it, use one of the following methods:

- The addDecorators() method accepts an array of decorator names and adds the corresponding decorators to the element. If you add a decorator that already exists, the decorator's settings will be overwritten with the values specified in the addDecorators() method.

- The clearDecorators() method removes all existing decorators for an element.

- The setDecorators() method accepts an array of decorator names, removes all existing decorators for an element, and attaches the new set of decorators to it.

TIP

To disable the default decorators for a particular form or form element, add a 'disableLoadDefaultDecorators' key to that form or form element's options array. Note that if you're disabling the default decorators, you should still add back the ViewHelper decorator with the addDecorators() or setDecorators() method, as this decorator produces the basic markup for the form and its elements.

To illustrate how these decorators can be used, consider the following example:

```php
<?php
class Form_Example extends Zend_Form
{
  public $formDecorators = array(
    array('FormElements'),
```

```
    array('Form'),
  );

public $elementDecorators = array(
  array('ViewHelper'),
  array('Label'),
  array('Errors'),
);

public $buttonDecorators = array(
  array('ViewHelper'),
  array('HtmlTag', array('tag' => 'p'))
);

public function init()
{
  // initialize form
  $this->setAction('/sandbox/example/form')
       ->setMethod('post')
       ->setDecorators($this->formDecorators);

  // create text input for name
  $name = new Zend_Form_Element_Text('name');
  $name->setLabel('Name:')
       ->setOptions(array('size' => '35'))
       ->setRequired(true)
       ->setDecorators($this->elementDecorators);

  // create text input for email address
  $email = new Zend_Form_Element_Text('email');
  $email->setLabel('Email address:');
  $email->setOptions(array('size' => '50'))
        ->setRequired(true)
        ->setDecorators($this->elementDecorators);

  // create checkbox for newsletter subscription
  $subscribe = new Zend_Form_Element_Checkbox('subscribe');
  $subscribe->setLabel('Subscribe to newsletter:')
            ->setCheckedValue('yes')
            ->setUncheckedValue('no')
            ->setDecorators($this->elementDecorators);

  // create submit button
  $submit = new Zend_Form_Element_Submit(
    'submit', array('class' => 'submit'));
  $submit->setLabel('Sign Up')
         ->setDecorators($this->buttonDecorators);
```

```
        // attach elements to form
        $this->addElement($name)
              ->addElement($email)
              ->addElement($subscribe)
              ->addElement($submit);
    }
}
```

This listing resets the default decorators with the `setDecorators()` method, removing the `<dt>...</dt>` and `<dd>...</dd>` elements around labels and input fields and instead adjusting the appearance of these elements with CSS, which offers more precise control. Consider Figure 3-23, which illustrates the revised source code, and Figure 3-24, which illustrates the rendered result.

As this example illustrates, decorators provide a solution to the problem of controlling form markup such that it conforms to the rest of your application's interface. And in case you find that the default decorators don't offer enough control for you, remember that you can always define your own form markup by creating a custom decorator class (simply extend the Zend_Form_Decorator_Abstract abstract class) and using that instead. You'll find links to articles on this topic at the end of the chapter.

```
    )

    input {
       width: 300px;
    }

    input[type='checkbox'] {
       width: auto;
    }

    input.submit  {
       width: 100px;
       margin-left: 210px;
    }

    label.required {
       color: red;
    }
    </style>
  </head>
  <body>
    <h2>Example Form</h2>
    <form enctype="application/x-www-form-urlencoded" action="/sandbox/example/form" method="post">
<label for="name" class="required">Name:</label>

<input type="text" name="name" id="name" value="" size="35" />
<ul class="errors"><li>Value is required and can't be empty</li></ul>
<label for="email" class="required">Email address:</label>

<input type="text" name="email" id="email" value="" size="50" />
<ul class="errors"><li>Value is required and can't be empty</li></ul>
<label for="subscribe" class="optional">Subscribe to newsletter:</label>

<input type="hidden" name="subscribe" value="no" /><input type="checkbox" name="subscribe" id="subscribe" value="yes" />
<p>
<input type="submit" name="submit" id="submit" value="Sign Up" class="submit" /></p></form>  </body>
</html>
```

Figure 3-23 The source code of a form using custom decorators

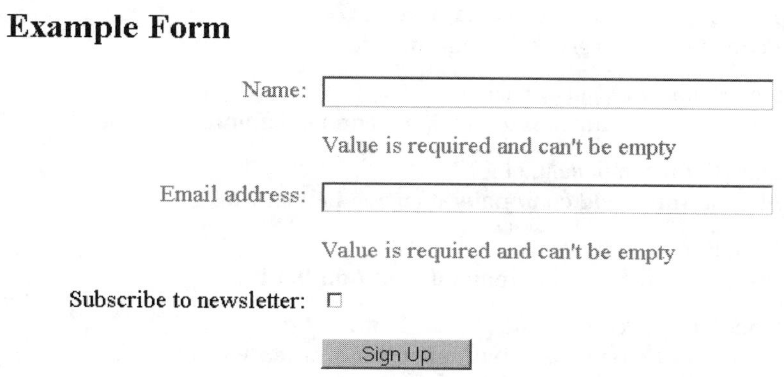

Example Form

Name: [   ]

Value is required and can't be empty

Email address: [   ]

Value is required and can't be empty

Subscribe to newsletter: ☐

[Sign Up]

Figure 3-24   The rendered version of the form in Figure 3-23

NOTE

Decorators are an extensive topic in themselves, and it isn't possible to cover them in exhaustive detail in this book. The material presented in the preceding section should be enough to get you started and to help you understand the relatively simple decorators used in this book. For more in-depth study, refer to the links at the end of this chapter.

Summary

This chapter focused on forms: creating them, validating them, and processing them. It introduced you to three of the most important components in the Zend Framework—Zend_Form, Zend_Validate, and Zend_Filter—and showed you how they can be used to securely request and handle user input. It then applied this knowledge to the SQUARE example application, guiding you through the process of registering a new namespace for custom objects, creating an email inquiry form, and transmitting the input received through this form as an email message using the Zend_Mail component. Finally, it took a quick look at some of the tools available to help you control the appearance of your forms, including display groups, decorators, and custom error messages; you'll see these tools in use throughout this book.

To learn more about the topics discussed in this chapter, consider visiting the following links:

- Wikipedia's discussion of CSRF and XSS attacks, at
  http://en.wikipedia.org/wiki/Cross-site_request_forgery and
  http://en.wikipedia.org/wiki/Cross-site_scripting

- Wikipedia's discussion of CAPTCHAs, at
  http://en.wikipedia.org/wiki/Captcha

- Wikipedia's discussion of fluent interfaces, at
  http://en.wikipedia.org/wiki/Fluent_interface

- The Zend Framework autoloader, at
  http://framework.zend.com/manual/en/zend.loader.autoloader.html

- The Zend_Form component, at
  http://framework.zend.com/manual/en/zend.form.html

- The Zend_Filter component, at
  http://framework.zend.com/manual/en/zend.filter.html

- The Zend_Validate component, at
  http://framework.zend.com/manual/en/zend.validate.html

- The Zend_Mail component, at
  http://framework.zend.com/manual/en/zend.mail.html

- A discussion of creating custom decorators (Matthew Weier O'Phinney), at
  http://weierophinney.net/matthew/archives/213-From-the-inside-out-How-to-layer-decorators.html

Chapter 4

Working with Models

Key Skills & Concepts

- Understand the role of models in the Model-View-Controller pattern
- Learn the benefits of the "fat model, skinny controller" approach
- Integrate the Doctrine Object Relational Mapping (ORM) toolkit with the Zend Framework
- Create models using the Doctrine model generator
- Use Doctrine models to retrieve records from a MySQL database
- Find out how to filter input with the Zend_Filter_Input component
- Tweak the application startup process with the Zend Framework bootstrapper

The previous chapter gave you a crash course in the basics of creating, validating, and processing forms using the Zend Framework. However, form input doesn't just disappear into a vacuum; it has to go somewhere. More often than not, that "somewhere" is a database, such as MySQL, SQLite, or PostgreSQL, so adding database support to an application becomes a key task for the application developer.

A database is only part of the puzzle, though: You also need *models* to interact with it. Models, which are logically independent of views and controllers, serve as the application's "data layer" and provide all the functions necessary to manipulate application data. The Zend Framework makes it easy to write models that are specific to your application's requirements; you can also integrate models generated by popular third-party tools such as Doctrine or Propel.

This chapter will take your Zend Framework skills up another couple of notches, by showing you how to create and add models to your application, and then use these models to retrieve data from a MySQL database. It will also introduce you to Doctrine, a powerful (and free) data mapping tool that can significantly simplify these tasks.

Understanding Models

By now, you should be reasonably familiar with views and controllers, which respectively represent the "user interface layer" and "processing layer" of an MVC-compliant application. Models represent the "data layer," responsible both for providing a channel through which data can be accessed and for maintaining and enforcing any business rules related to that data. So, for example, if you're building a check-in system for an online library, you might have a Transaction model that not only records the details of books checked in and out of the system, but also includes rules to disallow a single member from having more than five books checked out at any one time, or to autocalculate fees for late check-ins and debit them to the corresponding member account. Similarly, if you're building an airline ticketing application, you might have a Ticket model that is not only capable of saving and retrieving ticket purchase records, but can also automatically increase or decrease the price of a ticket depending on current passenger load for a particular flight.

Here's an example of a simple model:

```php
<?php
// model to handle member data
class MemberModel
{
  protected $db;

  public $id;
  public $name;
  public $age;
  public $type;
  private $rate;

  // constructor
  // initialize database connection
  public function __construct()
  {
    $this->db = new PDO('mysql:dbname=db;host=localhost', 'user',
'pass');
    $this->db->setAttribute(PDO::ATTR_ERRMODE, PDO::ERRMODE_EXCEPTION);
  }

  // get member record by id
  public function fetch($id)
  {
    $id = $this->db->quote($this->id);
    $rs = $this->db->query("SELECT * FROM member WHERE id = $id");
    return $rs->fetchAll(PDO::FETCH_ASSOC);
  }

  // get all member records
  public function fetchAll()
  {
    $rs = $this->db->query("SELECT * FROM member");
    return $rs->fetchAll(PDO::FETCH_ASSOC);
  }

  // add new member record
  public function save()
  {
    // filter input data
    $f = array();
    $f['name'] = htmlentities($this->name);
    $f['age']  = htmlentities($this->age);
```

```php
    $f['type'] = htmlentities($this->type);

  // validate age
  if ($f['age'] < 18) {
    throw new Exception('Member under 18');
  }

  // auto-calculate discount based on membership type
  switch ($f['type']) {
    case 'silver':
      $f['rate'] = 0;
      break;
    case 'gold':
      $f['rate'] = 0.10;
      break;
    case 'platinum':
      $f['rate'] = 0.25;
      break;
  }

  $this->db->exec(
    'INSERT INTO member (Name, Age, Type, DiscountRate) VALUES(' .
    $this->db->quote($f['name']) . ', ' .
    $this->db->quote($f['age']) . ', ' .
    $this->db->quote($f['type']) . ', ' .
    $this->db->quote($f['rate']) . ')'
  );
  return $this->db->lastInsertId();
  }
}
?>
```

As you can see, this model uses PHP's PDO abstraction layer to interact with a MySQL database. It exposes a number of methods for retrieving records from, and saving records to, the database. It also includes some business rules (autocalculating the discount rate based on the membership type) and some input validation rules (verifying that the member is 18 or older). As with all good models, its purpose begins and ends with data; it has nothing to say about how that data is formatted and displayed.

Here's how you would use it in an application:

```php
<?php
class Sandbox_ExampleController extends Zend_Controller_Action
{
  public function saveAction()
  {
    if ($this->getRequest()->isPost()) {
      if ($form->isValid($this->getRequest()->getPost())) {
        $model = new MemberModel;
        $model->name = $form->getValue('name');
```

```
        $model->age  = $form->getValue('age');
        $model->type = $form->getValue('type');
        $id = $model->save();
        $this->view->message = "Record saved with ID: $id";
      }
    }
  }
}
```

Model Patterns

When it comes to working with models, there are two commonly used patterns: the DataMapper pattern and the ActiveRecord pattern. The previous example is an illustration of the ActiveRecord pattern, in which a model class corresponds directly with a database table and exposes methods like `save()`, `update()`, and `delete()` to manipulate the records in that table. It should be clear that under this pattern, models and their underlying database tables are closely linked, and a change in one necessitates a change in the other.

The DataMapper pattern is slightly different, in that there need not exist a 1:1 correspondence between the model class and the underlying database table. Rather, this pattern uses an in-between layer (the "mapper" of the name) to handle the task of mapping data from the model class to database fields. In this case, it is the mapper class that exposes methods like `save()`, `update()`, and `fetch()`, and internally performs the translation necessary to correctly map class members to database fields. This pattern allows for greater flexibility and a wider variety of configurations than the ActiveRecord pattern; the separation of data from data storage also produces more readable and maintainable models. That said, it's also more complex to implement than the ActiveRecord pattern.

Which do you use when? There's no easy answer to that question, because it's a lot like asking which flavor of ice cream is best. The ActiveRecord pattern, by definition, assumes that you're using a database for data storage, and models based on this pattern are closely coupled with the underlying database structure. This is good for smaller projects or for projects where the key functions correspond closely to the standard `SELECT`, `INSERT`, `UPDATE`, and `DELETE` commands. The DataMapper pattern allows for explicit separation between application-level business rules and data storage, and it is the model itself, rather than the underlying database, that is considered the primary data definition agent. A corollary of this is that you're not limited only to a database; the mapper can just as easily map data to other types of storage, such as flat files, XML, or LDAP. This pattern is good for projects with sophisticated data structures and/or custom storage formats, or those where the key functions require more complex interactions between application entities.

Model Scope

It's often hard to draw a line between what goes into a model and what goes into a controller. For example, in the banking example described earlier, one might well argue that the validation related to amounts and locations should be in the controller, rather than in the model. In general, though, the developer community has largely adopted the "fat model, skinny controller" approach recommended by various thought leaders, including Martin

Fowler, Jamis Buck, and Chris Hartjes (you'll find links at the end of this chapter), which proposes that business logic should be located within models, rather than controllers, wherever possible. This approach offers a number of benefits:

- "Fat" models reduce duplication and help developers adhere to the Don't Repeat Yourself (DRY) maxim by encapsulating key business rules into reusable objects and object methods. Inheritance chains can then be used to apply these rules consistently across the application. Specifying models using OOP principles also makes it possible to extend base models with additional functionality as needed, and to make a distinction between public and private model attributes within the larger application space.

- Self-contained "fat" models that encapsulate all the business rules necessary for their proper functioning are more portable than "thin" models that rely on application controllers to enforce business rules. Since most of the application's business logic is in the model, rather than in the controller, switching to a different framework, for example, becomes much easier, as the model can simply be swapped in to the new system and will usually work without significant retrofitting required.

- When "fat" models handle most of the heavy lifting, controllers typically end up containing only a few lines of highly focused code. This makes them easier to understand and read, and contributes to better overall performance (because controllers are typically invoked more frequently than models). It also produces more maintainable code: For example, if you need to change the business rules for a particular application entity, you only need to update the model for that entity, not for all the controllers that use it.

- Debugging and testing become more transparent under the "fat model, skinny controller" approach, because it's usually very easy to identify whether the model or the controller is the source of an error, and to correct it with minimal impact on the rest of the application.

It's important to note, at this point, that the Zend Framework does not come with a Zend_Model component, or a set of predefined models, that you can "drop in" to your

Ask the Expert

Q: Is a "model" simply a set of prepackaged SQL statements?

A: No, definitely not. It's a common misconception that models are simply object representations of database tables, with methods corresponding to the SQL INSERT, SELECT, UPDATE, and DELETE statements. In reality, models are much more than Structured Query Language (SQL) wrappers. They can (and should) enforce application-specific business rules, perform calculations, handle conversions, apply filters, and perform any other required operations on data. Remember, the more intelligent your models, the less work for your controllers, and the more maintainable and portable your application.

application; you always need to create your own. The Zend Framework includes a number of tools that can assist you in this task, such as the Zend_Db_Adapter database abstraction layer and the Zend_Db_Table interface to table operations. However, you can also create your application models using third-party tools like Doctrine or Propel, and integrate them into your Zend Framework application. And that, in fact, is what the next section is all about.

Installing Doctrine

While you can certainly create your application models from scratch, using the components provided by the Zend Framework, there's an easier way: use an Object Relational Mapping (ORM) tool to automatically generate them for you. These tools can automatically scan an existing database and create model classes corresponding to the tables within it, using either the ActiveRecord or DataMapper pattern. It's then a simple task to add these autogenerated models to an application and extend them as needed to support specific requirements.

There are a large number of free, open-source ORM tools available for PHP, such as Propel, Doctrine, RedBean, and Qcodo. This book uses Doctrine, which is extremely popular among developers on account of its ease of use, flexibility, and extensive documentation. The Doctrine package includes a database abstraction layer, with support for most common RDBMS systems; a customized version of SQL called Doctrine Query Language (DQL); and tools to automatically generate model classes from an existing database schema. These model classes are based on the ActiveRecord pattern, and are fully compliant with the PHP 5.3.x object model.

To get started with Doctrine, download and install the latest version to your development environment by visiting the official Doctrine Web site and getting a copy of the most recent release of the software. Then, extract its contents to a temporary area on the file system.

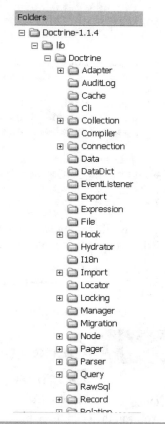

```
shell> cd /tmp
shell> tar -xzvf Doctrine-XX.tgz
```

You should end up with a directory structure that looks something like Figure 4-1. The *lib/* directory contains all the Doctrine components, while the *tests/* directory contains test cases.

The contents of the *lib/* directory should be moved to a location in your PHP "include path" list.

Figure 4-1   The contents of a Doctrine release archive

On UNIX/Linux systems, good possible locations for this are */usr/local/lib/php* or */usr/local/ share/php*. On Windows, consider using your PHP or PEAR installation directory, such as *C:\Program Files\PHP* or *C:\Program Files\PHP\PEAR*. Note that in case the target directory is not already part of your PHP "include path" list, you must add it before proceeding.

Here are example commands you can use to perform these tasks:

```
shell> cd Doctrine-XX
shell> mv lib /usr/local/lib/php/Doctrine
```

You should now be able to access Doctrine from within a PHP script. To verify this, create the following simple script, remembering to replace the access credentials with values appropriate to your system:

```php
<?php
// include main Doctrine class file
include_once 'Doctrine/Doctrine.php';
spl_autoload_register(array('Doctrine', 'autoload'));

// create Doctrine manager
$manager = Doctrine_Manager::getInstance();

// create database connection
$conn = Doctrine_Manager::connection(
  'mysql://root@localhost/test', 'doctrine');

// get and print list of databases
$databases = $conn->import->listDatabases();
print_r($databases);
?>
```

Save this script as */tmp/doctrine-test.php* and execute it at the command prompt using the PHP command-line interface (CLI), as follows:

```
shell> cd /tmp/
shell> php ./doctrine-test.php
```

Figure 4-2 illustrates an example of the output you will see.

Try This 4-1 Generating and Integrating Doctrine Models

Once you've got Doctrine installed and working, you're ready to start creating models with it. You can then add these models to the example application, and set things up so that they are automatically loaded as needed. The following sections discuss how to accomplish these tasks.

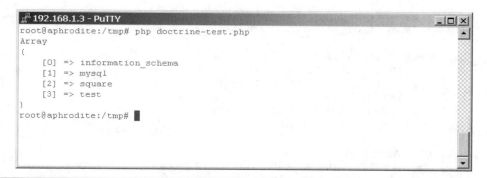

Figure 4-2 The list of available databases, as returned by Doctrine

Initializing the Application Database

The first step is to create a MySQL database for the application. To do this, drop to your command prompt, fire up the MySQL command-line client, and create a new database using the following commands:

```
shell> mysql -u root -p
Enter password: *****
Welcome to the MySQL monitor.  Commands end with ; or \g.
Your MySQL connection id is 17
Server version: 5.1.30-community MySQL Community Server (GPL)

mysql> CREATE DATABASE square;
Query OK, 0 rows affected (0.00 sec)
mysql> USE square;
Database changed
```

Add some tables to this database, as shown in the following code:

```
mysql> CREATE TABLE IF NOT EXISTS country (
    -> CountryID INT(11) NOT NULL AUTO_INCREMENT,
    -> CountryName VARCHAR(255) NOT NULL,
    -> PRIMARY KEY (CountryID)
    -> ) ENGINE=InnoDB  DEFAULT CHARSET=utf8;
Query OK, 0 rows affected (0.09 sec)

mysql> CREATE TABLE IF NOT EXISTS grade (
    -> GradeID INT(11) NOT NULL AUTO_INCREMENT,
    -> GradeName VARCHAR(255) NOT NULL,
    -> PRIMARY KEY (GradeID)
```

(continued)

```
    -> ) ENGINE=InnoDB DEFAULT CHARSET=utf8;
Query OK, 0 rows affected (0.09 sec)

mysql> CREATE TABLE IF NOT EXISTS type (
    -> TypeID INT(11) NOT NULL AUTO_INCREMENT,
    -> TypeName VARCHAR(255) NOT NULL,
    -> PRIMARY KEY (TypeID)
    -> ) ENGINE=InnoDB DEFAULT CHARSET=utf8;
Query OK, 0 rows affected (0.09 sec)

mysql> CREATE TABLE IF NOT EXISTS item (
    -> RecordID INT(11) NOT NULL AUTO_INCREMENT,
    -> RecordDate DATE NOT NULL,
    -> SellerName VARCHAR(255) NOT NULL,
    -> SellerEmail VARCHAR(255) NOT NULL,
    -> SellerTel VARCHAR(50) DEFAULT NULL,
    -> SellerAddress TEXT,
    -> Title VARCHAR(255) NOT NULL,
    -> `Year` INT(4) NOT NULL,
    -> CountryID INT(4) NOT NULL,
    -> Denomination FLOAT NOT NULL,
    -> TypeID INT(4) NOT NULL,
    -> GradeID INT(4) NOT NULL,
    -> SalePriceMin FLOAT NOT NULL,
    -> SalePriceMax FLOAT NOT NULL,
    -> Description TEXT NOT NULL,
    -> DisplayStatus TINYINT(1) NOT NULL,
    -> DisplayUntil DATE DEFAULT NULL,
    -> PRIMARY KEY (RecordID)
    -> ) ENGINE=InnoDB  DEFAULT CHARSET=utf8;
Query OK, 0 rows affected (0.09 sec)

mysql> CREATE TABLE IF NOT EXISTS user (
    -> RecordID INT(4) NOT NULL AUTO_INCREMENT,
    -> Username VARCHAR(10) NOT NULL,
    -> Password TEXT NOT NULL,
    -> PRIMARY KEY (RecordID)
    -> ) ENGINE=InnoDB  DEFAULT CHARSET=utf8;
Query OK, 0 rows affected (0.09 sec)
mysql> CREATE TABLE IF NOT EXISTS log (
    -> RecordID int(11) NOT NULL AUTO_INCREMENT,
    -> LogMessage text NOT NULL,
    -> LogLevel varchar(30) NOT NULL,
    -> LogTime varchar(30) NOT NULL,
    -> Stack text,
    -> Request text,
    -> PRIMARY KEY (RecordID)
    -> ) ENGINE=InnoDB  DEFAULT CHARSET=utf8;
Query OK, 0 rows affected (0.09 sec)
```

Table Name	Contains
item	List of stamps available for sale, together with seller contact information
user	List of authorized users
country	Master list of countries
grade	Master list of stamp grades
type	Master list of stamp types
log	Error log

Table 4-1 A Brief Description of the Application Database

Ask the Expert

Q: If the Zend Framework convention is to use upper camel-casing for entity names, why are the MySQL database and table names in this chapter specified in lowercase?

A: At the filesystem level, MySQL represents databases and tables as directories and files, respectively. Some file systems (for example Windows) don't make a distinction between upper- and lowercase filenames, while others (for example Linux) do. Therefore, to simplify moving databases and tables between different operating systems, it's generally recommended to lowercase all database and table names, and to ensure they consist only of alphanumeric and underscore characters. Obviously, you should also try to avoid using reserved MySQL keywords as database names.

Table 4-1 gives a brief description of these tables.

To better understand how these tables are connected, take a look at Figure 4-3, which presents an entity-relationship diagram of the MySQL database in this chapter.

Proceed to initialize the master tables with some records:

```
mysql> INSERT INTO country (CountryID, CountryName) VALUES
    -> (1, 'United States'),
    -> (2, 'United Kingdom'),
    -> (3, 'India'),
    -> (4, 'Singapore'),
    -> (5, 'Germany'),
    -> (6, 'France'),
    -> (7, 'Italy'),
```

(continued)

```
          -> (8, 'Spain'),
          -> (9, 'Hungary');
Query OK, 9 rows affected (0.09 sec)
Records: 9  Duplicates: 0  Warnings: 0

mysql> INSERT INTO grade (GradeID, GradeName) VALUES
          -> (1, 'Very Fine'),
          -> (2, 'Fine'),
          -> (3, 'Good'),
          -> (4, 'Average'),
          -> (5, 'Poor');
Query OK, 5 rows affected (0.09 sec)
Records: 5  Duplicates: 0  Warnings: 0

mysql> INSERT INTO type (TypeID, TypeName) VALUES
          -> (1, 'Commemorative'),
          -> (2, 'Decorative'),
          -> (3, 'Definitive'),
          -> (4, 'Special'),
          -> (5, 'Other');
```

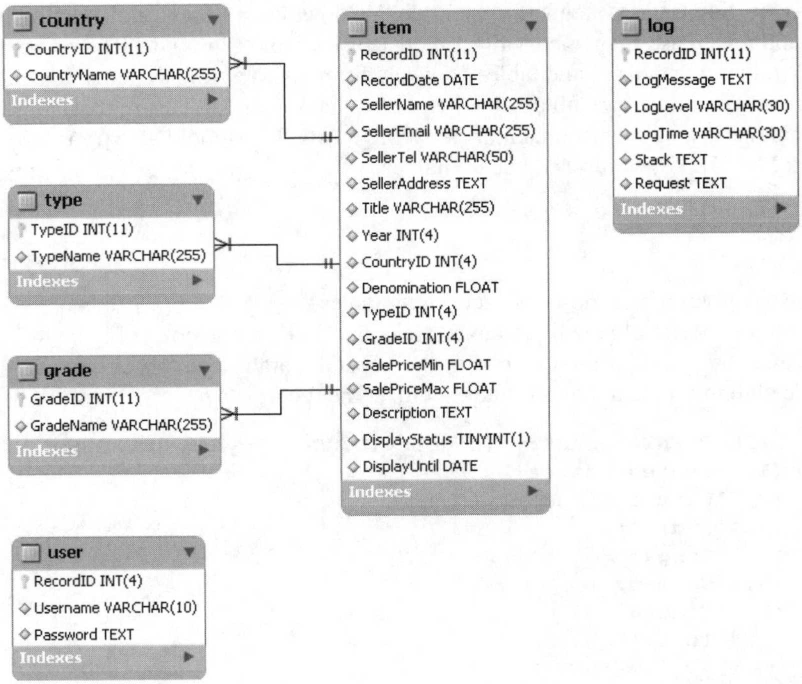

Figure 4-3   An entity-relationship diagram of the application database

```
Query OK, 5 rows affected (0.09 sec)
Records: 5  Duplicates: 0  Warnings: 0
```

You can also insert a couple of dummy records into the *item* table, just to get things rolling:

```
mysql> INSERT INTO item (RecordID, RecordDate, SellerName,
    -> SellerEmail, SellerTel, SellerAddress, Title,
    -> Year, CountryID, Denomination, TypeID, GradeID,
    -> SalePriceMin, SalePriceMax, Description,
    -> DisplayStatus, DisplayUntil) VALUES
    -> (1, '2009-12-06', 'John Doe', 'john@example.com',
    -> '+123456789102', '12 Green House, Red Road, Blue City',
    -> 'Himalayas - Silver Jubilee', 1958, 3, 5.00, 1, 2, 10, 15,
    -> 'Silver jubilee issue. Aerial view of snow-capped.
    -> Himalayan mountains. Horizontal orange stripe across
    -> top margin. Excellent condition, no marks.', 0, NULL);
Query OK, 1 row affected (0.02 sec)

mysql> INSERT INTO item (RecordID, RecordDate, SellerName,
    -> SellerEmail, SellerTel, SellerAddress, Title,
    -> Year, CountryID, Denomination, TypeID, GradeID,
    -> SalePriceMin, SalePriceMax, Description,
    -> DisplayStatus, DisplayUntil) VALUES
    -> (2, '2009-10-05', 'Susan Doe', 'susan@example.com',
    -> '+198765432198', '1 Tiger Place, Animal City 648392',
    -> 'Britain - WWII Fighter', 1966, 2, 1.00, 1, 4, 1.00, 2.00,
    -> 'WWII Fighter Plane overlaid on blue sky. Cancelled',
    -> 0, NULL);
Query OK, 1 row affected (0.02 sec)
```

For security reasons, it's also a good idea to create a dedicated MySQL user account with privileges to access only this database. Go ahead and do this using the following command:

```
mysql> GRANT ALL ON square.* TO square@localhost IDENTIFIED BY 'square';
Query OK, 1 row affected (0.00 sec)
```

Your database is now set up, and you're ready to start creating models from it!

Generating Doctrine Models

Doctrine comes with a powerful model generator, which can "read" an existing database and generate a set of model classes from it. To see it in action, create and run the following PHP script:

```php
<?php
// include main Doctrine class file
include_once 'Doctrine.php';
```

(continued)

```
spl_autoload_register(array('Doctrine', 'autoload'));

// create Doctrine manager
$manager = Doctrine_Manager::getInstance();

// create database connection
$conn = Doctrine_Manager::connection(
  'mysql://square:square@localhost/square', 'doctrine');

// auto-generate models
Doctrine::generateModelsFromDb('/tmp/models',
  array('doctrine'),
  array('classPrefix' => 'Square_Model_')
);
?>
```

This script sets up a connection to the database created in the previous section, and then uses the `generateModelsFromDb()` method to dynamically generate models corresponding to the tables in the database. These models will be saved to the directory named in the first argument to the method. Notice also that, in the array passed to the method as third argument, there's an option that tells Doctrine to prefix each model class name with a custom string. This is useful to have the models conform to the Zend Framework's autoloading subsystem.

Execute this script at the command prompt using the PHP CLI, as follows:

```
shell> cd /tmp
shell> php ./doctrine-models-generate
.php
```

If all goes well, Doctrine will write a set of models to the specified directory. Take a look, and you should see something like Figure 4-4.

These models should now be copied to the application directory. To do this, change to *$APP_DIR* and execute the following commands:

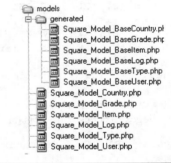

Figure 4-4 The autogenerated Doctrine models, in their original state

```
shell> mkdir library/Square/Model
shell> cp /tmp/models/* library/Square/Model
shell> cp /tmp/models/generated/* library/Square/Model
```

By default, the Doctrine model generator uses the model class name as the basis for the corresponding filename. So, for example, a model class named Square_Model_Item will be saved to a filename Square_Model_Item.php. Unfortunately, this arrangement does not sit well with the Zend Framework's autoloader, which expects a class named Square_Model_Item to be saved as *Square/Model/Item.php*. To resolve this, it's necessary to manually rename each of the generated model class files, removing the prefix that was automatically added by Doctrine. Here's an example:

```
shell> cd library/Square/Model
shell> mv Square_Model_BaseCountry.php BaseCountry.php
```

At the end of the process, you should have a structure that looks like Figure 4-5.

TIP

If you're using Doctrine v1.2, you can pass an additional `'classPrefixFiles'` option to the `generateModelsFromDb()` method. This specifies whether or not the class prefix should be added to the model filenames. Setting this to `'false'` reduces the work involved in getting Doctrine models integrated with your application, as it is no longer necessary to rename each model file to conform to Zend Framework conventions.

Notice that Doctrine maps each table in the database to two model classes: a base class and a child class. The base class extends the Doctrine_Record class, includes the table definition, and exposes (via inheritance) all the methods for common database operations. The child class is a stub class derived from the base class, and it serves as a container for any custom methods that you might want to add to the model.

Setting Model Relationships

Now, while Doctrine can produce models that correspond to individual tables and expose methods for common operations on those tables, it doesn't have the intelligence to automatically detect relationships between tables. However, these relationships are often critically important in practical use, so it's up to the application developer to define these relationships by linking models together.

Doctrine makes it possible to replicate all the different types of relationships possible in an RDBMS—one-to-one, one-to-many, many-to-many, and self-referencing—using just two methods: hasOne() and hasMany(). Both these methods take two arguments: the name of the other model to be used in the relationship, and an array of options specifying parameters for the relationship. To ensure that these relationships are automatically loaded when the model is instantiated, they should be used within the model's setUp() method.

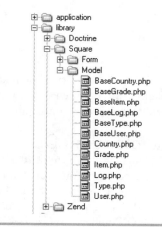

Figure 4-5 The autogenerated Doctrine models, after integration into the application

(continued)

To understand how this works, flip back a few pages to Figure 4-3, which illustrates the relationships between the various database tables. It should be clear from Figure 4-3 that there exists a *1:n* relationship between the *country*, *grade*, and *type* master tables on the one hand, and the *item* table on the other. This relationship makes use of the *item.CountryID*, *item.GradeID*, and *item.TypeID* foreign key fields, and it can be expressed in Doctrine by adding the following code to the Item model class:

```php
<?php
class Square_Model_Item extends Square_Model_BaseItem
{
    public function setUp()
    {
        $this->hasOne('Square_Model_Grade', array(
                'local' => 'GradeID',
                'foreign' => 'GradeID'
            )
        );
        $this->hasOne('Square_Model_Country', array(
                'local' => 'CountryID',
                'foreign' => 'CountryID'
            )
        );
        $this->hasOne('Square_Model_Type', array(
                'local' => 'TypeID',
                'foreign' => 'TypeID'
            )
        );
    }
}
```

Here, the `setUp()` method takes care of automatically defining the foreign key relationships between the Item model and the Country, Grade, and Item models. This comes in handy when joining these tables together in a Doctrine query (as you'll shortly see).

Autoloading Doctrine

All that's left now is to get the Zend Framework application and Doctrine talking nice to each other. There are a number of ways this can be done, but the recommended approach involves initializing Doctrine in the application bootstrap file and configuring it to "lazy load" models as needed. This approach is advocated by leading Zend Framework developers such as Matthew Weier O'Phinney and Eric LeClerc, and you'll find links to their work at the end of this chapter.

The first step is to decide whether to include the Doctrine libraries with your application or to allow users to download and install these libraries themselves. To understand the pros and cons of these options, revisit Chapter 1, when you had a similar decision to make for the Zend Framework libraries. In keeping with what was decided earlier, let's assume that the Doctrine libraries will be bundled with the application. Therefore, copy the contents of the Doctrine *lib/* directory to *$APP_DIR/library/Doctrine*, using the following command:

```
shell> cp -R /usr/local/lib/php/Doctrine library/
```

The next step is to update the application configuration file, at *$APP_DIR/application/ configs/application.ini*, with a Data Source Name (DSN) that Doctrine can use to connect to the MySQL database created earlier. To perform this update, open the application configuration file in a text editor and add the following lines to the [production] section:

```
doctrine.dsn = "mysql://square:square@localhost/square"
```

The final step is to initialize Doctrine by adding the necessary code to the application bootstrapper. As the name suggests, this component is automatically invoked on each request to "bootstrap" required application resources. It's defined as a class extending the Zend_ Application_Bootstrap_Bootstrap class, and it's located in *$APP_DIR/application/Bootstrap.php*.

Open this file in a text editor, and update it with a new _initDoctrine() method, as follows:

```php
<?php
class Bootstrap extends Zend_Application_Bootstrap_Bootstrap
{
    protected function _initDoctrine()
    {
        require_once 'Doctrine/Doctrine.php';
        $this->getApplication()
            ->getAutoloader()
            ->pushAutoloader(array('Doctrine', 'autoload'),
'Doctrine');

        $manager = Doctrine_Manager::getInstance();
        $manager->setAttribute(
            Doctrine::ATTR_MODEL_LOADING,
            Doctrine::MODEL_LOADING_CONSERVATIVE
        );

        $config = $this->getOption('doctrine');
        $conn = Doctrine_Manager::connection($config['dsn'],
'doctrine');
        return $conn;
    }

}
```

Under the Zend Framework's bootstrap system, any protected method belonging to the Bootstrap class and named with the special prefix _init* is considered a resource

(continued)

method and is automatically executed by the bootstrapper. The preceding listing defines the _initDoctrine() resource method, which starts off by including the main Doctrine class and configuring the autoloader with information on how to load Doctrine classes. It then creates an instance of the Doctrine_Manager class, configures Doctrine lazy loading, reads the DSN from the application configuration file, and opens a connection to the database.

Since this method will be automatically executed on every request, Doctrine models will be available for use in any application controller. With this, Doctrine is ready for use!

Working with Doctrine Models

Before going any further, let's take a quick diversion into the world of Doctrine models. As discussed earlier, Doctrine models implement the ActiveRecord pattern, wherein each instance of the model class represents a record of the underlying table, and each property of the instance represents a field of the record. Models extend the Doctrine_Record base class, which exposes a number of methods to simplify the work of adding, editing, deleting, and searching for records. The following sections examine these aspects in more detail.

Retrieving Records

There are a couple of different ways to retrieve records using a Doctrine model. If you have the record's primary key, one approach is to simply use the find() method, as follows:

```php
<?php
$member = Doctrine::getTable('Member')->find(1);
var_dump($member->toArray());
?>
```

If you'd instead prefer to fetch all the available records, you can use the findAll() method, as follows:

```php
<?php
$members = Doctrine::getTable('Members')->findAll();
var_dump($members->toArray());
?>
```

Doctrine comes with its own variant of SQL called Doctrine Query Language (DQL), which provides a flexible interface to creating and executing database queries. This offers an alternative, and more flexible, option for retrieving records from a database. Consider the following simple example, which retrieves all member records as an array:

```php
<?php
$q = Doctrine_Query::create()
        ->from('Member m');
$result = $q->fetchArray();
?>
```

Using Filters

The Doctrine_Query class exposes a fluent interface, which means it's very easy to add layers to this query. For example, let's suppose you wanted to retrieve only records of active member accounts. You can add this condition to the query with the where() method, as follows:

```php
<?php
$q = Doctrine_Query::create()
    ->from('Member m')
    ->where('m.Status = ?', 1);
$result = $q->fetchArray();
?>
```

You can attach multiple filters to a query in this manner with the addWhere() method. Here's an example that retrieves records of active members located in the United Kingdom:

```php
<?php
$q = Doctrine_Query::create()
    ->from('Member m')
    ->where('m.Status = ?', 1)
    ->addWhere('m.Location = ?', 'UK');
$result = $q->fetchArray();
?>
```

Grouping and Ordering Results

You can group and order the result set with the orderBy() and groupBy() methods. Here's an example of grouping and ordering members by country:

```php
<?php
$q = Doctrine_Query::create()
    ->from('Member m')
    ->where('m.Status = ?', 1)
    ->groupBy('m.Location')
    ->orderBy('m.Location DESC');
$result = $q->fetchArray();
?>
```

Joining Tables

You can also use DQL to perform joins between tables, using the leftJoin() and innerJoin() methods. Here's an example that creates a left join:

```php
<?php
$q = Doctrine_Query::create()
    ->from('Member m')
    ->leftJoin('m.Country c')
    ->leftJoin('m.OrgType o')
```

```
        ->where('o.DisplayStatus = 1');
$result = $q->execute();
?>
```

And here's an example of an inner join:

```php
<?php
$q = Doctrine_Query::create()
    ->from('Member m')
    ->innerJoin('m.Country c');
$result = $q->execute();
?>
```

The fields to use for the join are automatically set by Doctrine, based on the relationships defined in the source model's setUp() method.

TIP
When using DQL, you might need to review the autogenerated code for a particular query. Doctrine lets you do this via its getSql() method, which returns the raw SQL of a query for inspection.

Adding, Updating, and Deleting Records
Adding a new record to the database using a Doctrine model is simplicity itself: Simply instantiate an instance of the model class, set field values as model properties, and call the model's save() method. Here's an example:

```php
<?php
$member = new Member;
$member->FirstName  = 'Jack';
$member->LastName   = 'Frost';
$member->Email      = 'jack@example.com';
```

Ask the Expert

Q: **Does DQL support right joins?**

A: No. DQL currently only supports left joins and inner joins. But this shouldn't slow you down, because left and right joins are interchangeable, depending on which side of the join you're standing on. To illustrate, consider the following two queries, which are equivalent:

```
SELECT * FROM c LEFT JOIN a USING (id);
SELECT * FROM a RIGHT JOIN c USING (id);
```

```
$member->JoinDate    = '2009-11-11';
$member->Status      = 1;
$id = $member->save();
?>
```

To update an existing record, retrieve it using either the find() method or a DQL query, update the necessary properties, and save it back to the database using the save() method. Here's an example:

```
<?php
$member = Doctrine::getTable('Member')->find(1);
$member->FirstName  = 'John';
$member->Status     = 2;
$member->save();
?>
```

For more precise control, you can also update records using the DQL update() method. Here's an example, which is equivalent to the previous one:

```
<?php
$q = Doctrine_Query::create()
    ->update('Member m')
    ->set('m.FirstName', '?', 'John')
    ->set('m.Status', '?', '2')
    ->addWhere('m.RecordID = ?', 1);
$q->execute();
?>
```

In a similar vein, you can delete records either by calling the model's delete() method or by using a DQL query. The following listing illustrates both these approaches:

```
<?php
// using model methods
$member = Doctrine::getTable('Member')->find(11);
$member->delete();

// using DQL
$q = Doctrine_Query::create()
    ->delete('Member m')
    ->addWhere('m.RecordID = ?', 11);
$q->execute();
?>
```

While a full explanation of the Doctrine package is beyond the scope of this book, the preceding examples should have given you some insight into the basics of model operations and provided a foundation for you to understand the material in the following sections. For more information, and many more examples, refer to the links at the end of this chapter.

Try This 4-2 Retrieving Database Records

Now that you know a little bit about how Doctrine models work, how about doing something practical with that knowledge? The following section will show you how to use these models to retrieve individual stamp listings from the database, format them, and display them within the context of the SQUARE example application.

Creating a New Module

So far, all the examples you've seen have been created under the "default" module. However, one of the advantages of using a modular directory layout is that it allows you to group together logically related controllers and thereby produce a more maintainable and organized code tree. With this in mind, create a new module named "catalog," which will contain all the controllers and views related to adding, retrieving, searching, and manipulating the application's catalog of stamps for sale.

To create this new "catalog" module, change to *$APP_DIR/application/* and execute the following commands:

```
shell> mkdir modules/catalog
shell> mkdir modules/catalog/controllers
shell> mkdir modules/catalog/views
shell> mkdir modules/catalog/views/scripts
```

Defining a Custom Route

Next, let's define a route for display URLs. For simplicity, we'll assume that all display URLs will be of the form */catalog/item/display/xx*, where *xx* is a variable indicating the record ID. To set up a custom route to handle such URLs, add the following route definition to the application configuration file at *$APP_DIR/application/configs/application.ini*:

```
resources.router.routes.catalog-display.route = /catalog/item/
display/:id
resources.router.routes.catalog-display.defaults.module = catalog
resources.router.routes.catalog-display.defaults.controller = item
resources.router.routes.catalog-display.defaults.action = display
```

Defining the Controller

The next step is to define a controller and action corresponding to the route definition in the previous section. By convention, this controller will be located at *$APP_DIR/application/ modules/catalog/controllers/ItemController.php*. Here's what it looks like:

```php
<?php
class Catalog_ItemController extends Zend_Controller_Action
{
  public function init()
```

```
    {
    }

    // action to display a catalog item
    public function displayAction()
    {
      // set filters and validators for GET input
      $filters = array(
        'id' => array('HtmlEntities', 'StripTags', 'StringTrim')
      );
      $validators = array(
        'id' => array('NotEmpty', 'Int')
      );

      // test if input is valid
      // retrieve requested record
      // attach to view
      $input = new Zend_Filter_Input($filters, $validators);
      $input->setData($this->getRequest()->getParams());
      if ($input->isValid()) {
        $q = Doctrine_Query::create()
             ->from('Square_Model_Item i')
             ->leftJoin('i.Square_Model_Country c')
             ->leftJoin('i.Square_Model_Grade g')
             ->leftJoin('i.Square_Model_Type t')
             ->where('i.RecordID = ?', $input->id);

        $result = $q->fetchArray();
        if (count($result) == 1) {
          $this->view->item = $result[0];
        } else {
          throw new Zend_Controller_Action_Exception('Page not found', 404);
        }
      } else {
        throw new Zend_Controller_Action_Exception('Invalid input');
      }
    }
  }
}
```

NOTE

Under the Zend Framework, each module (except the "default" module) has its own namespace to prevent object and variable collisions. You can see this in the Catalog_ItemController, where the module name is prefixed to the controller name to create a custom namespace.

(continued)

In this example, the `displayAction()` method first retrieves the value of the input variable `$_GET['id']`, and then interpolates this value into a Doctrine query that attempts to find a matching record in the database. If the query returns a single record as the result, this result is assigned to the view as an associative array. If no matches, or multiple matches, are found, a 404 exception is raised and propagated forward to the default exception handler, which formats it into a readable error page and displays it to the client.

This listing also introduces a new component, the Zend_Filter_Input component. This component, as the name suggests, provides an alternative approach to filtering and validating input, and it is very useful in situations where the user's input doesn't come through a form (as in this example, where the record ID is submitted as a URL request parameter). All of the filters and validators discussed in Chapter 3 can also be used with Zend_Filter_Input.

How does it work? The Zend_Filter_Input class constructor accepts three arguments—an array of filters, an array of validators, and an array of input data to be tested—and runs the first and second of these on the third. You can also specify the array of input data separately, using the `setData()` method. In the previous listing, for example, the `$_GET['id']` variable is first filtered using the HTMLEntities, StripTags, and StringTrim filters, and is then checked to make sure it is an integer. As with Zend_Form, there's an `isValid()` method, which returns Boolean true or false depending on whether or not the data is valid; this can be used as a conditional wrapper around the action's business logic.

Defining the View

Assuming the requested record ID is valid and a record matching it is found in the database, the controller renders the corresponding view, which, by convention, should be stored at *$APP_DIR/application/modules/catalog/views/scripts/item/display.phtml*. Here's what it looks like:

```
<h2>View Item</h2>
<h3>
  FOR SALE:
  <?php echo $this->escape($this->item['Title']); ?> -
  <?php echo $this->escape($this->item['Year']); ?> -
  <?php echo $this->escape($this->item['Square_Model_Grade']
['GradeName']); ?>
</h3>

<div id="container">
  <div id="record">
    <table>
      <tr>
        <td class="key">Title:</td>
        <td class="value">
          <?php echo $this->escape($this->item['Title']); ?>
        </td>
      </tr>
      <tr>
        <td class="key">Type:</td>
        <td class="value">
```

```
        <?php echo $this->escape(
          $this->item['Square_Model_Type']['TypeName']); ?>
      </td>
    </tr>
    <tr>
      <td class="key">Year:</td>
      <td class="value">
        <?php echo $this->escape($this->item['Year']); ?>
      </td>
    </tr>
    <tr>
      <td class="key">Country:</td>
      <td class="value">
        <?php echo $this->escape(
          $this->item['Square_Model_Country']['CountryName']); ?>
      </td>
    </tr>
    <tr>
      <td class="key">Denomination:</td>
      <td class="value">
        <?php echo $this->escape(
          sprintf('%01.2f', $this->item['Denomination'])); ?>
      </td>
    </tr>
    <tr>
      <td class="key">Grade:</td>
      <td class="value">
        <?php echo $this->escape(
          $this->item['Square_Model_Grade']['GradeName']); ?>
      </td>
    </tr>
    <tr>
      <td class="key">Sale price:</td>
      <td class="value">
        $<?php echo $this->escape($this->item['SalePriceMin']); ?> -
        $<?php echo $this->escape($this->item['SalePriceMax']); ?>
      </td>
    </tr>
    <tr>
      <td class="key">Description:</td>
      <td class="value">
        <?php echo $this->escape($this->item['Description']); ?>
      </td>
    </tr>
  </table>
  </div>
</div>
```

(continued)

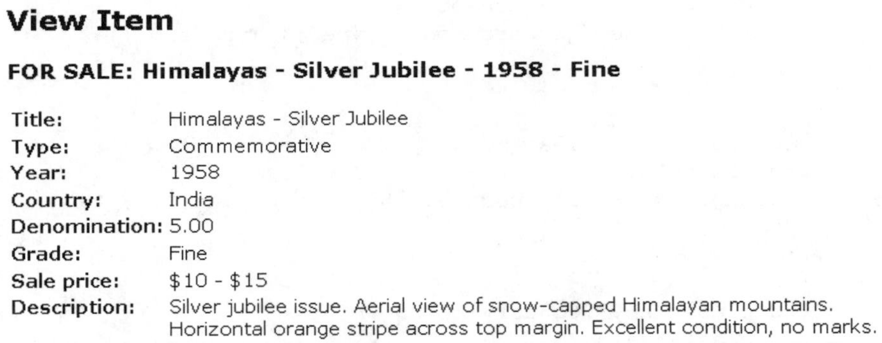

View Item

FOR SALE: Himalayas - Silver Jubilee - 1958 - Fine

Title:	Himalayas - Silver Jubilee
Type:	Commemorative
Year:	1958
Country:	India
Denomination:	5.00
Grade:	Fine
Sale price:	$10 - $15
Description:	Silver jubilee issue. Aerial view of snow-capped Himalayan mountains. Horizontal orange stripe across top margin. Excellent condition, no marks.

Figure 4-6   The result of successfully retrieving a database record

Nothing too complicated here. This view script simply reformats the record retrieved by the model in the previous step, and displays it in a usable and readable format. Notice the use of the escape() method to automatically escape the output of the view before displaying it to the user.

To see this in action, try accessing the URL **http://square.localhost/catalog/item/1** in your browser. If everything is working correctly, the controller will retrieve the record with ID #1 from the database (you'll remember that we manually added this record when initializing the database), assign it to the view, and render it. The output should look something like Figure 4-6.

As a test, you can also try accessing the same URL again, but with an invalid or missing record ID. You should see either a "Page not found" or an "Invalid input" error, as shown in Figure 4-7.

An error occurred

Application error

Exception information:

Message: Invalid input

Stack trace:

Request Parameters:

array (

Figure 4-7   The result of an unsuccessful retrieval attempt

Ask the Expert

Q: Why do I need to escape output before displaying it?

A: As a general rule, you shouldn't trust any data that comes from an external source. This is because it's always possible for attackers to embed malicious content into this data and, if you use it without first cleaning it, you might be putting your application's users at risk. A common example of this type of exploit is the "cross-site scripting attack," wherein an attacker is able to gain access to sensitive user data by piggybacking malicious JavaScript code or HTML form code into your Web pages. With this in mind, it's always essential to pass output through a sanitization routine before displaying it to the user.

Summary

While previous chapters have focused on views and controllers, this one focused on models: what they are, how they work, and what role they play in an MVC application. Although the Zend Framework doesn't come with a dedicated model component, it's nevertheless quite easy to create your own or to integrate third-party models, such as those generated by the Doctrine ORM package, into a Zend Framework application. This chapter demonstrated the process, showing you how to create Doctrine models and configure them to work in the context of a Zend Framework application. It also introduced you to the Zend_Filter_Input component, a useful tool for ad-hoc input filtering and validation, and the Bootstrap class, which provides a framework for initializing application resources at run time.

The SQUARE example application is now significantly smarter as well. It has a database for persistent storage, and a controller than can interact with it to retrieve and display database records. More importantly, it finally has a set of robust, extensible models. This will not only simplify data access and manipulation, but it will also provide a basis for the more advanced functionality discussed in later chapters of this book.

To learn more about the topics discussed in this chapter, consider visiting the following links:

- The official Doctrine Web site and manual, at **http://www.doctrine-project.org/** and **http://www.doctrine-project.org/documentation/manual/1_1/en**

- An introduction to Doctrine models, at **http://www.doctrine-project.org/documentation/manual/1_1/en/introduction-to-models**

- Information on how to express database relationships using Doctrine models, at **http://www.doctrine-project.org/documentation/manual/1_1/en/defining-models**

- Sample queries using Doctrine, at **http://www.doctrine-project.org/documentation/manual/1_0/en/working-with-models**

- Wikipedia's discussion of the ActiveRecord pattern, at
  http://en.wikipedia.org/wiki/Active_record_pattern

- Wikipedia's discussion of Object Relational Mapping, at
  http://en.wikipedia.org/wiki/Object-relational_mapping

- Wikipedia's discussion of CSRF and XSS attacks, at
  http://en.wikipedia.org/wiki/Cross-site_request_forgery and
  http://en.wikipedia.org/wiki/Cross-site_scripting

- The Zend_Filter_Input component, at
  http://framework.zend.com/manual/en/zend.filter.input.html

- The Bootstrap class, at
  http://framework.zend.com/manual/en/zend.application.theory-of-operation.html

- A discussion of the DataMapper pattern (Martin Fowler), at
  http://martinfowler.com/eaaCatalog/dataMapper.html

- A discussion of the Anemic Domain Model (Martin Fowler), at
  http://martinfowler.com/bliki/AnemicDomainModel.html

- Current thinking on the "fat models, skinny controllers" approach (Jamis Buck and Chris Hartjes), at
  http://weblog.jamisbuck.org/2006/10/18/skinny-controller-fat-model and
  http://www.littlehart.net/atthekeyboard/2007/04/27/fat-models-skinny-controllers/

- A discussion of autoloading Doctrine and Doctrine models in the context of a Zend Framework application (Matthew Weier O'Phinney and Eric Leclerc), at
  http://weierophinney.net/matthew/archives/220-Autoloading-Doctrine-and-Doctrine-entities-from-Zend-Framework.html and
  http://www.danceric.net/2009/06/06/doctrine-orm-and-zend-framework/

Chapter 5

Handling CRUD Operations

Key Skills & Concepts

- Understand and implement the four CRUD operations

- Learn different techniques of handling date input in Web forms

- Create multiple layout templates, and switch between them automatically

- Build a simple login/logout system

- Protect administrative actions with user authentication

Chances are you're already familiar with the acronym CRUD. It represents the four fundamental operations—Create, Read, Update, and Delete—that can be performed on application data. Most applications that use persistent data will also expose an interface that allows users to perform these four types of operations on the data. Models are an interface to an application's data, so no discussion of models is complete without an accompanying discussion of how they can be used to add CRUD functions to an application.

This chapter will focus squarely (pardon the pun!) on this aspect of application development, illustrating how to implement CRUD functions in the context of the SQUARE example application. It introduces you to the Zend_Auth component and shows you how to attach user authentication to application-level actions. And it also teaches you a little more about using models, controllers, views, and layouts in practice. So come on in, and let's get cracking!

Try This 5-1 Creating Database Records

You already know how to create and manipulate Web forms using the Zend Framework, and the previous chapter showed you how easy it is to integrate a Doctrine model into a Zend Framework controller. Let's now put those two things together and build a Web form that allows sellers to enter stamp information and have this information added to the application database.

Defining the Form

The first step is to define the input form that will form the basis for the catalog entry. Here's the form definition, which should be saved to *$APP_DIR/library/Square/Form/ItemCreate.php*:

```
<?php
class Square_Form_ItemCreate extends Zend_Form
{
  public function init()
  {
```

```php
// initialize form
$this->setAction('/catalog/item/create')
    ->setMethod('post');

// create text input for name
$name = new Zend_Form_Element_Text('SellerName');
$name->setLabel('Name:')
    ->setOptions(array('size' => '35'))
    ->setRequired(true)
    ->addValidator('Regex', false, array(
        'pattern' => '/^[a-zA-Z]+[A-Za-z\'\-\. ]{1,50}$/'
      ))
    ->addFilter('HtmlEntities')
    ->addFilter('StringTrim');

// create text input for email address
$email = new Zend_Form_Element_Text('SellerEmail');
$email->setLabel('Email address:');
$email->setOptions(array('size' => '50'))
    ->setRequired(true)
    ->addValidator('EmailAddress', false)
    ->addFilter('HtmlEntities')
    ->addFilter('StringTrim')
    ->addFilter('StringToLower');

// create text input for tel number
$tel = new Zend_Form_Element_Text('SellerTel');
$tel->setLabel('Telephone number:');
$tel->setOptions(array('size' => '50'))
    ->addValidator('StringLength', false, array('min' => 8))
    ->addValidator('Regex', false, array(
        'pattern'   => '/^\+[1-9][0-9]{6,30}$/',
        'messages'  => array(
          Zend_Validate_Regex::INVALID    =>
            '\'%value%\' does not match international number
             format +XXYYZZZZ',
          Zend_Validate_Regex::NOT_MATCH  =>
            '\'%value%\' does not match international number
             format +XXYYZZZZ'
        )
      ))
    ->addFilter('HtmlEntities')
    ->addFilter('StringTrim');

// create text input for address
$address = new Zend_Form_Element_TextArea('SellerAddress');
$address->setLabel('Postal address:')
```

(continued)

```
        ->setOptions(array('rows' => '6','cols' => '36'))
        ->addFilter('HtmlEntities')
        ->addFilter('StringTrim');

// create text input for item title
$title = new Zend_Form_Element_Text('Title');
$title->setLabel('Title:')
        ->setOptions(array('size' => '60'))
        ->setRequired(true)
        ->addFilter('HtmlEntities')
        ->addFilter('StringTrim');

// create text input for item year
$year = new Zend_Form_Element_Text('Year');
$year->setLabel('Year:')
      ->setOptions(array('size' => '8', 'length' => '4'))
      ->setRequired(true)
      ->addValidator('Between', false, array(
          'min' => 1700, 'max' => 2015))
      ->addFilter('HtmlEntities')
      ->addFilter('StringTrim');

// create select input for item country
$country = new Zend_Form_Element_Select('CountryID');
$country->setLabel('Country:')
         ->setRequired(true)
         ->addValidator('Int')
         ->addFilter('HtmlEntities')
         ->addFilter('StringTrim')
         ->addFilter('StringToUpper');
foreach ($this->getCountries() as $c) {
  $country->addMultiOption($c['CountryID'], $c['CountryName']);
}

// create text input for item denomination
$denomination = new Zend_Form_Element_Text('Denomination');
$denomination->setLabel('Denomination:')
              ->setOptions(array('size' => '8'))
              ->setRequired(true)
              ->addValidator('Float')
              ->addFilter('HtmlEntities')
              ->addFilter('StringTrim');

// create radio input for item type
$type = new Zend_Form_Element_Radio('TypeID');
$type->setLabel('Type:')
     ->setRequired(true)
     ->addValidator('Int')
```

```
        ->addFilter('HtmlEntities')
        ->addFilter('StringTrim');
foreach ($this->getTypes() as $t) {
  $type->addMultiOption($t['TypeID'], $t['TypeName']);
}
$type->setValue(1);

// create select input for item grade
$grade = new Zend_Form_Element_Select('GradeID');
$grade->setLabel('Grade:')
      ->setRequired(true)
      ->addValidator('Int')
      ->addFilter('HtmlEntities')
      ->addFilter('StringTrim');
foreach ($this->getGrades() as $g) {
  $grade->addMultiOption($g['GradeID'], $g['GradeName']);
};

// create text input for sale price (min)
$priceMin = new Zend_Form_Element_Text('SalePriceMin');
$priceMin->setLabel('Sale price (min):')
             ->setOptions(array('size' => '8'))
             ->setRequired(true)
             ->addValidator('Float')
             ->addFilter('HtmlEntities')
             ->addFilter('StringTrim');

// create text input for sale price (max)
$priceMax = new Zend_Form_Element_Text('SalePriceMax');
$priceMax->setLabel('Sale price (max):')
             ->setOptions(array('size' => '8'))
             ->setRequired(true)
             ->addValidator('Float')
             ->addFilter('HtmlEntities')
             ->addFilter('StringTrim');

// create text input for item description
$notes = new Zend_Form_Element_TextArea('Description');
$notes->setLabel('Description:')
      ->setOptions(array('rows' => '15','cols' => '60'))
      ->setRequired(true)
      ->addFilter('HTMLEntities')
      ->addFilter('StripTags')
      ->addFilter('StringTrim');

// create CAPTCHA for verification
$captcha = new Zend_Form_Element_Captcha('Captcha', array(
```

(continued)

```php
      'captcha' => array(
        'captcha' => 'Image',
        'wordLen' => 6,
        'timeout' => 300,
        'width'   => 300,
        'height'  => 100,
        'imgUrl'  => '/captcha',
        'imgDir'  => APPLICATION_PATH . '/../public/captcha',
        'font'    => APPLICATION_PATH .
                     '/../public/fonts/LiberationSansRegular.ttf',
      )
));

// create submit button
$submit = new Zend_Form_Element_Submit('submit');
$submit->setLabel('Submit Entry')
       ->setOrder(100)
       ->setOptions(array('class' => 'submit'));

// attach elements to form
$this->addElement($name)
     ->addElement($email)
     ->addElement($tel)
     ->addElement($address);

// create display group for seller information
$this->addDisplayGroup(
  array('SellerName', 'SellerEmail', 'SellerTel',
        'SellerAddress'), 'contact');
$this->getDisplayGroup('contact')
     ->setOrder(10)
     ->setLegend('Seller Information');

// attach elements to form
$this->addElement($title)
     ->addElement($year)
     ->addElement($country)
     ->addElement($denomination)
     ->addElement($type)
     ->addElement($grade)
     ->addElement($priceMin)
     ->addElement($priceMax)
     ->addElement($notes);

// create display group for item information
$this->addDisplayGroup(
```

```
        array('Title', 'Year', 'CountryID', 'Denomination',
              'TypeID', 'GradeID', 'SalePriceMin', 'SalePriceMax',
              'Description'), 'item');
    $this->getDisplayGroup('item')
          ->setOrder(20)
          ->setLegend('Item Information');

    // attach element to form
    $this->addElement($captcha);

    // create display group for CAPTCHA
    $this->addDisplayGroup(array('Captcha'), 'verification');
    $this->getDisplayGroup('verification')
          ->setOrder(30)
          ->setLegend('Verification Code');

    // attach element to form
    $this->addElement($submit);
}

public function getCountries() {
  $q = Doctrine_Query::create()
        ->from('Square_Model_Country c');
  return $q->fetchArray();
}

public function getGrades() {
  $q = Doctrine_Query::create()
        ->from('Square_Model_Grade g');
  return $q->fetchArray();
}

public function getTypes() {
  $q = Doctrine_Query::create()
        ->from('Square_Model_type t');
  return $q->fetchArray();
}

}
```

Much of this should be familiar to you from Chapter 3. This form contains a mixture of text input fields and selection lists, corresponding closely with the fields in the *item* database table created earlier in the chapter. All the fields use the HTMLEntities and StringTrim input filters, and many of them include input validators as well. In particular, notice the use of the Regex validator for validating names and telephone numbers using a custom pattern. As explained in Chapter 3, the form elements are organized into display groups for greater usability, and, in a few cases, custom error messages are used as well.

(continued)

The most interesting thing about this form definition in the preceding code, however, is the use of Doctrine models to populate the three selection lists. Notice that the class includes three ancillary methods, getCountries(), getGrades(), and getTypes(), which internally invoke the Doctrine models created in Chapter 4 to retrieve a list of options from the corresponding master tables. These options are then attached to form elements via the addMultiOption() method.

Defining Controllers and Views

The action URL for the form defined in the previous section is specified as */catalog/ item/create*. Under standard Zend Framework naming conventions, this corresponds to ItemController::createAction in the "catalog" module. This controller was created in Chapter 4; now it needs to be updated with the new action. Here's what the code looks like:

```php
<?php
class Catalog_ItemController extends Zend_Controller_Action
{
  public function createAction()
  {
    // generate input form
    $form = new Square_Form_ItemCreate;
    $this->view->form = $form;

    // test for valid input
    // if valid, populate model
    // assign default values for some fields
    // save to database
    if ($this->getRequest()->isPost()) {
      if ($form->isValid($this->getRequest()->getPost())) {
        $item = new Square_Model_Item;
        $item->fromArray($form->getValues());
        $item->RecordDate = date('Y-m-d', mktime());
        $item->DisplayStatus = 0;
        $item->DisplayUntil = null;
        $item->save();
        $id = $item->RecordID;
        $this->_helper->getHelper('FlashMessenger')->addMessage(
          'Your submission has been accepted as item #' . $id .
          '. A moderator will review it and, if approved,
          it will appear on the site within 48 hours.');
        $this->_redirect('/catalog/item/success');
      }
    }
  }

  public function successAction()
```

```
  {
    if ($this->_helper->getHelper('FlashMessenger')->getMessages()) {
      $this->view->messages = $this->_helper
        ->getHelper('FlashMessenger')->getMessages();
    } else {
      $this->_redirect('/');
    }
  }
}
```

Assuming the form input is valid, the `createAction()` method creates an instance of the Item model and populates it using the input submitted through the Web form. Any necessary custom adjustments to the input data—for example, setting the record's display status to hidden—are performed at this point as well, and the record is then saved to the database by calling the model's `save()` method, which formulates and executes the necessary INSERT query. Any errors in the process will be represented as Doctrine exceptions and propagated forward to the default exception handler for resolution.

If the record is saved successfully, a status message indicating this fact is added to the FlashMessenger and control is transferred to the `successAction()` method, which renders a success view. By convention, this view script is located at *$APP_DIR/application/modules/ catalog/views/scripts/item/success.phtml*. Here's what it looks like:

```
<h2>Success</h2>
<?php echo implode($this->messages); ?>
```

Ask the Expert

Q: Why are you redirecting to the `successAction()`, instead of simply rendering a success view within the `createAction()`, after saving the record in the previous example?

A: This is the recommended approach to follow after any successful POST operation, and is specifically done to avoid the so-called "double post problem." Consider that, in the scenario where the success view is rendered by the `createAction()`, if the application user hits the browser's Refresh/Reload button after the success view has been rendered, it will result in the same data being POST-ed to the server twice. However, by storing the success message in the FlashMessenger action helper and redirecting to the `successAction()` to render the success view, this problem is completely eliminated; reloading the page in this scenario will either generate the success view again (without causing a double post) or redirect the client back to the index page.

(continued)

Similarly, the view script for the input form is located at *$APP_DIR/application/modules/catalog/views/scripts/item/create.phtml*, and looks like this:

```
<h2>Add Item</h2>
<?php echo $this->form; ?>
```

And you're done! To see this in action, browse to the URL **http://square.localhost/catalog/item/create**, and you should be presented with a form like the one in Figure 5-1.

Enter values into the form and submit it. If your input passes validation, a new record will be created and inserted into the *item* table, and the success view will be rendered. Figure 5-2 illustrates the result of a successful submission.

You can verify that the record was successfully inserted by accessing the `ItemController::displayAction` from Chapter 4 at the URL **http://square .localhost/catalog/item/display/xx**, where **xx** is the ID of the newly inserted record.

If your input is invalid, the form will be re-rendered with error messages indicating what went wrong, as shown in Figure 5-3.

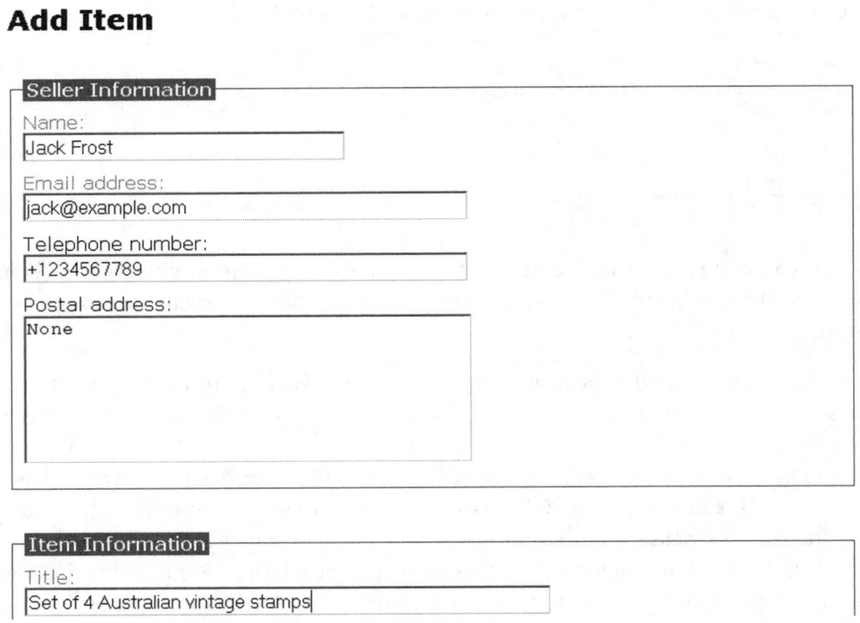

Add Item

Seller Information

Name:
Jack Frost

Email address:
jack@example.com

Telephone number:
+1234567789

Postal address:
None

Item Information

Title:
Set of 4 Australian vintage stamps

Figure 5-1 The form to add a new item to the SQUARE catalog

S Q U A R E
HOME
SERVICES
CONTACT
Success
Your submission has been accepted as item #5. A moderator will review it and, if approved, it will appear on the site within 48 hours.

Figure 5-2 The result of successfully adding a new item to the SQUARE catalog

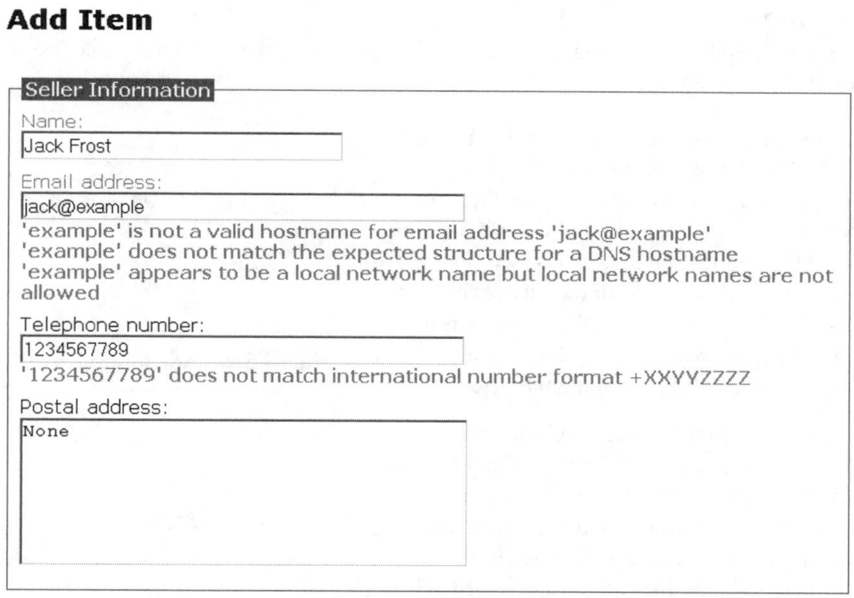

Add Item
Seller Information
Name:
Jack Frost
Email address:
jack@example
'example' is not a valid hostname for email address 'jack@example'
'example' does not match the expected structure for a DNS hostname
'example' appears to be a local network name but local network names are not allowed
Telephone number:
1234567789
'1234567789' does not match international number format +XXYYZZZZ
Postal address:
None

Figure 5-3 The result of submitting the form with invalid input values

Working with Administrative Actions

At this point, one of the key goals of the SQUARE example application—allowing sellers to directly upload listings of available stamps—has been met. However, these items aren't immediately visible in the public domain, because application administrators must still manually review uploaded items and either approve them for display or remove them from the database. And that's where the SQUARE administration panel comes in.

The SQUARE administration panel is a section of the application reserved specifically for application administrators. It provides an interface for administrators to view, update, and delete catalog items, and it's therefore the perfect place to illustrate how the remaining CRUD operations can be implemented. But before you dive into the code, it's a good idea to understand the different ways in which administrative actions can be handled in the context of a Zend Framework application. There are three aspects to consider here: structure, routing, and layout.

Structure

In a modular application, there are a number of ways in which administrative actions can be structured:

- Create a single controller in the default module that holds all the administrative actions for the application. Under this approach, a single controller would contain administrative actions for all the application's modules (see Figure 5-4). This approach is not recommended, except for very small applications, as the single controller could quickly grow to a very large size, affecting both performance and maintainability.

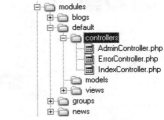

Figure 5-4 Administrative actions in a single controller

- Create a separate module that holds all the administrative actions for the application. Under this approach, the new module would contain individual controllers for the application's administrative actions, with one such controller per module (see Figure 5-5). This is a common approach, but it too is not very maintainable, because as Figure 5-5 illustrates, you end up with a single controller that must manage the information of the multiple controllers within each module. It's also not ideal when building self-contained modules, as the actions related to each module are not all stored in the same filesystem location.

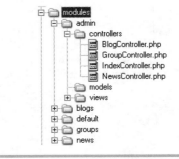

Figure 5-5 Administrative controllers in a separate module

- Create a separate controller within each module that holds all the administrative actions for that module. Under this approach, each module includes, at minimum, two controllers: one for public actions and the other for corresponding administrative actions (see Figure 5-6). This approach is recommended for various reasons: It makes sense from both logical and physical perspectives, as all the actions for a specific module are held in a single filesystem location; it's reasonably easy to maintain; and it is flexible enough to be adapted to different purposes.

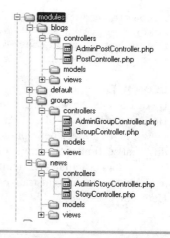

Figure 5-6 Administrative controllers within each module

Routing

To ensure consistency, it is generally a good idea for administrative routes to mimic their public counterparts. So, for example, if the public route to an action is */article/edit/5*, the corresponding administrative route might be of the form */admin/ article/edit/5*. The use of the */admin* prefix serves to mark the route as being administrative in nature, while simultaneously providing a clear and consistent interface to an application's functionality. This consistency is particularly important if, say, you later decide to expose REST or SOAP functionality as well.

Unlike some other frameworks, the Zend Framework doesn't come with built-in administrative routes. Therefore, it is necessary to manually configure these routes, either by specifying them in the application configuration file or by extending the base router to become "prefix-aware." An example of the former is shown in the following code; look at the end of this chapter for links to examples of the latter:

```
resources.router.routes.list.route = /admin/articles/index
resources.router.routes.list.defaults.module = system
resources.router.routes.list.defaults.controller = articles
resources.router.routes.list.defaults.action = list

resources.router.routes.view.route = /admin/articles/view/:id
resources.router.routes.view.defaults.module = system
resources.router.routes.view.defaults.controller = articles
resources.router.routes.view.defaults.action = display

resources.router.routes.update.route = /admin/articles/edit/:id
resources.router.routes.update.defaults.module = system
resources.router.routes.update.defaults.controller = articles
resources.router.routes.update.defaults.action = update
```

```
resources.router.routes.delete.route = /admin/articles/delete/:id
resources.router.routes.delete.defaults.module = system
resources.router.routes.delete.defaults.controller = articles
resources.router.routes.delete.defaults.action = delete
```

Layout

By default, all views will use the master layout defined in the application configuration file. However, customers often request a different look and feel for an application's administrative views, either for aesthetic purposes or to visually highlight to users that they've moved to a different section of the application.

It's not particularly difficult to do this with a Zend Framework application: Simply create a new layout for administrative views, and then switch to it as needed within individual actions. Here's an example:

```php
<?php
class Sandbox_ExampleController extends Zend_Controller_Action
{
  public function adminDeleteAction()
  {
    $this->_helper->layout->setLayout('admin');
    // continue
  }
}
```

This can be tedious (not to mention having the potential to become a maintenance nightmare) when dealing with a large number of actions. Therefore, an alternative approach is to examine the request URL and automatically switch the layout within the controller's `init()` or `preDispatch()` method, before rendering the view. This approach is discussed in detail in the next section.

Try This 5-2   Listing, Deleting, and Updating Database Records

With all this background information in mind, let's proceed to build the SQUARE administration panel. As noted earlier, to keep things simple, we'll assume that administrators only need to view, edit, and delete items from the catalog. The following sections discuss each of these functions in detail.

Setting the Administrative Layout

The first step is to define a new master layout for administrative views. Since the main purpose of this layout is simply to distinguish the administrative interface from the public one, it doesn't need to be particularly elaborate. Here's an example of what it might look like:

```
<!DOCTYPE html PUBLIC "-//W3C//DTD XHTML 1.0 Strict//EN" "http://www.
w3.org/TR/xhtml1/DTD/xhtml1-strict.dtd">
```

```html
<html xmlns="http://www.w3.org/1999/xhtml" xml:lang="en" lang="en">
  <head>
    <meta http-equiv="Content-Type" content="text/html; charset=utf-8"/>
    <base href="/" />
    <link rel="stylesheet" type="text/css" href="/css/master.css" />
    <link rel="stylesheet" type="text/css" href="/css/admin.css" />
    <script src="/js/form.js"></script>
  </head>
  <body>
    <div id="header">
      <div id="logo">
        <img src="/images/logo-admin.gif" />
      </div>

      <div id="menu">
        <a href="<?php echo $this->url(
          array(), 'admin-catalog-index'); ?>">CATALOG</a>
      </div>
    </div>

    <div id="content">
      <?php echo $this->layout()->content ?>
    </div>

    <div id="footer">
      <p>Created with <a href="http://framework.zend.com/">
      Zend Framework</a>. Licensed under
      <a href="http://www.creativecommons.org/">Creative Commons
      </a>.</p>
    </div>
  </body>
</html>
```

As you did in Chapter 2, save this layout template to the application's layout directory as *$APP_DIR/application/layouts/admin.phtml*.

You'll notice that the layout also makes use of three additional assets—a CSS stylesheet, a JavaScript code file, and a logo image. These files need to be located in the application's public area, so that they can be retrieved over HTTP by connecting clients. You'll find these assets in the code archive for this chapter, which can be downloaded from this book's companion Web site at `http://www.zf-beginners-guide.com/`.

The next step is to set things up so that the framework automatically switches the default layout to the new administrative layout whenever the router encounters a URL with the /admin prefix. As discussed earlier, one way to do this is to specify the new layout's name in each route definition. However, a simpler option is to perform this switch in the controller's `preDispatch()` method, which is automatically called before every action is invoked.

(continued)

Ask the Expert

Q: **What is the** `preDispatch()` **method?**

A: The `preDispatch()` method is a special "stub" method that is automatically executed by the controller before the requested action is invoked. It's particularly useful for preprocessing, logging, or otherwise manipulating the contents of a request before passing it on to the specified action. And, in case you're wondering, there's also a `postDispatch()` method, which is automatically executed by the controller after the requested action is invoked.

The code to do this should be added to the `Catalog_AdminItemController` at *$APP_DIR/application/modules/catalog/controllers/AdminItemController.php*, as shown in the following example:

```php
<?php
class Catalog_AdminItemController extends Zend_Controller_Action
{
  // action to handle admin URLs
  public function preDispatch()
  {
    // check URL for /admin pattern
    // set admin layout
    $url = $this->getRequest()->getRequestUri();
    $this->_helper->layout->setLayout('admin');

  }
}
```

This code checks the current request and switches to the administrative layout template using the `setLayout()` method.

Defining Custom Routes

The next step is to define custom routes for the administrative functions. It's necessary at this point to make some assumptions about what these routes will look like, so let's assume that

1. The summary listing URL will be of the form */admin/catalog/item/index*.

2. All display URLs will be of the form */admin/catalog/item/display/xx*, where *xx* is a variable indicating the record ID.

3. All update URLs will be of the form */admin/catalog/item/update/xx*, where *xx* is a variable indicating the record ID.

4. All delete URLs will be of the form */admin/catalog/item/delete/xx*, where *xx* is a variable indicating the record ID.

To set up custom routes corresponding to the URLs for the routes, add the following route definitions to the application configuration file at *$APP_DIR/application/configs/application.ini*:

```
resources.router.routes.admin-catalog-index.route = /admin/catalog/item/
index
resources.router.routes.admin-catalog-index.defaults.module = catalog
resources.router.routes.admin-catalog-index.defaults.controller = admin.
item
resources.router.routes.admin-catalog-index.defaults.action = index

resources.router.routes.admin-catalog-display.route =
/admin/catalog/item/display/:id
resources.router.routes.admin-catalog-display.defaults.module = catalog
resources.router.routes.admin-catalog-display.defaults.controller =
admin.item
resources.router.routes.admin-catalog-display.defaults.action = display

resources.router.routes.admin-catalog-update.route =
/admin/catalog/item/update/:id
resources.router.routes.admin-catalog-update.defaults.module = catalog
resources.router.routes.admin-catalog-update.defaults.controller =
admin.item
resources.router.routes.admin-catalog-update.defaults.action = update
resources.router.routes.admin-catalog-update.defaults.id = ""

resources.router.routes.admin-catalog-delete.route =
/admin/catalog/item/delete
resources.router.routes.admin-catalog-delete.defaults.module = catalog
resources.router.routes.admin-catalog-delete.defaults.controller =
admin.item
resources.router.routes.admin-catalog-delete.defaults.action = delete

resources.router.routes.admin-catalog-success.route =
/admin/catalog/item/success
resources.router.routes.admin-catalog-success.defaults.module = catalog
resources.router.routes.admin-catalog-success.defaults.controller =
admin.item
resources.router.routes.admin-catalog-success.defaults.action = success
```

(continued)

Defining the List Action and View

With all these pieces in place, we're now ready to begin writing some action code. Consider the following `Catalog_AdminItemController::indexAction`, which retrieves a list of records from the database using the Doctrine model and attaches them to the view:

```php
<?php
class Catalog_AdminItemController extends Zend_Controller_Action
{
  // action to display list of catalog items
  public function indexAction()
  {
    $q = Doctrine_Query::create()
          ->from('Square_Model_Item i')
          ->leftJoin('i.Square_Model_Grade g')
          ->leftJoin('i.Square_Model_Country c')
          ->leftJoin('i.Square_Model_Type t');
    $result = $q->fetchArray();
    $this->view->records = $result;
  }
}
```

The view then takes over and formats this information into a table to make it more readable. Here's what the view script looks like (as per convention, this should be saved as *$APP_DIR/application/modules/catalog/views/scripts/admin-item/index.php*):

```php
<h2>List Items</h2>
<?php if (count($this->records)): ?>
<div id="records">
  <form method="post" action="
    <?php echo $this->url(array(), 'admin-catalog-delete'); ?>">
    <table>
      <tr>
        <td></td>
        <td class="key">
          Item ID
        </td>
        <td class="key">
          Title
        </td>
        <td class="key">
          Denomination
        </td>
        <td class="key">
          Country
        </td>
        <td class="key">
          Grade
        </td>
```

```
          <td class="key">
            Year
          </td>
          <td></td>
          <td></td>
        </tr>
        <?php foreach ($this->records as $r):?>
        <tr>
          <td><input type="checkbox" name="ids[]"
          value="<?php echo $r['RecordID']; ?>" style="width:2px" />
          </td>
          <td><?php echo $this->escape($r['RecordID']); ?></td>
          <td><?php echo $this->escape($r['Title']); ?></td>
          <td><?php echo $this->escape(sprintf('%1.2f',
          $r['Denomination'])); ?></td>
          <td><?php echo $this->escape(
          $r['Square_Model_Country']['CountryName']); ?></td>
          <td><?php echo $this->escape(
          $r['Square_Model_Grade']['GradeName']); ?></td>
          <td><?php echo $this->escape($r['Year']); ?></td>
          <td><a href="<?php echo $this->url(array('id' =>
$r['RecordID']),
          'admin-catalog-display'); ?>">Display</a></td>
          <td><a href="<?php echo $this->url(array('id' =>
$r['RecordID']),
          'admin-catalog-update'); ?>">Update</a></td>
        </tr>
        <?php endforeach; ?>
        <tr>
          <td colspan="10"><input type="submit" name="submit"
          style="width:150px" value="Delete Selected" /></td>
        </tr>
      </table>
    </form>
</div>

<?php else: ?>
No records found
<?php endif; ?>
```

There are a few important points to note about this view:

- All field values are escaped before being rendered. As discussed in Chapter 4, this is a fundamental security precaution that you should take when working with output values, to reduce the risk of CSRF and XSS attacks.

(continued)

- The display `<table>` is enclosed within a `<form>`. This is necessary to handle the check boxes that appear next to each record, to enable multirecord deletion. Note that this form is manually generated inside the view script, rather than with Zend_Form, because there's no easy way to create this kind of form-plus-table combination in Zend_Form.

- Each record is displayed with "Update" and "Display" links. These correspond to the routes configured in the previous section, and they're dynamically generated at run time with the `url()` view helper. Notice that the record ID is included in the request URL as a `GET` parameter.

To see this view in action, fire up your browser and point it to **http://square.localhost/ admin/catalog/item/index**. You should be rewarded with a summary page like the one shown in Figure 5-7.

Defining the Delete Action

When the user selects one or more records for deletion, the selected record IDs are POST-ed as an array to the `Catalog_AdminItemController::deleteAction`. This `deleteAction()`

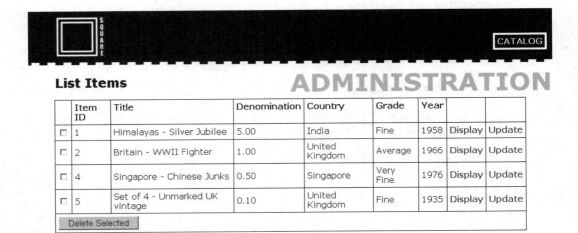

Figure 5-7 The catalog summary page in the SQUARE administration panel

method reads the selected IDs and uses the Doctrine model to formulate a DELETE query that removes them from the database. Here's what it looks like:

```php
<?php
class Catalog_AdminItemController extends Zend_Controller_Action
{
  // action to delete catalog items
  public function deleteAction()
  {
    // set filters and validators for POST input
    $filters = array(
      'ids' => array('HtmlEntities', 'StripTags', 'StringTrim')
    );
    $validators = array(
      'ids' => array('NotEmpty', 'Int')
    );
    $input = new Zend_Filter_Input($filters, $validators);
    $input->setData($this->getRequest()->getParams());

    // test if input is valid
    // read array of record identifiers
    // delete records from database
    if ($input->isValid()) {
      $q = Doctrine_Query::create()
            ->delete('Square_Model_Item i')
            ->whereIn('i.RecordID', $input->ids);
      $result = $q->execute();

      $this->_helper->getHelper('FlashMessenger')
        ->addMessage('The records were successfully deleted.');
      $this->_redirect('/admin/catalog/item/success');
    } else {
      throw new Zend_Controller_Action_Exception('Invalid input');
    }
  }

  // success action
  public function successAction()
  {
    if ($this->_helper->getHelper('FlashMessenger')->getMessages()) {
      $this->view->messages = $this->_helper
        ->getHelper('FlashMessenger')->getMessages();
    } else {
      $this->_redirect('/admin/catalog/item/index');
    }
  }
}
```

(continued)

Success

The records were successfully deleted.

Figure 5-8 The result of successfully deleting items in the SQUARE administration panel

To see this in action, select one or more records for deletion by ticking the corresponding check boxes in the summary page, and then submit the form using the Delete Selected button.

The records should be deleted from the database, and you should be presented with a success message, like the one shown in Figure 5-8.

Defining the Update Form

It's also quite common for administrators to have the ability to update more fields of a record than unprivileged users can update. For example, in the SQUARE application, in addition to the usual item description fields, administrators should also have the ability to update the item's display status and define the period for which the item is visible in the public catalog.

Zend_Form, with its object-oriented approach to form creation, is particularly good at meeting this requirement. Using OOP concepts of inheritance and extensibility, it's possible to extend a parent form class and derive different child form classes from it by adding and subtracting form elements via Zend_Form's addElement() and removeElement() methods.

To illustrate, consider the following ItemUpdate form class, which is derived from the ItemCreate form class created at the beginning of this chapter. This child class shares many input elements with its parent; however, since it's intended for use only by administrators, it removes some unwanted elements (the CAPTCHA input) and adds other necessary ones (display status and date inputs). Here's the code:

```php
<?php
class Square_Form_ItemUpdate extends Square_Form_ItemCreate
{
  public function init()
  {
    // get parent form
    parent::init();

    // set form action (set to false for current URL)
    $this->setAction('/admin/catalog/item/update');

    // remove unwanted elements
    $this->removeElement('Captcha');
    $this->removeDisplayGroup('verification');
```

```
// create hidden input for item ID
$id = new Zend_Form_Element_Hidden('RecordID');
$id->addValidator('Int')
   ->addFilter('HtmlEntities')
   ->addFilter('StringTrim');

// create select input for item display status
$display = new Zend_Form_Element_Select('DisplayStatus',
  array('onChange' =>
    "javascript:handleInputDisplayOnSelect('DisplayStatus',
      'divDisplayUntil', new Array('1'));"));
$display->setLabel('Display status:')
        ->setRequired(true)
        ->addValidator('Int')
        ->addFilter('HtmlEntities')
        ->addFilter('StringTrim');
$display->addMultiOptions(array(
  0 => 'Hidden',
  1 => 'Visible'
));

// create hidden input for item display date
$displayUntil = new Zend_Form_Element_Hidden('DisplayUntil');
$displayUntil->addValidator('Date')
             ->addFilter('HtmlEntities')
             ->addFilter('StringTrim');

// create select inputs for item display date
$displayUntilDay = new Zend_Form_Element_Select('DisplayUntil_day');
$displayUntilDay->setLabel('Display until:')
                ->addValidator('Int')
                ->addFilter('HtmlEntities')
                ->addFilter('StringTrim')
                ->addFilter('StringToUpper')
                ->setDecorators(array(
                  array('ViewHelper'),
                  array('Label', array('tag' => 'dt')),
                  array('HtmlTag',
                    array(
                      'tag' => 'div',
                      'openOnly' => true,
                      'id' => 'divDisplayUntil',
                      'placement' => 'prepend'
                    )
                  ),
                ));
for($x=1; $x<=31; $x++) {
  $displayUntilDay->addMultiOption($x, sprintf('%02d', $x));
}
```

(continued)

```
$displayUntilMonth = new Zend_Form_Element_Select('DisplayUntil_month');
$displayUntilMonth->addValidator('Int')
                  ->addFilter('HtmlEntities')
                  ->addFilter('StringTrim')
                  ->setDecorators(array(
                      array('ViewHelper')
                  ));
for($x=1; $x<=12; $x++) {
  $displayUntilMonth->addMultiOption(
    $x, date('M', mktime(1,1,1,$x,1,1)));
}

$displayUntilYear = new Zend_Form_Element_Select('DisplayUntil_year');
$displayUntilYear->addValidator('Int')
                 ->addFilter('HtmlEntities')
                 ->addFilter('StringTrim')
                 ->setDecorators(array(
                     array('ViewHelper'),
                     array('HtmlTag',
                       array(
                         'tag' => 'div',
                         'closeOnly' => true
                       )
                     ),
                 ));
for($x=2009; $x<=2012; $x++) {
  $displayUntilYear->addMultiOption($x, $x);
}

// attach element to form
$this->addElement($id)
     ->addElement($display)
     ->addElement($displayUntil)
     ->addElement($displayUntilDay)
     ->addElement($displayUntilMonth)
     ->addElement($displayUntilYear);

// create display group for status
$this->addDisplayGroup(
  array('DisplayStatus', 'DisplayUntil_day',
        'DisplayUntil_month', 'DisplayUntil_year',
        'DisplayUntil'), 'display');
$this->getDisplayGroup('display')
     ->setOrder(25)
     ->setLegend('Display Information');
  }
}
```

Save this form definition as *$APP_DIR/library/Square/Form/ItemUpdate.php*.

Handling Date Input

A word here about the date input fields in this form. As you may remember from Chapter 3, Zend_Form includes a Date validator, which can be used to check if a date is valid or not. If you take a look at the preceding form definition, you'll see that it includes three selection lists for date input, one each for the day, month, and year. There's also a hidden input field, which is used internally to store the composite date value created from the three selection lists, and which is associated with the aforesaid Date validator.

You're probably thinking that this seems unnecessarily complex, and you're right. Why? Well, at its default settings, the Date validator expects the date input to be formatted as a single string in YYYY-MM-DD format, and produces a validation error if this format is not met. In the real world, though, users often make errors when manually typing in date values as strings. Common errors include selecting a different format (for example, DD-MM-YYYY), forgetting to pad single-digit date and month values with zeroes (for example, entering 9 instead of 09), or using a different separator (for example, YYYY/MM/DD).

With this in mind, it's generally considered safer and more user-friendly to present a selection list or graphical calendar interface for date input, as this is less prone to user eccentricities, and then rewrite the input into the desired format programmatically. As you'll see in the next section, that's precisely what the updateAction() does. It uses the input from the three selection lists to create a composite date value in YYYY-MM-DD format, sets the hidden input field to this value, and then allows validation to proceed in the normal fashion.

Since the hidden input field is associated with a Date validator, an invalid date will fail validation and the Date validator will generate an error message, which will be visible when the form is re-rendered. If the date is valid, the input will pass validation and the remainder of the action code will be executed as normal.

TIP

There are other approaches to handling date input fields as well. One, suggested by leading Zend Framework developer Matthew Weier O'Phinney, involves extending the Zend_Form_Element base class to create a composite date input element (you'll find a link to this approach at the end of the chapter). Another technique, discussed in detail in Chapter 11, involves using a graphical calendar component in combination with a text input field to directly write the selected date to the form in the required format.

You'll notice that this form definition also makes use of the HtmlTag decorator. As explained in Chapter 3, this decorator controls the markup around form fields. In this particular case, it's used to wrap a <div> element around the three date selection lists, through selective use of the decorator's 'openOnly' and 'closeOnly' attributes. This <div> is used by the user-defined handleInputDisplayOnSelect() JavaScript function, which automatically hides or shows the group of date selectors depending on the item's display status.

(continued)

Defining the Update Action and View

Updating records typically involves two distinct queries:

1. The first query is a read query, occurring when the user selects a record for update. The `updateAction()` must read the selected record from the database, prepopulate a Web form with the field values currently stored in the database, and render this form to the user.

2. The second query is a write query, occurring when the user submits the form. The `updateAction()` must receive, filter, and validate the submitted values. If the values are valid, the action must write the new version of the record to the database.

   The `Catalog_AdminItemController::updateAction` performs both of these functions. Here's what it looks like:

```php
<?php
class Catalog_AdminItemController extends Zend_Controller_Action
{
  // action to modify an individual catalog item
  public function updateAction()
  {
    // generate input form
    $form = new Square_Form_ItemUpdate;
    $this->view->form = $form;

    if ($this->getRequest()->isPost()) {
      // if POST request
      // test if input is valid
      // retrieve current record
      // update values and replace in database
      $postData = $this->getRequest()->getPost();
      $postData['DisplayUntil'] = sprintf('%04d-%02d-%02d',
        $this->getRequest()->getPost('DisplayUntil_year'),
        $this->getRequest()->getPost('DisplayUntil_month'),
        $this->getRequest()->getPost('DisplayUntil_day')
      );
      if ($form->isValid($postData)) {
        $input = $form->getValues();
        $item = Doctrine::getTable('Square_Model_Item')
              ->find($input['RecordID']);
        $item->fromArray($input);
        $item->DisplayUntil =
          ($item->DisplayStatus == 0) ? null : $item->DisplayUntil;
        $item->save();
        $this->_helper->getHelper('FlashMessenger')
          ->addMessage('The record was successfully updated.');
        $this->_redirect('/admin/catalog/item/success');
      }
    } else {
      // if GET request
      // set filters and validators for GET input
```

```php
// test if input is valid
// retrieve requested record
// pre-populate form
$filters = array(
  'id' => array('HtmlEntities', 'StripTags', 'StringTrim')
);
$validators = array(
  'id' => array('NotEmpty', 'Int')
);
$input = new Zend_Filter_Input($filters, $validators);
$input->setData($this->getRequest()->getParams());
if ($input->isValid()) {
  $q = Doctrine_Query::create()
        ->from('Square_Model_Item i')
        ->leftJoin('i.Square_Model_Country c')
        ->leftJoin('i.Square_Model_Grade g')
        ->leftJoin('i.Square_Model_Type t')
        ->where('i.RecordID = ?', $input->id);
  $result = $q->fetchArray();
  if (count($result) == 1) {
    // perform adjustment for date selection lists
    $date = $result[0]['DisplayUntil'];
    $result[0]['DisplayUntil_day'] = date('d', strtotime($date));
    $result[0]['DisplayUntil_month'] = date('m', strtotime($date));
    $result[0]['DisplayUntil_year'] = date('Y', strtotime($date));
    $this->view->form->populate($result[0]);
  } else {
    throw new Zend_Controller_Action_Exception('Page not found', 404);
  }
} else {
  throw new Zend_Controller_Action_Exception('Invalid input');
}
}
}
}
```

Broadly speaking, this `updateAction()` method consists of two sections, divided by a conditional test:

1. If the request is a POST request, the action retrieves the POST input and performs the necessary adjustments to create a composite date string in YYYY-MM-DD format, as discussed in the preceding section. It then uses the Zend_Form object's `isValid()` method to test whether the submitted input is valid. Assuming that the input is valid, the action uses the Doctrine `find()` method to retrieve the selected record as an instance of the Item model class, and sets new values for the various fields of the record using the submitted input. The `save()` method is used to save the record back to the database, and control passes to the `successAction()`.

(continued)

2. If the request is a GET request, the action retrieves the record ID from the URL request string, validates it, and executes a Doctrine query to retrieve the corresponding record from the database. It performs the reverse adjustments for the date input values, and then uses the Zend_Form object's `populate()` method to prepopulate the input form with the current field values from the record.

Here's the corresponding view script, which should be saved as *$APP_DIR/application/ modules/catalog/views/scripts/admin-item/update.php*:

```
<h2>Update Item</h2>
<?php echo $this->form; ?>

<script>
handleInputDisplayOnSelect('DisplayStatus',
  'divDisplayUntil', new Array('1'));
</script>
```

To see this in action, use the "Update" link on the summary page to select one of the records for update, or use your browser to access an update URL, such as **http://square .localhost/admin/catalog/item/update/1**. You should be presented with a form that is already populated with the current contents of the record, as shown in Figure 5-9.

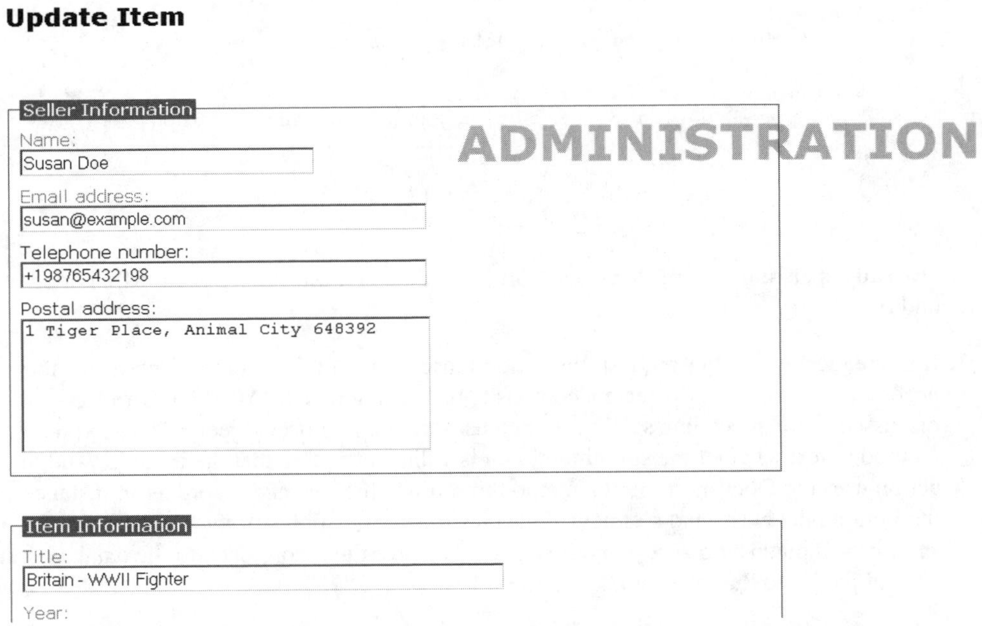

Figure 5-9 The form to update an existing item in the SQUARE administration panel

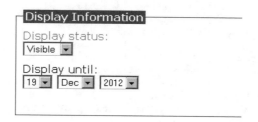

Figure 5-10   Additional options to define item visibility in the SQUARE update form

Notice that this form includes additional fields that allow you to control the item's display status (see Figure 5-10). If the status is set to visible, you will also have the option to define the date until which it should remain visible.

Make your changes and submit the form. Assuming your input passes validation, the record will be updated and you will be presented with a success message. Remember that you can also verify the update by browsing to the corresponding display URL, such as **http://square .localhost/catalog/item/display/1**.

Updating the Display Action

There's one final change to be made. In Chapter 4, you created a displayAction() that would accept an item ID and retrieve the corresponding record from the database using a Doctrine query. However, that query did not take account of the item's current display status. Since there now exists a mechanism for administrators to adjust an item's visibility status, it's a good idea to update this displayAction() to also take this status into account and display only those items which are set as publicly visible.

To do this, update the ItemController::displayAction, located at *$APP_DIR/ application/modules/catalog/controllers/ItemController.php*, such that it incorporates the visibility-adjusting condition in the Doctrine query:

```php
<?php
class Catalog_ItemController extends Zend_Controller_Action
{
  // action to display a catalog item
  public function displayAction()
  {
    // set filters and validators for GET input
    // ...


    // test if input is valid
    // retrieve requested record
    // attach to view
```

(continued)

```
if ($input->isValid()) {
  $q = Doctrine_Query::create()
        ->from('Square_Model_Item i')
        ->leftJoin('i.Square_Model_Country c')
        ->leftJoin('i.Square_Model_Grade g')
        ->leftJoin('i.Square_Model_Type t')
        ->where('i.RecordID = ?', $input->id)
        ->addWhere('i.DisplayStatus = 1')
        ->addWhere('i.DisplayUntilDate >= CURDATE()');
  $result = $q->fetchArray();
  if (count($result) == 1) {
    $this->view->item = $result[0];
  } else {
    throw new Zend_Controller_Action_Exception('Page not found', 404);
  }
} else {
  throw new Zend_Controller_Action_Exception('Invalid input');
}
  }
}
```

With this change, only items that have specifically been marked as visible will be accessible through the public interface. Any attempt to access items other than these will raise a 404 exception, which is propagated forward to the default exception handler for display to the requesting client.

NOTE
Are you wondering why this chapter doesn't include any coverage of reading individual records (the R in CRUD)? This aspect was already covered in Chapter 4, in the section entitled "Retrieving Database Records," which used a Doctrine model to read and display database records by ID. The administration panel discussed in this chapter includes a similar function, which you'll find in the code archive for this chapter. The code archive can be downloaded from this book's companion Web site at **http://www.zf-beginners-guide.com/**.

Adding User Authentication

At this point, the administration panel is complete, and administrators can perform read, update, and delete actions on records through a browser-based interface. However, these actions are currently unprotected and, as a result, any user can access them via their URL routes. This is obviously a security risk, so the next step must be to implement a mechanism that allows the application to distinguish between "unprivileged users" and "administrators," and only allow the latter group access to administrative functions.

The Zend Framework includes a component specifically designed to tackle user authentication tasks. This component, called Zend_Auth, provides an API and a set of adapters for verifying user credentials against a variety of data sources, including SQL-compliant database systems, text files, LDAP directories, and OpenID providers. Successfully authenticated identities are automatically stored in the session by Zend_Auth, and thus can be retrieved or reverified at any time by a controller or action.

NOTE

Out of the box, Zend_Auth only supports session-based storage. However, you can add support for other storage mechanisms simply by extending the Zend_Auth_Storage_ Interface class. More information, and examples of how to do this, can be found in the links at the end of this chapter.

To understand how this works in practice, consider the following example:

```php
<?php
class Sandbox_ExampleController extends Zend_Controller_Action
{
  public function authenticateAction()
  {
    // generate a login form
    $form = new Form_Example_Auth;
    $this->view->form = $form;
    if ($this->getRequest()->isPost()) {
      if ($form->isValid($this->getRequest()->getPost())) {
        // get credentials from user input
        // initialize authentication adapter
        // perform authentication and test result
        $values = $form->getValues();
        $adapter = new Zend_Auth_Adapter_DbTable($this->db);
        $adapter->setIdentity($values['username'])
                ->setCredential($values['password']);
        $auth = Zend_Auth::getInstance();
        $result = $auth->authenticate($adapter);
        if ($result->isValid()) {
          $this->_helper->getHelper('FlashMessenger')
                        ->addMessage('You were successfully logged
in.');
          $this->_redirect('/admin/index');
        } else {
          $this->view->message =
            'You could not be logged in. Please try again.';
        }
      }
    }
  }
}
```

This example makes use of the DbTable database authentication adapter, which is initialized with an instance of the Zend_Db_Adapter_Abstract class. This adapter is passed a set of user credentials, and the Zend_Auth singleton is then used to perform authentication against these credentials. The return value of the `Zend_Auth::authenticate` method is a Zend_Auth_Result object; this object can then be tested via its `isValid()` method to determine whether authentication succeeded or failed.

Zend_Auth also exposes a number of additional methods, which can be used from within individual controllers and actions to verify that an authenticated session exists. For example, the `hasIdentity()` method returns a Boolean value indicating whether an authenticated user session exists, while the `getIdentity()` method returns the identity of the authenticated user. These methods can be invoked from within individual actions to test whether or not the user has been authenticated, and therefore, to allow or disallow the action's execution.

Here's an example, which ensures that the `protectedAction()` is only available to authenticated users:

```php
<?php
class Sandbox_ExampleController extends Zend_Controller_Action
{
  public function protectedAction()
  {
    // check if user is authenticated
    // if no, redirect to login page
    // if yes, proceed as normal
    if (!Zend_Auth::getInstance()->hasIdentity()) {
      $this->_redirect('/admin/login');
    } else {
      $model = new MemberModel;
      $this->view->data = $model->fetchAll();
    }
  }
}
```

It's also possible to create custom authentication adapters that verify credentials against other data sources, simply by extending the base Zend_Auth_Adapter_Interface class. The child class must expose, at minimum, a constructor that accepts user credentials and an `authenticate()` method that verifies these credentials against an authentication provider. The return value of the `authenticate()` method must be an instance of the Zend_Auth_Result class, with a constant indicating whether or not authentication was successful. You'll see an example of one such custom authentication adapter in the next section.

Creating a Login/Logout System

Zend_Auth is one of those components that's hard to explain, and is better understood with a practical example. With this in mind, let's put it to work in a practical context by building a simple login/logout system to protect access to the SQUARE administration panel. The following sections will guide you through the process.

Defining Custom Routes

As always, a good place to begin is with the route definitions. Define login and logout routes for your administration panel by adding the following definitions to your application configuration file at *$APP_DIR/application/configs/application.ini*:

```
resources.router.routes.login.route = /admin/login
resources.router.routes.login.defaults.module = default
resources.router.routes.login.defaults.controller = login
resources.router.routes.login.defaults.action = login

resources.router.routes.login-success.route = /admin/login/success
resources.router.routes.login-success.defaults.module = default
resources.router.routes.login-success.defaults.controller = login
resources.router.routes.login-success.defaults.action = success

resources.router.routes.logout.route = /admin/logout
resources.router.routes.logout.defaults.module = default
resources.router.routes.logout.defaults.controller = login
resources.router.routes.logout.defaults.action = logout
```

Defining the Login Form

The next step is to define the login form itself. This doesn't need to be very complicated—all you really need is a field for the username, a field for the password, and a submit button. Here's the form definition, which should be saved as *$APP_DIR/library/Square/Form/Login.php*:

```php
<?php
class Square_Form_Login extends Zend_Form
{
  public function init()
  {
    // initialize form
    $this->setAction('/admin/login')
         ->setMethod('post');

    // create text input for name
    $username = new Zend_Form_Element_Text('username');
    $username->setLabel('Username:')
```

(continued)

```
            ->setOptions(array('size' => '30'))
            ->setRequired(true)
            ->addValidator('Alnum')
            ->addFilter('HtmlEntities')
            ->addFilter('StringTrim');

    // create text input for password
    $password = new Zend_Form_Element_Password('password');
    $password->setLabel('Password:')
            ->setOptions(array('size' => '30'))
            ->setRequired(true)
            ->addFilter('HtmlEntities')
            ->addFilter('StringTrim');

    // create submit button
    $submit = new Zend_Form_Element_Submit('submit');
    $submit->setLabel('Log In')
         ->setOptions(array('class' => 'submit'));

    // attach elements to form
    $this->addElement($username)
        ->addElement($password)
        ->addElement($submit);
    }
}
```

Defining the Authentication Adapter

The form in the previous section submits its data to the `LoginController::loginAction` in the "default" module. Before we get into the code for this action, though, we need to spend a few minutes creating an authentication adapter that knows how to verify the supplied username and password against the user table created in Chapter 4.

As discussed earlier, it's not very difficult to create a custom authentication adapter with Zend_Auth. It can be done simply by extending the base Zend_Auth_Adapter_Interface class and ensuring that the child class exposes an `authenticate()` method that knows how to perform the required authentication. The more important question is, why is it even necessary to create a custom adapter, when Zend_Auth already includes a built-in adapter for database authentication?

The reason has entirely to do with efficiency and consistency. To begin with, the Zend_Auth_Adapter_DbTable adapter only works with an instance of the Zend_Db class, and it cannot be used directly with a Doctrine model. Zend_Db, in turn, expects its database connection parameters to be specified in a format different from that used by Doctrine. Therefore, in order to use the Zend_Auth_Adapter_DbTable directly, it is necessary to either specify the same database connection parameters in two different formats in the application configuration file (not ideal, as it means updating two sets of parameters every time you, say, change the database password) or write code to "translate" the Doctrine DSN string to the array format expected by Zend_Db (tedious and error-prone due to the large number of DSN permutations possible).

There's also the small matter of consistency. Thus far, all database access has occurred through Doctrine models. Switching over to Zend_Db only for authentication-related queries is confusing; it's also inefficient because the application now has to load two sets of libraries instead of one for database operations. For all these reasons, it makes sense to create a custom authentication adapter that uses Doctrine internally, instead of using the provided Zend_Auth_Adapter_DbTable adapter.

With that explanation out of the way, let's proceed to the actual code. Consider the following listing, which creates a Doctrine-based authentication adapter that conforms to Zend_Auth conventions:

```php
<?php
class Square_Auth_Adapter_Doctrine implements Zend_Auth_Adapter_Interface
{
  // array containing authenticated user record
  protected $_resultArray;

  // constructor
  // accepts username and password
  public function __construct($username, $password)
  {
    $this->username = $username;
    $this->password = $password;
  }

  // main authentication method
  // queries database for match to authentication credentials
  // returns Zend_Auth_Result with success/failure code
  public function authenticate()
  {
    $q = Doctrine_Query::create()
         ->from('Square_Model_User u')
         ->where('u.Username = ? AND u.Password = PASSWORD(?)',
                 array($this->username, $this->password)
         );
    $result = $q->fetchArray();
    if (count($result) == 1) {
      return new Zend_Auth_Result(
        Zend_Auth_Result::SUCCESS, $this->username, array());
    } else {
      return new Zend_Auth_Result(
        Zend_Auth_Result::FAILURE, null,
          array('Authentication unsuccessful')
      );
    }
  }
}
```

(continued)

```
// returns result array representing authenticated user record
// excludes specified user record fields as needed
public function getResultArray($excludeFields = null)
{
  if (!$this->_resultArray) {
    return false;
  }

  if ($excludeFields != null) {
    $excludeFields = (array)$excludeFields;
    foreach ($this->_resultArray as $key => $value) {
      if (!in_array($key, $excludeFields)) {
        $returnArray[$key] = $value;
      }
    }
    return $returnArray;
  } else {
    return $this->_resultArray;
  }
}
}
```

Save this class as *$APP_DIR/library/Square/Auth/Adapter/Doctrine.php*.

The main workhorse in this class definition is the `authenticate()` method, which formulates and executes a Doctrine query to check if the supplied username and password are valid. The method returns an instance of the Zend_Auth_Result class with three properties: a result code indicating success or failure, the username (or other unique identity key) if successful, and an array containing error messages if unsuccessful.

TIP
Apart from simple success and failure indicators, a number of other result codes are also available. These can be used to provide more specific information on why the authentication attempt failed—for example, whether the failure was related to the username or to the password, whether the discovered user record was ambiguous, or whether some other type of error occurred. A complete list of these result codes can be found in the Zend Framework manual.

While the `authenticate()` method simply returns whether or not the user was authenticated, the `getResultArray()` method returns the complete user record for authenticated users, as an array. This method optionally accepts a list of fields to be excluded and strips these fields from the returned array. This is a handy method to include in your adapter, because it allows one-shot access to the entire user record and makes it easy to persist the user record in the session for use in other actions. You'll see an example of this in the next section.

Defining the Login Action and View

With most of the hard work delegated to the authentication adapter, creating the `LoginController::loginAction` becomes a piece of cake. Here's the code, which by convention should be saved as *$APP_DIR/application/modules/default/controllers/LoginController.php*:

```php
<?php
class LoginController extends Zend_Controller_Action
{
  public function init()
  {
    $this->_helper->layout->setLayout('admin');
  }

  // login action
  public function loginAction()
  {
    $form = new Square_Form_Login;
    $this->view->form = $form;
    // check for valid input
    // authenticate using adapter
    // persist user record to session
    // redirect to original request URL if present
    if ($this->getRequest()->isPost()) {
      if ($form->isValid($this->getRequest()->getPost())) {
        $values = $form->getValues();
        $adapter = new Square_Auth_Adapter_Doctrine(
          $values['username'], $values['password']
        );
        $auth = Zend_Auth::getInstance();
        $result = $auth->authenticate($adapter);
        if ($result->isValid()) {
          $session = new Zend_Session_Namespace('square.auth');
          $session->user = $adapter->getResultArray('Password');
          if (isset($session->requestURL)) {
            $url = $session->requestURL;
            unset($session->requestURL);
            $this->_redirect($url);
          } else {
            $this->_helper->getHelper('FlashMessenger')
                      ->addMessage('You were successfully logged in.');
            $this->_redirect('/admin/login/success');
          }
        } else {
          $this->view->message =
            'You could not be logged in. Please try again.';
        }
      }
    }
  }
}
```

(continued)

Ask the Expert

Q: Why is the LoginController part of the "default" module, rather than the "catalog" module?

A: The "catalog" module serves as a container for controllers, actions, and views related to catalog management. However, login/logout actions are not specific to catalog management, and are better situated at the global, or application, level. The "default" module is therefore a more logical location for these actions.

```
public function successAction()
{
  if ($this->_helper->getHelper('FlashMessenger')->getMessages()) {
    $this->view->messages = $this->_helper
                                  ->getHelper('FlashMessenger')
                                  ->getMessages();
  } else {
    $this->_redirect('/');
  }
 }
}
```

The loginAction() reads the credentials submitted through the login form, and uses the authentication adapter created in the previous step to verify them against the application database. If authentication fails, it re-renders the form with an error message. If not, it stores the user record in the session and then looks up the session namespace to see if there is an entry for the original request URL (more on this later). If there is, it redirects the client to that URL; if not, it forwards to the successAction() and renders the success view.

Here's what the login view script at *$APP_DIR/application/modules/default/views/login/login.phtml* looks like:

```
<h2>Login</h2>
<div style="color:red; font-weight:bolder">
  <?php echo $this->message; ?>
</div>
<?php echo $this->form; ?>
```

Defining the Logout Action

The corollary to the `loginAction()` is the `logoutAction()`, which destroys the authenticated session and clears the user's identity via the `Zend_Auth::clearIdentity` method. Here's what it looks like:

```php
<?php
class LoginController extends Zend_Controller_Action
{
  public function logoutAction()
  {
    Zend_Auth::getInstance()->clearIdentity();
    Zend_Session::destroy();
    $this->_redirect('/admin/login');
  }
}
```

Protecting Administrative Actions

The final step is to attach authentication checks to the actions you wish to protect. Since all the administrative actions created to date are located in a single controller, the Catalog_AdminItemController, these checks can conveniently be added to that controller's `preDispatch()` method. Here's what the updated `preDispatch()` method looks like:

```php
<?php
class Catalog_AdminItemController extends Zend_Controller_Action
{
  // action to handle admin URLs
  public function preDispatch()
  {
    // set admin layout
    // check if user is authenticated
    // if not, redirect to login page
    $url = $this->getRequest()->getRequestUri();
    $this->_helper->layout->setLayout('admin');
    if (!Zend_Auth::getInstance()->hasIdentity()) {
      $session = new Zend_Session_Namespace('square.auth');
      $session->requestURL = $url;
      $this->_redirect('/admin/login');
    }
  }
}
```

As a result of this change, whenever the router receives a request for an administrative action, the `preDispatch()` method will first check if the user's identity has been authenticated

(continued)

using the `Zend_Auth::hasIdentity` method. If no such identity exists, this method will return false. If this happens, the request URL will be stored in the session, and the client will be redirected to the login form.

Following a successful login, the request URL will be retrieved from the session by the `loginAction()` (discussed in the previous section) and the client will be redirected back to this URL. The `preDispatch()` method will again be executed, but this time, since the user's identity has already been confirmed, the `hasIdentity()` will return true, and the requested action will be dispatched in the normal manner.

Updating the Master Layout

As illustrated in the preceding section, the Zend_Auth object's `hasIdentity()` method provides a convenient test for whether or not the user has been authenticated. This fact can be put to good use in the administrative layout, to selectively display certain menu items depending on whether the user is logged in or not. Here's an example, which updates the administrative layout at *$APP_DIR/application/layouts/admin.phtml* to display a "Logout" item in the main menu when the user is logged in, and a "Login" item otherwise. The changes to the layout are highlighted in bold.

```
<!DOCTYPE html PUBLIC "-//W3C//DTD XHTML 1.0 Strict//EN" "http://www.w3.org/TR/
xhtml1/DTD/xhtml1-strict.dtd">
<html xmlns="http://www.w3.org/1999/xhtml" xml:lang="en" lang="en">
  <head>
    <meta http-equiv="Content-Type" content="text/html; charset=utf-8"/>
    <base href="/" />
    <link rel="stylesheet" type="text/css" href="/css/master.css" />
    <link rel="stylesheet" type="text/css" href="/css/admin.css" />
    <link rel="stylesheet" type="text/css" href="/css/yui/calendar.css"/>
    <script src="/js/form.js"></script>
  </head>
  <body>
    <div id="header">
      <div id="logo">
        <img src="/images/logo-admin.gif" />
      </div>

      <div id="menu">
        <?php if (Zend_Auth::getInstance()->hasIdentity()): ?>
        <a href="<?php echo $this->url(array(),
        'admin-catalog-index'); ?>">CATALOG</a>
        <a href="<?php echo $this->url(array(), 'logout'); ?>">LOGOUT</a>
        <?php else: ?>
```

```
      <a href="<?php echo $this->url(array(), 'login'); ?>">LOGIN</a>
      <?php endif; ?>
    </div>
  </div>

  <div id="content">
    <?php echo $this->layout()->content ?>
  </div>

  <div id="footer">
    <p>Created with <a href="http://framework.zend.com/">
    Zend Framework</a>. Licensed under
    <a href="http://www.creativecommons.org/">Creative Commons
    </a>.</p>
  </div>
 </body>
</html>
```

And you're done! To see this in action, try accessing the summary page at **http://square .localhost/admin/catalog/item/index**. You should be presented with a login form, as in Figure 5-11.

Once you submit valid credentials through this form, you should be automatically redirected to the summary page. The main menu should also reflect your logged-in status by displaying a new "Logout" link, as shown in Figure 5-12.

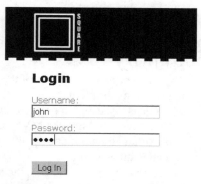

Figure 5-11 The login form for the SQUARE administration panel

Figure 5-12 The post-login menu in the SQUARE administration panel

Ask the Expert

Q: Can I use Zend_Auth to grant or deny access to application resources on the basis of user roles or privileges?

A: No. As the Zend Framework manual points out, Zend_Auth is concerned with *user authentication* (verifying that a user is who he or she claims to be) and not with *user access control* (verifying that a user has rights to access specific application resources). In practical terms, this means that once authenticated, a user can access any or all of the protected actions; the system does not allow for fine-grained control over which user has access to which action(s). If your application needs to control access to specific actions based on user roles, you should consider using the Zend_Acl component instead.

Summary

This chapter focused on two of the most common tasks you'll encounter when building Web applications: implementing CRUD operations and authenticating users. Building on the techniques discussed in previous chapters, it showed you how to list, create, update, and delete database records using the MVC paradigm. It also introduced you to the Zend_Auth component and explained how it can be used to protect access to specified actions with a simple user authentication system.

At the end of this chapter, the SQUARE example application has a lot of meat on its bones. Users are now able to directly add stamps for sale to the online catalog, while administrators have the capability to review these listings, approve them for display, modify them, or delete them through a reasonably full-fledged administration panel. Access to these administrative functions is protected through a basic login/logout system, and there are even a couple of nice touches, such as the ability to automatically redirect to the originally requested action post-login and a main menu that "knows" whether or not a user is currently logged in.

Implementing these functions should have given you some insight into how the different components of the Zend Framework can be combined to satisfy real-world requirements. Remember that you can read more about the topics discussed in this chapter by visiting the following links:

● The Zend_Controller component, at
http://framework.zend.com/manual/en/zend.controller.html

● The Zend_Layout component, at
http://framework.zend.com/manual/en/zend.layout.html

● The Zend_Auth component, at
http://framework.zend.com/manual/en/zend.auth.html

- A more sophisticated Doctrine authentication adapter (Jason Eisenmenger and David Werner), at **http://framework.zend.com/wiki/pages/viewpage.action?pageId=3866950**

- A discussion of creating simple, extensible CRUD with the Zend Framework (Ryan Mauger), at **http://www.rmauger.co.uk/2009/06/creating-simple-extendible-crud-using-zend-framework/**

- A discussion of creating composite date input elements (Matthew Weier O'Phinney), at **http://weierophinney.net/matthew/archives/217-Creating-composite-elements.html**

- More information on creating a login/logout system (Matthew Weier O'Phinney), at **http://weierophinney.net/matthew/archives/165-Login-and-Authentication-with-Zend-Framework.html**

- A discussion of enhancing the base router (Michael Sheakoski), at **http://framework.zend.com/wiki/display/ZFUSER/MJS_Controller_PathRouter+-+An+enhanced+RewriteRouter?focusedCommentId=9437448**

- A discussion of using a database for Zend_Auth identity storage (Branko Ajzele), at **http://inchoo.net/zend/zend-authentication-component-zend_auth-database-storage-class/**

Chapter 6

Indexing, Searching, and Formatting Data

Key Skills & Concepts

- Dynamically generate and execute database search queries
- Learn to store and index different types of data
- Create a full-text search engine with the Zend_Search_Lucene component
- Understand how to enable output type switching at run time
- Express the same output in many different formats, including XML

H ave you ever seen a sponge in a bucket of water? For the first minute or two, while it's still mostly dry, it floats happily on the surface, without a care in the world. As it soaks up more and more water, though, it gradually submerges, until it's finally completely wet and ready for use. A user-facing Web application is a lot like this. When it's first launched on the Web, it's usually little more than an empty shell, waiting for the world to notice it. As it attracts users, it begins soaking up data, and positive network effects start to take over: The more people who use it, the more valuable it becomes to others.

What does this have to do with anything? Well, as your application starts accumulating user content, it becomes more and more important to have this content searchable and accessible in different formats, so that users can exploit it for different purposes (for example, mashing it up with content from other services). Simply providing a browsable index of database contents won't cut it; you also need to offer users different ways to search data and filter results, and different formats in which to express these search results.

That's where this chapter comes in. Over the next few pages, it will introduce you to the basics of adding search functionality to a Web application, with examples of both filter-based searchs and full-text searchs. It will also discuss the Zend Framework's ContextSwitch helper, which provides a flexible and extensible system for handling multiple output types, including XML and JSON.

Try This 6-1 Searching and Filtering Database Records

In the previous chapter, you built an interface for users to upload items to the product catalog and for administrators to review and approve these items for display on the public Web site. This section will build on the work done in the previous chapter, by creating an interface for users to browse approved items and filter them by various criteria.

Defining the Search Form

For this illustrative example, let's keep the search form as simple as possible by assuming that users will only need to search for stamps by three criteria: year, price, and grade. Here's what the search form definition looks like:

```php
<?php
class Square_Form_Search extends Zend_Form
{
  public $messages = array(
      Zend_Validate_Int::INVALID    =>
         '\'%value%\' is not an integer',
      Zend_Validate_Int::NOT_INT  =>
         '\'%value%\' is not an integer'
  );


  public function init()
  {
    // initialize form
    $this->setAction('/catalog/item/search')
         ->setMethod('get');

    // set form decorators
    $this->setDecorators(array(
        array('FormErrors',
          array('markupListItemStart' => '', 'markupListItemEnd' =>
'')),
        array('FormElements'),
        array('Form')
    ));

    // create text input for year
    $year = new Zend_Form_Element_Text('y');
    $year->setLabel('Year:')
            ->setOptions(array('size' => '6'))
            ->addValidator('Int', false,
               array('messages'  => $this->messages))
            ->addFilter('HtmlEntities')
            ->addFilter('StringTrim');

    // create text input for price
    $price = new Zend_Form_Element_Text('p');
    $price->setLabel('Price:')
            ->setOptions(array('size' => '8'))
            ->addValidator('Int', false,
               array('messages'  => $this->messages))
            ->addFilter('HtmlEntities')
            ->addFilter('StringTrim');

    // create select input for grade
    $grade = new Zend_Form_Element_Select('g');
    $grade->setLabel('Grade:')
         ->addValidator('Int', false,
```

(continued)

```
                        array('messages'  => $this->messages))
                ->addFilter('HtmlEntities')
                ->addFilter('StringTrim')
                ->addMultiOption('', 'Any');
        foreach ($this->getGrades() as $g) {
          $grade->addMultiOption($g['GradeID'], $g['GradeName']);
        };

        // create submit button
        $submit = new Zend_Form_Element_Submit('submit');
        $submit->setLabel('Search')
                ->setOptions(array('class' => 'submit'));

        // attach elements to form
        $this->addElement($year)
                ->addElement($price)
                ->addElement($grade)
                ->addElement($submit);

        // set element decorators
        $this->setElementDecorators(array(
            array('ViewHelper'),
            array('Label', array('tag' => '<span>'))
        ));
        $submit->setDecorators(array(
            array('ViewHelper'),
         ));
    }


    public function getGrades()
    {
        $q = Doctrine_Query::create()
            ->from('Square_Model_Grade g');
        return $q->fetchArray();
    }
}
```

This is a fairly standard form definition, of the type you should be familiar with by now: two text input fields, one selection list, and one submit button, all wrapped inside an init() method. Notice that the default Label decorator has been modified to wrap each element label in a <span> element (instead of the default <dt> element), thereby ensuring that the form elements are rendered horizontally instead of vertically.

There is one other point of note. So far, in all the previous examples, validation errors have been automatically displayed to the user under the corresponding input element. Often, however, application or user interface requirements dictate that these errors should be displayed together, in a single block at the top of the form instead of under individual elements. This is not very difficult to do—there is a built-in FormErrors decorator that does this for you automatically—but accomplishing it requires you to disable the Errors decorator that is attached to each element by default. The form definition in the preceding code does both these tasks by adding the FormErrors decorator via the Zend_Form object's `setDecorators()` method and then specifically excluding the Errors decorator from the list of decorators applied to each element via the Zend_Form object's `setElementDecorators()` method.

Once you've understood the form definition, save it as *$APP_DIR/library/Square/Form/ Search.php*.

Defining the Controller and View

The next step is to define the action and view for the browse/search interface. Update the Catalog_ItemController class at *$APP_DIR/modules/catalog/controllers/ItemController.php* with the following `searchAction()` method:

```php
<?php
class Catalog_ItemController extends Zend_Controller_Action
{

  public function searchAction()
  {
    // generate input form
    $form = new Square_Form_Search;
    $this->view->form = $form;

    // check for valid input
    // generate base query
    if ($form->isValid($this->getRequest()->getParams())) {
      $input = $form->getValues();
      $q = Doctrine_Query::create()
            ->from('Square_Model_Item i')
            ->leftJoin('i.Square_Model_Country c')
            ->leftJoin('i.Square_Model_Grade g')
            ->leftJoin('i.Square_Model_Type t')
            ->where('i.DisplayStatus = 1')
            ->addWhere('i.DisplayUntil >= CURDATE()');

      // attach criteria to base query
      if (!empty($input['y'])) {
        $q->addWhere('i.Year = ?', $input['y']);
      }
```

(continued)

```
    if (!empty($input['g'])) {
      $q->addWhere('i.GradeID = ?', $input['g']);
    }
    if (!empty($input['p'])) {
      $q->addWhere('? BETWEEN i.SalePriceMin AND i.SalePriceMax',
        $input['p']);
    }

    // execute query and attach results to view
    $results = $q->fetchArray();
    $this->view->results = $results;
  }

  }

}
```

The searchAction() method first formulates a base query that returns a list of all the approved items in the catalog. Based on the input entered by the user, it then attaches Where clauses to this query to further filter the result set by the specified criteria. Once the query is executed, the results are assigned to a view variable. If the submitted input is invalid, the list of validation error messages is likewise assigned to a view variable.

The view script takes care of iterating over the result set and formatting each record for display. Errors, if any, are displayed at the top of the results page via the FormErrors decorator. Here's the view script, which should be saved as *$APP_DIR/modules/catalog/views/scripts/search php*:

```
<h2>Search</h2>
<?php echo $this->form; ?>

<h2>Search Results</h2>
<p><?php echo count($this->results); ?> result(s) found.</p>

<?php if (count($this->results)): ?>
  <?php $x=1; ?>
  <?php foreach ($this->results as $r): ?>

  <div>
  <?php echo $x; ?>.
    <a href="<?php echo $this->url(array('id' =>
      $this->escape($r['RecordID'])), 'catalog-display'); ?>">
      <?php echo $this->escape($r['Title']); ?>
      (<?php echo $this->escape($r['Year']); ?>)
    </a>
    <?php if (!empty($r['Description'])): ?>
    <br/><?php echo $this->escape($r['Description']); ?>
    <?php endif; ?>
```

```
    <br/>
    <strong>
    Grade:
    <?php echo $this->escape($r['Square_Model_Grade']['GradeName']);
?> |
    Country:
    <?php echo $this->escape($r['Square_Model_Country']
['CountryName']); ?> |
    Sale price:
    $<?php echo sprintf('%0.2f', $this->escape($r['SalePriceMin']));
?> to
    $<?php echo sprintf('%0.2f', $this->escape($r['SalePriceMax']));
?>
    </strong>
  </div>
  <br/>
    <?php $x++; ?>
  <?php endforeach; ?>
<?php endif; ?>

<div>
  <a href="<?php echo $this->url(array(
    'module' => 'catalog',
    'controller' => 'item',
    'action' => 'create'),
    null, true); ?>">Add Item</a>
</div>
```

Updating the Master Layout

All that's left now is to update the navigation links in the application's main menu to reflect the
new browse/search form using the url() helper method. To do this, update the master layout,
at *$APP_DIR/application/layouts/master.phtml*, with the changes highlighted in bold:

```
<!DOCTYPE html PUBLIC "-//W3C//DTD XHTML 1.0 Strict//EN" "http://www.
w3.org/TR/xhtml1/DTD/xhtml1-strict.dtd">
<html xmlns="http://www.w3.org/1999/xhtml" xml:lang="en" lang="en">
...

    <div id="menu">
      <a href="<?php echo $this->url(array(), 'home'); ?>">HOME</a>
      <a href="<?php echo $this->url(array('page' => 'services'),
      'static-content'); ?>">SERVICES</a>
      <a href="<?php echo $this->url(array('module' => 'catalog',
      'controller' => 'item', 'action' => 'search'), 'default', true);
      ?>">CATALOG</a>
```

(continued)

```
        <a href="<?php echo $this->url(array(), 'contact');
?>">CONTACT</a>
      </div>
    </div>

...
</html>
```

NOTE
Pay attention to the arguments passed to the `url()` view helper in the previous listing. The second argument, as you already know, specifies the route name to use for URL generation. If this argument is null, the view helper will use the route that generated the current URL as the basis for the new URL. Since this can produce odd errors when working with routes that reset the URL request, it's a good idea to explicitly tell the framework to use its standard, or "default," route, corresponding to a URL of the form /module/controller/action, in these cases.

If you now try visiting the URL **http://square.localhost/catalog/item/search** through your Web browser, you should see a form like the one in Figure 6-1.

Enter values into the search input fields and submit the form, and if all goes well, you should see a revised list of items matching your search parameters, as shown in Figure 6-2.

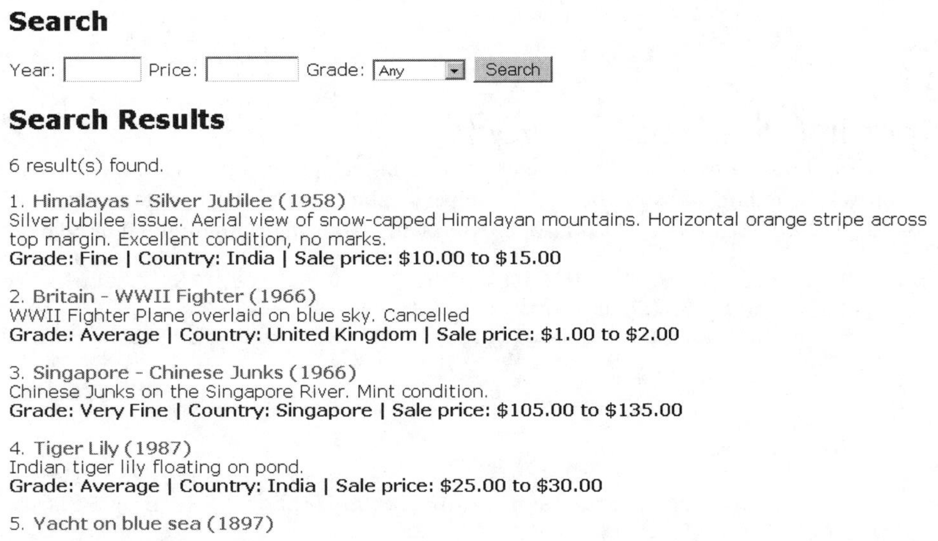

Search

Year: [   ] Price: [   ] Grade: [Any ▼] [Search]

Search Results

6 result(s) found.

1. Himalayas - Silver Jubilee (1958)
Silver jubilee issue. Aerial view of snow-capped Himalayan mountains. Horizontal orange stripe across top margin. Excellent condition, no marks.
Grade: Fine | Country: India | Sale price: $10.00 to $15.00

2. Britain - WWII Fighter (1966)
WWII Fighter Plane overlaid on blue sky. Cancelled
Grade: Average | Country: United Kingdom | Sale price: $1.00 to $2.00

3. Singapore - Chinese Junks (1966)
Chinese Junks on the Singapore River. Mint condition.
Grade: Very Fine | Country: Singapore | Sale price: $105.00 to $135.00

4. Tiger Lily (1987)
Indian tiger lily floating on pond.
Grade: Average | Country: India | Sale price: $25.00 to $30.00

5. Yacht on blue sea (1897)

Figure 6-1 The SQUARE catalog search form

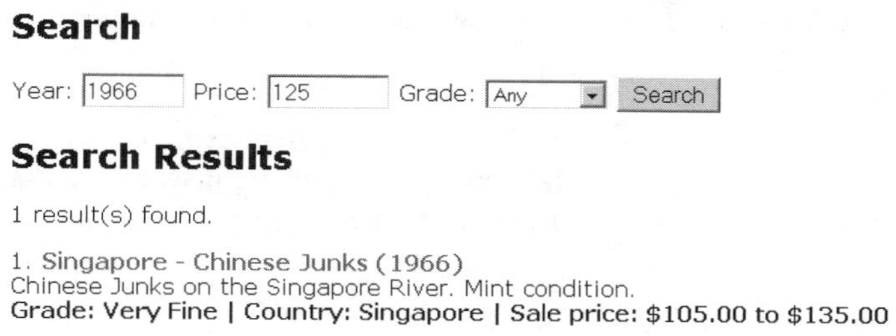

Search

Year: [1966] Price: [125] Grade: [Any ▼] [Search]

Search Results

1 result(s) found.

1. Singapore - Chinese Junks (1966)
Chinese Junks on the Singapore River. Mint condition.
Grade: Very Fine | Country: Singapore | Sale price: $105.00 to $135.00

Figure 6-2   A list of catalog items matching the search criteria entered into the search form

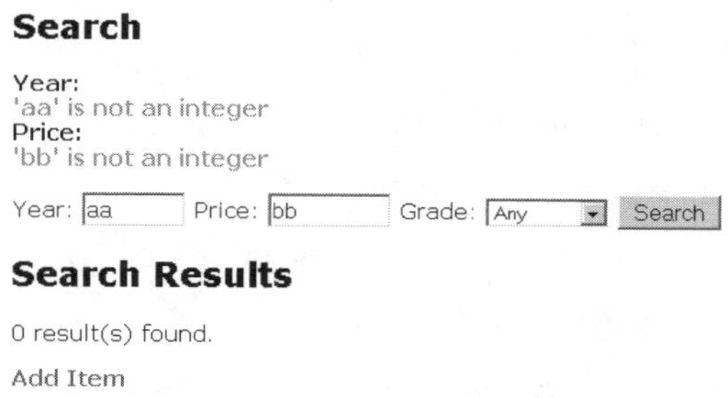

Search

Year:
'aa' is not an integer
Price:
'bb' is not an integer

Year: [aa] Price: [bb] Grade: [Any ▼] [Search]

Search Results

0 result(s) found.

Add Item

Figure 6-3   Validation errors in search input, captured and emitted in a single block

You can also try submitting the form with invalid values. The built-in validators will catch your invalid input and display error messages at the top of the page in a single block, as shown in Figure 6-3.

Adding Full-Text Search

When you're building an application search engine, there are a couple of different ways you can go. You can create a filter-based search engine, wherein specific criteria entered by the user are used to filter the list of search results, as shown in the previous section. Or, you can create a full-text search engine, which indexes application content and finds matches on the basis of keywords entered by the user. In modern Web applications, a full-text search is often preferred, because it's typically faster and produces more accurate results than a database search.

The Zend Framework comes with a very capable full-text search component, known as Zend_Search_Lucene. A PHP-only implementation of the Apache Lucene Project, this component can be used both to index various document types (including text, HTML, and some Microsoft Office 2007 formats) as well as to perform different types of search queries on the indexed data.

There are two primary operations involved in implementing full-text search with Zend_Search_Lucene: indexing data and searching data. Indexing involves scanning a set of documents and creating an index of their contents; searching involves looking up this index to find documents matching various user-specified criteria. The following sections provide an overview of these two operations.

Indexing Data

A Zend_Search_Lucene index is composed of individual documents, each of which may be further broken into fields. When you're building an index, Zend_Search_Lucene allows users precise control over how each field of a document should be treated. The two basic parameters here are indexing and storage: Indexed fields can be used in searches, while stored fields can be displayed in search results. There are five basic types of fields:

- *Keyword* fields are not tokenized, but are indexed and stored within the index.
- *Text* fields are tokenized, indexed, and stored.
- *UnStored* fields are tokenized and indexed, but not stored.
- *UnIndexed* fields are tokenized and stored, but not indexed.
- *Binary* fields are not tokenized or indexed, but are stored.

When you're making a determination as to which field types to use in your Zend_Search_ Lucene index, it's important to have a clear idea of which fields you'll be using as search criteria and which fields you plan to display in search results. To illustrate how this works in practice, assume for a moment that you have a collection of XML documents in the following format:

```xml
<?xml version='1.0'?>
<document>
  <id>5468</id>
  <from>Jim Doe <jim@example.com></from>
  <to>Jane Doe <jane@example.com></to>
  <subject>Re: Hello</subject>
  <date>Tuesday, February 27, 2008 10:45 PM</date>
  <body>Lorem ipsum dolor sit amet, consectetur adipisicing elit,
  sed do eiusmod tempor incididunt ut labore et dolore magna aliqua.
  Ut enim ad minim veniam, quis nostrud exercitation ullamco laboris
  nisi ut aliquip ex ea commodo consequat. Duis aute irure dolor
  in reprehenderit in voluptate velit esse cillum dolore eu fugiat
  nulla pariatur. Excepteur sint occaecat cupidatat non proident, sunt
  in culpa qui officia deserunt mollit anim id est laborum</body>
</document>
```

Here's some example code that illustrates how a collection of these documents could be indexed:

```php
<?php
class Sandbox_ExampleController extends Zend_Controller_Action
{
  public function indexAction()
  {
    // get index directory
    $index = Zend_Search_Lucene::create('/tmp/indexes');

    foreach (glob('*.xml') as $file) {
      // read source xml
      $xml = simplexml_load_file($file);

      // create new document in index
      $doc = new Zend_Search_Lucene_Document();

      // index and store fields
      $doc->addField(Zend_Search_Lucene_Field::UnIndexed('id', $xml->id));
      $doc->addField(Zend_Search_Lucene_Field::Text('from', $xml->from));
      $doc->addField(Zend_Search_Lucene_Field::Text('to', $xml->to));
      $doc->addField(Zend_Search_Lucene_Field::Text(
        'date', strtotime($xml->date)));
      $doc->addField(Zend_Search_Lucene_Field::UnStored(
        'subject', $xml->subject));
      $doc->addField(Zend_Search_Lucene_Field::UnStored('body', $xml->body));

      // save result to index
      $index->addDocument($doc);
    }

    // set number of documents in index
    $count = $index->count();
  }
}
```

Each document in the index is represented as a Zend_Search_Lucene_Document object, and the individual fields of each message are represented as Zend_Search_Lucene_Field objects. These fields are indexed and added to the document with the Zend_Search_ Lucene_Document::addField() method, and the final document is then added to the index with the Zend_Search_Lucene::addDocument() method.

Defining which fields should be searchable and which fields should be displayed in search results is a key task when indexing data. The previous example supposes that recipient, date, subject, and body fields should be searchable, while only recipient and date fields should be displayed in search results. Marking the body and subject fields as UnStored fields makes them searchable while reducing the disk space consumed by the index, while marking the recipient and date fields as Text fields makes it possible to both search them and display them in search results.

Searching Data

Once the data has been indexed, the next step is to search it. Zend_Search_Lucene comes with a full-featured query engine that can be used to perform both simple and complex queries on an index. Queries may be created either by applying the built-in query parser to user input or by programmatically generating them using API methods. For simple keyword queries, the standard query parser is suitable; more complex queries that include modifiers, proximity constraints, subqueries, or field groups should be created using API methods.

Here's some example code that illustrates how to search a collection of indexed documents and display matching results:

```php
<?php
class Sandbox_ExampleController extends Zend_Controller_Action
{
  public function searchAction()
  {
    // get query string from $_GET['query']
    // if valid, open index and parse query string
    // execute query and return array of result objects
    $input->setData($this->getRequest()->getParams());
    if ($input->isValid()) {
      $index = Zend_Search_Lucene::open('/tmp/indexes');
      $results = $index->find(
        Zend_Search_Lucene_Search_QueryParser::parse($input->query));
      $this->view->results = $results;
    }
  }
}
```

As illustrated in the preceding code, the first step is to open a handle to the index created earlier using the Zend_Search_Lucene::open() method. Next, the query string is passed to the Zend_Search_Lucene object's find() method to scan the index for matching documents. Matches are returned as Zend_Search_Lucene_Search_QueryHit objects, and are ranked by score. Each of these objects exposes the document number and the document score as object properties. Other stored fields of the document can also be accessed as object properties, as shown in the previous example. All field values are automatically encoded to UTF-8.

The query string passed to the find() method may contain keywords, phrases, wildcards, range constraints, proximity modifiers, and Boolean operators like AND, OR, and NOT. When this query string is submitted directly by the user, it's a good idea to pass it through the Zend_Search_Lucene_Search_QueryParser::parse() method, which takes care of automatically parsing and tokenizing the query string and converting it into a set of query objects. This also reduces the amount of input validation needed.

Ask the Expert

Q: How do I sort or limit search results from a Zend_Search_Lucene search?

A: By default, Zend_Search_Lucene returns all matching documents, sorted by score. If this is not to your taste, you can define the sort field and sort order by passing additional parameters to the `find()` method. Similarly, you can restrict the number of matches returned by specifying a limit via the `setResultSetLimit()` method.

NOTE
A full discussion of the query language supported by Zend_Search_Lucene is not possible within the limited scope of this book. However, you can look up detailed information on this topic using the links at the end of this chapter.

Try This 6-2   Creating a Full-Text Search Engine

With all this background information at hand, let's see how Zend_Search_Lucene works in a practical context. This next section replaces the filter-based search engine, created for the SQUARE application earlier in this chapter, with a full-text search system based on Zend_Search_Lucene.

Defining the Index Location

Zend_Search_Lucene full-text search indices are stored as disk files, and so one of the first tasks is to define a location for these files. So, create the *$APP_DIR/data/indexes/* directory, which is the default location for search index files under the Zend Framework's recommended directory layout.

```
shell> cd /usr/local/apache/htdocs/square
shell> mkdir data
shell> mkdir data/indexes
```

It's also a good idea to update the application configuration file, at *$APP_DIR/application/configs/application.ini*, with this location, so that it can be used from within actions. Open this file and update it with the following configuration directive:

```
indexes.indexPath = APPLICATION_PATH "/../data/indexes"
```

(continued)

Defining Custom Routes

While you're updating the application configuration, it's also a good idea to add a route for the `createFulltextIndexAction()`. Since index creation is typically an administrative task, this action should be part of the Catalog_AdminItemController. Here's the corresponding route definition:

```
resources.router.routes.admin-fulltext-index-create.route =
/admin/catalog/fulltext-index/create
resources.router.routes.admin-fulltext-index-create.defaults.module =
catalog
resources.router.routes.admin-fulltext-index-create.defaults.
controller =
admin.item
resources.router.routes.admin-fulltext-index-create.defaults.action =
create.fulltext.index
```

Defining the Index Action and View

The next step is to actually build a full-text index of the content stored in the application database. The easiest way to do this is to perform a Doctrine query to retrieve records from the database, and then feed these to the Zend_Search_Lucene indexer in a loop. Here's the code for the `createFulltextIndexAction()` method, which is responsible for this task:

```php
<?php
class Catalog_AdminItemController extends Zend_Controller_Action
{

  // action to create full-text indices
  public function createFulltextIndexAction()
  {
    // create and execute query
    $q = Doctrine_Query::create()
         ->from('Square_Model_Item i')
         ->leftJoin('i.Square_Model_Country c')
         ->leftJoin('i.Square_Model_Grade g')
         ->leftJoin('i.Square_Model_Type t')
         ->where('i.DisplayStatus = 1')
         ->addWhere('i.DisplayUntil >= CURDATE()');
    $result = $q->fetchArray();

    // get index directory
    $config = $this->getInvokeArg('bootstrap')->getOption('indexes');
    $index = Zend_Search_Lucene::create($config['indexPath']);

    foreach ($result as $r) {
      // create new document in index
      $doc = new Zend_Search_Lucene_Document();
```

```
      // index and store fields
      $doc->addField(Zend_Search_Lucene_Field::Text('Title',
$r['Title']));
      $doc->addField(
        Zend_Search_Lucene_Field::Text('Country',
        $r['Square_Model_Country']['CountryName']));
      $doc->addField(
        Zend_Search_Lucene_Field::Text('Grade',
        $r['Square_Model_Grade']['GradeName']));
      $doc->addField(Zend_Search_Lucene_Field::Text('Year',
$r['Year']));
      $doc->addField(Zend_Search_Lucene_Field::UnStored(
        'Description', $r['Description']));
      $doc->addField(Zend_Search_Lucene_Field::UnStored(
        'Denomination', $r['Denomination']));
      $doc->addField(Zend_Search_Lucene_Field::UnStored(
        'Type', $r['Square_Model_Type']['TypeName']));
      $doc->addField(Zend_Search_Lucene_Field::UnIndexed(
        'SalePriceMin', $r['Denomination']));
      $doc->addField(Zend_Search_Lucene_Field::UnIndexed(
        'SalePriceMax', $r['Denomination']));
      $doc->addField(Zend_Search_Lucene_Field::UnIndexed(
       'RecordID', $r['RecordID']));

      // save result to index
      $index->addDocument($doc);
    }

    // set number of documents in index
    $count = $index->count();
    $this->_helper->getHelper('FlashMessenger')
      ->addMessage("The index was successfully created
                   with $count documents.");
    $this->_redirect('/admin/catalog/item/success');
  }

}
```

Here, the `createFulltextIndexAction()` first executes a Doctrine query to retrieve a list of all approved catalog items. It then initializes a new Zend_Search_Lucene index with the index location specified in the previous step (notice how the configuration file value is retrieved using the `getInvokeArg()` method), and then iterates over the records returned by the Doctrine query, feeding each one to the indexer as a separate document. For each such document, the title, description, country, grade, year, denomination, and type are indexed; of these, only the title, country, grade, and year are stored in the index for display in search results, together with the record ID and sale price range. Once indexing is complete, a success view is generated, summarizing the number of documents indexed.

(continued)

Updating the Summary View

It's also a good idea to update the administrative summary page, at *$APP_DIR/application/modules/catalog/views/scripts/admin-item/index.phtml,* to display a link to the new action. The changes to the view script are highlighted in bold.

```
<h2>List Items</h2>
<?php if (count($this->records)): ?>
<div id="records">
  <form method="post" action="<?php echo $this->url(array(),
  'admin-catalog-delete'); ?>">
    <table>

      ...
      <tr>
        <td colspan="7"><input type="submit" name="submit"
style="width:150px" value="Delete Selected" /></td>
        <td colspan="2"><a href="<?php echo $this->url(array(),
'admin-fulltext-index-create'); ?>">Update full-text indices</a></td>
      </tr>
    </table>
  </form>
</div>

<?php else: ?>
No records found
<?php endif; ?>
```

Updating the Search Form

Once the indexing end of things is handled, there's just the searching end left to handle. Begin by updating the search form definition, at *$APP_DIR/library/Square/Form/Search.php,* such that it contains only a single text input field for search keywords. Here's the revised form definition:

```
<?php
class Square_Form_Search extends Zend_Form
{
public function init()
  {
    // initialize form
    $this->setAction('/catalog/item/search')
        ->setMethod('get');

    // create text input for keywords
    $query = new Zend_Form_Element_Text('q');
    $query->setLabel('Keywords:')
            ->setOptions(array('size' => '20'))
            ->addFilter('HtmlEntities')
            ->addFilter('StringTrim');
    $query->setDecorators(array(
            array('ViewHelper'),
```

```
                    array('Errors'),
                    array('Label', array('tag' => '<span>')),
            ));

    // create submit button
    $submit = new Zend_Form_Element_Submit('submit');
    $submit->setLabel('Search')
            ->setOptions(array('class' => 'submit'));
    $submit->setDecorators(array(
                array('ViewHelper'),
            ));

    // attach elements to form
    $this->addElement($query)
        ->addElement($submit);
    }
}
```

Updating the Search Action and View

The final step is to update the `Catalog_ItemController::searchAction` to use Zend_
Search_Lucene's full-text index instead of a Doctrine query. Here's the revised code:

```php
<?php
class Catalog_ItemController extends Zend_Controller_Action
{

    // action to perform full-text search
    public function searchAction()
    {
        // generate input form
        $form = new Square_Form_Search;
        $this->view->form = $form;

        // get items matching search criteria
        if ($form->isValid($this->getRequest()->getParams())) {
            $input = $form->getValues();
            if (!empty($input['q'])) {
                $config = $this->getInvokeArg('bootstrap')-
>getOption('indexes');
                $index = Zend_Search_Lucene::open($config['indexPath']);
                $results = $index->find(
                    Zend_Search_Lucene_Search_QueryParser::parse($input['q']));
                $this->view->results = $results;
            }
        }
    }

}
```

(continued)

The return value of the Zend_Search_Lucene find() method is different from that of the Doctrine fetchArray() method; field values are now exposed as object properties instead of array elements. Therefore, it is necessary to update the corresponding view script, at *$APP_DIR/modules/catalog/views/scripts/item/search.phtml*, as follows:

```
<h2>Search</h2>
<?php echo $this->form; ?>

<h2>Search Results</h2>
<p><?php echo count($this->results); ?> result(s) found.</p>

<?php if (count($this->results)): ?>
  <?php $x=1; ?>
  <?php foreach ($this->results as $r): ?>
  <div>
  <?php echo $x; ?>.
    <a href="<?php echo $this->url(
    array('id' => $this->escape($r->RecordID)),
    'catalog-display'); ?>">
      <?php echo $this->escape($r->Title); ?>
      (<?php echo $this->escape($r->Year); ?>)
    </a>
    <br/>
    Score: <?php printf('%1.4f', $this->escape($r->score)); ?>
    <br/>
    <strong>
    Grade: <?php echo $this->escape($r->Grade); ?> |
    Country: <?php echo $this->escape($r->Country); ?> |
    Sale price:
    $<?php echo sprintf('%0.2f', $this->escape($r->SalePriceMin)); ?>
to
    $<?php echo sprintf('%0.2f', $this->escape($r->SalePriceMax)); ?>
    </strong>
  </div>
  <br/>
    <?php $x++; ?>
  <?php endforeach; ?>
<?php endif; ?>


<div>
  <a href="<?php echo $this->url(array(
    'module' => 'catalog',
    'controller' => 'item',
    'action' => 'create'),
    null, true); ?>">Add Item</a>
</div>
```

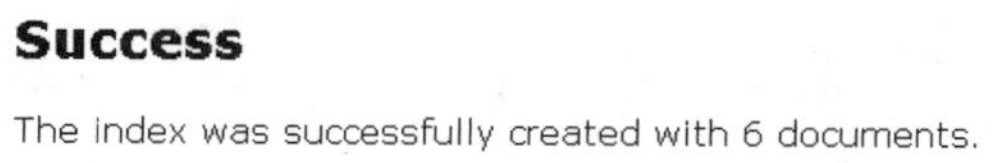

Success

The index was successfully created with 6 documents.

Figure 6-4   The result of successfully creating a full-text index of catalog contents

To see this in action, first log in to the SQUARE administration panel and create the full-text indices by browsing to the URL **http://square.localhost/admin/catalog/fulltext-index/create**. Once the index creation process is complete, you should see a success page, like the one displayed in Figure 6-4.

You can now try searching the index by visiting the URL **http://square.localhost/catalog/item/search** through your Web browser. You should see a revised search form, like the one in Figure 6-5.

Enter one or more keywords into the input field and submit it and, if all goes well, you should see a list of items matching your keywords, as shown in Figure 6-6.

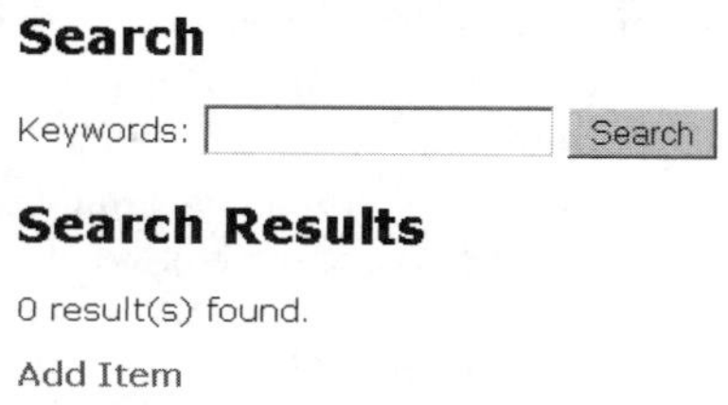

Search

Keywords: [   ] [Search]

Search Results

0 result(s) found.

Add Item

Figure 6-5   The revised SQUARE catalog search form

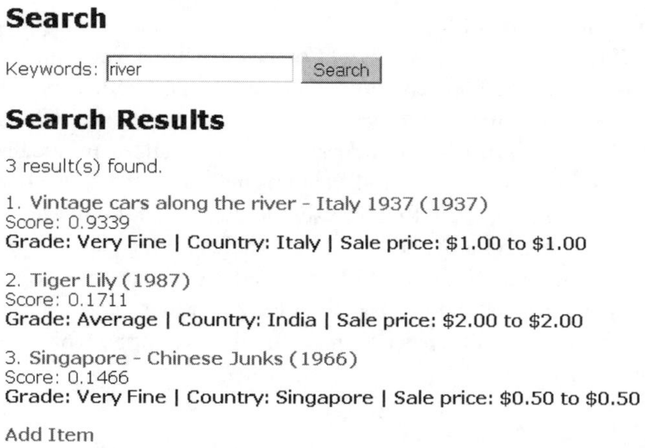

Search

Keywords: [river   ] [Search]

Search Results

3 result(s) found.

1. Vintage cars along the river - Italy 1937 (1937)
Score: 0.9339
Grade: Very Fine | Country: Italy | Sale price: $1.00 to $1.00

2. Tiger Lily (1987)
Score: 0.1711
Grade: Average | Country: India | Sale price: $2.00 to $2.00

3. Singapore - Chinese Junks (1966)
Score: 0.1466
Grade: Very Fine | Country: Singapore | Sale price: $0.50 to $0.50

Add Item

Figure 6-6   A list of catalog items matching the full-text search criteria entered into the search form

Ask the Expert

Q: Which is better: full-text search using disk indices or filter-based search using database queries?

A: As a general rule, full-text search produces better quality results than database search, for a couple of reasons. It's not usually practical to allow users to search by *every* single facet of a database record, and besides, the full-text search capabilities built into most RDBMSes aren't as sophisticated or as efficient as those found in more focused full-text search tools like Lucene, Sphinx, or Solr. It's also typically faster than database search, as the search is performed using disk-based indices rather than over a database connection. That said, full-text search relies on static disk indices created from the source content, and therefore, in situations where the source content is subject to frequent updates, full-text search results can lag behind the actual, available content. A database search, because it runs directly on the content, does not suffer from this lag. As with most questions, therefore, the answer to this one is subjective and depends on the exact balance you wish to achieve between performance and accuracy.

Handling Multiple Output Types

Modern Web applications do not just speak HTML—they're also usually capable of serving up RSS, JSON, XML, and a variety of other formats as well. Since the MVC pattern distinguishes between data and presentation, it's ideally suited to this sort of thing; supporting a new output type now becomes as simple as creating a new view containing the appropriate formatting codes and/or markup. Most importantly, these changes are localized to the view layer, and can be accomplished without any modifications needed in the controller and model layers.

The Zend Framework comes with a built-in handler for multiple output types, or *contexts*, known as the ContextSwitch helper. This helper handles all the tasks involved in switching to a different output format, including disabling the default layout, selecting the appropriate view script, and sending the correct headers for the selected format.

To illustrate how this works, consider the following example, which sets up a new context for YAML output:

```php
<?php
class Sandbox_ExampleController extends Zend_Controller_Action
{
  public function init()
  {
    // initialize context switch helper
    $contextSwitch = $this->_helper->getHelper('contextSwitch');
    $contextSwitch->addContext(
      'yaml',
      array(
```

```
        'suffix' => 'yaml',
        'headers' => array('Content-Type' => 'text/yaml')
      )
    );
    $contextSwitch->addActionContext('list', 'yaml')
                  ->initContext();
  }
}
```

There are four basic steps to be followed when supporting a new output type with the ContextSwitch helper:

1. *Define the context parameters.* The ContextSwitch helper comes with an addContext() method that can be used to define a new context. This addContext() method accepts two arguments: a string holding the name of the new output type, and an array containing additional configuration information, such as the headers to be sent to the requesting client and the filename suffix to look for in view scripts. In the previous example, the addContext() method specifies a view filename suffix of *.yaml* and a 'Content-Type' header of *text/yaml*.

NOTE

This step can be omitted when working with the predefined XML and JSON contexts.

2. *Link the context with one or more actions.* Once the output type has been defined, the ContextSwitch helper's addActionContext() method can be used to map it to one or more actions. In the previous example, the addActionContext() method specifies that the listAction() can also return output in YAML format.

TIP

In case you have a number of different contexts and actions to deal with, consider using the addActionContexts() method, which accepts an array of context-action pairs and serves as a convenient shortcut to map multiple contexts and actions in a single method call.

3. *Create a view script for the context.* The next step is to create a view script for each action and context. By default, this view script is named with the suffix specified in the addContext() method, and it contains all the formatting codes, markup, and business logic needed to generate output in the specified format. To illustrate, consider that in the previous example, the view script *list.yaml.phtml* would be responsible for generating a YAML view of the listAction() method's output. Similarly, if the required output type was XLS, the view script would be named *list.xls.phtml*, and it would contain the PHP code necessary to generate spreadsheets in Microsoft Excel format.

4. *Initialize the context.* This is the final step, and also the simplest, because it simply entails calling the ContextSwitch helper's `initContext()` method. When called without any arguments, this method initializes all the defined contexts and gets the ball rolling. You can now attach the special *?format=context-name* parameter to the action's URL string to indicate the required output type to the ContextSwitch helper— for example, *?format=yaml* for YAML output or *?format=xls* for XLS output.

Try This 6-3   Expressing Search Results in XML

To illustrate how the ContextSwitch helper works in practice, let's enhance the search engine created earlier in the chapter with support for XML output. The following sections guide you through the process.

Enabling the XML Context

Since the ContextSwitch helper comes with built-in definitions for XML and JSON contexts, it isn't necessary to define them with the `addContext()` method. Instead, we can skip directly to mapping the XML context to the `searchAction()` method with the `addActionContext()` method. Add this method invocation to the Catalog_ItemController class's `init()` method, as follows:

```php
<?php
class Catalog_ItemController extends Zend_Controller_Action
{
  public function init()
  {
    // initialize context switch helper
    $contextSwitch = $this->_helper->getHelper('contextSwitch');
    $contextSwitch->addActionContext('search', 'xml')
                ->initContext();
  }
}
```

Defining the XML View

Once the XML context has been mapped and initialized, any request for search results in XML format will be served by the corresponding XML view script. By convention, this view should be saved as *$APP_DIR/application/modules/catalog/views/scripts/item/search.xml.phtml*. Here's what it should contain:

```php
<?php
// create XML document
$dom = new DOMDocument('1.0', 'utf-8');
```

```
// create root element
$root = $dom->createElementNS(
  'http://square.localhost', 'square:document');
$dom->appendChild($root);

// convert to SimpleXML
$xml = simplexml_import_dom($dom);

// add summary element
$xml->addChild('matches', count($this->results));
$xml->addChild('searchTime', time());

// add resultset elements
$results = $xml->addChild('results');
foreach ($this->results as $r) {
  $result = $results->addChild('result');
  $result->addChild('score', $this->escape($r->score));
  $result->addChild('id', $this->escape($r->RecordID));
  $result->addChild('title', $this->escape($r->Title));
  $result->addChild('year', $this->escape($r->Year));
  $result->addChild('grade', $this->escape($r->Grade));
  $result->addChild('country', $this->escape($r->Country));
  $price = $result->addChild('price');
  $price->addChild('min', $this->escape($r->SalePriceMin));
  $price->addChild('max', $this->escape($r->SalePriceMax));
}

// return output
echo $xml->asXML();
?>
```

If you're familiar with PHP's SimpleXML and DOM extensions, the preceding script should be fairly easy to read. It begins by using PHP's DOM extension to generate a new XML document and prolog, and to define a custom namespace for the XML data that will follow. This document is then converted to a SimpleXML object (for convenience), and the result set returned by the `searchAction()` action method is processed and presented as a series of XML elements. Once the entire result set has been processed, the SimpleXML `asXML()` method is used to output the final XML document tree to the requesting client.

To see this in action, try performing a search by visiting the search URL at **http://square .localhost/catalog/item/search** and entering a set of keywords. You should be presented with the search results in HTML format, as shown in Figure 6-6.

Now, request the same search results in XML format by appending an additional *?format=xml* parameter to the URL string. On detecting this parameter, the ContextSwitch

(continued)

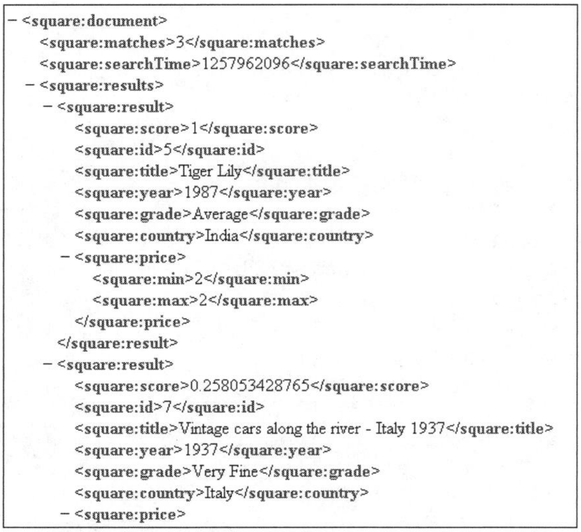

```
− <square:document>
    <square:matches>3</square:matches>
    <square:searchTime>1257962096</square:searchTime>
  − <square:results>
    − <square:result>
        <square:score>1</square:score>
        <square:id>5</square:id>
        <square:title>Tiger Lily</square:title>
        <square:year>1987</square:year>
        <square:grade>Average</square:grade>
        <square:country>India</square:country>
      − <square:price>
          <square:min>2</square:min>
          <square:max>2</square:max>
        </square:price>
      </square:result>
    − <square:result>
        <square:score>0.258053428765</square:score>
        <square:id>7</square:id>
        <square:title>Vintage cars along the river - Italy 1937</square:title>
        <square:year>1937</square:year>
        <square:grade>Very Fine</square:grade>
        <square:country>Italy</square:country>
      − <square:price>
```

Figure 6-7 Results of a search, expressed in XML

helper will automatically switch the output type and present you with the search results in XML format, as shown in Figure 6-7.

TIP
The `'format'` parameter passed to the ContextSwitch helper need not only be specified as a GET parameter. It can come from any valid parameter source, including the route definition itself.

Summary
Once your application's basic CRUD functions are up and running, users and administrators are free to add data to it. This begets a new problem, that of making application data accessible, searchable, and exportable to a number of common formats. This chapter focused specifically on this problem, guiding you through the process of adding search capabilities to an application and showing you how to use the Zend_Search_Lucene component. It also demonstrates the ContextSwitch helper, which makes it easy to support different output formats such as XML, RSS, JSON, and others.

To read more about the topics discussed in this chapter, consider visiting the following links:

- The Zend_Search_Lucene component, at **http://framework.zend.com/manual/en/zend .search.lucene.html**

- The Zend_Search_Lucene query language, at **http://framework.zend.com/manual/en/ zend.search.lucene.query-language.html**

- The ContextSwitch helper, at **http://framework.zend.com/manual/en/zend.controller .actionhelpers.html**

- PHP's SimpleXML extension, at **http://www.php.net/simplexml**

- PHP's DOM extension, at **http://www.php.net/dom**

- A discussion of using the ContextSwitch helper to output Microsoft Excel spreadsheets (Pablo Viquez), at **http://www.pabloviquez.com/2009/08/export-excel-spreadsheets- using-zend-framework/**

- A discussion of using the ContextSwitch helper to change layouts on the fly (Phil Brown), at **http://morecowbell.net.au/2009/02/changing-layouts-with-zend-contextswitch/**

- A discussion of creating a REST API with the ContextSwitch helper (Chris Danielson), at **http://www.chrisdanielson.com/2009/09/02/creating-a-php-rest-api-using-the-zend- framework/**

- A comparison of indexing email messages with Zend_Search_Lucene and Sphinx (Vikram Vaswani), at **http://devzone.zend.com/article/4887-Indexing-Email-Messages-with- PHP-Zend-Lucene-and-Sphinx**

Chapter 7

Paging, Sorting, and Uploading Data

Key Skills & Concepts

- Page and sort database result sets
- Filter, validate, and process file uploads through Web forms
- Read and write configuration files in INI and XML formats

When you're building a software application, one of your most important tasks is to identify which aspects of the application's behavior should be configurable by the user. For example, if you're building a content management system, you will probably want to allow the application administrator leeway to decide how dates and times should be displayed, whether or not images can be attached to posts, and whether or not comments should be subject to moderator review and approval. However, you will probably *not* want the administrator fiddling with the file format in which data is stored, or the manner in which exceptions are handled, as these aspects are internal to the application and (usually) not appropriate for user-level configuration.

Identifying which aspects of an application should be user-configurable isn't as easy as it sounds. In order to perform the analysis correctly, the developer requires a thorough understanding of both the software's goals and the end-user requirements it is built to address. Once the analysis is complete, however, things become much easier. The identified variables can be relocated to a separate storage area (usually one or more configuration files), and it's now up to the developer to present an interface for application administrators to manipulate these variables at run time.

The Zend Framework includes a Zend_Config component, which provides a full-featured API for reading and writing configuration files in various formats. This chapter examines this component in detail, discussing how it can be used to manage configuration data in the context of the SQUARE example application. It also revisits two components from previous chapters, Zend_Form and Doctrine, and illustrates how they can be used to satisfy two common requirements: enabling file uploads, and paging and sorting large result sets.

Try This 7-1 Paging and Sorting Database Records

When you're dealing with large data sets within a Web application, it's generally considered a Bad Thing to simply dump all the available data into a single page willy-nilly and let the user sort it out for himself or herself. Pagination, which involves breaking large data sets into smaller chunks, or *pages*, is a common user interface pattern for improving readability and navigation in these situations. Pagination is important because it allows the user to exert some degree of control over which segment of the data set is visible at any given moment, and thus avoid drowning in a never-ending sea of data. When used with a database server, pagination also helps reduce server load by producing smaller result sets.

The interesting thing about pagination is that the program code needed to implement this pattern is reasonably standard, and is unlikely to change from project to project. This makes it the ideal kind of thing to implement as a reusable component, and, in fact, most frameworks and database abstraction layers come with a ready-made pagination component. For example, the Zend Framework includes a Zend_Paginator component, which comes with adapters (including one for Zend_Db) for different data sources. Similarly, Doctrine comes with a Doctrine_Pager component, which can be used to directly process and page Doctrine queries.

There isn't much to choose between Zend_Paginator and Doctrine_Pager: Both components work by segmenting a single data set into smaller subsets, and by generating navigation links to move back and forth between the different subsets. However, since pagination is most commonly associated with database result sets, it usually makes sense to use the pager component that is recommended by, or included with, the database abstraction layer in use. Since this book recommends Doctrine for all database access operations, the following discussion will focus on the Doctrine_Pager and Doctrine_Query components, illustrating how they can be used to page and sort database result sets in the context of the SQUARE example application.

Adding Page Numbers to Routes

The typical operation of a pagination component is quite simple. The component is first configured with the number of items to be displayed per page. It then calculates the total number of pages by dividing the total number of items present in the data set by the number of items requested per page, and then it dynamically generates a set of navigation links for movement between these pages. Each link contains an additional GET parameter (the page number) that the page controller can use to determine which subset of data is being requested.

To illustrate how this works, open the application configuration file at *$APP_DIR/ application/configs/application.ini* and update the route definition for the administrative summary page with an additional parameter, as follows:

```
resources.router.routes.admin-catalog-index.route =
/admin/catalog/item/index/:page
resources.router.routes.admin-catalog-index.defaults.module = catalog
resources.router.routes.admin-catalog-index.defaults.controller =
admin.item
resources.router.routes.admin-catalog-index.defaults.action = index
resources.router.routes.admin-catalog-index.defaults.page = 1
```

Updating the Index Controller and View

The next step is to update the Catalog_AdminItemController::indexAction to use this parameter when formulating its SELECT query. This is where the Doctrine_Pager component comes in. Here's what the updated action code looks like:

```php
<?php
class Catalog_AdminItemController extends Zend_Controller_Action
{
```

(continued)

```php
// action to display list of catalog items
public function indexAction()
{
  // set filters and validators for GET input
  $filters = array(
    'page' => array('HtmlEntities', 'StripTags', 'StringTrim')
  );
  $validators = array(
    'page' => array('Int')
  );
  $input = new Zend_Filter_Input($filters, $validators);
  $input->setData($this->getRequest()->getParams());

  // test if input is valid
  // create query and set pager parameters
  if ($input->isValid()) {
    $q = Doctrine_Query::create()
          ->from('Square_Model_Item i')
          ->leftJoin('i.Square_Model_Grade g')
          ->leftJoin('i.Square_Model_Country c')
          ->leftJoin('i.Square_Model_Type t');

    $perPage = 5;
    $numPageLinks = 5;

    // initialize pager
    $pager = new Doctrine_Pager($q, $input->page, $perPage);

    // execute paged query
    $result = $pager->execute(array(), Doctrine::HYDRATE_ARRAY);

    // initialize pager layout
    $pagerRange = new Doctrine_Pager_Range_Sliding(
      array('chunk' => $numPageLinks), $pager);
    $pagerUrlBase = $this->view->url(
      array(), 'admin-catalog-index', 1) . "/{%page}";
    $pagerLayout = new Doctrine_Pager_Layout(
      $pager, $pagerRange, $pagerUrlBase);

    // set page link display template
    $pagerLayout->setTemplate('<a href="{%url}">{%page}</a>');
    $pagerLayout->setSelectedTemplate(
      '<span class="current">{%page}</span>');
    $pagerLayout->setSeparatorTemplate(' ');

    // set view variables
    $this->view->records = $result;
    $this->view->pages = $pagerLayout->display(null, true);
```

```
    } else {
        throw new Zend_Controller_Action_Exception('Invalid input');
    }
  }
}
```

This code differs from the original in that the query is routed through the Doctrine_Pager component, which is initialized with the query, the page number, and the number of items per page (in this case, four). When the query is executed through this component's `execute()` method, it is automatically constrained to retrieve only the set of records corresponding to the specified page offset.

However, there's still the small matter of generating navigation links so that users can access other pages of the data set. This is handled by the Doctrine_Pager_Layout component, which accepts a URL template containing a variable placeholder, and then dynamically generates a set of navigation links from this template, replacing the variable placeholder with actual page numbers as needed. The number of navigation links, and the HTML formatting to be applied to each link, can be configured using Doctrine_Pager_Layout methods. The final output of the new Doctrine_Pager_Layout object's `display()` method is a block of HTML code that can be directly incorporated into the view, as follows:

```
<h2>List Items</h2>
<?php if (count($this->records)): ?>
<div id="pager">
  Pages: <?php echo $this->pages; ?>
</div>

<div id="records">

...
</div>

<div id="pager">
  Pages: <?php echo $this->pages; ?>
</div>
<?php else: ?>
No records found
<?php endif; ?>
```

To see this in action, visit the catalog summary page in the SQUARE administration panel by browsing to **http://square.localhost/admin/catalog/item/index**. Assuming that you have more than four items in the catalog, you should see a set of page navigation links, which can be used to page through the result set. Figure 7-1 has an example of the result:

Notice that each page link includes the corresponding page number in its URL, as a GET parameter.

More information on how the Doctrine_Pager_Layout component can be used to define the layout of navigation links is available in the links at the end of this chapter.

(continued)

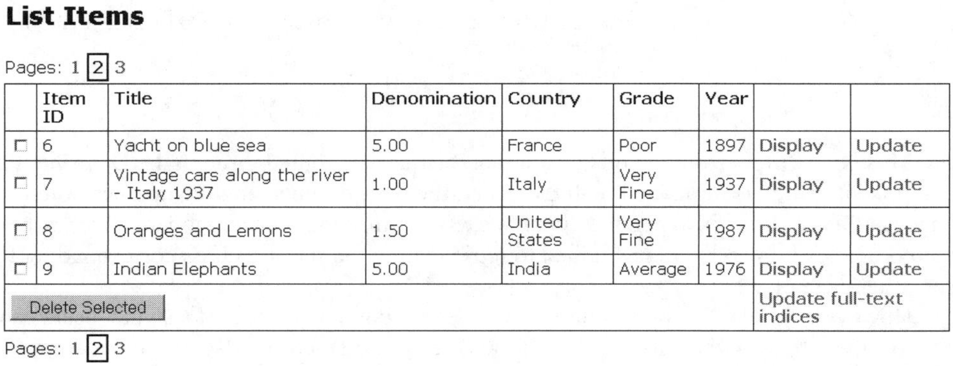

List Items

Pages: 1 [2] 3

	Item ID	Title	Denomination	Country	Grade	Year		
☐	6	Yacht on blue sea	5.00	France	Poor	1897	Display	Update
☐	7	Vintage cars along the river - Italy 1937	1.00	Italy	Very Fine	1937	Display	Update
☐	8	Oranges and Lemons	1.50	United States	Very Fine	1987	Display	Update
☐	9	Indian Elephants	5.00	India	Average	1976	Display	Update
Delete Selected							Update full-text indices	

Pages: 1 [2] 3

Figure 7-1   The catalog summary view, with paging enabled

Adding Sort Criteria to Routes

Paging is one way of slicing and dicing a data set, but there are others. Another extremely common requirement involves allowing users to sort the data set by one of its fields. Here too, additional parameters indicating the field and direction to sort by are appended to the URL request, and the page controller is configured to sort the data by these parameters before handing it off to the view for display.

To see how this works, go back to the application configuration file at *$APP_DIR/ application/configs/application.ini* and further revise the route definition with two additional parameters, as shown in the following example:

```
resources.router.routes.admin-catalog-index.route =
/admin/catalog/item/index/:page/:sort/:dir
resources.router.routes.admin-catalog-index.defaults.module = catalog
resources.router.routes.admin-catalog-index.defaults.controller =
admin.item
resources.router.routes.admin-catalog-index.defaults.action = index
resources.router.routes.admin-catalog-index.defaults.page = 1
resources.router.routes.admin-catalog-index.defaults.sort = RecordID
resources.router.routes.admin-catalog-index.defaults.dir = asc
```

Updating the Controller and View

These parameters should be incorporated into the Doctrine query generated by the `Catalog_ AdminItemController::indexAction`. The InArray validator can be used to ensure that only valid parameters make it through to the main body of the action. The revised action code is shown in the following example:

```
<?php
class Catalog_AdminItemController extends Zend_Controller_Action
```

```
{
  // action to display list of catalog items
  public function indexAction()
  {
    // set filters and validators for GET input
    $filters = array(
      'sort' => array('HtmlEntities', 'StripTags', 'StringTrim'),
      'dir'  => array('HtmlEntities', 'StripTags', 'StringTrim'),
      'page' => array('HtmlEntities', 'StripTags', 'StringTrim')
    );

    $validators = array(
      'sort' => array(
        'Alpha',
        array('InArray', 'haystack' =>
          array('RecordID', 'Title', 'Denomination',
                'CountryID', 'GradeID', 'Year'))
      ),
      'dir'  => array(
        'Alpha',
        array('InArray', 'haystack' =>
          array('asc', 'desc'))
      ),
      'page' => array('Int')
    );
    $input = new Zend_Filter_Input($filters, $validators);
    $input->setData($this->getRequest()->getParams());

    // test if input is valid
    // create query and set pager parameters
    if ($input->isValid()) {
      $q = Doctrine_Query::create()
           ->from('Square_Model_Item i')
           ->leftJoin('i.Square_Model_Grade g')
           ->leftJoin('i.Square_Model_Country c')
           ->leftJoin('i.Square_Model_Type t')
           ->orderBy(sprintf('%s %s', $input->sort, $input->dir));

      $perPage = 4;
      $numPageLinks = 5;

      // initialize pager
      $pager = new Doctrine_Pager($q, $input->page, $perPage);

      // execute paged query
      $result = $pager->execute(array(), Doctrine::HYDRATE_ARRAY);
```

(continued)

```
        // initialize pager layout
        $pagerRange = new Doctrine_Pager_Range_Sliding(array('chunk' =>
$numPageLinks), $pager);
        $pagerUrlBase = $this->view->url(array(), 'admin-catalog-index',
1) . "/{%page}/{$input->sort}/{$input->dir}";
        $pagerLayout = new Doctrine_Pager_Layout($pager, $pagerRange,
$pagerUrlBase);

        // set page link display template
        $pagerLayout->setTemplate('<a href="{%url}">{%page}</a>');
        $pagerLayout->setSelectedTemplate('<span
class="current">{%page}</span>');
        $pagerLayout->setSeparatorTemplate(' ');

        // set view variables
        $this->view->records = $result;
        $this->view->pages = $pagerLayout->display(null, true);
    } else {
        throw new Zend_Controller_Action_Exception('Invalid input');
    }
  }
}
```

Note that the URL template used by the Doctrine_Pager_Layout component to generate page links should also be updated to include the necessary sorting parameters, so that sorting criteria are not "lost" when moving between pages.

The final step is to update the view and include links for the user to sort the different fields of the data set. Here's the revised view script:

```
<h2>List Items</h2>
<?php if (count($this->records)): ?>
<div id="pager">
  Pages: <?php echo $this->pages; ?>
</div>

<div id="records">
  <form method="post" action="<?php echo $this->url(array(), 'admin-
catalog-delete'); ?>">
    <table>
      <tr>
        <td></td>
        <td class="key">
          Item ID
          <a href="<?php echo $this->url(array('sort' => 'RecordID',
'dir' => 'asc'), 'admin-catalog-index'); ?>">&uArr;</a>
          <a href="<?php echo $this->url(array('sort' => 'RecordID',
'dir' => 'desc'), 'admin-catalog-index'); ?>">&dArr;</a>
        </td>
```

```
        <td class="key">
          Title
          <a href="<?php echo $this->url(array('sort' => 'Title', 'dir'
=> 'asc'), 'admin-catalog-index'); ?>">&uArr;</a>
          <a href="<?php echo $this->url(array('sort' => 'Title', 'dir'
=> 'desc'), 'admin-catalog-index'); ?>">&dArr;</a>
        </td>
        <td class="key">
          Denomination
          <a href="<?php echo $this->url(array('sort' => 'Denomination',
'dir' => 'asc'), 'admin-catalog-index'); ?>">&uArr;</a>
          <a href="<?php echo $this->url(array('sort' => 'Denomination',
'dir' => 'desc'), 'admin-catalog-index'); ?>">&dArr;</a>
        </td>
        <td class="key">
          Country
          <a href="<?php echo $this->url(array('sort' => 'CountryID',
'dir' => 'asc'), 'admin-catalog-index'); ?>">&uArr;</a>
          <a href="<?php echo $this->url(array('sort' => 'CountryID',
'dir' => 'desc'), 'admin-catalog-index'); ?>">&dArr;</a>
        </td>
        <td class="key">
          Grade
          <a href="<?php echo $this->url(array('sort' => 'GradeID',
'dir' => 'asc'), 'admin-catalog-index'); ?>">&uArr;</a>
          <a href="<?php echo $this->url(array('sort' => 'GradeID',
'dir' => 'desc'), 'admin-catalog-index'); ?>">&dArr;</a>
        </td>
        <td class="key">
          Year
          <a href="<?php echo $this->url(array('sort' => 'Year', 'dir'
=> 'asc'), 'admin-catalog-index'); ?>">&uArr;</a>
          <a href="<?php echo $this->url(array('sort' => 'Year', 'dir'
=> 'desc'), 'admin-catalog-index'); ?>">&dArr;</a>
        </td>
        <td></td>
        <td></td>
      </tr>
      <?php foreach ($this->records as $r):?>

        ...
      <td><?php echo $this->escape($r['RecordID']); ?></td>
      <td><?php echo $this->escape($r['Title']); ?></td>
        ...

      </tr>
```

(continued)

```php
<?php endforeach; ?>
    <tr>
      <td colspan="7">
        <input type="submit" name="submit" style="width:150px"
        value="Delete Selected" />
      </td>
      <td colspan="2">
        <a href="<?php echo $this->url(array(),
        'admin-fulltext-index-create'); ?>">Update full-text indices</
a>
      </td>
    </tr>
  </table>
 </form>
</div>

<div id="pager">
  Pages: <?php echo $this->pages; ?>
</div>
<?php else: ?>
No records found
<?php endif; ?>
```

And now, when you revisit the URL at **http://square.localhost/admin/catalog/item/index**, you'll see that you can sort the data set by various fields, in either ascending or descending order. This sorting selection is retained even as you move between the pages of the data set. If no sorting criteria are stated, the route defaults will ensure that the data set is automatically sorted by item ID in ascending order.

Figure 7-2 has an example of the output, sorted by grade (look at the URL in your browser address bar to better understand how this works).

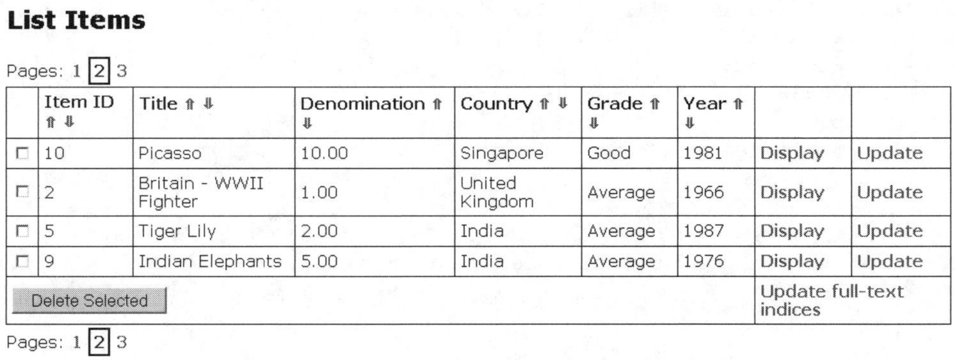

List Items

Pages: 1 [2] 3

	Item ID ⇑ ⇓	Title ⇑ ⇓	Denomination ⇑ ⇓	Country ⇑ ⇓	Grade ⇑ ⇓	Year ⇑ ⇓		
☐	10	Picasso	10.00	Singapore	Good	1981	Display	Update
☐	2	Britain - WWII Fighter	1.00	United Kingdom	Average	1966	Display	Update
☐	5	Tiger Lily	2.00	India	Average	1987	Display	Update
☐	9	Indian Elephants	5.00	India	Average	1976	Display	Update
Delete Selected							Update full-text indices	

Pages: 1 [2] 3

Figure 7-2 The catalog summary view, with sorting and paging enabled

Working with File Uploads

In Chapter 3, you got a crash course in how to create and process forms with the Zend_Form component, and subsequent chapters have further increased your knowledge of Zend_Form by applying those techniques to different types of forms. However, there's one fairly common requirement that hasn't been covered to date: handling file uploads through forms.

PHP has, of course, supported file upload through forms for many years, and offers both the special $_FILES superglobal and a number of built-in methods, such as `is_uploaded_file()` and `move_uploaded_file()`, to assist in the task of managing uploaded files securely and efficiently. Under the Zend Framework, similar functionality is available through the Zend_File_Transfer component, which provides a full-fledged API for receiving, validating, and processing uploaded files. This component also works seamlessly to handle file transfers initiated through Zend_Form elements.

CAUTION

While PHP natively supports POST and PUT file uploads, the Zend_File_Transfer component currently only supports POST uploads.

The best way to understand how file transfers work under Zend_Form is with an example. Consider the following code, which sets up a simple form consisting of a file upload element and a submit button:

```php
<?php
class Form_Example extends Zend_Form
{
  public function init()
  {
    // initialize form
    $this->setAction('/sandbox/example/form')
         ->setMethod('post');

    // create file input for photo upload
    $photo = new Zend_Form_Element_File('photo');
    $photo->setLabel('Photo:')
          ->setDestination('/tmp/upload');

    // create submit button
    $submit = new Zend_Form_Element_Submit('submit');
    $submit->setLabel('Submit');

    // attach elements to form
    $this->addElement($photo)
         ->addElement($submit);

    return $this;
  }
}
```

Figure 7-3 illustrates what this form looks like.

The `setDestination()` method defines the target directory for uploaded files. Note that this directory should already exist prior to initializing the Zend_Form object in an action; if it doesn't, the object will throw an exception. It's also a good idea to make sure that the target directory is writable by the Web server, to avoid any unexpected failures when processing the upload.

When the form is submitted, calling its `getValues()` method inside an action will automatically receive and transfer the file to the specified destination. Here's an example:

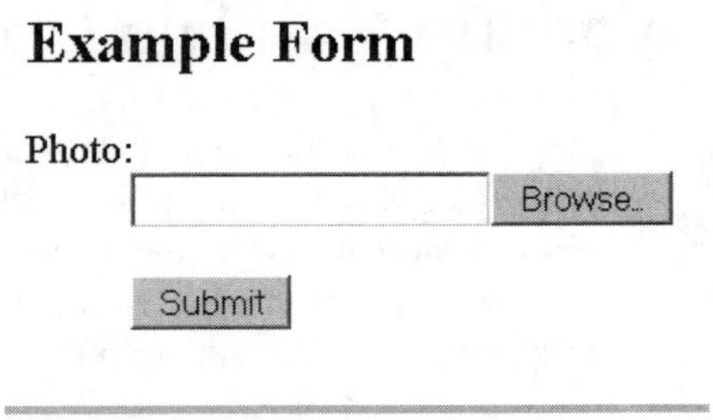

Example Form

Photo:

[Browse...]

[Submit]

Figure 7-3   A form with a file input field

```php
<?php
class Sandbox_ExampleController extends Zend_Controller_Action
{
  public function formAction()
  {
    $form = new Form_Example;
    $this->view->form = $form;

    if ($this->getRequest()->isPost()) {
      if ($form->isValid($this->getRequest()->getPost())) {
        $values = $form->getValues();
        $this->_redirect('/form/success');
      }
    }
  }
}
```

For security reasons, it's not a good idea to receive files without first validating them. There may also be application-level constraints that need to be satisfied by the uploaded files, such as constraints on the file size or file type. These requirements are satisfied by the diverse array of file-specific input validators that are included in the Zend Framework, as shown in Table 7-1.

It may also be necessary to perform various types of operations on the uploaded files before saving them to disk, such as renaming them, modifying their contents, or encrypting them. The file-specific input filters that are included in the Zend Framework (see Table 7-2) can take care of these requirements.

To illustrate these filters and validators in action, consider a revised version of the form definition shown previously. This version uses a combination of filters and

Validator Name	Description
Exists	Returns false if argument is not a valid file
Count	Returns false if number of uploaded files is outside the range specified in argument
Size	Returns false if uploaded file size is outside the range specified in argument
FilesSize	Returns false if uploaded file size total is outside the range specified in argument
Extension	Returns false if uploaded file extension does not match those specified in argument
MimeType	Returns false if uploaded file MIME type does not match those specified in argument
IsCompressed	Returns false if uploaded file is not a compressed archive file
IsImage	Returns false if uploaded file is not an image file
ImageSize	Returns false if uploaded image dimensions are outside the range specified in argument
Crc32, Md5, Sha1, Hash	Returns false if uploaded file content does not match the hash value specified in argument (supports crc32, md5, and sha1 hash algorithms)
ExcludeExtension	Returns false if uploaded file extension matches those specified in argument
ExcludeMimeType	Returns false if uploaded file MIME type matches those specified in argument
WordCount	Returns false if number of words in uploaded file is outside the range specified in argument

Table 7-1   File Upload Validators Included with the Zend Framework

Filter Name	Description
Encrypt	Encrypts contents of uploaded file
Decrypt	Decrypts contents of uploaded file
LowerCase	Converts contents of uploaded file to lowercase
UpperCase	Converts contents of uploaded file to uppercase
Rename	Renames uploaded file

Table 7-2   File Upload Filters Included with the Zend Framework

validators to restrict uploads to JPEG images under 40KB in size and rename them to a unique filename.

```php
<?php
class Form_Example extends Zend_Form
{
  public function init()
  {
    // initialize form
    $this->setAction('/sandbox/example/form')
         ->setMethod('post');

    // create file input for photo upload
    $photo = new Zend_Form_Element_File('photo');
    $photo->setLabel('Photo:')
          ->setDestination('/tmp/upload')
          ->addFilter('Rename',
              sprintf('p-%s.jpg', uniqid(md5(time()), true)))
          ->addValidator('Extension', false, 'jpg')
          ->addValidator('MimeType', false, 'image/jpeg')
          ->addValidator('Size', false, 40000);

    // create submit button
    $submit = new Zend_Form_Element_Submit('submit');
    $submit->setLabel('Submit');

    // attach elements to form
    $this->addElement($photo)
         ->addElement($submit);

    return $this;
  }
}
```

Figure 7-4 has an example of the output seen when attempting to upload a file that does not match the specified constraints.

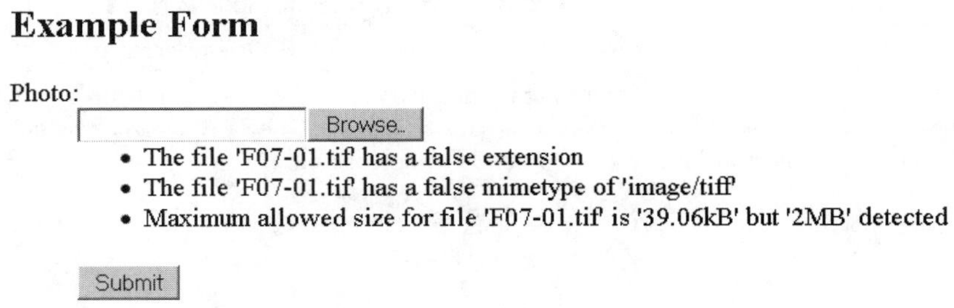

Example Form

Photo:

[_____] Browse...

- The file 'F07-01.tif' has a false extension
- The file 'F07-01.tif' has a false mimetype of 'image/tiff'
- Maximum allowed size for file 'F07-01.tif' is '39.06kB' but '2MB' detected

[Submit]

Figure 7-4 The result of uploading an invalid file

Try This 7-2 Enabling Image Uploads

With all this background information at hand, let's consider updating the SQUARE example application by allowing sellers to add up to three photographs to their catalog entries. The following sections discuss how to enable this feature.

Defining the Upload Destination

The first step is to define a destination for uploaded images. Since these images will eventually be displayed in the public catalog and therefore must be accessible through unauthenticated URL requests, it makes sense to store them under the *$APP_DIR/public/* directory hierarchy. So, create the *$APP_DIR/public/uploads/*, as follows:

```
shell> cd /usr/local/apache/htdocs/square/public
shell> mkdir uploads
```

Since different controllers and actions will require this information, it also makes sense to centralize it in the application configuration file. Accordingly, open the application configuration file, at *$APP_DIR/application/configs/application.ini*, and add the following directive to it:

```
uploads.uploadPath = APPLICATION_PATH "/../public/uploads"
```

Updating the Form Definition

The next step is to update the form for creating new catalog entries with additional file upload elements. To do this, update the form definition, at *$APP_DIR/library/Square/Form/ItemCreate .php*, with the changes highlighted in bold:

```php
<?php
class Square_Form_ItemCreate extends Zend_Form
{
  public function init()
  {
    // initialize form
    $this->setAction('/catalog/item/create')
         ->setMethod('post');

    // -------------- //
    // element definitions abbreviated due to space constraints //
    // refer to Chapter 4 or the code archive //
    // for the complete form definition //
    // ------------ //

    // create file input for item images
    $images = new Zend_Form_Element_File('images');
    $images->setMultiFile(3)
```

(continued)

```
                    ->addValidator('IsImage')
                    ->addValidator('Size', false, '204800')
                    ->addValidator('Extension', false, 'jpg,png,gif')
                    ->addValidator('ImageSize', false, array(
                        'minwidth'  => 150,
                        'minheight' => 150,
                        'maxwidth'  => 150,
                        'maxheight' => 150
                      ))
                    ->setValueDisabled(true);

            // attach element to form
            $this->addElement($images);

            // create display group for file elements
            $this->addDisplayGroup(array('images'), 'files');
            $this->getDisplayGroup('files')
                  ->setOrder(40)
                  ->setLegend('Images');

            // attach element to form
            $this->addElement($submit);
        }
    }
```

This change adds a set of three file upload elements to the form, via the `setMultiFile()` method. A set of validators is used to ensure that these elements can only be used to upload

Ask the Expert

Q: **Why are you calling the Zend_Form_Element_File object's** `setValueDisabled()` **method?**

A: This call prevents the files from being automatically received when the `getValues()` method is called in the action. That's simple, but the really interesting question is, why should the files not be automatically received? And therein lies a tale. You see, the Rename filter does not actually support multifile uploads. However, our application requirements dictate that uploaded files should be renamed to a specific format. To reconcile these two facts, Thomas Wiedner, a well-known Zend Framework developer, suggests dynamically setting the Rename filter on each individual file of the multifile upload, and then manually receiving it using the Zend_File_Transfer HTTP adapter's `receive()` method. So, the call to `setValueDisabled()` ensures that the files are not automatically received in the action and provides room for this manual receive-and-rename process.

image files in JPEG, GIF, or PNG format, each under 2MB in size and each with dimensions of 150×150 pixels. It's also a good idea to rename uploaded images to conform to a standard naming format before saving them to disk, and this is handled by the Rename filter (discussed in the next section).

Updating the Create Action

The next step is to update the `Catalog_ItemController::createAction` to receive the uploaded images, rename them to conform to a standard format, and save them to disk. To accomplish this, revise the action code, at *$APP_DIR/application/modules/catalog/controllers/ItemController.php*, with the changes highlighted in bold:

```php
<?php
class Catalog_ItemController extends Zend_Controller_Action
{
  public function createAction()
  {
    // generate input form
    $form = new Square_Form_ItemCreate;
    $this->view->form = $form;

    // test for valid input
    // if valid, populate model
    // assign default values for some fields
    // save to database
    if ($this->getRequest()->isPost()) {
      if ($form->isValid($this->getRequest()->getPost())) {
        $item = new Square_Model_Item;
        $item->fromArray($form->getValues());
        $item->RecordDate = date('Y-m-d', mktime());
        $item->DisplayStatus = 0;
        $item->DisplayUntil = null;
        $item->save();
        $id = $item->RecordID;
        $config = $this->getInvokeArg('bootstrap')-
>getOption('uploads');
        $form->images->setDestination($config['uploadPath']);
        $adapter = $form->images->getTransferAdapter();
        for($x=0; $x<$form->images->getMultiFile(); $x++) {
          $xt = @pathinfo($adapter->getFileName('images_'.$x.'_'),
              PATHINFO_EXTENSION);
          $adapter->clearFilters();
          $adapter->addFilter('Rename', array(
            'target' => sprintf('%d_%d.%s', $id, ($x+1), $xt),
            'overwrite' => true
          ));
          $adapter->receive('images_'.$x.'_');
        }
```

(continued)

```
        $this->_helper->getHelper('FlashMessenger')->addMessage(
          'Your submission has been accepted as item #' . $id .
          '. A moderator will review it and, if approved, it will
          appear on the site within 48 hours.');
        $this->_redirect('/catalog/item/success');
      }
    }
  }
}
```

Here, the Zend_Form_Element_File object's getTransferAdapter() method returns an instance of the Zend_File_Transfer HTTP adapter. This adapter serves as a control point for receiving, validating, and processing multifile uploads. It exposes a receive() method, which can be used to manually receive the individual elements of a multifile upload. The use of the Rename filter on each file ensures that these files are automatically renamed using a particular naming convention that incorporates both the entry's record ID and the file sequence ID in the filename. The renamed files are then saved to disk, in the destination directory specified by the Zend_Form_Element_File object's setDestination() method.

CAUTION

When you're storing uploaded files with their original name, remember to validate the filename before receiving the file with the receive() method. This is to eliminate the possibility of files being injected into the server's file system through the use of filenames like '../etc/passwd' or '../index.php', which would obviously cause serious problems on a badly configured server.

Updating the Display Action and View

Most of the heavy lifting is now over. The next step is to update the Catalog_ItemController::displayAction to display uploaded images together with the other details of an entry. Here's the revised code for the displayAction() method.

```php
<?php
class Catalog_ItemController extends Zend_Controller_Action
{
  // action to display a catalog item
  public function displayAction()
  {
    // set filters and validators for GET input
    $filters = array(
      'id' => array('HtmlEntities', 'StripTags', 'StringTrim')
    );
    $validators = array(
      'id' => array('NotEmpty', 'Int')
    );
```

```
$input = new Zend_Filter_Input($filters, $validators);
$input->setData($this->getRequest()->getParams());

// test if input is valid
// retrieve requested record
// attach to view
if ($input->isValid()) {
  $q = Doctrine_Query::create()
        ->from('Square_Model_Item i')
        ->leftJoin('i.Square_Model_Country c')
        ->leftJoin('i.Square_Model_Grade g')
        ->leftJoin('i.Square_Model_Type t')
        ->where('i.RecordID = ?', $input->id)
        ->addWhere('i.DisplayStatus = 1')
        ->addWhere('i.DisplayUntil >= CURDATE()');
    $result = $q->fetchArray();
    if (count($result) == 1) {
      $this->view->item = $result[0];
      $this->view->images = array();
      $config = $this->getInvokeArg('bootstrap')-
>getOption('uploads');
      foreach (glob("{$config['uploadPath']}/
        {$this->view->item['RecordID']}_*") as $file)
      {
        $this->view->images[] = basename($file);
      }
    } else {
      throw new Zend_Controller_Action_Exception('Page not found',
404);
    }
  } else {
    throw new Zend_Controller_Action_Exception('Invalid input');
  }
}
}
```

The additional code reads the location of the upload directory from the application configuration file, uses PHP's glob() function to retrieve a list of all files corresponding to the item ID in that directory, and then sends the resulting file list to the view as an array. The view script can now process this array and display the images in a gallery, as follows:

```
<h2>View Item</h2>
<h3>
  FOR SALE:
  <?php echo $this->escape($this->item['Title']); ?> -
  <?php echo $this->escape($this->item['Year']); ?> -
  <?php echo $this->escape($this->item['Square_Model_Grade']
```

(continued)

```
['GradeName']); ?>
</h3>

<div id="container">
  <div id="images">
    <?php foreach ($this->images as $image): ?>
    <img src="/uploads/<?php echo $this->escape($image); ?>"
    width="150" height="150" />
    <?php endforeach; ?>
  </div>
  <div id="record">
    <table>
      <tr>
        <td class="key">Title:</td>
        <td class="value">
          <?php echo $this->escape($this->item['Title']); ?>
        </td>
      </tr>

      ...
      <tr>
        <td class="key">Description:</td>
        <td class="value">
          <?php echo $this->escape($this->item['Description']); ?>
        </td>
      </tr>
    </table>
  </div>
</div>
```

In a similar manner, you should update the `Catalog_AdminItemController::`
`displayAction` and corresponding view script to display the images associated with each
item. You'll find the necessary code in this chapter's code archive, which can be downloaded
from this book's companion Web site at **http://www.zf-beginners-guide.com/**.

Updating the Delete Action

Finally, you should also update the `Catalog_AdminItemController::deleteAction`
to automatically remove the uploaded images associated with a catalog item when the item
is deleted. This is not very difficult to do, and the relevant code is shown in the following
example:

```php
<?php
class Catalog_AdminItemController extends Zend_Controller_Action
{
  // action to delete catalog items
  public function deleteAction()
```

```
  {
    // set filters and validators for GET input
    $filters = array(
      'ids' => array('HtmlEntities', 'StripTags', 'StringTrim')
    );
    $validators = array(
      'ids' => array('NotEmpty', 'Int')
    );
    $input = new Zend_Filter_Input($filters, $validators);
    $input->setData($this->getRequest()->getParams());

    // test if input is valid
    // read array of record identifiers
    // delete records from database
    if ($input->isValid()) {
    $q = Doctrine_Query::create()
            ->delete('Square_Model_Item i')
            ->whereIn('i.RecordID', $input->ids);
      $result = $q->execute();
      $config = $this->getInvokeArg('bootstrap')-
>getOption('uploads');
      foreach ($input->ids as $id) {
        foreach (glob("{$config['uploadPath']}/{$id}_*") as $file) {
          unlink($file);
        }
      }
      $this->_helper->getHelper('FlashMessenger')
      ->addMessage('The records were successfully deleted.');
      $this->_redirect('/admin/catalog/item/success');
    } else {
      throw new Zend_Controller_Action_Exception('Invalid input');
    }
  }
}
}
```

To see all of this in action, try adding a new entry to the catalog by visiting the URL **http://square.localhost/catalog/item/create**. As shown in Figure 7-5, the input form will now display a set of three additional file upload elements.

Enter details for a new entry, attach one or more images, and submit the entry. If the images don't correspond to the specified formats and dimensions, you'll be presented with an error, as shown in Figure 7-6.

(continued)

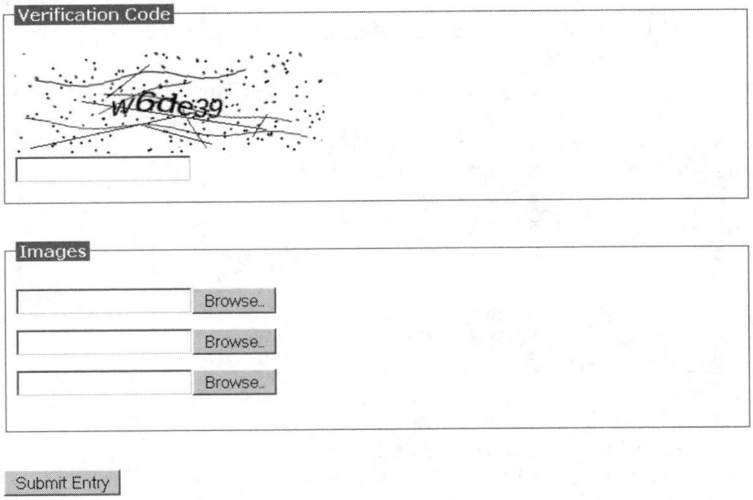

Figure 7-5 The form to add a new item to the SQUARE catalog, with additional file upload elements

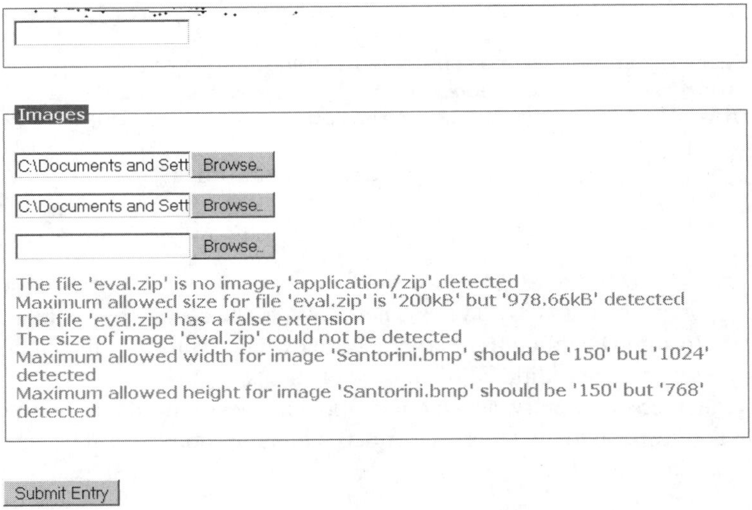

Figure 7-6 The result of attempting to upload invalid files

Following a successful submission, you should be able to find the uploaded images in the application's directory, renamed to the standard format (see Figure 7-7). You can now log in to the application's administration panel, find the newly added item, and make it visible in the public catalog. Then, visit the item's display URL and you should be presented with a page containing the item details and the set of images that you uploaded. Figure 7-8 has an example of the output.

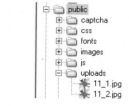

Figure 7-7   Uploaded images, renamed to a standard format

And finally, if you try deleting the item through the administration panel and then check the *$APP_DIR/public/uploads/* directory, you'll find that the image files have also been removed.

View Item

FOR SALE: Indian otters - 1941 - Good

Title:	Indian otters
Type:	Commemorative
Year:	1941
Country:	India
Denomination:	3.00
Grade:	Good
Sale price:	$10 - $15
Description:	Smooth Indian otters. Set of two, cancelled

Figure 7-8   The detail page for a catalog entry, complete with user-supplied images

Working with Configuration Data

As explained earlier, an application developer must usually define which aspects of an application's behavior should be configurable by the user. This information, or *configuration data*, should be stored within the application's data store (which could be a database, a flat file, or some other form of permanent storage), and accessed as needed by different application components.

The Zend Framework makes the task of handling configuration files a little easier, with its Zend_Config component. This component provides a full-featured API for reading and writing configuration files, using an adapter-based approach. As of this writing, the component comes with adapters for both INI and XML formats, and it's reasonably easy to write new adapters for other custom formats as well.

The best way to illustrate how Zend_Config works is with a few examples. The following sections will get you started.

Reading Configuration Files

Zend_Config can be used to read and parse configuration files expressed either in XML or INI format. To illustrate how this works, assume for a moment that you have an INI configuration file named *example.ini*, containing the following data:

```
[object]
shape = 'square'
size = '10'
color = 'red'
typeface.name = 'Mono'
typeface.size = 19
typeface.units = 'px'
typeface.color = 'white'
```

This data can be read into a Zend_Config object, and the individual configuration variables can then be accessed as object properties using standard object notation. Here's an example, which illustrates this:

```php
<?php
class Sandbox_ExampleController extends Zend_Controller_Action
{
  public function configAction()
  {
    // initialize configuration object
    $config = new Zend_Config_Ini(APPLICATION_PATH . "/configs/
example.ini");

    // sets $view->a to 'square'
    $this->view->a = $config->object->shape;
```

```
    // sets $view->b to 'white'
    $this->view->b = $config->object->typeface->color;
  }
}
```

CAUTION

By default, configuration data represented in a Zend_Config object is read-only, and any attempt to modify it will produce an exception. To allow modifications, pass an additional options array to the Zend_Config object as third argument, specifying the 'allowModifications' key as true. More information on this can be obtained from the links at the end of this chapter.

There's also a Zend_Config_Xml adapter designed to handle XML-encoded configuration data. Consider the following XML file:

```xml
<?xml version="1.0"?>
<configuration>
  <application>
    <name>SomeApp</name>
    <version>2.3</version>
    <window>
      <height>600</height>
      <width>500</width>
      <titlebar>
        <title>Export Data</title>
        <foreColor>#ffffff</foreColor>
        <backColor>#0000ff</backColor>
      </titlebar>
    </window>
  </application>
</configuration>
```

Here's an example of reading this file and accessing configuration values from within it using the Zend_Config_Xml adapter:

```php
<?php
class Sandbox_ExampleController extends Zend_Controller_Action
{
  public function configAction()
  {
    // initialize configuration object
    $config = new Zend_Config_Xml(APPLICATION_PATH . "/configs/
example.xml");

    // sets $view->a to '2.3'
    $this->view->a = $config->application->version;
```

```
    // sets $view->b to 'Export Data'
    $this->view->b = $config->application->window->titlebar->title;
  }
}
```

Writing Configuration Files

That takes care of reading files, but how about writing them? Zend_Config includes a writer component, Zend_Config_Writer, which can be used to create configuration files in PHP, XML, or INI formats. Configuration data can be arranged hierarchically, or in sections, for greater readability.

Here's an example that illustrates how Zend_Config_Writer can be used to produce a configuration file in INI format:

```php
<?php
class Sandbox_ExampleController extends Zend_Controller_Action
{
  public function configAction()
  {
    // create configuration object
    $config = new Zend_Config(array(), 1);

    // create section
    $config->blog = array();
    $config->blog->allowComments = 'yes';
    $config->blog->displayComments = 'yes';
    $config->blog->allowTrackbacks = 'yes';
    $config->blog->defaultAuthor = 'Jack Frost';
    $config->blog->numPostsOnIndexPage = 5;

    // create section
    $config->calendar = array();
    $config->calendar->weekStartsOn = 'Monday';
    $config->calendar->highlightToday = 1;

    // create subsection
    $config->calendar->events = array();
    $config->calendar->events->displayTitle = 1;
    $config->calendar->events->displayStartTime = 1;
    $config->calendar->events->displayEndTime = 0;
    $config->calendar->events->displayLocation = 1;

    // write data to file
    $writer = new Zend_Config_Writer_Ini();
    $writer->write(APPLICATION_PATH . "/configs/example.ini", $config);
  }
}
```

The first step is to initialize a Zend_Config object, which represents the configuration data. This object should be initialized with an array containing configuration data (or an empty array if no such data exists), and with a Boolean argument indicating whether or not the configuration data can be modified. Once the Zend_Config object has been initialized, individual configuration variables can be set as object properties using standard object notation. Hierarchical data structures are supported, simply by chaining properties together; depending on the output format chosen, this hierarchy is represented either with separators (INI) or nesting (XML).

The configuration file generated by the preceding code is as follows:

```
[blog]
allowComments = "yes"
displayComments = "yes"
allowTrackbacks = "yes"
defaultAuthor = "Jack Frost"
numPostsOnIndexPage = 5

[calendar]
weekStartsOn = "Monday"
highlightToday = 1
events.displayTitle = 1
events.displayStartTime = 1
events.displayEndTime = 0
events.displayLocation = 1
```

XML configuration files are quite popular for Web-based applications, because most languages include XML parsing support (PHP, in particular, comes with a number of extensions for XML data parsing, including the SimpleXML, DOM, and XMLReader extensions). To present the same configuration data in XML format, simply update the action code to use the Zend_Config_Writer_Xml adapter, as follows:

```php
<?php
class Sandbox_ExampleController extends Zend_Controller_Action
{
  public function configAction()
  {
    // create configuration object
    $config = new Zend_Config(array(), 1);

    // create section
    $config->blog = array();
    $config->blog->allowComments = 'yes';
    $config->blog->displayComments = 'yes';
    $config->blog->allowTrackbacks = 'yes';
    $config->blog->defaultAuthor = 'Jack Frost';
    $config->blog->numPostsOnIndexPage = 5;
```

```
    // create section
    $config->calendar = array();
    $config->calendar->weekStartsOn = 'Monday';
    $config->calendar->highlightToday = 1;

    // create subsection
    $config->calendar->events = array();
    $config->calendar->events->displayTitle = 1;
    $config->calendar->events->displayStartTime = 1;
    $config->calendar->events->displayEndTime = 0;
    $config->calendar->events->displayLocation = 1;

    // write data to file
    $writer = new Zend_Config_Writer_Xml();
    $writer->write(APPLICATION_PATH . "/configs/example.xml",
$config);
  }
}
```

And here's what the resulting file looks like:

```xml
<?xml version="1.0"?>
<zend-config xmlns:zf="http://framework.zend.com/xml/zend-config-
xml/1.0/">
  <blog>
    <allowComments>yes</allowComments>
    <displayComments>yes</displayComments>
    <allowTrackbacks>yes</allowTrackbacks>
    <defaultAuthor>Jack Frost</defaultAuthor>
    <numPostsOnIndexPage>5</numPostsOnIndexPage>
  </blog>
  <calendar>
    <weekStartsOn>Monday</weekStartsOn>
    <highlightToday>1</highlightToday>
    <events>
      <displayTitle>1</displayTitle>
      <displayStartTime>1</displayStartTime>
      <displayEndTime>0</displayEndTime>
      <displayLocation>1</displayLocation>
    </events>
  </calendar>
</zend-config>
```

There are also cases where you might prefer to store configuration data as a native PHP array, which can be read into the application environment with a simple include() or `require()`. To do this, update the action code to use the Zend_Config_Writer_Array adapter, and you should see something like this in the output file:

```php
<?php
return array (
  'blog' =>
  array (
    'allowComments' => 'yes',
    'displayComments' => 'yes',
    'allowTrackbacks' => 'yes',
    'defaultAuthor' => 'Jack Frost',
    'numPostsOnIndexPage' => 5,
  ),
  'calendar' =>
  array (
    'weekStartsOn' => 'Monday',
    'highlightToday' => 1,
    'events' =>
    array (
      'displayTitle' => 1,
      'displayStartTime' => 1,
      'displayEndTime' => 0,
      'displayLocation' => 1,
    ),
  ),
);
```

TIP
Expressing configuration data as a native PHP array offers a performance advantage, as this data is immediately cacheable by an opcode cache such as APC, with no further intervention by the developer. INI- and XML-based configuration files cannot be cached in this manner without explicit intervention by the developer.

Try This 7-3   Configuring Application Settings

Now that the basics of Zend_Config are clear, let's look at using it in a practical context, by creating a simple configuration panel for the SQUARE application. The following sections walk you through the process.

Defining the Configuration Form
The first step is to define a configuration form. Typically, you would only be able to do this after having performed some analysis to determine which aspects of the application should be

(continued)

configurable, and after having decided how these configuration options should be presented. In this case, let's assume that the following aspects of the application are configurable:

● The email address for messages sent through the contact form

● The default, or fallback, email address for all application and user messages

● The number of items to display per page in the administration control panel

● The visibility of seller names and addresses in the public catalog

● The logging of exceptions to a disk file

Here's the corresponding form definition, which should be saved to *$APP_DIR/library/ Square/Form/Configure.php*:

```php
<?php
class Square_Form_Configure extends Zend_Form
{
  public function init()
  {
    // initialize form
    $this->setAction('/admin/config')
         ->setMethod('post');

    // create text input for default email
    $default = new Zend_Form_Element_Text('defaultEmailAddress');
    $default->setLabel('Fallback email address for all operations:')
            ->setOptions(array('size' => '40'))
            ->setRequired(true)
            ->addValidator('EmailAddress')
            ->addFilter('HtmlEntities')
            ->addFilter('StringTrim');

    // create text input for sales email
    $sales = new Zend_Form_Element_Text('salesEmailAddress');
    $sales->setLabel('Default email address for sales enquiries:')
          ->setOptions(array('size' => '40'))
          ->addValidator('EmailAddress')
          ->addFilter('HtmlEntities')
          ->addFilter('StringTrim');

    // create text input for number of items per page in admin summary
    $items = new Zend_Form_Element_Text('itemsPerPage');
    $items->setLabel('Number of items per page in administrative
views:')
          ->setOptions(array('size' => '4'))
          ->setRequired(true)
          ->addValidator('Int')
```

```
                ->addFilter('HtmlEntities')
                ->addFilter('StringTrim');

    // create radio button for display of seller name and address
    $seller = new Zend_Form_Element_Radio('displaySellerInfo');
    $seller->setLabel('Seller name and address visible in public
catalog:')
                ->setRequired(true)
                ->setMultiOptions(array(
                '1'     => 'Yes',
                '0'     => 'No'
                ));


    // create radio button for exception logging
    $log = new Zend_Form_Element_Radio('logExceptionsToFile');
    $log->setLabel('Exceptions logged to file:')
            ->setRequired(true)
            ->setMultiOptions(array(
                '1'     => 'Yes',
                '0'     => 'No'
                ));

    // create submit button
    $submit = new Zend_Form_Element_Submit('submit');
    $submit->setLabel('Save configuration')
                ->setOptions(array('class' => 'submit'));

    // attach elements to form
    $this->addElement($sales)
            ->addElement($default)
            ->addElement($items)
            ->addElement($seller)
            ->addElement($log)
            ->addElement($submit);
    }
}
```

Defining the Configuration File

The next step is to define the file in which user-level configuration settings will be stored. The
Zend Framework recommends the *$APP_DIR/application/configs/* directory for all configuration
data, so let's use this directory. Open the main application configuration file at *$APP_DIR/
application/configs/application.ini*, and add the following directive to it to define the location of
the user-level configuration file:

```
configs.localConfigPath = APPLICATION_PATH "/configs/square.ini"
```

(continued)

Defining Custom Routes

The next step is to define a route to the configuration controller. Since the configuration panel isn't specific to any particular module, this controller can be placed in the all-purpose "default" module. Here's the route definition, which should be added to the application configuration file at *$APP_DIR/application/configs/application.ini*:

```
resources.router.routes.admin-config.route = /admin/config
resources.router.routes.admin-config.defaults.module = default
resources.router.routes.admin-config.defaults.controller = config
resources.router.routes.admin-config.defaults.action = index

resources.router.routes.admin-config-success.route = /admin/config/
success
resources.router.routes.admin-config-success.defaults.module = default
resources.router.routes.admin-config-success.defaults.controller =
config
resources.router.routes.admin-config-success.defaults.action = success
```

Ask the Expert

Q: I'm confused. Why are you storing the location of one configuration file in another?

A: The application configuration file, at *$APP_DIR/application/configs/application.ini*, is a global file that is read by the Zend Framework application. Typically, it contains numerous settings that are defined by the application designer and that should not be modified without due consideration. That said, every application has various user-level settings that should be configurable by application users and/or administrators. For the SQUARE application, these settings are stored in a separate user-level configuration file, at *$APP_DIR/application/configs/square.ini*.

Separating system-level settings from user-level settings in this manner is generally recommended, because it allows these two types of variables to be manipulated independently without risk of corruption. However, there also needs to be a link between the two, so that actions and controllers that rely on user-level settings know where to find this information. Since the application configuration file *application.ini* is globally available to all actions and controllers, the path to the user-level configuration file *square.ini* can be conveniently stored within it.

If you're still confused, here's another way to look at it: Changes in the *application.ini* global configuration may also require alteration of application code, but changes in the user-level configuration file should never have this effect.

Defining the Controller and View

The next step is to define the action and view for the configuration interface. Here's the code for the ConfigController, which should be saved as *$APP_DIR/application/modules/default/controllers/ConfigController.php*:

```php
<?php
class ConfigController extends Zend_Controller_Action
{
  protected $localConfigPath;

  public function init()
  {
    // set doctype
    $this->view->doctype('XHTML1_STRICT');

    // retrieve path to local config file
    $config = $this->getInvokeArg('bootstrap')->getOption('configs');
    $this->localConfigPath = $config['localConfigPath'];
  }

  // action to handle admin URLs
  public function preDispatch()
  {
    // set admin layout
    // check if user is authenticated
    // if not, redirect to login page
    $url = $this->getRequest()->getRequestUri();
    $this->_helper->layout->setLayout('admin');
    if (!Zend_Auth::getInstance()->hasIdentity()) {
      $session = new Zend_Session_Namespace('square.auth');
      $session->requestURL = $url;
      $this->_redirect('/admin/login');
    }
  }

  // action to save configuration data
  public function indexAction()
  {
    // generate input form
    $form = new Square_Form_Configure();;
    $this->view->form = $form;

    // if config file exists
    // read config values
    // pre-populate form with values
    if (file_exists($this->localConfigPath)) {
      $config = new Zend_Config_Ini($this->localConfigPath);
```

(continued)

```
        $data['defaultEmailAddress'] = $config->global-
>defaultEmailAddress;
        $data['salesEmailAddress'] = $config->user->salesEmailAddress;
        $data['itemsPerPage'] = $config->admin->itemsPerPage;
        $data['displaySellerInfo'] = $config->user->displaySellerInfo;
        $data['logExceptionsToFile'] = $config->global-
>logExceptionsToFile;
        $form->populate($data);
    }

    // test for valid input
    // if valid, create new config object
    // create config sections
    // save config values to file,
    // overwriting previous version
    if ($this->getRequest()->isPost()) {
      if ($form->isValid($this->getRequest()->getPost())) {
        $values = $form->getValues();
        $config = new Zend_Config(array(), true);
        $config->global = array();
        $config->admin = array();
        $config->user = array();
        $config->global->defaultEmailAddress =
$values['defaultEmailAddress'];
        $config->user->salesEmailAddress =
$values['salesEmailAddress'];
        $config->admin->itemsPerPage = $values['itemsPerPage'];
        $config->user->displaySellerInfo =
$values['displaySellerInfo'];
        $config->global->logExceptionsToFile =
$values['logExceptionsToFile'];
        $writer = new Zend_Config_Writer_Ini();
        $writer->write($this->localConfigPath, $config);
        $this->_helper->getHelper('FlashMessenger')->addMessage(
          'Thank you. Your configuration was successfully saved.');
        $this->_redirect('/admin/config/success');
      }
    }
  }

  // success action
  public function successAction()
  {
    if ($this->_helper->getHelper('FlashMessenger')->getMessages()) {
      $this->view->messages =
        $this->_helper->getHelper('FlashMessenger')->getMessages();
    } else {
```

```
        $this->_redirect('/');
    }
  }
}
```

The main workhorse in this controller is the `indexAction()` method, which is responsible for validating the input received through it and for writing the configuration data to an INI file using the Zend_Config_Writer component. When initializing the configuration form, the `indexAction()` method also reads the source configuration file (if available) with the Zend_Config component, and then prepopulates then form with the current configuration settings.

The location of the configuration file is read directly from the application configuration file and stored as a protected class property, in the controller's `init()` method. Since this controller is intended for use only by administrators, the `preDispatch()` method checks for an authenticated user and redirects to the login page if not present.

Here's the corresponding view script, which should be saved as *$APP_DIR/application/ modules/default/views/scripts/config/index.phtml*:

```
<h2>Edit Settings</h2>
<?php echo $this->form; ?>
```

Updating the Master Layout

All that's left is to update the administrative layout at *$APP_DIR/application/layouts/admin .phtml* to display a "Settings" item in the main menu when the user is logged in. The revision to the layout is highlighted in bold in the following example:

```
<!DOCTYPE html PUBLIC "-//W3C//DTD XHTML 1.0 Strict//EN" "http://www.
w3.org/TR/xhtml1/DTD/xhtml1-strict.dtd">
<html xmlns="http://www.w3.org/1999/xhtml" xml:lang="en" lang="en">

    ...
    <div id="menu">
      <?php if (Zend_Auth::getInstance()->hasIdentity()): ?>
      <a href="<?php echo $this->url(array(),
      'admin-catalog-index'); ?>">CATALOG</a>
      <a href="<?php echo $this->url(array(),
      'admin-config'); ?>">SETTINGS</a>
      <a href="<?php echo $this->url(array(), 'logout'); ?>">LOGOUT</a>
      <?php else: ?>
      <a href="<?php echo $this->url(array(), 'login'); ?>">LOGIN</a>
      <?php endif; ?>
    </div>

    ...
</html>
```

(continued)

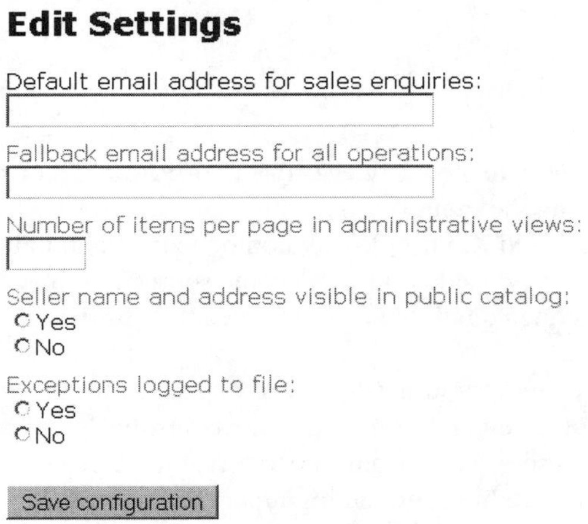

Edit Settings

Default email address for sales enquiries:

Fallback email address for all operations:

Number of items per page in administrative views:

Seller name and address visible in public catalog:
 ○ Yes
 ○ No

Exceptions logged to file:
 ○ Yes
 ○ No

[Save configuration]

Figure 7-9   The SQUARE application configuration form

You can now try this out, by logging in to the application's administration panel and browsing to the URL **http://square.localhost/admin/config**. Figure 7-9 illustrates the configuration form that you should see.

Enter values into this configuration form and submit it. The data should now be saved to the file *$APP_DIR/application/configs/square.ini*. Look inside this file, and you should see the data in INI format, as shown in Figure 7-10.

If you now revisit the URL **http://square.localhost/admin/config**, you'll see that the configuration form is automatically prepopulated with the settings saved earlier. Figure 7-11 displays the output.

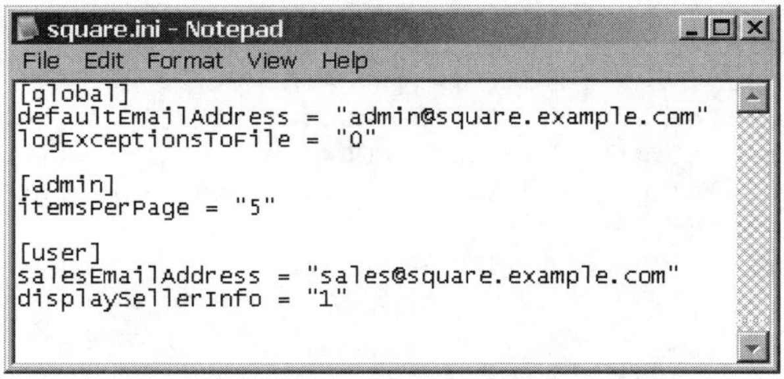

```
square.ini - Notepad                          _ □ X
File  Edit  Format  View  Help
[global]
defaultEmailAddress = "admin@square.example.com"
logExceptionsToFile = "0"

[admin]
itemsPerPage = "5"

[user]
salesEmailAddress = "sales@square.example.com"
displaySellerInfo = "1"
```

Figure 7-10   Example configuration data in INI format

Edit Settings

Default email address for sales enquiries:

```
sales@square.example.com
```

Fallback email address for all operations:

```
admin@square.example.com
```

Number of items per page in administrative views:

```
5
```

Seller name and address visible in public catalog:
⦿ Yes
○ No

Exceptions logged to file:
○ Yes
⦿ No

Save configuration

Figure 7-11   The SQUARE application configuration form, prepopulated with current settings

Using Configuration Data

Successfully reading and writing configuration data is only half the battle won—you still need to make use of this data to inform the behavior of specific controllers and actions. As an example, consider that the ContactController::indexAction should now be modified to read the user-level configuration file and send its email messages to the sales address specified in that file. Here's the revised ContactController::indexAction:

```php
<?php
class ContactController extends Zend_Controller_Action
{
  public function indexAction()
  {
    $form = new Square_Form_Contact();;
    $this->view->form = $form;
    if ($this->getRequest()->isPost()) {
      if ($form->isValid($this->getRequest()->getPost())) {
        $values = $form->getValues();
        $configs = $this->getInvokeArg('bootstrap')-
>getOption('configs');
        $localConfig = new Zend_Config_Ini($opt['localConfigPath']);
        $to = (!empty($localConfig->user->salesEmailAddress)) ?
          $localConfig->user->salesEmailAddress :
          $localConfig->global->defaultEmailAddress;
        $mail = new Zend_Mail();
        $mail->setBodyText($values['message']);
```

(continued)

```
        $mail->setFrom($values['email'], $values['name']);
        $mail->addTo($to);
        $mail->setSubject('Contact form submission');
        $mail->send();
        $this->_helper->getHelper('FlashMessenger')->addMessage(
        'Thank you. Your message was successfully sent.');
        $this->_redirect('/contact/success');
      }
    }
  }
}
```

In a similar vein, the `Catalog_ItemController::displayAction` should be updated to check whether seller information should be visible in the public catalog, and to display this information accordingly. Here's the revised `Catalog_ItemController::displayAction`, which sets a flag for the view after reading the user-level configuration file:

```
<?php
class Catalog_ItemController extends Zend_Controller_Action
{
  // action to display a catalog item
  public function displayAction()
  {
    // set filters and validators for GET input
    $filters = array(
      'id' => array('HtmlEntities', 'StripTags', 'StringTrim')
    );
    $validators = array(
      'id' => array('NotEmpty', 'Int')
    );
    $input = new Zend_Filter_Input($filters, $validators);
    $input->setData($this->getRequest()->getParams());

    // test if input is valid
    // retrieve requested record
    // attach to view
    if ($input->isValid()) {
      $q = Doctrine_Query::create()
          ->from('Square_Model_Item i')
          ->leftJoin('i.Square_Model_Country c')
          ->leftJoin('i.Square_Model_Grade g')
          ->leftJoin('i.Square_Model_Type t')
          ->where('i.RecordID = ?', $input->id)
          ->addWhere('i.DisplayStatus = 1')
          ->addWhere('i.DisplayUntil >= CURDATE()');
      $result = $q->fetchArray();
      if (count($result) == 1) {
```

```
        $this->view->item = $result[0];
        $this->view->images = array();
        $config = $this->getInvokeArg('bootstrap')-
>getOption('uploads');
        foreach (glob("{$config['uploadPath']}/
          {$this->view->item['RecordID']}_*") as $file)
        {
            $this->view->images[] = basename($file);
        }
        $configs = $this->getInvokeArg('bootstrap')-
>getOption('configs');
        $localConfig = new Zend_Config_Ini($configs['localConfigPath']
);

        $this->view->seller = $localConfig->user->displaySellerInfo;
      } else {
        throw new Zend_Controller_Action_Exception('Page not found',
404);
      }
    } else {
      throw new Zend_Controller_Action_Exception('Invalid input');
    }
  }
}
```

And here's the corresponding view, which uses the flag set by the controller to determine whether or not seller information is included in the output page:

```
<h2>View Item</h2>
<h3>
  FOR SALE:
  <?php echo $this->escape($this->item['Title']); ?> -
  <?php echo $this->escape($this->item['Year']); ?> -
  <?php echo $this->escape($this->item['Square_Model_Grade']
['GradeName']); ?>
</h3>

<div id="container">
  <div id="images">
    <?php foreach ($this->images as $image): ?>
    <img src="/uploads/<?php echo $this->escape($image); ?>"
    width="150" height="150" />
    <?php endforeach; ?>
  </div>
  <div id="record">
    <table>
      <tr>
        <td class="key">Title:</td>
        <td class="value">
```

(continued)

```php
        <?php echo $this->escape($this->item['Title']); ?>
      </td>
    </tr>
    <!-- other display fields -->

    <tr>
      <td class="key">Description:</td>
      <td class="value">
        <?php echo $this->escape($this->item['Description']); ?>
      </td>
    </tr>
    <?php if ($this->seller == 1): ?>
    <tr>
      <td class="key">Seller:</td>
      <td class="value">
        <?php echo $this->escape($this->item['SellerName']); ?>,
        <?php echo $this->escape($this->item['SellerAddress']); ?>
      </td>
    </tr>
    <?php endif; ?>
    </table>
  </div>
</div>
```

It's also quite easy to integrate the user-level configuration with the behavior of the Doctrine_Pager component in the `Catalog_AdminItemController::indexAction`. This ensures that the number of items displayed on each page reflects the value specified by the user, rather than an arbitrary value set by the application designer. The code is not included here due to space constraints, but you'll find it in this chapter's code archive.

TIP

If you have a number of different controllers and actions reading data from the same user-level configuration file, you can save yourself some code duplication by having the application bootstrapper automatically read this file into the local resource registry. This registry can be accessed from anywhere in the application using the `getResource()` method of the Zend_Application_Bootstrap_Bootstrap class. Internally, the registry is represented as an instance of the Zend_Registry component, which provides an application-level storage area for global objects or variables. More information on the application bootstrapper and the Zend_Registry component is available through the links at the end of this chapter, and you'll also find numerous examples of using Zend_Registry in subsequent chapters of this book.

Summary

This chapter focused on three components, all of which are new to you: the Doctrine_Pager component, which provides a framework for paginating large database result sets; the Zend_File_Transfer component, which provides a full-featured API for validating, filtering, and receiving files uploaded through Web forms; and the Zend_Config component, which makes it easy to handle configuration data expressed in different formats. All of these components were illustrated with practical reference to the SQUARE example application, which now sports paging and sorting features, a configuration panel, and an image upload system.

To learn more about the topics discussed in this chapter, consider visiting the following links:

- The Doctrine_Pager component, at **http://www.doctrine-project.org/documentation/manual/1_1/en/utilities#pagination:working-with-pager**

- The Zend_Paginator component, at **http://framework.zend.com/manual/en/zend.paginator.html**

- The Zend_File_Transfer component, at **http://framework.zend.com/manual/en/zend.file.html**

- Filters and validators for the Zend_File_Transfer components, at **http://framework.zend.com/manual/en/zend.file.transfer.filters.html** and **http://framework.zend.com/manual/en/zend.file.transfer.validators.html**

- The Zend_Config component, at **http://framework.zend.com/manual/en/zend.config.html**

- The Zend_Registry component, at **http://framework.zend.com/manual/en/zend.registry.html**

- The Bootstrap class and the local resource registry, at **http://framework.zend.com/manual/en/zend.application.theory-of-operation.html**

- An explanation of the Registry pattern (Martin Fowler), at **http://martinfowler.com/eaaCatalog/registry.html**

- A discussion of creating a custom resource plug-in for the Zend Framework bootstrapper (Stefan Schmalhaus), at **http://blog.log2e.com/2009/06/01/creating-a-custom-resource-plugin-in-zend-framework-18/**

- A tutorial on the Zend_Config component (Aaron Wormus), at **http://devzone.zend.com/article/1264**

Chapter 8

Logging and Debugging Exceptions

Key Skills & Concepts

- Learn about the PHP 5.x exception model
- Understand how exceptions are handled in a Zend Framework application
- Integrate custom exceptions classes with the default Zend Framework error handler
- Control the visibility of error information in production environments
- Maintain a permanent record of exceptions by logging them to a file or a database
- Enhance log messages with additional debugging information
- Track exceptions in real time with the Firebug console debugger

A common misconception, especially among less experienced developers, is that a "good" program is one that works without errors. In fact, this is not strictly true: A better definition might be that a good program is one that anticipates all possible error conditions ahead of time and deals with them in a consistent manner.

Writing "intelligent" programs that conform to this definition is as much art as science. Experience and imagination play important roles in assessing potential causes of error and defining corrective action, but no less important is the programming framework itself, which defines the tools and functions available to trap and resolve errors.

By developing applications with the Zend Framework, error handling is less of a concern than with many other frameworks. The default error handler supplied with the Zend Framework can handle most common situations out of the box, and there are a number of other components, such as Zend_Log and Zend_Debug, which can be used to provide additional information to developers and administrators. This chapter will introduce you to all of these tools, and explain how they can be used in a practical context.

Understanding Exceptions

PHP 5.x introduced a new exception model, similar to that used by other programming languages like Java and Python. In this exception-based approach, program code is wrapped in a `try` block, and exceptions generated by it are "caught" and resolved by one or more `catch` blocks. Because multiple `catch` blocks are possible, developers can trap different types of exceptions and handle each type differently.

To illustrate how this works, consider the following listing, which attempts to access a nonexistent array element using an ArrayIterator:

```php
<?php
// define array
$cities = array(
  'London',
  'Washington',
  'Paris',
  'Delhi'
);

// try accessing a non-existent array element
// generates an OutOfBoundsException
try {

  $iterator = new ArrayIterator($cities);
  $iterator->seek(10);

} catch (Exception $e) {
  echo "ERROR: Something went wrong!\n";
  echo "Error message: " . $e->getMessage() . "\n";
  echo "Error code: " . $e->getCode() . "\n";
  echo "File name: " . $e->getFile() . "\n";
  echo "Line: " . $e->getLine() . "\n";
  echo "Backtrace: " . $e->getTraceAsString() . "\n";
}
?>
```

When PHP encounters code wrapped within a `try-catch` block, it first attempts to execute the code within the `try` block. If this code is processed without any exceptions being generated, control transfers to the lines following the `try-catch` block. However,

Ask the Expert

Q: I've seen that uncaught exceptions generate a fatal error that causes the script to end abruptly. Can I change this?

A: Yes and no. PHP offers the `set_exception_handler()` function, which allows you to replace PHP's default exception handler with your own custom code, in much the same way as `set_error_handler()` does. However, there's an important caveat to be aware of here. PHP's default exception handler displays a notification and then terminates script exception. Using a custom exception handler allows limited control over this behavior: While you can change the manner and appearance of the notification display, you can't make the script continue executing beyond the point where the exception was generated.

Method Name	Description
getMessage()	Returns a message describing what went wrong
getCode()	Returns a numeric error code
getFile()	Returns the disk path and name of the script that generated the exception
getLine()	Returns the number of the line that generated the exception
getTrace()	Returns a backtrace of the calls that led to the error, as an array
getTraceAsString()	Returns a backtrace of the calls that led to the error, as a string

Table 8-1   Methods of the PHP Exception Object

if an exception is generated while running the code within the `try` block (as happens in the preceding listing), PHP stops execution of the block at that point and begins checking each `catch` block to see if there is a handler for the exception. If a handler is found, the code within the appropriate `catch` block is executed and then the lines following the `try` block are executed; if not, a fatal error is generated and script execution stops at the point of error.

Every Exception object includes some additional information that can be used for debugging the source of the error. This information can be accessed via the Exception object's built-in methods and includes a descriptive error message, an error code, the filename and the number of the line in which the error occurred, and a backtrace of the function invocations leading to the error. Table 8-1 lists these methods.

A more sophisticated approach is to subclass the generic Exception object and create specific Exception objects for each possible error. This approach is useful when you need to treat different types of exceptions differently, as it allows you to use a separate `catch` block (and separate handling code) for each exception type. Here's a revision of the preceding example, which illustrates this approach:

```php
<?php
// subclass Exception
class MissingFileException extends Exception { }
class DuplicateFileException extends Exception { }
class FileIOException extends Exception { }

// set file name
// attempt to copy and then delete file
$file = 'dummy.txt';
try {

  if (!file_exists($file)) {
    throw new MissingFileException($file);
  }
  if (file_exists("$file.new")) {
    throw new DuplicateFileException("$file.new");
```

```
    }
    if (!copy($file, "$file.new")) {
      throw new FileIOException("$file.new");
    }
    if (!unlink($file)) {
      throw new FileIOException($file);
    }

} catch (MissingFileException $e) {
  echo 'ERROR: Could not find file \'' . $e->getMessage() . '\'';
  exit();
} catch (DuplicateFileException $e) {
  echo 'ERROR: Destination file \'' . $e->getMessage() . '\' already exists';
  exit();
} catch (FileIOException $e) {
  echo 'ERROR: Could not perform file input/output operation on file \'' .
    $e->getMessage() . '\'';
  exit();
} catch (Exception $e) {
  echo 'ERROR: Something bad happened on line ' . $e->getLine() . ': ' .
    $e->getMessage();
  exit();
}
echo 'SUCCESS: File operation successful.';
?>
```

This script extends the base Exception class to create three new Exception types, each representing a different possible error. A separate `catch` block for each Exception now makes it possible to customize how each of these three Exceptions is treated. The last `catch` block is a generic "catch-all" handler: Exceptions that are not handled by the more specific blocks above it will fall through to, and be dealt with by, this handler.

The exception-based approach offers a number of benefits:

- Without exception handling, it is necessary to check the return value of every function called to identify if an error occurred and take corrective action. This produces unnecessarily complicated code and deeply nested code blocks. In the exception-based model, a single `catch` block can be used to trap any error that occurs in the preceding code block. This eliminates the need for multiple cascading error tests, and it produces simpler and more readable code.

- In the absence of exceptions, error handling is prescriptive by nature: It requires the developer to think through all possible errors that might occur, and write code to handle each of these possibilities. By contrast, the exception-based approach is more flexible. A generic exception handler works like a safety net, catching and handling even those errors for which no specific handling code has been written. This only helps to make application code more robust and resilient to unforeseen situations.

- Because the exception model used an object-based approach, developers can use OOP concepts of inheritance and extensibility to subclass the base Exception object and create different Exception objects for different types of exceptions. This makes it possible to distinguish between different types of errors and to handle each type differently.

- The exception-based approach forces developers to make hard decisions about how to handle different types of errors. Where exceptions are not available, developers can easily omit (by accident or design) tests to check the return value of functions. However, exceptions are not so easy to ignore. By requiring developers to create and populate catch blocks, the exception model forces them to think about the causes and consequences of errors and ultimately results in better design and more robust implementation.

All Zend Framework components are explicitly designed to use the exception-based model by default, with each component extending the base Zend_Exception class as needed. So, regardless of whether you're using Zend Framework components as stand-alone pieces of a larger application, or within the context of a Zend Framework MVC application, this consistency in approach can significantly reduce the time spent on developing application-level error-handling features.

Understanding the Default Error-Handling Process

Let's now look a little more closely at exception handling within a Zend Framework MVC application. By default, whenever an action throws an exception, this exception "bubbles up" through the execution chain until it reaches the front controller. The front controller includes an error-handler plug-in (automatically registered as part of the bootstrap process) which takes care of forwarding the exception to the application's default error controller. The error controller then checks the exception type and displays an appropriate error view to the requesting client.

Where does this error controller come from? For projects created with the *zf* command-line script, it's automatically included in the default project layout. For projects created manually, it must be manually generated. In either case, it's represented as a separate controller and action, ErrorController::errorAction, and located within the application's "default" module. Here's an example of what it typically looks like:

```php
<?php
class ErrorController extends Zend_Controller_Action
{
  public function errorAction()
  {
    $errors = $this->_getParam('error_handler');

    switch ($errors->type) {
        case Zend_Controller_Plugin_ErrorHandler::EXCEPTION_NO_CONTROLLER:
        case Zend_Controller_Plugin_ErrorHandler::EXCEPTION_NO_ACTION:

            // 404 error -- controller or action not found
            $this->getResponse()->setHttpResponseCode(404);
            $this->view->message = 'Page not found';
            break;
```

```
        default:
            // application error
            $this->getResponse()->setHttpResponseCode(500);
            $this->view->message = 'Application error';
            break;
    }

    $this->view->exception = $errors->exception;
    $this->view->request   = $errors->request;
  }
}
```

This default error controller is designed to handle two types of situations: invalid HTTP requests, and exceptions generated by action code. It responds to the former with a 404 error code, and to the latter with a 500 error code. To see this in action, consider the following example:

```php
<?php
class Sandbox_ExampleController extends Zend_Controller_Action
{
  public function failAction()
  {
    // try accessing a non-existent array element
    // generates an OutOfBoundsException
    $cities = array(
      'London',
      'Washington',
      'Paris',
      'Delhi'
    );
    $iterator = new ArrayIterator($cities);
    $iterator->seek(10);
  }
}
```

In this case, any request for the action will result in an exception, and this exception will be propagated through the execution chain until it reaches the ErrorController::errorAction. This action will check the exception type and respond by setting the server response code to 500 (internal server error), and then rendering the error view. Figure 8-1 shows an example of the error view generated by the previous code listing.

If you were instead to try accessing a nonexistent controller or action, you'd be handed a 404 (page not found) error. Figure 8-2 shows an example.

Notice that in addition to the error message, the default view also contains a stack trace of the internal requests that led to the exception and a list of the parameters included in the original HTTP request. This is useful information when you're trying to identify the source of an error.

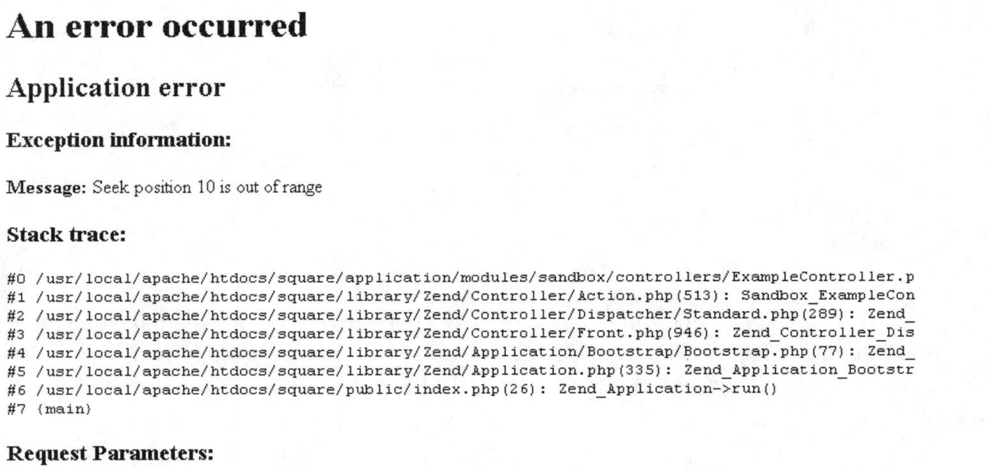

An error occurred

Application error

Exception information:

Message: Seek position 10 is out of range

Stack trace:

```
#0 /usr/local/apache/htdocs/square/application/modules/sandbox/controllers/ExampleController.p
#1 /usr/local/apache/htdocs/square/library/Zend/Controller/Action.php(513): Sandbox_ExampleCon
#2 /usr/local/apache/htdocs/square/library/Zend/Controller/Dispatcher/Standard.php(289): Zend_
#3 /usr/local/apache/htdocs/square/library/Zend/Controller/Front.php(946): Zend_Controller_Dis
#4 /usr/local/apache/htdocs/square/library/Zend/Application/Bootstrap/Bootstrap.php(77): Zend_
#5 /usr/local/apache/htdocs/square/library/Zend/Application.php(335): Zend_Application_Bootstr
#6 /usr/local/apache/htdocs/square/public/index.php(26): Zend_Application->run()
#7 {main}
```

Request Parameters:

Figure 8-1 The result of an internal error thrown by the application

TIP

The behavior of the default error controller fits the needs of the vast majority of Zend Framework applications—in most cases, a 500 response for application-level exceptions and a 404 response for invalid requests is the expected, standards-compliant behavior—and so you won't often need to modify it. However, if your application uses custom exception classes, you might want to modify the default handler and switch to different handling routines based on the exception type. This is examined in the following section.

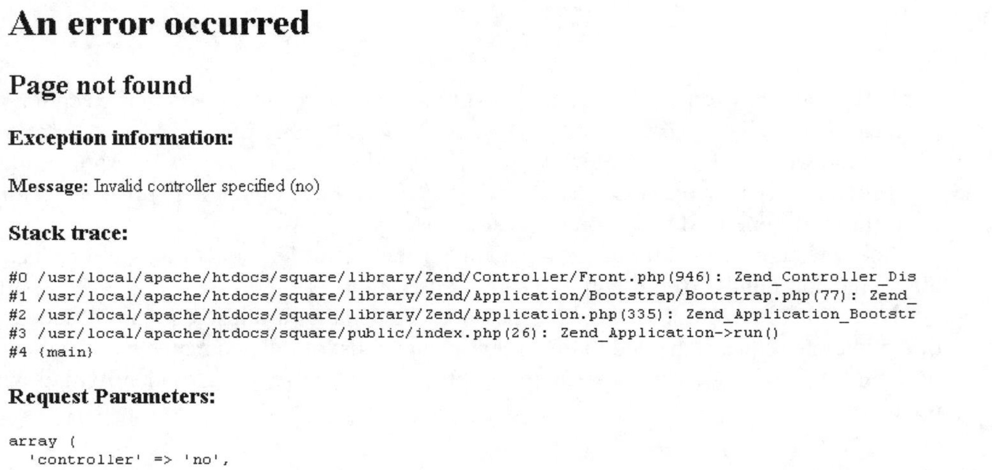

An error occurred

Page not found

Exception information:

Message: Invalid controller specified (no)

Stack trace:

```
#0 /usr/local/apache/htdocs/square/library/Zend/Controller/Front.php(946): Zend_Controller_Dis
#1 /usr/local/apache/htdocs/square/library/Zend/Application/Bootstrap/Bootstrap.php(77): Zend_
#2 /usr/local/apache/htdocs/square/library/Zend/Application.php(335): Zend_Application_Bootstr
#3 /usr/local/apache/htdocs/square/public/index.php(26): Zend_Application->run()
#4 {main}
```

Request Parameters:

```
array (
  'controller' => 'no',
```

Figure 8-2 The result of a request for an invalid or missing application resource

Fatal error: Uncaught exception 'Zend_Controller_Dispatcher_Exception' with message 'Invalid controller specified (no)' in /usr/local/apache/htdocs/square/library/Zend/Controller/Dispatcher/Standard.php:242 Stack trace: #0 /usr/local/apache/htdocs /square/library/Zend/Controller/Front.php(946): Zend_Controller_Dispatcher_Standard->dispatch(Object(Zend_Controller_Request_Http), Object(Zend_Controller_Response_Http)) #1 /usr/local/apache/htdocs/square/library/Zend/Application/Bootstrap /Bootstrap.php(77): Zend_Controller_Front->dispatch() #2 /usr/local/apache/htdocs/square/library /Zend/Application.php(335): Zend_Application_Bootstrap_Bootstrap->run() #3 /usr/local/apache/htdocs/square/public /index.php(26): Zend_Application->run() #4 {main} thrown in **/usr/local/apache/htdocs/square/library/Zend/Controller /Dispatcher/Standard.php** on line **242**

Figure 8-3 The result of disabling the default error controller and allowing exceptions to be handled by PHP

If you'd like to disable the default error controller and have exceptions handled by PHP in the default manner, update your application configuration file to include the following directive:

```
resources.frontController.throwExceptions = 1
```

With this change, the onus is now on the developer to catch and resolve exceptions locally, within the scope of the action that produced them. Uncaught exceptions will produce a fatal error and halt script execution at the point where the exception was raised. Figure 8-3 has an example of how uncaught exceptions behave when the default error handler is disabled.

Using Custom Exception Classes

If your application makes use of custom exception classes, it often makes sense to alter the default error controller to switch its behavior depending on the type of exception caught. This approach allows the developer to go beyond the two basic error types handled by the default controller and provides more fine-grained control over how different types of exceptions are handled.

To illustrate how this works, consider the following variant of the previous code listing, which throws a custom exception depending on whether the required file is present or absent:

```php
<?php
class Sandbox_ExampleController extends Zend_Controller_Action
{
  public function failAction()
  {
    $this->file = APPLICATION_PATH . '/configs/no.such.file.xml';
    if (!file_exists($this->file)) {
      throw new Example_Invalid_File_Exception(
        'File does not exist: ' . $this->file);
    }
    if (file_exists($this->file)) {
      throw new Example_Duplicate_File_Exception(
        'File already exists: ' . $this->file);
    }
  }
}
```

When you're using custom exceptions in this manner, it's quite common to change the default error controller and add in specific handling code for different exception types. Here's an example of how to do this:

```php
<?php
class ErrorController extends Zend_Controller_Action
{
  public function errorAction()
  {
    $errors = $this->_getParam('error_handler');
    $this->view->exception = $errors->exception;
    $this->view->request    = $errors->request;
    switch (get_class($errors->exception)) {
      // handle invalid file exceptions
      case 'Example_Invalid_File_Exception':
          $this->getResponse()->setHttpResponseCode(500);
          $this->view->title = 'File Not Found';
          $this->view->message =
            'There was an error reading a file needed by the application.';
          break;

      // handle duplicate file exceptions
      case 'Example_Duplicate_File_Exception':
          $this->getResponse()->setHttpResponseCode(500);
          $this->view->title = 'File Already Exists';
          $this->view->message =
            'There was an error writing a file needed by the application.';
          break;

      // handle 404 exceptions
      case 'Zend_Controller_Dispatcher_Exception':
        $this->getResponse()->setHttpResponseCode(404);
        $this->view->title = 'Page Not Found';
        $this->view->message = 'The requested page could not be found.';
        break;

      // handle generic action exceptions
      case 'Zend_Controller_Action_Exception':
        if ($errors->exception->getCode() == 404) {
          $this->getResponse()->setHttpResponseCode(404);
          $this->view->title = 'Page Not Found';
          $this->view->message = 'The requested page could not be found.';
        } else {
          $this->getResponse()->setHttpResponseCode(500);
          $this->view->title = 'Internal Server Error';
          $this->view->message =
            'Due to an application error, the requested page could
            not be displayed.';
        }
        break;

      // handle everything else
      default:
```

```
            $this->getResponse()->setHttpResponseCode(500);
            $this->view->title = 'Internal Server Error';
            $this->view->message =
               'Due to an application error, the requested page could
               not be displayed.';
          break;
      }
    }
  }
}
```

Here, the `errorAction()` begins by first retrieving the exception object thrown by the source action controller, via the `'error_handler'` request parameter. It then examines the exception class and switches to a different code branch depending on the exception class name. In this example, in addition to the standard cases (requests for invalid resources and generic uncaught exceptions), the controller also has specific branches for the custom exception classes used by the application. Needless to say, this `switch-case()` routine can be extended to support as many custom exception classes as are required.

Controlling Exception Visibility

As a general rule, it's not a good idea to include stack traces and other debugging information in error messages once an application has been transferred to a production environment. This information sometimes contains sensitive information, such as SQL query output, file locations, and/or user passwords, which can be used by malicious users to identify an application's weak points and mount attacks on it remotely. Hiding this information in production environments is thus an important step in improving overall application security.

The typical Zend Framework application comes with configuration settings for four environments: development, testing, staging, and production. Under the default settings, error display in these environments is handled as follows:

- In both development and testing environments, the PHP `'display_errors'` and `'display_startup_errors'` configuration variables are set to true, resulting in error messages being displayed to the user. In staging and production environments, these variables are set to false and, as a result, error messages are hidden from the user.

Ask the Expert

Q: How do I switch between production and development environments?

A: Information about the current environment is specified in the application's *.htaccess* file, as a server environment variable named APPLICATION_ENV. On every request, the *index.php* script checks for this variable and passes it to the Zend_Application component. Zend_ Application then reads the appropriate block of the application configuration file, and sets up application variables as per the directives specified in this block. So, to switch from one environment to another, simply edit the application's *.htaccess* file and set the value of the APPLICATION_ENV variable to the required environment name.

● In the development environment, the default error view includes the error message, a stack trace, and a variable dump of the request space. In production, staging, and testing environments, only the error message is displayed to the user.

These settings can be adjusted by modifying the appropriate block in the application configuration file and by altering the error view to display more or less information depending on which environment is currently in use (there's an example of this in the next section).

Try This 8-1 Creating a Custom Error Page

With all this information at hand, let's try creating a custom error page for the SQUARE example application.

Since we don't have any special exception-handling requirements, we can leave the error controller largely untouched, with just one minor change: adding a view script variable for the page title. You'll see this minor modification in the section entitled "Try This 8-2," and you'll also find it in the code archive for this chapter.

We can now proceed to customize the error view by updating the default error view script, at *$APP_DIR/application/modules/default/views/scripts/error/error.phtml*, to include some additional debugging information:

```
<div>
  <div id="error-image">
    <img src="/images/error.gif" />
  </div>
  <div id="error-message">
    <h1><?php echo $this->title; ?></h1>
    <?php echo $this->message; ?>
  </div>
</div>

<?php if ('development' == APPLICATION_ENV): ?>
<div id="error-data">
  <h2>Exception message:</h2>
  <pre><?php echo $this->exception->getMessage(); ?></pre>

  <h2>Stack trace:</h2>
  <pre><?php echo $this->exception->getTraceAsString() ?></pre>

  <h2>Request method:</h2>
  <pre><?php echo $this->request->getMethod(); ?></pre>

  <h2>Request parameters:</h2>
  <?php Zend_Debug::dump($this->request->getParams()); ?>

  <h2>Server environment:</h2>
  <?php Zend_Debug::dump($this->request->getServer()); ?>

  <h2>System environment:</h2>
  <?php Zend_Debug::dump($this->request->getEnv()); ?>
  <?php endif ?>
</div>
```

Figure 8-4 Error output in a production environment

This error view displays one of two messages, depending on whether the error is a 404 or 500 server error. The amount of information displayed also differs depending on the environment in use. For example, Figure 8-4 illustrates the output when running in a production environment, while Figure 8-5 illustrates the output when running in a development environment.

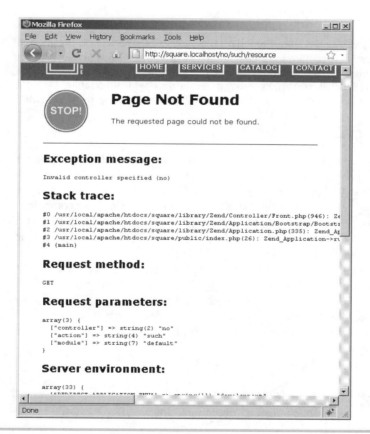

Figure 8-5 Error output in a development environment

Ask the Expert

Q: What is Zend_Debug?

A: The Zend_Debug component provides a convenient way to inspect variables in PHP. It exposes a single static method, `dump()`, which can be used to "dump" the contents of a variable to the standard output device. This method is commonly used to quickly look inside variables, especially when debugging and logging errors. Internally, `Zend_Debug::dump()` works as a wrapper around the PHP `var_dump()` function, adding `<pre>...</pre>` tags around the output and cleaning up line breaks for better formatting.

TIP

The Zend_Controller_Request_Http object exposes various methods to get information about the current request, and some of these are used in the previous code listing. The `getParams()` method returns an array of the current request parameters, the `getServer()` method returns an array of server environment variables (`$_SERVER`), and the `getEnv()` method returns an array of the current environment (`$_ENV`).

Logging Data

You've already seen, in the previous section, how it's possible to alter the amount of debugging information presented to the user in production environments. However, even though this information shouldn't be shown to the user, it does have value to the application developer and administrator. And so, the Zend Framework includes a Zend_Log component, which provides a general-purpose logging framework to log any type of data (including, but not limited to, exceptions) to disk files or other data storage. This information is typically analyzed and used for debugging, auditing, or reporting purposes.

The Zend_Log component is remarkably flexible. It supports multiple log destinations (standard output device, file, database, email address, or system log), multiple output formats (single line ASCII, XML, or custom), and multiple log priorities (ranging from "informational" to "emergency"). Some of its other features include user-defined priority levels; user-defined log formats; priority-based log filters; and support for Firebug (the Firefox browser debugger) console output.

The following sections examine these features in greater detail.

Writing Log Messages

Here's a simple example of using Zend_Log to log a message to a file in a specified format:

```php
<?php
class Sandbox_ExampleController extends Zend_Controller_Action
{
  public function logAction()
  {
```

```
    // initialize logging engine
    $logger = new Zend_Log();

    // attach writer to logging engine
    $writer = new Zend_Log_Writer_Stream(
      APPLICATION_PATH . '/../data/logs/example.log');
    $logger->addWriter($writer);

    // attach formatter to writer
    $format = '%timestamp%: %priorityName%: %message%' . PHP_EOL;
    $formatter = new Zend_Log_Formatter_Simple($format);
    $writer->setFormatter($formatter);

    // write log message
    $logger->log('Body temperature critical', Zend_Log::EMERG);
  }
}
```

Figure 8-6 illustrates what the output looks like.

It should be clear from the preceding example that there are various objects involved in writing log messages:

- The Zend_Log object serves as the primary control point for generating log messages. It exposes a `log()` method that initiates the log write operation.

- The Zend_Log_Writer object takes care of writing the log message to the specified data storage destination, be it a file, a database, an email address, or the system log. It is attached to the Zend_Log object with the latter's `addWriter()` method. Multiple writers may be attached to a single Zend_Log object. Table 8-2 shows a list of the built-in writers included with the Zend Framework.

- The Zend_Log_Formatter object takes care of reformatting the log message, either into XML or a user-defined format. It is always associated with a writer, and is attached to one with the latter's `setFormatter()` method. Only one formatter is permitted per writer. Table 8-3 provides a list of the built-in formatters included with the Zend Framework.

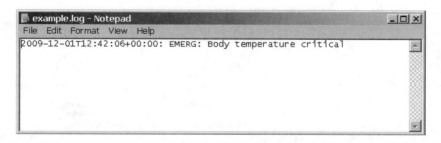

Figure 8-6   An example log message, written to a file

Writer	Description
Zend_Log_Writer_Stream	Writes log messages to PHP streams (output device, error device, URLs, or local files)
Zend_Log_Writer_Db	Writes log messages to a database
Zend_Log_Writer_Firebug	Writes log messages to the Firebug console
Zend_Log_Writer_Mail	Writes log messages to an email address
Zend_Log_Writer_Mock	Writes log messages back to itself for testing purposes
Zend_Log_Writer_Null	Writes log messages to */dev/null*
Zend_Log_Writer_Syslog	Writes log messages to the system logger (*syslogd* on UNIX and the Event Viewer on Windows)

Table 8-2 Log Writers Included with the Zend Framework

Notice also the second parameter passed to the Zend_Log object's `log()` method. This parameter specifies the message priority, and it can be any one of eight predefined priority levels. These levels are listed in Table 8-4, and they correspond closely to the levels used by the UNIX system logger (*syslog*). They can be specified by the developer on a per-message basis, depending on the importance of the message being logged.

To log messages to a database instead of a file (recommended in situations where logging concurrency is high), use the Zend_Log_Writer_Db writer. This writer is initialized with an instance of the Zend_Db_Adapter class (representing the database connection to be used), the destination table, and an array specifying which fields should be used for the different elements of the log message. Here's an example:

```php
<?php
class Sandbox_ExampleController extends Zend_Controller_Action
{
  public function logAction()
  {
    // initialize logging engine
    $logger = new Zend_Log();

    // define database mapping
```

Formatter	Description
Zend_Log_Formatter_Simple	Formats log messages into a user-defined format
Zend_Log_Formatter_Firebug	Formats log messages for the Firebug console
Zend_Log_Formatter_Xml	Formats log messages into XML

Table 8-3 Log Formatters Included with the Zend Framework

Log Level	Description
DEBUG	Debug notice
INFO	Informational notice
NOTICE	Notice
WARNING	Warning notice
ERR	Error notice
CRIT	Critical error notice
ALERT	Alert notice
EMERG	Emergency error notice

Table 8-4 Log Levels Supported by the Zend_Log Component

```
    $table = 'log';
    $fields = array(
      'LogLevel'    => 'priority',
      'LogMessage'  => 'message',
      'LogTime'     => 'timestamp'
    );

    // attach writer to logging engine
    $writer = new Zend_Log_Writer_Db($this->adapter, $table, $fields);
    $logger->addWriter($writer);

    // write log message
    $logger->log('Body temperature critical', Zend_Log::EMERG);
  }
}
```

CAUTION
It is not possible to use a formatter with the database log writer. Attempting to do so will result in an exception.

It's also possible to log messages to an email address with the Zend_Log_Writer_Mail writer, which accepts a configured Zend_Mail component as input. This is shown in the next listing:

```
<?php
class Sandbox_ExampleController extends Zend_Controller_Action
{
  public function logAction()
  {
    // create email message template
```

```
    $mail = new Zend_Mail();
    $mail->setFrom('error-bot@host.example.com')
        ->addTo('admin@host.example.com');
    $mail->setSubject('Email error log');

    // initialize logging engine
    $logger = new Zend_Log();

    // attach writer to logging engine
    $writer = new Zend_Log_Writer_Mail($mail);
    $logger->addWriter($writer);

    // write log message
    // note: a mail transport must be defined for this to work
    $logger->log('Body temperature critical', Zend_Log::EMERG);
  }
}
```

CAUTION
Email logging can be a major drag on performance, particularly when the mail server used is not on the same host as the application.

To write messages directly to the system logger (*syslogd* on UNIX and the Event Viewer on Windows), use the Zend_Log_Writer_Syslog writer, as shown in the following example. Note the use of the setFacility() method, which is used to set the log event's *facility*, or category, for the UNIX system logger.

```
<?php
class Sandbox_ExampleController extends Zend_Controller_Action
{
  public function logAction()
  {
    // initialize logging engine
    $logger = new Zend_Log();

    // attach writer to logging engine
    $writer = new Zend_Log_Writer_Syslog();
    $writer->setFacility(LOG_USER);
    $logger->addWriter($writer);

    // write log message
    $logger->log('Body temperature critical', Zend_Log::EMERG);
  }
}
```

It's worth pointing out here that in case none of the techniques in the preceding examples fit your application's requirements, it's also quite easy to create custom log writers for other data storage destinations, simply by extending the base Zend_Log_Writer_Abstract class. The child class must expose, at minimum, a protected _write() method that accepts the log message as an input argument, and writes it to the specified destination. You'll see an example of one such custom log writer in the next section.

Adding Data to Log Messages

By default, every log message contains four keys: the log message, the log priority (as a number and as a string), and a timestamp indicating when the message was generated. However, it's possible to add user-defined keys to this message, via the Zend_Log object's setEventItem() method. This method accepts two parameters—a key and a value—and attaches this key/value pair to the log message. This is particularly useful if you need to include additional debugging information in a log message.

Here's an example, which adds the client IP address and request URL to the log message:

```php
<?php
class Sandbox_ExampleController extends Zend_Controller_Action
{
  public function logAction()
  {
    // initialize logging engine
    $logger = new Zend_Log();

    // attach writer to logging engine
    $writer = new Zend_Log_Writer_Mock();
    $logger->addWriter($writer);

    // add client IP and request URL to log message
    $logger->setEventItem('request', $this->getRequest()->getRequestUri());
    $logger->setEventItem('host', $this->getRequest()->getClientIp());

    // write log message
    $logger->log('Body temperature critical', Zend_Log::EMERG);
  }
}
```

Formatting Log Messages

The keys included in a log message serve a dual purpose: They can also be used as format specifiers to create a custom format string for log messages. The Zend_Log_Formatter_Simple object uses this format string to control the format in which log messages are written to the destination. Format specifiers are enclosed in percentage (%) symbols (see the very first code listing in this section for an example).

The default format string contains a timestamp, the log level (as both a number and a string), and the log message. However, it is possible to modify this format and rearrange items to suit application-specific requirements. To illustrate, here's another example, this one making use of additional keys set with the `setEventItem()` method:

```php
<?php
class Sandbox_ExampleController extends Zend_Controller_Action
{
  public function logAction()
  {
    // initialize logging engine
    $logger = new Zend_Log();

    // attach writer to logging engine
    $writer = new Zend_Log_Writer_Stream(
      APPLICATION_PATH . '/../data/logs/example.log');
    $logger->addWriter($writer);

    // attach formatter to writer
    $format = '%timestamp%: %priorityName%: %request%:
            %host%: %message%' . PHP_EOL;
    $formatter = new Zend_Log_Formatter_Simple($format);
    $writer->setFormatter($formatter);

    // add client IP and request URL to log message
    $logger->setEventItem('request', $this->getRequest()->getRequestUri());
    $logger->setEventItem('host', $this->getRequest()->getClientIp());

    // write log message
    $logger->log('Body temperature critical', Zend_Log::EMERG);
  }
}
```

Figure 8-7 illustrates what the output of the previous listing might look like.

CAUTION

When you're using the Zend_Log_Formatter_Simple formatter, additional keys specified with the `setEventItem()` method will not be written to the log by default. To include these items in the log, explicitly include them in the format string passed to the formatter.

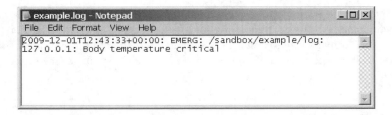

Figure 8-7 An example log message, with extra information added

To log data in XML, rather than plain-text format, switch to the Zend_Log_Formatter_ Xml formatter, as follows:

```php
<?php
class Sandbox_ExampleController extends Zend_Controller_Action
{
  public function logAction()
  {
    // initialize logging engine
    $logger = new Zend_Log();

    // attach writer to logging engine
    $writer = new Zend_Log_Writer_Stream(
      APPLICATION_PATH . '/../data/logs/example.log');
    $logger->addWriter($writer);

    // attach formatter to writer
    $formatter = new Zend_Log_Formatter_Xml();
    $writer->setFormatter($formatter);

    // add client IP and request URL to log message
    $logger->setEventItem('request', $this->getRequest()->getRequestUri());
    $logger->setEventItem('host', $this->getRequest()->getClientIp());

    // write log message
    $logger->log('Body temperature critical', Zend_Log::EMERG);
  }
}
```

In this case, log messages are formatted as XML entries, suitable for parsing in any XML processor. Figure 8-8 shows an example of the output.

As with the Zend_Log_Formatter_Simple formatter, it's possible to customize the output XML by specifying different element names. This information should be passed to the Zend_ Log_Formatter_Simple object constructor as an array. Here's an example illustrating this feature:

```php
<?php
class Sandbox_ExampleController extends Zend_Controller_Action
{
  public function logAction()
  {
    // initialize logging engine
    $logger = new Zend_Log();

    // attach writer to logging engine
    $writer = new Zend_Log_Writer_Stream(
      APPLICATION_PATH . '/../data/logs/example.log');
    $logger->addWriter($writer);

    // set XML element configuration
    $xml = array(
```

```
        'data'    => 'message',
        'time'    => 'timestamp',
        'level'   => 'priorityName',
        'request' => 'request',
        'host'    => 'host',
    );

    // attach formatter to writer
    $formatter = new Zend_Log_Formatter_Xml('entry', $xml);
    $writer->setFormatter($formatter);

    // add client IP and request URL to log message
    $logger->setEventItem('request', $this->getRequest()->getRequestUri());
    $logger->setEventItem('host', $this->getRequest()->getClientIp());

    // write log message
    $logger->log('Body temperature critical', Zend_Log::EMERG);
  }
}
```

Figure 8-9 shows an example of the revised output.

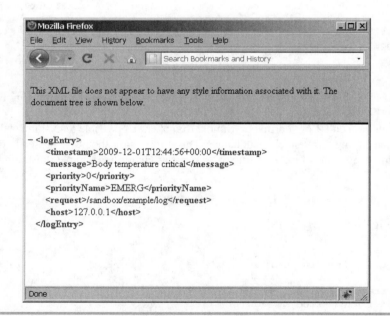

Figure 8-8   An example log message, formatted as XML

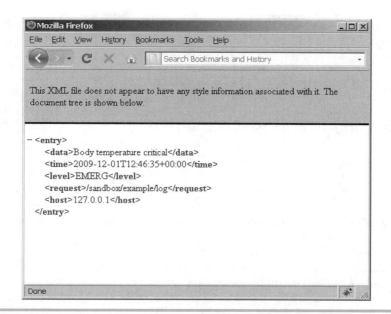

Figure 8-9 An example log message, formatted as XML with custom element names

Try This 8-2 Logging Application Exceptions

Let's now put all of this information in a practical context by updating the SQUARE example application with a full-fledged exception-logging system, one that logs exception data to the file, the database, and the Firebug console. As you will see, this is actually quite simple and can be accomplished relatively easily. The following sections will guide you through the process.

NOTE
The following sections includes a discussion of how to log exception data to Firebug, the Firefox browser debugger. It assumes that you have a working installation of the Firefox browser, together with the Firebug and FirePHP extensions. In case you don't already have these components, you can download them from the Web using the links at the end of the chapter.

Defining the Log Location
The first step is to define a location for the file-based log. So, create the *$APP_DIR/data/logs/* directory, which is the default location for log files under the Zend Framework's recommended directory layout.

```
shell> cd /usr/local/apache/htdocs/square/data
shell> mkdir logs
```

(continued)

It's also a good idea to update the application configuration file, at *$APP_DIR/application/configs/application.ini*, with this location, so that it can be used from within actions. Open this file and update it with the following configuration directive:

```
logs.logPath = APPLICATION_PATH "/../data/logs"
```

Defining the Database Log Writer

The next step is to create a log writer that will integrate with Doctrine to write log entries to the database.

As discussed earlier, this is not very difficult: It can be done simply by extending the base Zend_Log_Writer_Abstract class and ensuring that the child class exposes a _write() method that knows how to actually perform the log write operation. However, you might be wondering why this is even necessary, given that Zend_Log already comes with the Zend_Log_Writer_Db writer.

As explained in detail in Chapter 5, the reasons have to do with efficiency and consistency. Consistency, because all database queries are currently being performed through Doctrine models, and adding Zend_Db at this point simply muddies the waters. Efficiency, because using one database access library instead of two reduces the number of components the application has to load and the amount of configuration information that must be duplicated.

With this explanation in mind, proceed to create a custom log writer class named Square_Log_Writer_Doctrine containing the following code:

```php
<?php
class Square_Log_Writer_Doctrine extends Zend_Log_Writer_Abstract
{
  // constructor
  // accepts model name and column map
  public function __construct($modelName, $columnMap)
  {
    $this->_modelName = $modelName;
    $this->_columnMap = $columnMap;
  }

  // stub function
  // to deny formatter coupling
  public function setFormatter($formatter)
  {
    require_once 'Zend/Log/Exception.php';
    throw new Zend_Log_Exception(get_class() . ' does not support formatting');
  }

  // main log write method
  // maps database fields to log message fields
  // saves log messages as database records using model methods
  protected function _write($message)
  {
    $data = array();
```

```
    foreach ($this->_columnMap as $messageField => $modelField) {
      $data[$modelField] = $message[$messageField];
    }
    $model = new $this->_modelName();
    $model->fromArray($data);
    $model->save();
  }

  // static factory method
  static public function factory($config)
  {
    return new self(self::_parseConfig($config));
  }
}
```

Save this class as *$APP_DIR/library/Square/Log/Writer/Doctrine.php*.

This class is based on the Zend_Log_Writer_Doctrine prototype created by Matthew Lurz on the Zend Framework community wiki (see the link at the end of the chapter). Its main workhorse is the _write() method, which initializes the named Doctrine model and populates it with the keys of the log message. The model's save() method is then used to write the log message to the database.

Updating the Error Controller

All that's left now is to update the ErrorController::errorAction such that it automatically logs exceptions to the file, the database, and the Firebug console. Here's the revised controller from *$APP_DIR/application/modules/default/controllers/ErrorController .php*, with modifications highlighted in bold:

```
<?php
class ErrorController extends Zend_Controller_Action
{
  public function errorAction()
  {
    $errors = $this->_getParam('error_handler');
    switch ($errors->type) {
        case Zend_Controller_Plugin_ErrorHandler::EXCEPTION_NO_CONTROLLER:
        case Zend_Controller_Plugin_ErrorHandler::EXCEPTION_NO_ACTION:

            // 404 error -- controller or action not found
            $this->getResponse()->setHttpResponseCode(404);
            $this->view->title = 'Page Not Found';
            $this->view->message = 'The requested page could not be found.';
            break;
        default:
            // application error
            $this->getResponse()->setHttpResponseCode(500);
            $this->view->title = 'Internal Server Error';
            $this->view->message =
                'Due to an application error, the requested page could
```

(continued)

```
            not be displayed.';
          break;
    }

    $this->view->exception = $errors->exception;
    $this->view->request    = $errors->request;

    // initialize logging engine
    $logger = new Zend_Log();

    // add XML writer
    $config = $this->getInvokeArg('bootstrap')->getOption('logs');
    $xmlWriter = new Zend_Log_Writer_Stream(
      $config['logPath'] . '/error.log.xml');
    $logger->addWriter($xmlWriter);
    $formatter = new Zend_Log_Formatter_Xml();
    $xmlWriter->setFormatter($formatter);

    // add Doctrine writer
    $columnMap = array(
      'message' => 'LogMessage',
      'priorityName' => 'LogLevel',
      'timestamp' => 'LogTime',
      'stacktrace' => 'Stack',
      'request' => 'Request',
    );
    $dbWriter = new Square_Log_Writer_Doctrine('Square_Model_Log', $columnMap);
    $logger->addWriter($dbWriter);

    // add Firebug writer
    $fbWriter = new Zend_Log_Writer_Firebug();
    $logger->addWriter($fbWriter);

    // add additional data to log message - stack trace and request parameters
    $logger->setEventItem('stacktrace',
      $errors->exception->getTraceAsString());
    $logger->setEventItem('request',
      Zend_Debug::dump($errors->request->getParams()));

    // log exception to writer
    $logger->log($errors->exception->getMessage(), Zend_Log::ERR);
  }
}
```

This code initializes an instance of the Zend_Log component and attaches three writers to it: the standard file writer, the Doctrine-compliant database writer created in the previous section, and the Firebug console writer. The Zend_Log object's setEventItem() method is used to attach two additional pieces of information to the log message, namely a stack trace of the exception and the list of request parameters. As a result of these modifications, any exception that bubbles up to the ErrorController::errorAction will be automatically logged to three different destinations.

Figure 8-10 An application exception, logged to a file in XML format

To see this in action, try accessing a nonexistent application URL, such as **http://square .localhost/no/such/resource**. An exception will be raised to the error controller, and a 404 response will be sent back to the requesting client. This exception will also be logged to a file (Figure 8-10), to the application database (Figure 8-11), and to the Firebug console (Figure 8-12).

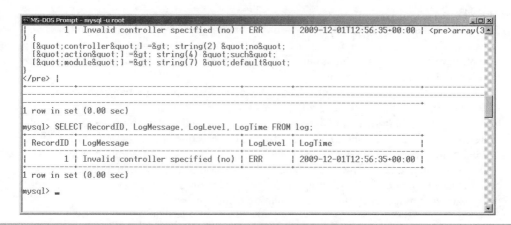

Figure 8-11 An application exception, logged to the application database

(continued)

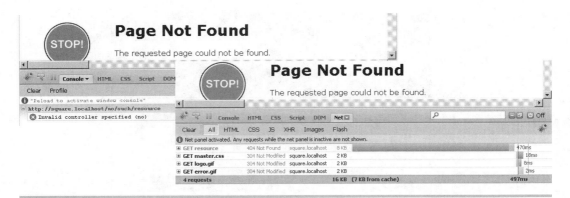

Figure 8-12 An application exception, logged to the Firebug console

---

CAUTION

It should be noted that logging exceptions to three different destinations, as discussed in this section, is not recommended in production environments. Logging data to a file or database can affect performance due to file locking or network latency issues, while logging data to the Firebug console increases the size of the response packet sent to the client by the server. These and other performance issues must be carefully explored when adding logging capabilities to a Zend Framework application.

Summary

This chapter marks the end of first section of this book, which was intended to teach you basic application development techniques with the Zend Framework. Fittingly, it covered exception handling, an important part of application development and an area that every developer should be familiar with.

This chapter began with an introduction to the new exception model introduced in PHP 5.x, outlining its benefits and advantages vis-à-vis the older PHP 4.x model. With this background information at hand, it then proceeded to examine the default exception-handling system built into the Zend Framework, outlining the functions of the default error controller and examining how the default process can be adjusted to cover different situations. It also took a quick look at how exception handling can (and should) be modified depending on whether the application is running in a development or production environment, and demonstrated a practical application of creating a custom error page.

The second half of the chapter focused specifically on the Zend_Log component, which provides a full-featured framework for logging messages in a Zend Framework application. This component can be used to log messages to a variety of different storage media, including file, database, email address, system logger, and Firebug console, and it can also be easily extended to support new log destinations. Some of these features were demonstrated in a practical context, by adding exception logging code to the SQUARE example application.

To learn more about the topics discussed in this chapter, consider visiting the following links:

- An overview of exceptions and exception handling in PHP 5.x, at **http://www.php.net/ manual/en/language.exceptions.php**

- An overview of exceptions and exception handling in the Zend Framework, at **http:// framework.zend.com/manual/en/zend.controller.exceptions.html**

- The Zend Framework error handler plug-in, at **http://framework.zend.com/manual/en/ zend.controller.plugins.html**

- The Zend_Log component, at **http://framework.zend.com/manual/en/zend.log.html**

- The Zend_Debug component, at **http://framework.zend.com/manual/en/zend.debug.html**

- The Firefox Web browser, at **http://www.mozilla.com/firefox**

- The Firebug console debugger, at **http://www.getfirebug.com/**

- The FirePHP extension, at **http://www.firephp.org/**

- A discussion of using the Firebug and FirePHP components with the Zend Framework (Christoph Dorn), at **http://www.christophdorn.com/Blog/2008/09/02/firephp-and-zend-framework-16/**

- A discussion of handling errors in a Zend Framework application (Jani Hartikainen), at **http://codeutopia.net/blog/2009/03/02/handling-errors-in-zend-framework/**

- A more advanced Zend Framework exception formatter (Larry Root), at **http://code .google.com/p/zend-framework-exception-formatter/**

- The original proposal and source for the Doctrine-based log writer (Matthew Lurz), at **http://framework.zend.com/wiki/display/ZFPROP/Zend_Log_Writer_Doctrine+-+Matthew+Lurz**

Chapter 9

Understanding Application Localization

Key Skills & Concepts

- Localize your application to different regions of the world

- Automatically apply local conventions for dates, currencies, temperatures, and measurements

- Build a multilingual Web application

One of the nicest things about the Web is that it's global: People from around the world can access and use Web applications with nothing more complicated than a browser and an Internet connection. The popularity and rapid growth of applications like Flickr, Google, Twitter, MySpace, and Facebook are testaments to the Web's global reach and to its popularity as a medium for communication and collaboration.

If you're a developer building a Web application, this fact has one important implication. Once your application is out on the Web, it's quite likely to receive visits from users who don't necessarily speak the same language as you, or even live in the same country. To make your application accessible to these users, it's necessary to support the local languages, symbols, and formatting conventions of each user's home country. This is the approach followed by some of today's most popular applications; look at any of the applications mentioned in the previous paragraph, and chances are you'll find a version in your local language or dialect.

The Zend Framework provides an easy way to perform application-level localization with its Zend_Locale component, and many other components, such as Zend_Date and Zend_Currency, can also automatically adjust their behavior to reflect the user's current region. There's also the Zend_Translate component, which provides a full-fledged API for managing and using translation strings in different languages. This chapter examines these components in detail, illustrating how they can be combined to build a localized, multilingual application.

Understanding Localization and Locales

The pundits of globalization would have us believe that the world is becoming an increasingly homogenous place, but in reality, each country still has a distinct identity and set of cultural mores. These differences exist both at the perceptual level—for example, the Italians are perceived as having a keen eye for fashion, while the French are perceived as a nation of gourmets—and in more prosaic cultural artifacts such as language, currency, measurements, and calendars. For example, in the United States, July 4th 2011 would be written as 7/4/2011, while in India the same date would be expressed as 4/7/2011. Similarly, distances are expressed in kilometers in Germany, France, Italy, India, and many other countries, while they are expressed in miles in the United States.

Localization is the process of adapting an application to the conventions of a particular geographic region, country, and/or language. This might be as simple as ensuring that dates, times, and currencies are displayed in the correct format for the selected region, or as complex as translating application labels, menus, and messages into the native language(s) of that region. The rationale is simple: The more "local" the application, the easier it is for users in different regions to understand it and begin making use of it. Most popular Web applications do this as a matter of routine: To illustrate, consider Figure 9-1, which displays the Google.com search engine as it appears in three different countries of the world: United States, France, and India.

Central to the process of localization is the concept of *locales* and *locale identifiers*. A locale identifier is a string representing the user's language and geographic region. This identifier consists of a language code and a country code, separated with an underscore. This identifier is intended to provide the application with precise information about the user's current location and language, and thereby enable it to present its information in the usual conventions of that location and language.

An example will make this clearer. Consider, for example, an application that is set to the locale *en_US* (language: English, country: United States). If the application is locale-aware, it will use this information to ensure that, for example, dates are presented in MM-DD-YYYY format and currencies are prefixed with the dollar ($) symbol. If the same application is reconfigured to the locale *de_AT* (language: German, country: Austria), it will automatically perform the necessary internal adjustments to present dates in DD-MM-YYYY format and prefix currencies with the euro (€) symbol.

Figure 9-1   The Google search engine, as it appears in different countries

Locale	Language	Country
en_US	English	United States
en_GB	English	United Kingdom
fr_FR	French	France
fr_CA	French	Canada
fr_BE	French	Belgium
fr_CH	French	Switzerland
de_DE	German	Germany
it_IT	Italian	Italy
es_ES	Spanish	Spain
es_US	Spanish	United States
cs_CZ	Czech	Czech Republic
hi_IN	Hindi	India
mr_IN	Marathi	India
en_IN	English	India
pt_BR	Portuguese	Brazil
zh_CN	Chinese	China

Table 9-1   Common Locale Identifiers

Table 9-1 provides a list of common locale identifiers, together with a description of the languages and countries they represent.

NOTE
A complete list of the language codes found in locale identifiers is available in the ISO 639 standard, while a corresponding list of country codes is available in the ISO 3166 standard. You'll find links to both these standards at the end of the chapter.

Setting the Application Locale

The Zend Framework includes a component named Zend_Locale, which can be used to define the application's locale. This component can be used to set the application locale, either manually or through a process of automatic detection at run time. Here's an example of manually setting the locale to *fr_FR* (language: French, country: France):

```php
<?php
class Sandbox_ExampleController extends Zend_Controller_Action
{
  public function localeAction()
```

```
  {
    $locale = new Zend_Locale('fr_FR');
  }
}
```

The individual components of a locale identifier can be retrieved with the Zend_Locale object's getLanguage() and getRegion() methods, as follows:

```
<?php
class Sandbox_ExampleController extends Zend_Controller_Action
{
  public function localeAction()
  {
    // define locale
    $locale = new Zend_Locale('fr_BE');

    // result: 'fr'
    $this->view->message = $locale->getLanguage();

    // result: 'BE'
    $this->view->message = $locale->getRegion();
  }
}
```

Typically, the Zend_Locale object is initialized in the application bootstrapper and made persistent through the application registry. Once registered in this manner, other locale-aware Zend Framework components, such as Zend_Date and Zend_Form, will automatically read the selected locale and adjust themselves to display information in the conventions for that locale. Here's an illustrative example, and you'll see this used many times throughout this chapter.

```
<?php
class Bootstrap extends Zend_Application_Bootstrap_Bootstrap
{
  protected function _initLocale()
  {
    // define locale
    $locale = new Zend_Locale('fr_FR');

    // register locale
    $registry = Zend_Registry::getInstance();
    $registry->set('Zend_Locale', $locale);
  }
}
```

Unless you're very sure that your application will only be used in a single locale, manually setting the application locale at design time is not recommended. Zend_Locale includes an automatic locale detection feature, which can dynamically set the locale at run time after inspecting the following information sources:

- **The locale settings of the client environment**   Most modern Web clients allow users to choose their preferred language and locale for viewing Web pages. This information is accessible within a PHP application in the `$_SERVER['HTTP_ACCEPT_LANGUAGES']` array. Whenever this information is available, Zend_Locale will use it to automatically set the application locale. When the user has specified multiple preferred languages and locales, the first valid locale will be used.

- **The locale settings of the host environment**   When client settings are not available, Zend_Locale will inspect the server environment and set the application locale based on the host system's locale. This information can be accessed and modified within PHP with the `setlocale()` function.

To use automatic locale detection, the Zend_Locale object must be initialized with one of the special locales `'browser'`, `'environment'`, or `'auto'`. Using the `'browser'` locale restricts locale detection to the user's browser only, while using the `'environment'` locale restricts it to the host server only. Using the special `'auto'` locale (or, alternatively, passing no arguments at all to the object constructor) tells Zend_Locale to check both the user's browser and the host environment for locale information.

Here is an example that illustrates these in action:

```php
<?php
class Bootstrap extends Zend_Application_Bootstrap_Bootstrap
{
  protected function _initLocale()
  {
    // detect locale from user's browser
    $locale = new Zend_Locale('browser');

    // detect locale from server environment
    $locale = new Zend_Locale('environment');

    // detect locale automatically from browser and then server
    $locale = new Zend_Locale('auto');

    // detect locale automatically from browser and then server
    $locale = new Zend_Locale();

    // register locale
    $registry = Zend_Registry::getInstance();
    $registry->set('Zend_Locale', $locale);
  }
}
```

If locale autodetection fails, Zend_Locale will throw an exception indicating this fact. The general practice in this situation is to catch the exception and manually set the locale to a reasonable value, based on a "best guess" assumption about the application's primary audience. For example, if the application is an e-commerce store aimed at users in India, it is reasonable to set the default locale to *hi_IN* in cases where no other locale information can be detected. Here's an example of how this can be done:

```php
<?php
class Bootstrap extends Zend_Application_Bootstrap_Bootstrap
{
  protected function _initLocale()
  {
    // try to auto-detect locale
    // if fail, set locale manually
    try {
      $locale = new Zend_Locale('browser');
    } catch (Zend_Locale_Exception $e) {
      $locale = new Zend_Locale('hi_IN');
    }

    // register locale
    $registry = Zend_Registry::getInstance();
    $registry->set('Zend_Locale', $locale);
  }
}
```

CAUTION

It is important to note that Zend_Locale will *not* throw an exception if the locale identifier detected contains only the language code and not the region code. For example, some client and/or server environments may simply return the locale *en* or *fr*. This situation can sometimes create a problem when Zend_Locale is used with other locale-aware classes that expect a complete locale identifier, such as Zend_Currency. There is no real solution to this problem, apart from manually setting the locale based on available facts and a "best guess" estimate. A proposed new feature in Zend_Locale will, in the future, allow "locale upgrading," wherein partially qualified locale identifiers (for example, *en*) will be automatically converted to fully qualified locale identifiers (for example, *en_US*).

Localizing Numbers

The Zend_Locale component includes a subcomponent, Zend_Locale_Format, which is designed expressly to assist in the task of localizing numeric values. This component includes a static toNumber() method that can be used to present numbers in locale-specific conventions. Here's an example:

```php
<?php
class Sandbox_ExampleController extends Zend_Controller_Action
{
```

```php
public function numberAction()
{
    // localize number
    // result: '195,740.676'
    $this->view->message = Zend_Locale_Format::toNumber(195740.676,
array('locale' => 'en_GB'));

    // result: '1,95,740.676'
    $this->view->message = Zend_Locale_Format::toNumber(
                            195740.676, array('locale' => 'en_GB'));

    }
}
```

It is worth pointing out that, unlike Zend_Date and Zend_Currency, Zend_Locale_Format cannot directly retrieve the application locale from the registry. It is therefore mandatory to pass a locale identifier to the static toNumber() method as an argument.

It is also possible to further customize the output number by specifying a custom format and precision. These options can be passed to the toNumber() method in the options array. Here are some examples:

```php
<?php
class Sandbox_ExampleController extends Zend_Controller_Action
{
  public function numberAction()
  {
    // use custom number format
    // result: '1,95,740.67'
    $this->view->message = Zend_Locale_Format::toNumber(195740.676, array(
                            'locale'        => 'en_GB,
                            'number_format' => '##,##,##0.00'
                           ));
  }
}
```

The other method of note in the Zend_Locale_Format component is the static convertNumerals() method, which makes it possible to convert numbers between Arabic and Latin scripts. Note that this requires PHP's PCRE extension to be compiled with UTF-8 support (Windows PHP installations often lack this support). Here's an example of it in action:

```php
<?php
class Sandbox_ExampleController extends Zend_Controller_Action
{
  public function numberAction()
  {
    // convert between numeric scripts
    $this->view->message =
      Zend_Locale_Format::convertNumerals('1956', 'Latn', 'Thai');
    $this->view->message =
```

```
        Zend_Locale_Format::convertNumerals('6482093.6498', 'Latn', 'Deva');
    }
}
```

TIP

You can obtain a complete list of the numeric scripts supported by Zend_Locale_
Format::convertNumerals by calling Zend_Locale::getTranslationList('
script').

Localizing Dates and Times

The Zend Framework comes with a component specifically designed to handle temporal display
and manipulation. This component, Zend_Date, provides a simple API to create and format
date and time values; it also supports a much wider range of timestamps than PHP's built-in
mktime() function, and it can automatically detect the application locale (if set with Zend_
Locale) and present date and time values according to the local conventions of that locale.

Here's a simple example of Zend_Date in action:

```php
<?php
class Sandbox_ExampleController extends Zend_Controller_Action
{
  public function dateAction()
  {
    // set date to now
    $date = new Zend_Date();

    // result: 'Dec 18, 2009 5:58:38 AM'
    $this->view->message = $date;
  }
}
```

As these examples illustrate, a Zend_Date object is automatically initialized to the
current date and time. It is also possible to initialize it to a specific date and time by passing
the constructor a human-readable date string, a UNIX timestamp, or an array of date/time
segments. Here are some examples:

```php
<?php
class Sandbox_ExampleController extends Zend_Controller_Action
{

  public function dateAction()
  {
    // set date using UNIX timestamp
    $date = new Zend_Date(1261125725);
```

```php
// result: '2009-12-18T08:42:05+00:00'
$this->view->message = $date->get(Zend_Date::ISO_8601);

// set date using string
// result: '2010-12-25T15:56:00+00:00'
$date->set('25/12/2010 15:56');
$this->view->message = $date->get(Zend_Date::ISO_8601);

// set date using array
// returns '2010-06-24T16:35:00+00:00'
$date->set(
  array(
    'year' => 2010,
    'month' => 6,
    'day' => 24,
    'hour' => 16,
    'minute' => 35,
    'second' => 0
));
  $this->view->message = $date->get(Zend_Date::ISO_8601);
  }
}
```

CAUTION

Avoid creating multiple instances of Zend_Date, because each instance incurs a significant startup cost. So, where multiple instances are required, it is much more efficient to reset an existing instance than to instantiate multiple instances.

As illustrated in the previous example, Zend_Date includes a set of predefined constants for common date formats such as ISO 8601 and UNIX timestamps. These can be passed to the Zend_Date object's get() method to retrieve date and time output in the correct format. The following listing demonstrates some of these formatting constants, with examples of the resulting output:

```php
<?php
class Sandbox_ExampleController extends Zend_Controller_Action
{
  public function dateAction()
  {
    // set date using string
    $date = new Zend_Date('25/12/2010 15:56');

    // result: '2010-12-25T15:56:00+00:00'
    $this->view->message = $date->get(Zend_Date::ISO_8601);

    // result: 'Sat, 25 Dec 2010 15:56:00 +0000'
    $this->view->message = $date->get(Zend_Date::RFC_2822);
```

```
    // result: 'Saturday, 25-Dec-10 15:56:00 UTC'
    $this->view->message = $date->get(Zend_Date::RFC_850);

    // result: '2010-12-25T15:56:00+00:00'
    $this->view->message = $date->get(Zend_Date::ATOM);

    // returns '2010-06-24T16:35:00+00:00'
    $this->view->message = $date->get(Zend_Date::ISO_8601);

    // result: 'Saturday, December 25, 2010'
    $this->view->message = $date->get(Zend_Date::DATE_FULL);

    // result: 'December 25, 2010 3:56:00 PM UTC'
    $this->view->message = $date->get(Zend_Date::DATETIME_LONG);
  }
}
```

TIP

If the predefined formats don't meet your needs, you can also create your own custom formats, using either Zend_Date or PHP date() format specifiers. The Zend Framework manual has more information on this, and you'll find a link to the relevant section at the end of this chapter.

Zend_Date is also fully locale-aware: The component will automatically look for a registered Zend_Locale object and, if available, will use the specified locale when formatting date and time values. It's also possible to explicitly specify a locale identifier as an argument to the Zend_Date object constructor, and then have Zend_Date use that value instead. Consider the following example, which illustrates both these scenarios:

```php
<?php
class Sandbox_ExampleController extends Zend_Controller_Action
{
  public function dateAction()
  {
    // define and register locale
    $locale = new Zend_Locale('fr_FR');
    $registry = Zend_Registry::getInstance();
    $registry->set('Zend_Locale', $locale);

    // create date object
    // locale will be automatically detected
    $date = new Zend_Date();

    // result: 'vendredi 18 décembre 2009'
    $this->view->message = $date->get(Zend_Date::DATE_FULL);
```

```
    // create date object
    // pass it locale or locale object
    $locale = new Zend_Locale('de_DE');
    $date = new Zend_Date($locale);

    // result: 'Freitag, 18. Dezember 2009 '
    $this->view->message = $date->get(Zend_Date::DATE_FULL);
  }
}
```

Zend_Date also natively supports time zones via its `getTimezone()` and `setTimezone()` methods, and automatically adjusts dates and times based on the selected time zone. Here's a simple example that illustrates this:

```
<?php
class Sandbox_ExampleController extends Zend_Controller_Action
{
  public function dateAction()
  {
    // set date using string
    $date = new Zend_Date('25/12/2010 15:56');

    // set time zone to UTC
    $date->setTimezone('UTC');

    // result: '2010-12-25T15:56:00+00:00'
    $this->view->message = $date->get(Zend_Date::ISO_8601);

    // set time zone to IST
    $date->setTimezone('Asia/Calcutta');

    // result: '2010-12-25T21:26:00+05:30'
    $this->view->message = $date->get(Zend_Date::ISO_8601);
  }
}
```

Localizing Currencies

Every country (with the exception of the Eurozone) has its own currency, making currency localization a key aspect of application development. As with dates and times, Zend_Framework includes a Zend_Currency component designed specifically to handle this task. This component provides methods to create currency strings that conform to local conventions, complete with currency symbol and short or long name. It also exposes methods to retrieve information on the regions where a specified currency is in circulation, and to list the currencies that are in circulation in a specified region.

By default, a newly instantiated Zend_Currency object will check if the application contains a registered Zend_Locale object and, if it does, it will use this registered locale when localizing currency values. It's also possible to override this behavior and explicitly specify a locale identifier as argument to the Zend_Currency object constructor. In either case, Zend_Currency will automatically select the appropriate currency for that locale. Localized currency values can now be obtained by calling the Zend_Currency object's toCurrency() method, which accepts a currency value as argument.

Consider the following example, which illustrates this in practice:

```php
<?php
class Sandbox_ExampleController extends Zend_Controller_Action
{
  public function currencyAction()
  {
    // initialize currency object
    $currency = new Zend_Currency('fr_FR');

    // result: '990,65 €'
    $this->view->message = $currency->toCurrency(990.65);
  }
}
```

CAUTION

When you are passing a locale identifier to Zend_Currency, it is mandatory to include both the language code and the region code. Omitting either one of these two codes will result in an exception, as Zend_Currency requires the complete locale identifier to correctly identify the corresponding currency.

For regions that have more than one currency, or to override the default currency selection, the Zend_Currency object constructor will accept a currency code as additional optional argument. Here's an example:

```php
<?php
class Sandbox_ExampleController extends Zend_Controller_Action
{
  public function currencyAction()
  {
    // initialize currency object
    $currency = new Zend_Currency('fr_FR', 'FRF');

    // result: '990,65 F'
    $this->view->message = $currency->toCurrency(990.65);
  }
}
```

It is also possible to customize the currency string returned by Zend_Currency by using the setFormat() method to adjust the position of the currency symbol, the name of the currency, the number precision, and the visibility of the three-character currency code. This method accepts an array of key-value pairs and reformats the currency string accordingly. The following examples illustrate this:

```php
<?php
class Sandbox_ExampleController extends Zend_Controller_Action
{
  public function currencyAction()
  {
    // initialize currency object
    $currency = new Zend_Currency('hi_IN');

    // adjust currency format
    $currency->setFormat(
      array(
        'position'  => Zend_Currency::RIGHT,
        'display'   => Zend_Currency::USE_NAME,
        'precision' => 2,
      )
    );

    // result: '990.65 भारतीय रूपया '
    $this->view->message = $currency->toCurrency(990.65);

    // create custom currency format
    $currency->setFormat(
      array(
        'position'  => Zend_Currency::LEFT,
        'display'   => Zend_Currency::USE_SYMBOL,
        'precision' => 4,
        'name'      => 'Driit',
        'symbol'    => 'DRT'
      )
    );

    // result: 'DRT 990.6500'
    $this->view->message = $currency->toCurrency(990.65);
  }
}
```

TIP

Zend_Currency includes the ability to perform exchange rate conversions on currency values before localizing them. Alternatively, consider using the PEAR Services_ ExchangeRates package, which provides an API to perform real-time currency conversion using current exchange rates. You'll find links with more information at the end of this chapter.

Localizing Measurements

Weights and measures are another area where localization is often necessary, and here too the Zend Framework has a solution: Zend_Measure, a component designed to help in converting between different measurement units and presenting the result as per local conventions. The component supports more than 30 different measurement types, ranging from common types such as length, weight, volume, and temperature to more unusual ones such as acceleration, illumination, power, frequency, and energy.

To initialize a Zend_Measure object, it is necessary to pass the object constructor two arguments: a numeric measurement and a constant indicating the measurement scale it is expressed in. Consider the following example, which illustrates by creating a Zend_Measure_ Temperature object:

```php
<?php
class Sandbox_ExampleController extends Zend_Controller_Action
{
  public function measureAction()
  {
    // initialize measure object
    $tempF = new Zend_Measure_Temperature(
              98.6, Zend_Measure_Temperature::FAHRENHEIT);

    // result: '98.6 °F'
    $this->view->message = $tempF;
  }
}
```

Here's another example, this one creating Zend_Measure_Length and Zend_Measure_ Weight objects:

```php
<?php
class Sandbox_ExampleController extends Zend_Controller_Action
{
  public function measureAction()
  {
    // initialize measure object
    $lengthCm = new Zend_Measure_Length(2540, Zend_Measure_Length::CENTIMETER);

    // result: '2,540 cm'
    $this->view->message = $lengthCm;
```

```php
      // initialize measure object
      $weightKg = new Zend_Measure_Weight(6500, Zend_Measure_Weight::KILOGRAM);

      // result: '6,500 kg'
      //$this->view->message = $weightKg;
  }
}
```

Each Zend_Measure object exposes a `convertTo()` method, which can be used to convert from one unit of measurement to another. The target unit of measurement must be specified as an argument to the `convertTo()` method. Here are some examples that illustrate this method in action:

```php
<?php
class Sandbox_ExampleController extends Zend_Controller_Action
{
  public function measureAction()
  {
    // convert temperature
    // result: '37.0 °C'
    $tempF = new Zend_Measure_Temperature(
             98.6, Zend_Measure_Temperature::FAHRENHEIT);
    $this->view->message = $tempF->convertTo(
                           Zend_Measure_Temperature::CELSIUS);

    // convert length
    // result: '1,000.0 in'
    $lengthCm = new Zend_Measure_Length(2540, Zend_Measure_Length::CENTIMETER);
    $this->view->message = $lengthCm->convertTo(Zend_Measure_Length::INCH);

    // convert weight
    // result: '6,500,000.0 g'
    $weightKg = new Zend_Measure_Weight(6500, Zend_Measure_Weight::KILOGRAM);
    $this->view->message = $weightKg->convertTo(Zend_Measure_Weight::GRAM);
  }
}
```

CAUTION
Zend_Measure does not allow you to convert from one measurement type to another. So, for example, any attempt to convert from length to weight, or from speed to frequency, will result in an exception.

Like Zend_Date and Zend_Currency, Zend_Measure is locale-aware. A locale identifier may be passed to the Zend_Measure object constructor as optional third argument or, if this is not present, Zend_Measure can also use the value specified in the registered Zend_Locale instance. Here's an example illustrating both these scenarios:

```php
<?php
class Sandbox_ExampleController extends Zend_Controller_Action
{
  public function measureAction()
  {
    // define and register locale
    $locale = new Zend_Locale('pt_BR');
    $registry = Zend_Registry::getInstance();
    $registry->set('Zend_Locale', $locale);

    // convert temperature using default locale
    // result: '37,0 °C'
    $tempF = new Zend_Measure_Temperature(
            98.6, Zend_Measure_Temperature::FAHRENHEIT);
    $this->view->message = $tempF->convertTo(Zend_Measure_Temperature::CELSIUS);

    // convert length using custom locale
    // result: '1'000.0 in'
    $lengthCm = new Zend_Measure_Length(
            2540, Zend_Measure_Length::CENTIMETER, 'fr_CH');
    $this->view->message = $lengthCm->convertTo(Zend_Measure_Length::INCH);
  }
}
```

Localizing Strings

While English is the language you're most likely to see on the Web, it's important to remember that there is still a large percentage of Internet users for whom English is not their native language. This fact assumes particular significance when localizing a Web application, as the biggest component of any localization project usually consists of translating the application's textual content into multiple languages.

The Zend Framework offers a comprehensive API for managing translation strings in different languages, via its Zend_Translate component. This component supports a wide variety of translation data sources, including CSV files, PHP arrays, and GNU gettext files, and it can also be readily extended to support other data sources (for example, translation strings from a database). Like other Zend Framework components discussed in this chapter, it is fully locale-aware and can dynamically select the appropriate language for the application based on a registered Zend_Locale object, or from client locale settings.

The best way to understand Zend_Translate is with an example. Assume for a moment that there are translation source files for different languages, as follows:

```php
<?php
// languages/messages.fr_FR.php
return array(
  'welcome'  => 'Bienvenue',
  'dog'      => 'chien',
  'cat'      => 'chat',
  'one'      => 'un',
  'two'      => 'deux',
  'three'    => 'trois'
);
```

```php
<?php
// languages/messages.de_DE.php
return array(
  'welcome'  => 'Wilkommen',
  'dog'      => 'hund',
  'cat'      => 'katz',
  'one'      => 'eins',
  'two'      => 'zwei',
  'three'    => 'drei'
);
```

```php
<?php
// languages/messages.es_ES.php
return array(
  'welcome'  => 'Bienvenido',
  'dog'      => 'gato',
  'cat'      => 'perro',
  'one'      => 'un',
  'two'      => 'dos',
  'three'    => 'tres'
);
```

This is the simplest possible format for a translation file, consisting of a PHP associative array with keys mapping to the corresponding local language strings. Zend_Translate can now be configured to read these files and dynamically translate strings at run time based on the selected locale. Here's an example:

```php
<?php
class Sandbox_ExampleController extends Zend_Controller_Action
{
  public function translateAction()
  {
    // create translation object
    // specify translation adapter
    // specify source files for each locale
    $translate = new Zend_Translate('array', APPLICATION_PATH .
                    '/../languages/messages.es_ES.php', 'es_ES');
    $translate->addTranslation(APPLICATION_PATH .
                    '/../languages/messages.de.php', 'de_DE');
    $translate->addTranslation(APPLICATION_PATH .
                    '/../languages/messages.fr_FR.php', 'fr_FR');

    // set current locale
    $translate->setLocale('fr_FR');

    // translate string
    // result: 'un, deux, trois'
    $this->view->message = sprintf('%s, %s, %s',
                            $translate->_('one'),
                            $translate->_('two'),
                            $translate->_('three')
                            );

    // set current locale
    $translate->setLocale('de_DE');

    // translate string
    // result: 'eins, zwei, drei'
    $this->view->message = sprintf('%s, %s, %s',
                            $translate->_('one'),
                            $translate->_('two'),
                            $translate->_('three')
                            );
  }
}
```

A Zend_Translate object is initialized with three arguments: the type of translation adapter to use, the location of the translation source files, and the locale for the file. The setLocale() method is then used to define the current locale. With this information at hand, Zend_Translate is able to look up the appropriate translation file and return the correct translation for each string.

TIP

If Zend_Translate is unable to find a translation source for the specified locale, it will return the original translation key and generate a PHP error notice. To disable this notice, pass the special 'disableNotices' option in the fourth argument to the Zend_Translate object constructor.

Working with Adapters and Data Sources

Zend_Translate supports a number of different adapters for translation source files. The previous example used the Array adapter, which is suitable in most scenarios. However, there exist other options too, as shown in Table 9-2.

Zend_Translate can also recursively scan a directory tree and attach all found translation sources to the Zend_Translate object, through a process of automatic source detection. The locale for each translation file is autodetected based on the corresponding file and/or

Adapter	Description
Zend_Translate_Adapter_Array	Reads translation sources expressed as a PHP array
Zend_Translate_Adapter_Csv	Reads translation sources expressed in CSV format
Zend_Translate_Adapter_Ini	Reads translation sources expressed in INI format
Zend_Translate_Adapter_Gettext	Reads translation sources expressed in GNU gettext binary format
Zend_Translate_Adapter_Tbx	Reads translation sources expressed in TermBase eXchange (TBX) format
Zend_Translate_Adapter_Tmx	Reads translation sources expressed in Translation Memory eXchange (TMX) format
Zend_Translate_Adapter_Qt	Reads translation sources expressed in QtLinguist format
Zend_Translate_Adapter_Xliff	Reads translation sources expressed in the XML Localization Interchange File Format (XLIFF)
Zend_Translate_Adapter_XmlTm	Reads translation sources expressed in XML Text Memory (XML:TM) format

Table 9-2   Translation Adapters Included with the Zend Framework

Figure 9-2 Translation sources in separate directories

directory names. This eliminates the need to manually add translation sources with the addTranslation() method.

To illustrate, consider Figure 9-2, which illustrates the use of locale-specific directories for translation source files, and the following code listing, which configures Zend_Translate to automatically scan this directory structure and incorporate all found translation sources:

```php
<?php
class Sandbox_ExampleController extends Zend_Controller_Action
{
  public function translateAction()
  {
    // create translation object
    // specify translation adapter
    // automatically find source files for each locale
    $translate = new Zend_Translate('array', APPLICATION_PATH .
                '/../languages', null,
                array('scan' => Zend_Translate:: LOCALE_DIRECTORY));
  }
}
```

Notice that, in this case, the second argument to the Zend_Translate object constructor is simply the root of the directory tree to scan, and the additional fourth argument indicates that locale information should be read from each directory's name.

Figure 9-3 Translation sources in separate files

An alternative approach is to use a file-based structure, wherein each filename incorporates the locale identifier for the corresponding translation source. Figure 9-3 illustrates such a system, and the following code listing demonstrates how to use Zend_Translate with it:

```php
<?php
class Sandbox_ExampleController extends Zend_Controller_Action
{
  public function translateAction()
  {
```

```
      // create translation object
      // specify translation adapter
      // automatically find source files for each locale
      $translate = new Zend_Translate('array', APPLICATION_PATH .
                       '/../languages', null,
                       array('scan' => Zend_Translate::LOCALE_FILENAME));
  }
}
```

Of course, these are not the only two options available. There are a number of standard directory layouts supported by Zend_Translate for translation source files, and you should choose one that is most appropriate for the size and scale of your project. You can read more about these layouts, and also see some examples, using the links at the end of this chapter.

Using the Application Locale

Like many other Zend_Framework components, Zend_Translate is locale-aware: If a registered Zend_Locale instance is available, it can automatically use this locale as the default for all translation operations. This is convenient, because it allows the locale to be set just once (in the application bootstrapper) and then have that locale applied to all Zend_Translate operations across the entire application.

Ask the Expert

Q: What is GNU gettext and how do I use it?

A: GNU gettext is part of the GNU Translation Project, and provides a standard way of creating and using translation tables for an application. Under this system, translation strings for different languages are specified in human-readable message template (*.po) files, one for each language. These files are then converted to binary catalog (*.mo) files, which are distributed with the application.

By convention, GNU gettext uses a directory-based layout for *.mo translation files, wherein translation files for different languages are stored in separate directories named according to locale or language (Figure 9-4 shows an example). It is worth noting that Zend_Translate's source detection feature can recognize and use this directory layout automatically, thereby allowing developers to use existing GNU gettext sources in a PHP application with no additional modification.

Figure 9-4 The conventional GNU gettext directory layout for translation sources

The following example demonstrates this in action, by registering the *de_DE* (language: German, country: Germany) locale in the application registry and having Zend_Translate automatically detect and use it:

```php
<?php
class Sandbox_ExampleController extends Zend_Controller_Action
{
  public function localeAction()
  {
    // define and register locale
    $locale = new Zend_Locale('de_DE');
    $registry = Zend_Registry::getInstance();
    $registry->set('Zend_Locale', $locale);

    // create translation object
    // specify translation adapter
    // automatically find source files for each locale
    $translate = new Zend_Translate('array', APPLICATION_PATH .
                '/../languages', null,
                array('scan' => Zend_Translate::LOCALE_FILENAME));

    // translate string
    // result: 'eins, zwei, drei'
    $this->view->message = sprintf('%s, %s, %s',
                          $translate->_('one'),
```

```
                                  $translate->_('two'),
                                  $translate->_('three')
                                  );
  }
}
```

It's important to note that if Zend_Translate is unable to find a translation source for a fully qualified locale, it will automatically "degrade" the locale and use the translation source that best matches the degraded locale. So, for example, if the application locale is set to *fr_LU* (language: French, country: Luxembourg) but no translation source is available for the *fr_LU* locale, Zend_Translate will automatically use the translation source for the *fr* locale instead, if available.

Using the Translation View Helper

The examples in the previous sections have demonstrated translation operations within the scope of the controller. In reality, however, the correct approach is to perform translation operations within the scope of the view script rather than that of the controller. Zend_Translate includes a translation view helper, which can be used to perform these operations within a view script.

To use the translation view helper, it is necessary to first register the Zend_Translate object in the application registry, such that it is accessible throughout the application. Here's an example of how to do this:

```php
<?php
class Bootstrap extends Zend_Application_Bootstrap_Bootstrap
{
  protected function _initTranslate()
  {
    // initialize and register translation object
    $translate = new Zend_Translate('array',
                    APPLICATION_PATH . '/../languages/',
                    null,
                    array('scan' => Zend_Translate::LOCALE_FILENAME));
    $registry->set('Zend_Translate', $translate)
  }
}
```

Once this is done, translation can be performed within a view script simply by calling the view object's translate() method, as shown in the following code. When invoked in this manner, the translation view helper will retrieve the corresponding local-language string and interpolate it into the view script before rendering the view.

```php
<div id="header">
  <?php echo $this->translate('welcome'); ?>
</div>
```

Once a Zend_Translate object has been registered with the application registry, other Zend Framework components can also use it for string localization. The best example of this is Zend_Form, which can automatically use a registered Zend_Translate object to prepare localized versions of form field and button labels, option elements, fieldset legends, and validation error messages. You'll see an example of this in the next section.

Try This 9-1 Localizing the Example Application

As the previous sections have illustrated, the Zend Framework offers a comprehensive API for application localization. Now that you know the theory, let's apply it in a practical context by localizing the SQUARE example application to support three different languages: English (both UK and US), French, and German.

Setting the Application Locale

The first step in application localization is to define the application's locale. This locale information can then be used by other components, such as Zend_Date and Zend_Translate. The recommended way to do this is to first attempt locale autodiscovery from the user's client, or failing that, manually set the locale to a reasonable value.

Begin by editing the application bootstrapper, at *$APP_DIR/application/Bootstrap.php*, and adding a method to perform locale autodiscovery, as follows:

```php
<?php
class Bootstrap extends Zend_Application_Bootstrap_Bootstrap
{
  protected function _initLocale()
  {
    try {
      $locale = new Zend_Locale('browser');
    } catch (Zend_Locale_Exception $e) {
      $locale = new Zend_Locale('en_GB');
    }
    $registry = Zend_Registry::getInstance();
    $registry->set('Zend_Locale', $locale);
  }
}
```

In this case, Zend_Locale will attempt to automatically detect the user's current locale and, if unable to do so, will set the locale to *en_GB* (language: English, country: United Kingdom). The locale will be registered in the application registry via Zend_Registry so that other locale-aware components can use it as well.

Localizing Numbers and Dates

With locale definition out of the way, the next step is to look through the application and begin the process of localizing numbers and dates. If you take a look at the stamp catalog views, you'll see that each stamp record includes some numeric values: the stamp's denomination and the stamp's minimum and maximum sale prices. Ideally, these values should be formatted to reflect the user's current locale conventions.

Another item that's currently missing from each stamp's detail page is the date on which it was offered for sale. This is useful information for potential buyers, as it allows them to judge how "fresh" the listing is. Ideally, this date value should also be presented in the user's local language and convention.

The Zend_Locale_Format component provides the tools needed to localize numbers via its `toNumber()` static method, while the Zend_Date component can handle date localization and formatting. To use these tools, update the `Catalog_ItemController::displayAction` at *$APP_DIR/application/modules/catalog/controllers/ItemController.php* as shown in the following example:

```php
<?php
class Catalog_ItemController extends Zend_Controller_Action
{
  // action to display a catalog item
  public function displayAction()
  {
    // set filters and validators for GET input
    $filters = array(
      'id' => array('HtmlEntities', 'StripTags', 'StringTrim')
    );
    $validators = array(
      'id' => array('NotEmpty', 'Int')
    );
    $input = new Zend_Filter_Input($filters, $validators);
    $input->setData($this->getRequest()->getParams());

    // test if input is valid
    // retrieve requested record
    // attach to view
    if ($input->isValid()) {
      $q = Doctrine_Query::create()
            ->from('Square_Model_Item i')
            ->leftJoin('i.Square_Model_Country c')
            ->leftJoin('i.Square_Model_Grade g')
            ->leftJoin('i.Square_Model_Type t')
            ->where('i.RecordID = ?', $input->id)
            ->addWhere('i.DisplayStatus = 1')
            ->addWhere('i.DisplayUntil >= CURDATE()');
      $result = $q->fetchArray();
      if (count($result) == 1) {
        $this->view->item = $result[0];
        $this->view->images = array();
        $config = $this->getInvokeArg('bootstrap')->getOption('uploads');
        foreach (glob("{$config['uploadPath']}/
          {$this->view->item['RecordID']}_*") as $file) {
          $this->view->images[] = basename($file);
        }
```

(continued)

```
        $configs = $this->getInvokeArg('bootstrap')->getOption('configs');
        $localConfig = new Zend_Config_Ini($configs['localConfigPath']);
        $this->view->seller = $localConfig->user->displaySellerInfo;
        $registry = Zend_Registry::getInstance();
        $this->view->locale = $registry->get('Zend_Locale');
        $this->view->recordDate = new Zend_Date($result[0]['RecordDate']);
    } else {
        throw new Zend_Controller_Action_Exception('Page not found', 404);
    }
  } else {
    throw new Zend_Controller_Action_Exception('Invalid input');
  }
 }
}
```

Here, the `displayAction()` method retrieves the current locale from the application registry, and assigns it to a view variable. It also retrieves the date on which the record was saved and assigns it to a Zend_Date object. It is now possible to localize these dates and numbers within the corresponding view script, at *$APP_DIR/application/modules/catalog/views/scripts/item/display.phtml*, as follows:

```
<h2>View Item</h2>
<h3>
  FOR SALE:
  <?php echo $this->escape($this->item['Title']); ?> -
  <?php echo $this->escape($this->item['Year']); ?> -
  <?php echo $this->escape($this->item['Square_Model_Grade']['GradeName']); ?>
</h3>

<div id="container">
  <div id="images">
    <?php foreach ($this->images as $image): ?>
    <img src="/uploads/<?php echo $this->escape($image); ?>"
    width="150" height="150" />
    <?php endforeach; ?>
  </div>
  <div id="record">
    <table>

      ...
    <tr>
      <td class="key">Denomination:</td>
      <td class="value">
        <?php echo $this->escape(
          Zend_Locale_Format::toNumber($this->item['Denomination'],
            array(
              'locale' => $this->locale,
              'precision' => 2
            )
          )); ?>
      </td>
```

```
      </tr>
      <tr>
        <td class="key">Grade:</td>
        <td class="value">
          <?php echo $this->escape(
            $this->item['Square_Model_Grade']['GradeName']); ?>
        </td>
      </tr>
      <tr>
        <td class="key">Sale price:</td>
        <td class="value">
          $<?php echo $this->escape(
            Zend_Locale_Format::toNumber($this->item['SalePriceMin'],
              array(
                'locale' => $this->locale,
                'precision' => 2
              )
          )); ?> -
          $<?php echo $this->escape(
            Zend_Locale_Format::toNumber($this->item['SalePriceMax'],
              array(
                'locale' => $this->locale,
                'precision' => 2
              )
          )); ?>
        </td>
      </tr>
      <tr>
        <td class="key">Description:</td>
        <td class="value">
          <?php echo $this->escape($this->item['Description']); ?>
        </td>
      </tr>
      <tr>
        <td class="key">Date posted:</td>
        <td class="value">
          <?php echo $this->escape($this->recordDate->get(
          Zend_Date::DATE_FULL)); ?>
        </td>
      </tr>
      <?php if ($this->seller == 1): ?>
      <tr>
        <td class="key">Seller:</td>
        <td class="value">
          <?php echo $this->escape($this->item['SellerName']); ?>,
          <?php echo $this->escape($this->item['SellerAddress']); ?>
        </td>
      </tr>
      <?php endif; ?>
    </table>
  </div>
</div>
```

(continued)

Defining String Localization Targets

With the dates and numbers handled, the next step is to perform string localization. Given the limited space constraints of this book, it isn't possible to localize every single string in the application, and so, this example will assume that string localization is restricted to only the following three targets: the application's main menu, page footer, and contact form.

To perform string localization, it is necessary to edit each application layout and view, and use the translation view helper to dynamically interpolate translation strings into it. A good place to begin is the application's master layout, which contains the main menu. Edit this file, which is located at *$APP_DIR/application/layouts/master.phtml*, with the revisions highlighted in bold:

```
<!DOCTYPE html PUBLIC "-//W3C//DTD XHTML 1.0 Strict//EN"
"http://www.w3.org/TR/xhtml1/DTD/xhtml1-strict.dtd">
<html xmlns="http://www.w3.org/1999/xhtml" xml:lang="en" lang="en">

...

    <div id="menu">
      <a href="<?php echo $this->url(array(), 'home'); ?>">
        <?php echo $this->translate('menu-home'); ?>
      </a>
      <a href="<?php echo $this->url(array('page' => 'services'),
      'static-content'); ?>">
        <?php echo $this->translate('menu-services'); ?>
      </a>
      <a href="<?php echo $this->url(array('module' => 'catalog',
      'controller' => 'item', 'action' => 'search'), 'default', true); ?>
      ">
        <?php echo $this->translate('menu-catalog'); ?>
        </a>
      <a href="<?php echo $this->url(array(), 'contact'); ?>">
        <?php echo $this->translate('menu-contact'); ?>
      </a>
    </div>
  </div>

  <div id="content">
    <?php echo $this->layout()->content ?>
  </div>

  <div id="footer">
    <p>
      <?php echo $this->translate('created-with'); ?>
      <a href="http://framework.zend.com/">Zend Framework</a>.
      <?php echo $this->translate('licensed-under'); ?>
      <a href="http://www.creativecommons.org/">Creative Commons</a>.
    </p>
  </div>
  </body>
</html>
```

Next up, the application's contact form. This form definition is created using Zend_Form, which can automatically detect and use a registered Zend_Translate object to perform run-time string localization. So all that's really required here is to replace each element's label with a string identifier, which will be automatically replaced by the translated value at run time. Edit the form definition, at *$APP_DIR/library/Square/Form/Contact.php*, and make the changes highlighted in bold:

```php
<?php
class Square_Form_Contact extends Zend_Form
{
  public function init()
  {
    // initialize form
    $this->setAction('/contact/index')
         ->setMethod('post');

    // create text input for name
    $name = new Zend_Form_Element_Text('name');
    $name->setLabel('contact-name')
         ->setOptions(array('size' => '35'))
         ->setRequired(true)
         ->addValidator('NotEmpty', true)
         ->addValidator('Alpha', true)
         ->addFilter('HTMLEntities')
         ->addFilter('StringTrim');

    // create text input for email address
    $email = new Zend_Form_Element_Text('email');
    $email->setLabel('contact-email-address');
    $email->setOptions(array('size' => '50'))
          ->setRequired(true)
          ->addValidator('NotEmpty', true)
          ->addValidator('EmailAddress', true)
          ->addFilter('HTMLEntities')
          ->addFilter('StringToLower')
          ->addFilter('StringTrim');

    // create text input for message body
    $message = new Zend_Form_Element_Textarea('message');
    $message->setLabel('contact-message')
            ->setOptions(array('rows' => '8','cols' => '40'))
            ->setRequired(true)
            ->addValidator('NotEmpty', true)
            ->addFilter('HTMLEntities')
            ->addFilter('StringTrim');
```

(continued)

```php
// create captcha
$captcha = new Zend_Form_Element_Captcha('captcha', array(
    'captcha' => array(
        'captcha' => 'Image',
        'wordLen' => 6,
        'timeout' => 300,
        'width'   => 300,
        'height'  => 100,
        'imgUrl'  => '/captcha',
        'imgDir'  => APPLICATION_PATH . '/../public/captcha',
        'font'    => APPLICATION_PATH .
                     '/../public/fonts/LiberationSansRegular.ttf',
    )
));
$captcha->setLabel('contact-verification');

// create submit button
$submit = new Zend_Form_Element_Submit('submit');
$submit->setLabel('contact-send-message')
       ->setOptions(array('class' => 'submit'));

// attach elements to form
$this->addElement($name)
     ->addElement($email)
     ->addElement($message)
     ->addElement($captcha)
     ->addElement($submit);
    }
}
```

Creating Translation Sources

Once the various view elements have been configured for localization, the next step is to create translation source files for each language. To keep things simple, express these translation source files as PHP arrays, with locales specified within the filename.

Begin by creating a directory for these translation sources by changing to the *$APP_DIR* directory and executing the following command:

```
shell> mkdir languages
```

Then, go ahead and create translation source files for each language that should be supported. Here's an example of the French translation source file, which should be saved as *$APP_DIR/languages/messages.fr.php*:

```php
<?php
return array(
    'menu-home'          => 'ACCUEIL',
    'menu-services'      => 'SERVICES',
```

```
'menu-catalog'          => 'BROCHURE',
'menu-contact'          => 'CONTACTEZ-NOUS',
'welcome'               => 'Bienvenue',
'created-with'          => 'Créé avec',
'licensed-under'        => 'Sous license',
'contact-name'          => 'Nom:',
'contact-email-address' => 'Adresse email:',
'contact-message'       => 'Message:',
'contact-verification'  => 'Vérification:',
'contact-send-message'  => 'Envoyer Message',
'contact-title'         => 'Contactez-Nous',
);
```

Once you're done, you should have a directory structure like the one shown in Figure 9-5.

TIP

To avoid data corruption, use UTF-8 encoding when creating translation files containing non-Latin characters. Some free and commercial text editors with UTF-8 encoding support include gedit on UNIX and Notepad2 on Microsoft Windows. Download links can be found at the end of this chapter.

Figure 9-5   The application's translation sources, each in a separate file

Ask the Expert

Q: Why do you have a separate translation file for the *en* locale in addition to files for the *en_US* and *en_GB* locales?

A: As explained earlier in the chapter, if Zend_Translate is unable to find a translation source file for a locale identifier, it will automatically degrade the locale identifier to just the language code and use the general translation source file for that language, if available. Therefore, it's recommended to always include a general translation file for every language that you plan to support in the application, in addition to the more specific translation files. This is the reason for including an *en* language file in addition to the *en_US* and *en_GB* language files.

(continued)

Registering the Translation Object

The final step is to update the application bootstrapper and configure and register an instance of the Zend_Translate object. This instance will then become available in all application controllers and views, enabling the use of the translation view helper and Zend_Form's autotranslation features.

To do this, update the application bootstrapper, at *$APP_DIR/application/Bootstrap.php*, and add the following method to it:

```php
<?php
class Bootstrap extends Zend_Application_Bootstrap_Bootstrap
{
  protected function _initTranslate()
  {
    $translate = new Zend_Translate('array',
                 APPLICATION_PATH . '/../languages/',
                 null,
                 array('scan' => Zend_Translate::LOCALE_FILENAME,
                       'disableNotices' => 1));
    $registry = Zend_Registry::getInstance();
    $registry->set('Zend_Translate', $translate);
  }
}
```

TIP
Instead of getting the Zend_Registry instance, you can directly access registry values with the shorthand `Zend_Registry::get($index)` and `Zend_Registry::set($index, $value)` methods.

And you're done! To see this in action, configure your browser settings and add French or German as your preferred language. Figure 9-6 shows an example of how to do this in Mozilla Firefox, while Figure 9-7 shows an example of how to do this in Microsoft Internet Explorer.

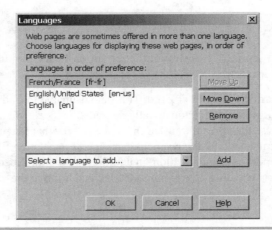

Figure 9-6 Configuring page languages in Mozilla Firefox

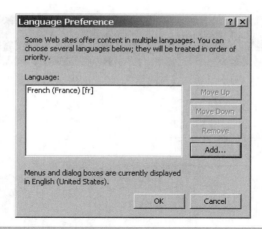

Figure 9-7   Configuring page languages in Microsoft Internet Explorer

Then, browse to the application index page at **http://square.localhost/** and you should be presented with something like Figure 9-8. Notice that the main menu and footer are presented in the selected local language.

Browse to the contact form at **http://square.localhost/contact**, and you'll see that the field labels have also been automatically translated by Zend_Form (see Figure 9-9).

Figure 9-8   The application's index page, automatically localized to French

(continued)

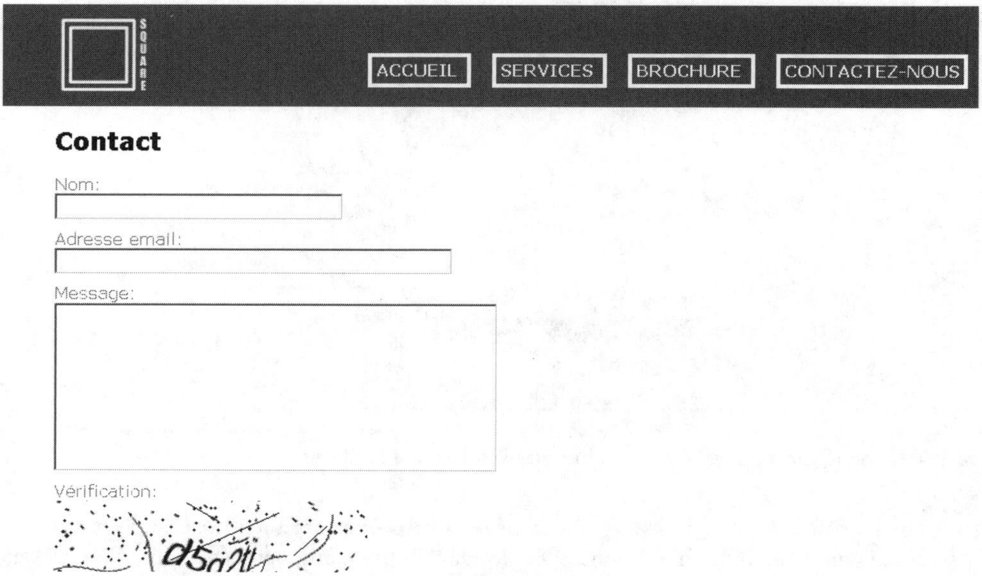

Figure 9-9 The application's contact form, automatically localized to French

If you adjust your browser settings to use another preferred language, and if Zend_ Translate is able to find a translation source for that language, content will be automatically translated into the selected language (see Figure 9-10). If, on the other hand, Zend_Translate is not able to find a translation source for that language, translation will not be possible and the original string identifiers will be displayed instead (see Figure 9-11). Finally, if your browser is not set to use any particular language, locale autodetection will fail and the fallback locale of *en_GB* will be used instead by both Zend_Locale and Zend_Translate (see Figure 9-12).

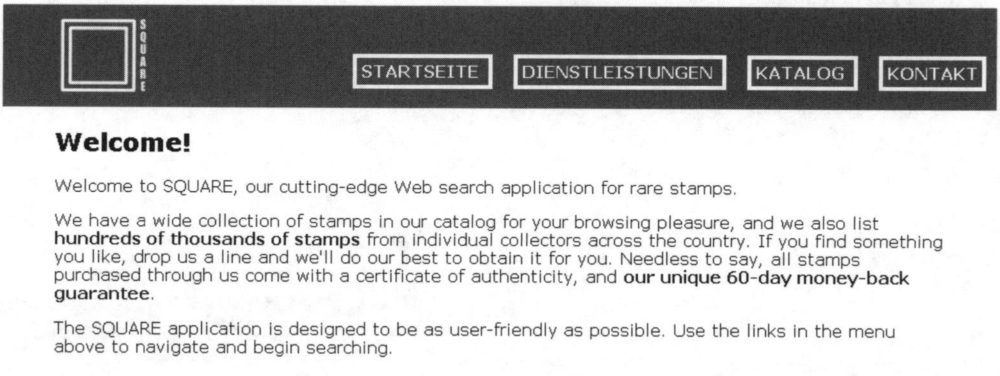

Figure 9-10 The application's index page, automatically localized to German

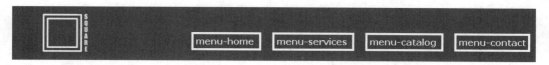

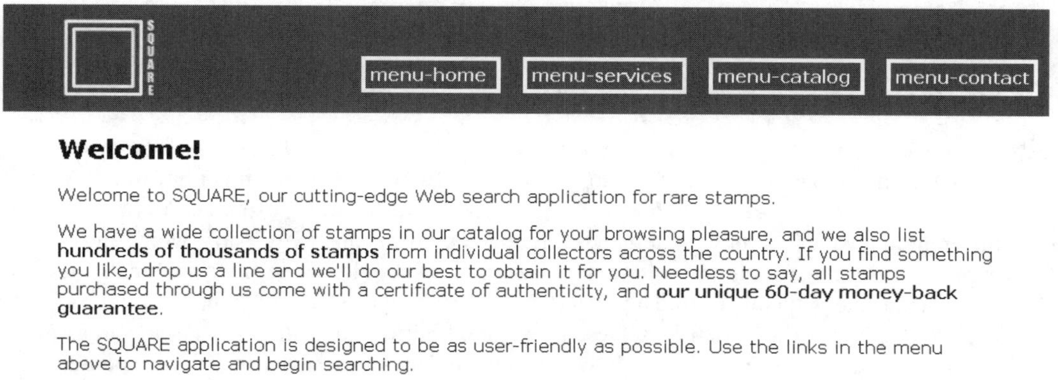

SQUARE
menu-home
menu-services
menu-catalog
menu-contact
Welcome!
Welcome to SQUARE, our cutting-edge Web search application for rare stamps.
We have a wide collection of stamps in our catalog for your browsing pleasure, and we also list hundreds of thousands of stamps from individual collectors across the country. If you find something you like, drop us a line and we'll do our best to obtain it for you. Needless to say, all stamps purchased through us come with a certificate of authenticity, and our unique 60-day money-back guarantee.
The SQUARE application is designed to be as user-friendly as possible. Use the links in the menu above to navigate and begin searching.

Figure 9-11 The application's index page, when no translation is available

NOTE

You'll notice that the static page content is still presented in US English, regardless of the locale autodetection. It isn't possible to cover this aspect of localization in the limited space available in this chapter, but you can easily handle it by creating separate static pages for each language and adjusting the static page controller to render the page corresponding to the current locale or language. This method is preferable to creating translation keys containing the content for each static page, as maintaining such large blocks of localized content can quickly become a problem.

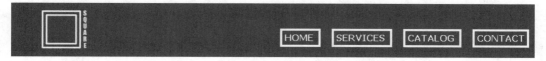

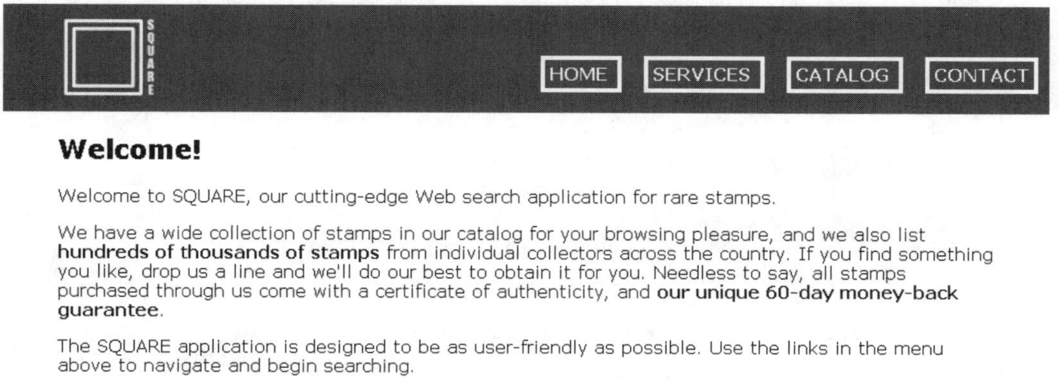

SQUARE
HOME
SERVICES
CATALOG
CONTACT
Welcome!
Welcome to SQUARE, our cutting-edge Web search application for rare stamps.
We have a wide collection of stamps in our catalog for your browsing pleasure, and we also list hundreds of thousands of stamps from individual collectors across the country. If you find something you like, drop us a line and we'll do our best to obtain it for you. Needless to say, all stamps purchased through us come with a certificate of authenticity, and our unique 60-day money-back guarantee.
The SQUARE application is designed to be as user-friendly as possible. Use the links in the menu above to navigate and begin searching.

Figure 9-12 The application's index page, manually set to UK English when no locale autodetection is possible

(continued)

Ask the Expert

Q: Should translation keys be lowercased?

A: There is no convention that requires you to only use lowercase for translation keys. Doing so would mean that you would need to wrap `translate()` calls within application views in calls to `strtoupper()` and/or `ucfirst()`, which is a tedious exercise. Additionally, different languages might well demand different capitalizations of the same word, and applying case transformations within application views would not permit this. Finally, if Zend_Translate is unable to find a translation source for the selected language, it will fall back to displaying the keys themselves. Therefore, limiting translation keys to lowercase is usually undesirable. You should, however, ensure that your translation keys are named correctly, so that they serve as a viable fallback option for Zend_Translate.

Supporting Manual Locale Selection

Now, while locale autodetection is fine and dandy, you may also want users to be able to manually select their desired language and locale. More often than not, this feature is implemented in the application user interface as a string of clickable flag icons; clicking one of these icons switches the application to the corresponding language.

To add this feature, define a new LocaleController in the application's "default" module, which will be responsible for manually setting the locale to that selected by the user, and fill it with the following code:

```php
<?php
class LocaleController extends Zend_Controller_Action
{
  // action to manually override locale
  public function indexAction()
  {
    // if supported locale, add to session

    if (Zend_Validate::is(
      $this->getRequest()->getParam('locale'), 'InArray',
        array('haystack' => array('en_US', 'en_GB', 'de_DE', 'fr_FR'))
    )) {
      $session = new Zend_Session_Namespace('square.l10n');
      $session->locale = $this->getRequest()->getParam('locale');
    }

    // redirect to requesting URL
    $url = $this->getRequest()->getServer('HTTP_REFERER');
    $this->_redirect($url);
  }
}
```

Save this file as *$APP_DIR/application/modules/default/controllers/LocaleController.php*.

When the `LocaleController::indexAction` is invoked, it first retrieves the URL of the referring script and stores this in a local variable. It then looks up the URL request for a `$_GET['locale']` parameter, checks if the requested locale is supported, and if it is, stores this locale in the session. Finally, it redirects the client back to the referring script.

This is only part of the puzzle, though. It's also necessary to now update the application bootstrapper and modify the `_initLocale()` method to first check if a locale identifier is present in the session and, if it is, to give this locale priority over the autodetected locale. Here's the revised `_initLocale()` method:

```php
<?php
class Bootstrap extends Zend_Application_Bootstrap_Bootstrap
{
  protected function _initLocale()
  {
    $session = new Zend_Session_Namespace('square.l10n');
    if ($session->locale) {
      $locale = new Zend_Locale($session->locale);
    }

    if ($locale === null) {
      try {
        $locale = new Zend_Locale('browser');
      } catch (Zend_Locale_Exception $e) {
        $locale = new Zend_Locale('en_GB');
      }
    }

    $registry = Zend_Registry::getInstance();
    $registry->set('Zend_Locale', $locale);
  }
}
```

Updating the Master Layout

The final step is to add the string of flag icons to the application's main menu, and link it to the `LocaleController::indexAction`. To do this, update the master layout, at *$APP_DIR/ application/layouts/master.phtml*, with the changes highlighted in bold:

```html
<!DOCTYPE html PUBLIC "-//W3C//DTD XHTML 1.0 Strict//EN"
"http://www.w3.org/TR/xhtml1/DTD/xhtml1-strict.dtd">
<html xmlns="http://www.w3.org/1999/xhtml" xml:lang="en" lang="en">
...
    <div id="menu-locale-container">
      <div id="locale">
        <a href="<?php echo $this->url(array('module' => 'default',
          'controller' => 'locale', 'action' => 'index',
          'locale' => 'en_GB'), 'default', true); ?>">
```

(continued)

```
            <img src="/images/locale/en_gb.gif" />
        </a>
        <a href="<?php echo $this->url(array('module' => 'default',
            'controller' => 'locale', 'action' => 'index',
            'locale' => 'en_US'), 'default', true); ?>">
            <img src="/images/locale/en_us.gif" />
        </a>
        <a href="<?php echo $this->url(array('module' => 'default',
            'controller' => 'locale', 'action' => 'index',
            'locale' => 'fr_FR'), 'default', true); ?>">
            <img src="/images/locale/fr_fr.gif" />
        </a>
        <a href="<?php echo $this->url(array('module' => 'default',
            'controller' => 'locale', 'action' => 'index',
            'locale' => 'de_DE'), 'default', true); ?>">
            <img src="/images/locale/de_de.gif" />
        </a>
    </div>
...

</html>
```

You'll notice that the master layout makes use of various images from the *$APP_DIR/ public/images/locale/* directory. You'll find these images and the corresponding stylesheet rules in the code archive for this chapter, which can be downloaded from this book's companion Web site at http://www.zf-beginners-guide.com/.

And now, when you revisit the application index page at **http://square.localhost/**, you'll see that you have the ability to manually select a language from the menu bar that appears on every page. This language selection overrides the locale that is autodetected from the browser settings, and it persists throughout your visit to the site. Figure 9-13 illustrates what the output looks like.

Figure 9-13 The application's index page, with controls for manual language selection

Summary

As this chapter demonstrates, the Zend Framework includes everything you need to fully localize your application to different languages and countries. The Zend_Locale component provides a framework for defining the application locale, either through a manual setting at design time or through a process of autodetection at run time. In either case, other Zend Framework components, such as Zend_Date, Zend_Currency, and Zend_Measure, have the ability to automatically detect this locale and adjust their behavior to reflect local conventions for dates, currencies, and measurements.

The most complex aspect of any localization project involves translating application strings to different languages, and here too, the Zend Framework offers a solution in the form of Zend_Translate. Zend_Translate provides a flexible API for working with translation sources in many different formats, and it can automatically integrate with Zend_View via the translation view helper to simplify the task of run-time string localization.

All these aspects of localization were illustrated in the SQUARE example application which, at the end of this chapter, now supports four different locales and is capable of presenting dates, numbers, and (some) content in the user's current or selected language. While a complete localization exercise is not possible within the limited confines of this book, this exercise should nevertheless give you some insight into the process, and set the foundation for future research.

To learn more about the topics discussed in this chapter, consider visiting the following links:

- The Zend_Locale component, at **http://framework.zend.com/manual/en/zend.locale.html**

- The Zend_Date component, at **http://framework.zend.com/manual/en/zend.date.html**

- Zend_Date format specifiers, at **http://framework.zend.com/manual/en/zend.date .constants.html**

- The Zend_Currency component, at **http://framework.zend.com/manual/en/zend .currency.html**

- Zend_Currency exchange rate conversion, at **http://framework.zend.com/manual/en/ zend.currency.exchange.html**

- The Zend_Measure component, at **http://framework.zend.com/manual/en/zend .measure.html**

- The Zend_Translate component, at **http://framework.zend.com/manual/en/zend .translate.html**

- Zend_Translate directory layouts for translation source files, at **http://framework.zend .com/manual/en/zend.translate.using.html**

- The GNU gettext project, at **http://www.gnu.org/software/gettext/**

- The ISO 639 standard (language codes), at **http://www.iso.org/iso/support/faqs/faqs_ widely_used_standards/widely_used_standards_other/language_codes.htm**

- The ISO 3166 standard (country codes), at **http://www.iso.org/iso/support/faqs/faqs_ widely_used_standards/widely_used_standards_other/country_name_codes.htm**

- The ISO 4217 standard (currency codes), at **http://www.iso.org/iso/support/faqs/faqs_widely_used_standards/widely_used_standards_other/currency_codes.htm**

- The PEAR Services_ExchangeRates package, at **http://pear.php.net/package/Services_ExchangeRates/**

- The gedit text editor, at **http://www.gnome.org/projects/gedit/**

- The Notepad2 text editor, at **http://www.flos-freeware.ch/notepad2.html**

- A discussion of building multilingual Web sites with the Zend Framework (Jason Gilmore), at **http://www.developer.com/design/article.php/3683571/Build-Multi-lingual-Websites-With-the-Zend-Framework.htm**

- A discussion of string localization with gettext and the Zend Framework (Peter Törnstrand), at **http://www.tornstrand.com/2008/03/29/string-localization-with-gettext-and-zend-framework/**

Chapter 10

Working with News Feeds and Web Services

Key Skills & Concepts

- Generate and read news feeds in Atom and RSS formats

- Understand the different types of Web service architecture

- Integrate search results and data from Google, Amazon, and Twitter

- Access third-party Web services using SOAP and REST

- Implement a simple REST API

If you've ever tried getting two (or more) disparate Web applications to work together harmoniously, you probably already know how difficult and frustrating the process can be. In the multiplatform, multilingual world of the Web, exchanging data between applications written in different programming languages is often the biggest stumbling block to achieving true application interoperability.

In recent years, a number of technologies and protocols have emerged that attempt to solve this problem. Web Distributed Data eXchange (WDDX), Simple Object Access Protocol (SOAP), Really Simple Syndication (RSS), Atom Syndication Format (ASF), and others provide a language- and platform-independent framework for data exchange between Web applications. Typically, this exchange occurs over HTTP, with requests and responses transferred back and forth using an XML variant. These technologies are in common use today for news feed syndication and Web service implementation.

The Zend Framework includes a number of components that can come in handy when working with Web services and news feeds. First, the Zend_Feed and Zend_Feed_Reader components make it easy to create, modify, parse, and process news feeds in RSS and Atom formats. Next, the Zend_Rest_Client component allows access to existing REST-based Web services, while the Zend_Rest_Controller component simplifies the task of implementing new REST-based Web services. And, finally, a comprehensive set of Zend_Service implementations eases integration with popular Web applications such as Twitter, Technorati, Google, and Flickr. This chapter examines all of these components in detail.

Working with News Feeds

If you've ever had your own weblog, you already know what a news feed is. It's a way for content publishers to distribute information about what's new and interesting on a particular site at any given time. This information, which is typically a list of chronologically ordered news headlines and snippets, is published as machine-readable XML that can be parsed by third-party Web sites or feed reader applications.

The Zend Framework comes with a couple of components that help in working with such news feeds. The Zend_Feed_Reader component provides an API to read and parse news feeds in the two most common formats, while the Zend_Feed component makes it possible to generate new feeds or modify existing feeds from native PHP data structures. The following sections examine these components in detail.

Understanding News Feed Formats

Typically, news feeds are published in either Really Simple Syndication (RSS) format or Atom Syndication Format (ASF or, more commonly, "Atom"). Both formats are XML-based and contain a marked-up list of resources, each of which is tagged with descriptive information such as a title, description, URL, and date. Both formats can also reference a variety of different resource types, including documents (usually blog entries or news items), images, and video and audio streams.

Like RSS feeds, Atom feeds contain summary information about the resources they describe; however, Atom feeds are slightly more complex than RSS feeds, and the Atom syndication format has also been accepted as an Internet Engineering Task Force (IETF) standard, a feat yet to be matched by the RSS format. The differences are not unintentional: The Atom syndication format was conceived in 2003 as an alternative to the RSS format, which was originally devised by Netscape Communications in early 1997. Since its introduction, the RSS format has been through multiple iterations and competing versions, and the Atom format was conceived as a fresh approach that had the advantage of not requiring backward compatibility with existing feeds.

Figure 10-1 illustrates the similarities (and differences) between the RSS and Atom feed formats.

Consuming News Feeds

The easiest way to integrate news feeds into a Zend Framework application is with the Zend_Feed_Reader component, which provides a simple, extensible framework for parsing feed and entry data. This component can handle both Atom and RSS feeds, and it supports all existing versions of both formats. This is a significant time-saver, given the numerous RSS variants currently in use. The Zend Framework manual specifies the component's design philosophy best when it states, "you should not have to care whether a feed is RSS or Atom so long as you can extract the information you want."

Consider the following example, which illustrates the process of using Zend_Feed_Reader:

```php
<?php
class Sandbox_ExampleController extends Zend_Controller_Action
{
  public function feedAction()
  {
    // import feed from URL
    $feed = Zend_Feed_Reader::import(
      'http://news.google.com/news?hl=en&topic=w&output=rss');

    // get feed-level summary elements
    $this->view->feed = array(
```

```
<rss version="2.0">                                                     RSS Example
  <channel>
    <title>Recent Posts</title>
    <link>http://www.melonfire.com</link>
    <language>en</language>
    <pubDate>Tue, 26 Jan 2010 10:47:47 GMT+00:00</pubDate>
    <item>
      <title>Building A PHP-Based Mail Client (part 1)</title>
      <link>http://www.melonfire.com/community/columns/trog/article.php?id=100</link>
      <category>PHP</category>
      <pubDate>Tue, 26 Jan 2010 09:17:54 GMT+00:00</pubDate>
      <description>Ever wondered how Web-based mail clients work? Find out here.</description>
    </item>
    <item>
      <title>Access Granted</title>
      <link>http://www.melonfire.com/community/columns/trog/article.php?id=62</link>
      <category>MySQL</category>
      <pubDate>Mon, 25 Jan 2010 16:17:54 GMT+00:00</pubDate>
      <description>Precisely control access to information with the MySQL grant tables.</description>
    </item>
  </channel>
</rss>

<feed xmlns="http://www.w3.org/2005/Atom">                 Atom Syndication Format Example
  <id>1264503315014</id>
  <title>Recent Posts</title>
  <link rel="self" type="application/atom+xml" href="http://www.melonfire.com/feed.php?format=atom"></link>
  <author>
    <name>Melonfire</name>
    <email>example@example.com</email>
  </author>
  <updated>2010-01-26T10:55:15Z</updated>
  <entry>
    <id>tag:melonfire.com,2010-01-26:/community/columns/trog/article.php#100</id>
    <title>Building A PHP-Based Mail Client (part 1)</title>
    <category>PHP</category>
    <updated>2010-01-26T09:17:54Z</updated>
    <link rel="alternate" href="http://www.melonfire.com/community/columns/trog/article.php?id=100" />
    <content>Ever wondered how Web-based mail clients work? Find out here.</content>
  </entry>
  <entry>
    <id>tag:melonfire.com,2010-01-25:/community/columns/trog/article.php#62</id>
    <title>Access Granted</title>
    <category>PHP</category>
    <updated>2010-01-25T16:17:54Z</updated>
    <link rel="alternate" href="http://www.melonfire.com/community/columns/trog/article.php?id=62" />
    <content>Precisely control access to information with the MySQL grant tables.</content>
  </entry>
</feed>
```

Figure 10-1 Example RSS and Atom feeds

```
        'title'       => $feed->getTitle(),
        'description' => $feed->getDescription(),
        'url'         => $feed->getLink(),
        'generator'   => $feed->getGenerator(),
        'numEntries'  => $feed->count()
    );

    // get first entry in feed
    $feed->rewind();
    $entry = $feed->current();
    $this->view->entries = array(
      array(
        'title'       => $entry->getTitle(),
        'description' => $entry->getDescription(),
        'body'        => $entry->getContent(),
        'url'         => $entry->getLink(),
        'date'        => $entry->getDateModified()
      )
    );
  }
}
```

As this example illustrates, the first step to consume a news feed with Zend_Feed_Reader is to import it with the `import()` method. This method accepts a URL to the feed and, depending on the feed type being imported, returns either a Zend_Feed_Reader_Feed_Rss or Zend_Feed_Reader_Feed_Atom object. This object is the primary entry point to feed and entry data, and it exposes various methods to access feed summary information, such as the `getTitle()`, `getLink()`, and `getDescription()` methods.

Entries within a feed can be accessed by iterating over the primary feed object. Individual entry objects expose similar methods to the primary feed object. In particular, pay attention to the `getTitle()`, `getDescription()`, `getLink()`, `getDateModified()`, `getDateCreated()`, and `getContent()` methods, which return the entry title, description, URL, last modification date, creation date, and entry content, respectively. These methods will suffice for most common requirements.

It's also possible to access the underlying XML representation of a feed as a DOMDocument, DOMXPath, or DOMElement object. This is useful for occasions when you need to work directly with the feed XML, and this can be accomplished with the feed object's `getDomDocument()`, `getElement()`, and `getXpath()` methods. Here's an example that illustrates this in action:

```php
<?php
class Sandbox_ExampleController extends Zend_Controller_Action
{
  public function feedAction()
  {
    // import feed from URL
```

```php
$feed = Zend_Feed_Reader::import(
    'http://news.google.com/news?hl=en&topic=w&output=rss');

    // get underlying XPath object
    $xpath = $feed->getXpath();

    // query for list of all item titles
    $titles = $xpath->query('//item/title');

    // return third item in list
    $this->view->title = $titles->item(2)->nodeValue;
    }
}
```

NOTE

It's also possible to import a news feed from a file or string, using the `Zend_Feed_Reader::importFile()` and `Zend_Feed_Reader::importString()` methods, respectively.

In addition to Zend_Feed_Reader, the Zend Framework also includes the Zend_Feed component, which provides a comprehensive API for feed generation and modification. While Zend_Feed can also be used for parsing feeds, Zend_Feed_Reader is usually a better alternative because of its simpler API and ability to autodetect the feed type. Nevertheless, an example of consuming an RSS feed with Zend_Feed is included for completeness:

```php
<?php
class Sandbox_ExampleController extends Zend_Controller_Action
{
  public function feedAction()
  {
    // import feed from URL
    $feed = Zend_Feed::import(
      'http://news.google.com/news?hl=en&topic=w&output=rss');

    // get feed-level summary elements
    $this->view->feed = array(
      'title'       => $feed->title(),
      'description' => $feed->description(),
      'url'         => $feed->link(),
      'generator'   => $feed->generator(),
      'numEntries'  => $feed->count()
    );

    // get first entry in feed
    $feed->rewind();
    $entry = $feed->current();
    $this->view->entries = array(
```

```
       array(
          'title'          => $entry->title(),
          'description' => $entry->description(),
          'url'            => $entry->link(),
          'date'           => $entry->pubDate()
       )
     );
   }
}
```

Notice that, when Zend_Feed is used, the content of individual feed-level and entry-level elements is accessed using `$object->method` syntax, where the method name corresponds to the element name. So, for example, `$feed->title()` retrieves the content of the feed `<title>` element, while `$entry->description()` retrieves the content of the entry's `<description>` element.

Creating News Feeds

So that takes care of reading existing feeds. Now, how about creating new ones?

Creating a new feed is trivial and is most easily accomplished with Zend_Feed. To do this, simply pass the `Zend_Feed::importArray` method an array representation of the feed and the output format (RSS or Atom) required, and it will produce a correctly encoded feed in the specified format, suitable for use in any standards-compliant feed reader. Here's an example, which illustrates by building an Atom feed from a database result set:

```php
<?php
class Sandbox_ExampleController extends Zend_Controller_Action
{
  public function feedAction()
  {
    // query for 10 most recent articles
    $q = Doctrine_Query::create()
          ->from('App_Model_Posts p')
          ->where('p.status = 1')
          ->orderBy('p.date desc')
          ->limit(10);
    $result = $q->fetchArray();

    // generate output array
    // set feed-level elements
    $output = array(
      'title'   => 'Newest posts on melonfire.com/trog',
      'link'    => 'http://www.melonfire.com/community/columns/trog/',
      'author'  => 'Melonfire Feed Generator/1.0',
      'charset' => 'UTF-8',
      'entries' => array()
    );
```

```
      // iterate over result set
      // set entry-level elements as nested array
      foreach ($result as $r) {
        $entry = array(
            'title' => $r['title'],
            'link'  => 'http://www.melonfire.com/community/columns/trog/'.
                       $r['id'],
            'description' => $r['abstract'],
            'lastUpdate' => strtotime($r['date']),
        );
        $output['entries'][] = $entry;
      }

      // import array into Zend_Feed and convert to Atom feed
      $feed = Zend_Feed::importArray($output, 'atom');

      // disable layout and view rendering
      $this->_helper->layout->disableLayout();
      $this->getHelper('viewRenderer')->setNoRender(true);

      // send feed to client
      $feed->send();
      exit();
    }
}
```

TIP

The Zend_Feed send() method will set its own headers, so if this is not what you want, or if you want to set your own custom headers, consider setting the headers manually with header() and then using the saveXml() method to send the feed XML to the requesting client.

The previous listing first builds a nested array containing feed and entry content, and then passes this array to the Zend_Feed::importArray method for conversion into an Atom feed. The return value of this method is a Zend_Feed_Atom object, which exposes two very useful methods, send() and saveXml(). The send() method sends the feed to a client with the correct HTTP headers, while the saveXml() method returns an XML representation of the feed for further processing.

Figure 10-2 displays an example of the Atom feed produced by the previous example.

NOTE

Newer versions of the Zend Framework also include a Zend_Feed_Writer component, which provides an alternative API for creating and modifying feeds.

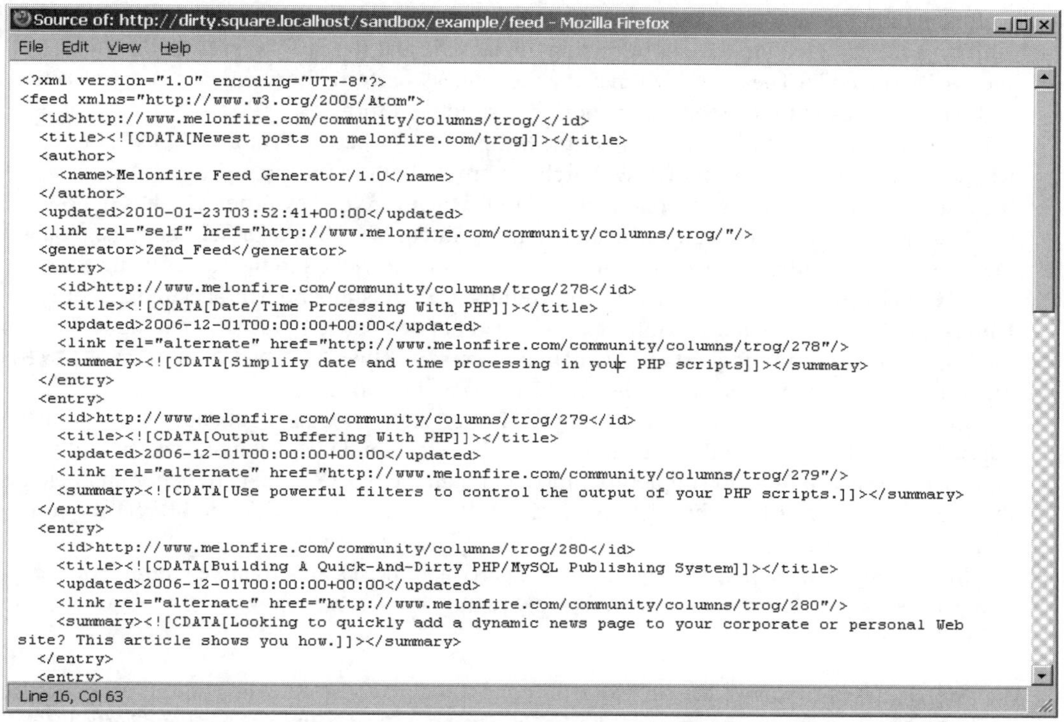

Figure 10-2   A dynamically generated Atom feed

Accessing Web Services

In recent years, it's become almost *de rigueur* for consumer-facing Web applications to expose some or all of their functions and/or data for third-party use through Web services. Google, Facebook, Twitter, Technorati, and Flickr are just some of the many hundreds of thousands of Web applications that today allow such access to their innards. As an application developer, it's quite likely that you'll find yourself either integrating these Web services into your application, or creating your own Web services for others to access and consume.

The Zend Framework comes with implementations for many common Web services (including all the ones mentioned in the previous paragraph, and a few more besides). It also offers generic SOAP and REST clients for accessing SOAP- and REST-based Web services. The following sections examine these components in greater detail.

Understanding Web Services

Think of a Web service as a "remote API," which allows a client to request an action or perform a query on a remote server. The nature of the request can vary; common examples include looking up and returning a database record that matches a particular identifier, verifying a credit card number, or retrieving the latitude and longitude corresponding to a specific postal code. The server will receive the request, perform the necessary query or action, and return the result to the requesting client in a structured format.

Web services may be based on either the Simple Object Access Protocol (SOAP) or Representational State Transfer (REST) architecture. In both cases, clients transmit service requests and receive service responses over HTTP. However, the key difference lies in how these requests and responses are encoded and transmitted. With SOAP-based services, request messages are typically encoded in XML envelopes and transmitted to the server using the HTTP POST method, and responses are transmitted back in similar XML packaging. With REST-based services, requests, and responses need not be encoded in XML, and the HTTP method used to transmit requests from client to server (whether GET, POST, PUT, or DELETE) plays an active role in determining the server action and response.

Because the REST model uses existing HTTP verbs, such as GET (get data), POST (create data), PUT (update data), and DELETE (remove data) to communicate intent, it is generally considered easier to use and simpler to implement than the SOAP model. To better appreciate this, consider Figure 10-3, which illustrates the difference between SOAP and REST request and response packets.

In case you're ever asked the question at a party and there's an attractive member of the opposite sex within earshot, here are a few key points of difference between the SOAP and REST approaches:

● SOAP makes extensive use of XML for request and response encoding, and it uses strong data typing to ensure the integrity of the data being passed between client and server. REST requests and responses, on the other hand, can be transmitted in ASCII, XML, JSON, or any other format that is understandable by both client and server. Additionally, the REST model also has no built-in data typing requirements. As a result, REST request and response packets are typically much smaller than the corresponding SOAP packets.

● Under the SOAP model, the HTTP transport layer is mostly a passive spectator, with its role limited to the transmission of SOAP requests from client to server using the POST method. The details of the service request, such as the remote procedure name and input arguments, are encoded within the request body. REST architecture, on the other hand, treats the HTTP transport layer as an active participant in the transaction, making use of existing HTTP method "verbs" such as GET, POST, PUT, and DELETE to indicate the type of service required. From a development perspective, therefore, REST requests are generally easier to formulate and understand, as they piggyback on existing, well-understood HTTP interfaces.

● The SOAP model supports some degree of introspection, by allowing service developers to describe the service API in a Web Service Description Language (WSDL) file. These files are reasonably complex to create; however, the effort is often worth it, because SOAP clients can then automatically obtain detailed information on method names and signatures, input and output data types, and return values through this WSDL file. The

```
<?xml version="1.0" encoding="UTF-8"?>
<SOAP-ENV:Envelope                                                    Example SOAP Request and Response
 xmlns:SOAP-ENV="http://schemas.xmlsoap.org/soap/envelope/"
 xmlns:ns1="http://rpc.geocoder.us/Geo/Coder/US/"
 xmlns:xsd="http://www.w3.org/2001/XMLSchema"
 xmlns:xsi="http://www.w3.org/2001/XMLSchema-instance"
 xmlns:SOAP-ENC="http://schemas.xmlsoap.org/soap/encoding/"
 SOAP-ENV:encodingStyle="http://schemas.xmlsoap.org/soap/encoding/">
 <SOAP-ENV:Body>
  <ns1:geocode>
   <location xsi:type="xsd:string">1600 Pennsylvania Av, Washington, DC</location>
  </ns1:geocode>
 </SOAP-ENV:Body>
</SOAP-ENV:Envelope>

<?xml version="1.0" encoding="UTF-8"?>
<soap:Envelope
 xmlns:xsi="http://www.w3.org/2001/XMLSchema-instance"
 xmlns:soapenc="http://schemas.xmlsoap.org/soap/encoding/"
 xmlns:xsd="http://www.w3.org/2001/XMLSchema"
 soap:encodingStyle="http://schemas.xmlsoap.org/soap/encoding/"
 xmlns:soap="http://schemas.xmlsoap.org/soap/envelope/">
 <soap:Body>
  <geocodeResponse xmlns="http://rpc.geocoder.us/Geo/Coder/US/">
   <geo:results soapenc:arrayType="geo:GeocoderAddressResult[1]"
    xsi:type="soapenc:Array"
    xmlns:geo="http://rpc.geocoder.us/Geo/Coder/US/">
    <geo:item xsi:type="geo:GeocoderAddressResult" xmlns:geo="http://rpc.geocoder.us/Geo/Coder/US/">
     <geo:number xsi:type="xsd:int">1600</geo:number>
     <geo:lat xsi:type="xsd:float">38.898748</geo:lat>
     <geo:street xsi:type="xsd:string">Pennsylvania</geo:street>
     <geo:state xsi:type="xsd:string">DC</geo:state>
     <geo:city xsi:type="xsd:string">Washington</geo:city>
     <geo:zip xsi:type="xsd:int">20502</geo:zip>
     <geo:suffix xsi:type="xsd:string">NW</geo:suffix>
     <geo:long xsi:type="xsd:float">-77.037684</geo:long>
     <geo:type xsi:type="xsd:string">Ave</geo:type>
     <geo:prefix xsi:type="xsd:string" />
    </geo:item>
   </geo:results>
  </geocodeResponse>
 </soap:Body>
</soap:Envelope>

                                                                      Example REST Request and Response
GET http://geocoder.us/service/rest/geocode?
    address=1600+Pennsylvania+Ave,+Washington+DC

<?xml version="1.0"?>
<rdf:RDF
 xmlns:dc="http://purl.org/dc/elements/1.1/"
 xmlns:geo="http://www.w3.org/2003/01/geo/wgs84_pos#"
 xmlns:rdf="http://www.w3.org/1999/02/22-rdf-syntax-ns#">
 <geo:Point rdf:nodeID="aid47091944">
  <dc:description>1600 Pennsylvania Ave NW, Washington DC 20502</dc:description>
  <geo:long>-77.037684</geo:long>
  <geo:lat>38.898748</geo:lat>
 </geo:Point>
</rdf:RDF>
```

Figure 10-3   Example SOAP and REST transactions

REST model, on the other hand, eschews WSDL-level complexity in favor of a simpler, more intuitive interface based on standard HTTP methods, as described earlier.

● REST revolves around the concept of *resources*, while SOAP uses interfaces based on *objects* and *methods*. A SOAP interface can have a potentially unlimited number of methods; however, a REST interface is limited to four possible operations, corresponding to the four HTTP "verbs."

Consuming Web Services

The Zend Framework includes generic clients for REST- and SOAP-based Web services, as well as a number of service-specific client implementations that can be used to directly communicate with popular Web services. The following sections examine these aspects in greater detail.

Using Service-Specific Client Implementations

The Zend Framework includes a number of preconfigured clients for popular Web services, such as those exposed by Google, Amazon, Flickr, Technorati, and others. Using these service-specific client implementations can reduce the time and effort involved in integrating data from these services into a Web application. In most cases, these implementations provide an object-oriented API, with service responses returned as native PHP objects or arrays.

Table 10-1 lists the service-specific implementations currently included in the Zend Framework.

While a complete description of each of these implementations is not possible within the limited confines of this chapter, a few examples will be illustrative. Consider the following

Ask the Expert

Q: If I'm building a Web service, which should I use: SOAP or REST?

A: As with all questions of this sort, the answer really depends on your requirements and goals. For transactional or e-commerce services, or in situations where the service is part of a larger, distributed platform, SOAP's strict data typing and formal service description often make it a better choice than REST. On the other hand, if your goal is simply to enable quick-and-dirty access to your application's innards, with ease of use and format flexibility as the key factors in your choice, then REST is probably a better option. That said, it's worth noting that the REST approach is gradually overtaking the SOAP approach in popularity, both because it cleverly leverages existing technologies and because it is significantly simpler to use and understand.

Client Class	Description
Zend_Service_Akismet	A client for the Akismet spam-blocking application
Zend_Service_Amazon	A client for the Amazon Web Services API, with specific implementations for Amazon EC2, Amazon SQS, and Amazon S3
Zend_Service_AudioScrobbler	A client for the Last.fm music search engine
Zend_Service_Delicious	A client for the del.icio.us social bookmarking application
Zend_Service_Flickr	A client for the Flickr photo-sharing application
Zend_Service_Nirvanix	A client for the Nirvanix data storage application
Zend_Service_ReCaptcha	A client for the ReCaptcha CAPTCHA generator
Zend_Service_Simpy	A client for the Simpy social bookmarking application
Zend_Service_SlideShare	A client for the SlideShare presentation-sharing application
Zend_Service_StrikeIron	A client for the StrikeIron commercial database aggregator
Zend_Service_Technorati	A client for the Technorati weblog search engine
Zend_Service_Twitter	A client for the Twitter micro-blogging service
Zend_Service_Yahoo	A client for the Yahoo! Search APIs
Zend_Gdata	A client for the Google Data APIs, with specific implementations for Google applications such as Notebook, Calendar, YouTube, Base, Spreadsheets, and Documents

Table 10-1   Web Service Client Implementations Included with the Zend Framework

listing, which uses the Zend_Service_Delicious component to retrieve a list of the user's tags and bookmarks on the del.icio.us service:

```php
<?php
class Sandbox_ExampleController extends Zend_Controller_Action
{
  public function deliciousAction()
  {
    // initialize service object
    $client = new Zend_Service_Delicious('username', 'password');

    // get all tags created by user with frequency
    $this->view->tags = $client->getTags();

    // get all posts tagged with PHP
    $this->view->posts = $client->getPosts('php');
  }
}
```

Here's another example, this one using the Zend_Gdata component to query the YouTube service for a list of the five most popular videos at the current time:

```php
<?php
class Sandbox_ExampleController extends Zend_Controller_Action
{
  public function youtubeAction()
  {
    // initialize service object
    $client = new Zend_Gdata_YouTube();

    // get feed of five most popular videos
    $feed = $client->getVideoFeed(
      'http://gdata.youtube.com/feeds/api/standardfeeds/most_popular?
      max-results=5');

    // process feed and get individual entries
    // for each entry, get title, category, rating, view count and url
    $this->view->mostViewed = array();
    foreach ($feed as $entry) {
      $this->view->mostViewed[] = array(
        'title'    => $entry->getVideoTitle(),
        'rating'   => $entry->getVideoRatingInfo(),
        'category' => $entry->getVideoCategory(),
        'views'    => $entry->getVideoViewCount(),
        'watch'    => $entry->getVideoWatchPageUrl()
      );
    }
  }
}
```

In this example, the `getVideoFeed()` method returns an Atom feed of YouTube video results; this feed is automatically parsed and converted into an array of Zend_Gdata_YouTube_VideoEntry objects, each representing one entry in the feed. It's now a simple matter to iterate over this array, retrieve the details of each entry using object properties, and represent it as a Web page.

And finally, here's an example of using the Zend_Service_Amazon implementation to search Amazon.com for books by a particular author:

```php
<?php
class Sandbox_ExampleController extends Zend_Controller_Action
{
  public function amazonAction()
  {
    // initialize service object
    $client = new Zend_Service_Amazon('ACCESS-KEY', 'US', 'SECRET-KEY');
```

```
    // search for items on Amazon.com by attributes
    $items = $client->itemSearch(array(
        'SearchIndex'   => 'Books',
        'Author'        => 'Dan Brown',
        'ResponseGroup' => 'Large'
    ));

    // process search results
    $this->view->results = array();
    foreach ($items as $i) {
      $this->view->results[] = array (
        'asin' => $i->ASIN,
        'title' => $i->Title,
        'author' => $i->Author,
        'url' => $i->DetailPageURL,
        'rating' => $i->AverageRating,
        'salesRank' => $i->SalesRank,
      );
    }
  }
}
```

Here, the service object's `itemSearch()` method queries the Amazon Web service for a list of products matching the specified parameters, and returns an array of Zend_Service_Amazon_Item objects, each containing information on the corresponding item. It's quite easy to iterate over this array of objects, extracting the relevant information for display.

Using Generic Client Implementations

If you're trying to access a Web service for which no predefined service implementation exists, don't lose heart: The Zend Framework also includes generic SOAP and REST clients for accessing such services. These clients are implemented in the Zend_Soap_Client and Zend_Rest_Client components, respectively.

To illustrate these in action, consider the following example, which uses the generic SOAP client to access the GeoCoder Web service and return the latitude and longitude corresponding to a particular address:

```php
<?php
class Sandbox_ExampleController extends Zend_Controller_Action
{
  public function soapAction()
  {
    // initialize SOAP client
    $soap = new Zend_Soap_Client(
      'http://geocoder.us/dist/eg/clients/GeoCoderPHP.wsdl', array(
      'soap_version' => SOAP_1_1,
      'compression' => SOAP_COMPRESSION_ACCEPT,
    ));
```

```
    // get latitude/longitude results for address
    $response = $soap->geocode('E Capitol St NE & 1st St NE, Washington,
DC');
    $this->view->results = array();
    foreach ($response as $r) {
      $this->view->results[] = array(
        'zip' => $r->zip,
        'latitude' => $r->lat,
        'longitude' => $r->long
      );
    }

    // get SOAP request and response for debugging
    $this->view->request = $soap->getLastRequest();
    $this->view->response = $soap->getLastResponse();
  }
}
```

This example creates a new Zend_Soap_Client object and instantiates it with the URL
to the Web service's WSDL file. As discussed earlier, the WSDL file allows the client to
automatically obtain information on available methods, expected data types, and content of
input and output arguments. The second argument to the object constructor is an array of
configuration options, which can be used to define various aspects of client behavior.

NOTE

It's also possible to use Zend_Soap_Client in non-WSDL mode by omitting the WSDL
URL and directly specifying the SOAP service URL (*endpoint*) as an argument in the
options array.

Once the Zend_Soap_Client object has been instantiated, remote service methods can
be accessed "by proxy," by calling the corresponding object method. The Zend_Soap_Client
object will automatically take care of creating the SOAP message packet, transmitting it to the
server via POST, receiving a response packet, and decoding the response packet into a native
PHP Zend_Soap_Client_Response object. This is visible in the previous example, which
invokes the service's geocode() method, passes it an address string (actually, the address of
the U.S. Capitol in Washington, D.C.), and retrieves the postal code, latitude, and longitude
from the response.

CAUTION

The Zend_Soap_Client component makes use of PHP's ext/soap extension and will not
function if your PHP environment does not include this extension.

In a similar vein, it's possible to use the Zend_Rest_Client implementation to access
REST-based Web services in a generic and consistent manner. Consider this next
example, which illustrates by attempting to access the GeoNames REST service for
country information:

```php
<?php
class Sandbox_ExampleController extends Zend_Controller_Action
{
  public function restAction()
  {
    // initialize REST client
    $client = new Zend_Rest_Client('http://ws.geonames.org/countryInfo');

    // set arguments
    $client->country('IN');

    // make GET request for country information
    // parse results
    $result = $client->get();
    $this->view->countryName = $result->countryName();
    $this->view->countryCode = $result->countryCode();
    $this->view->capital = $result->capital();
    $this->view->areaKM = $result->areaInSqKm();
    $this->view->population = $result->population();
    $this->view->languages = $result->languages();
    $this->view->mapCoordinates = array(
      $result->bBoxWest(),
      $result->bBoxEast(),
      $result->bBoxNorth(),
      $result->bBoxSouth()
    );

    // get REST request and response for debugging
    $this->view->request = $client->getLastRequest();
    $this->view->response = $client->getLastResponse();
  }
}
```

As before, the first step is to initialize the REST client by creating an instance of the Zend_Rest_Client object and passing the object constructor the URL to the REST service. Arguments are specified using a fluent interface that proxies argument names to object methods, and actual request transmission is performed using the get(), post(), put(), or delete() method, which is internally translated to the corresponding HTTP method. This is clearly visible in the previous listing, which formulates a GET request for the GeoNames country information service, passing it the country code for India as an argument: **http://ws.geonames.org/countryInfo?country=IN**.

The response to a Zend_Rest_Client request is presented as an instance of the Zend_Rest_Client_Response object, and is typically represented as a SimpleXML object or array of objects. Individual elements of the response can be accessed either by using SimpleXML notation, or by directly accessing the element name as a method. Under the latter method, an XPath query will be used to return all matching elements, regardless of their hierarchical position in the XML document tree.

As these two examples illustrate, the Zend Framework makes it easy to access any SOAP- or REST-based Web service, even if a service-specific implementation does not already exist and without requiring extensive knowledge of service internals. This makes it a valuable tool for rapid and efficient integration of third-party Web services into a PHP application.

TIP

Notice the getLastRequest() and getLastResponse() methods in the previous two listings. These methods come in very handy for debugging SOAP and REST transactions, and for verifying the contents of request and response packets.

Try This 10-1 Integrating Twitter and Blog Search Results

With all this background information at hand, let's see how it plays out in the real world. The following sections will illustrate how the components discussed in preceding sections can be combined to display recent news, blog posts, and Twitter updates related to the subject of philately within the SQUARE example application.

Defining Custom Routes

The first step is, as always, to define a custom route for the news page. Edit the application configuration file, at *$APP_DIR/application/configs/application.ini*, and add the following route definition to it:

```
resources.router.routes.news.route = /news
resources.router.routes.news.defaults.module = default
resources.router.routes.news.defaults.controller = news
resources.router.routes.news.defaults.action = index
```

Defining the Controller and View

The next step is to define the action and view for the news interface. Here's the code for the NewsController, which should be saved as *$APP_DIR/application/modules/default/ controllers/NewsController.php*:

```php
<?php
class NewsController extends Zend_Controller_Action
{
  public function indexAction()
  {
    // get Twitter search feed
    $q = 'philately';
    $this->view->q = $q;
    $twitter = new Zend_Service_Twitter_Search();
    $this->view->tweets = $twitter->search($q,
      array('lang' => 'en', 'rpp' => 8, 'show_user' => true));
```

```
    // get Google News Atom feed
    $this->view->feeds = array();
    $gnewsFeed = "http://news.google.com/news?hl=en&q=$q&output=atom";
    $this->view->feeds[0] = Zend_Feed_Reader::import($gnewsFeed);

    // get BPMA RSS feed
    $bpmaFeed = "http://www.postalheritage.org.uk/news/RSS";
    $this->view->feeds[1] = Zend_Feed_Reader::import($bpmaFeed);
  }
}
```

The indexAction() method is responsible for accessing and importing various news feeds and Web service feeds.

● The Zend_Service_Twitter implementation makes it possible to perform a Twitter search for recent status updates containing the word 'philately'. The object's search() method accepts a query term, and an options array that specifies the language filter, the number of results to return, and whether or not each result entry should include the source user's Twitter username. The return value of this method is a nested array of results matching the search term, and this is then attached to the view for further processing.

● The Zend_Feed_Reader implementation is used to import two news feeds. The first is an Atom feed containing the latest news headlines related to 'philately' from Google News, and the second is a list of recent posts from the official British Postal Museum and Archive (BPMA) blog. The resulting feed objects are then assigned as view script variables.

Here's the corresponding view script, which should be saved as *$APP_DIR/application/ modules/default/views/scripts/news/index.phtml*:

```
<h2>News</h2>
<div id="newsfeeds">

  <div id="posts">
  <strong>Recent news about
    <a href="http://news.google.com/news?hl=en&q=<?php echo $this->q; ?>">
      '<?php echo $this->q; ?>'
    </a>:
  </strong>
  <p id="hdiv"></p>
  <?php $count = 0; ?>
  <?php foreach ($this->feeds[0] as $entry):?>
    <?php if ($count >= 5) break; ?>
    <p class="post">
    <span class="text">
```

(continued)

```php
          <a href="<?php echo $entry->getLink(); ?>">
            <?php echo $entry->getTitle(); ?>
          </a>
        </span>
        <span class="time">
          <?php echo $entry->getDateModified(); ?>
        </span>
        </p>
        <?php $count++; ?>
    <?php endforeach; ?>

    <p style="padding-top: 4px"/>

    <strong>Recent posts from
      <a href="http://www.postalheritage.org.uk/">
        the British Postal Museum and Archive
      </a> blog:
    </strong>
    <p id="hdiv"></p>
    <?php $count = 0; ?>
    <?php foreach ($this->feeds[1] as $entry):?>
      <?php if ($count >= 5) break; ?>
      <p class="post">
      <span class="text">
        <a href="<?php echo $entry->getLink(); ?>">
          <?php echo $entry->getTitle(); ?>
        </a>
      </span>
      <span class="time">
        <?php echo $entry->getDateModified(); ?>
      </span>
      </p>
      <?php $count++; ?>
    <?php endforeach; ?>
    </div>

    <div id="tweets">
    <strong>Recent tweets about
      <a href="http://search.twitter.com/search?q=<?php echo $this->q; ?>">
        '<?php echo $this->q; ?>'
      </a>:
    </strong>
    <?php foreach ($this->tweets['results'] as $tweet):?>
      <p class="tweet">
      <span class="image">
        <img src="<?php echo $tweet['profile_image_url']; ?>" />
      </span>
      <span class="user">
        <?php echo $tweet['from_user'] . ': '; ?>
      </span>
      <span class="text">
```

```
    <?php echo $tweet['text']; ?>
  </span>
  <span class="time">
    <?php echo $tweet['created_at']; ?>
  </span>
  </p>
<?php endforeach; ?>
</div>

</div>
```

Nothing very complicated here. The view script merely iterates over the result objects assigned in the controller, extracting the necessary information from each and displaying it in a neatly formatted two-column layout.

Updating the Master Layout

All that's left is to update the master layout at *$APP_DIR/application/layouts/master.phtml* to display a link to the news page in the main menu. The revision to the layout is highlighted in bold in the following listing:

```
<!DOCTYPE html PUBLIC "-//W3C//DTD XHTML 1.0 Strict//EN"
"http://www.w3.org/TR/xhtml1/DTD/xhtml1-strict.dtd">
<html xmlns="http://www.w3.org/1999/xhtml" xml:lang="en" lang="en">

    <div id="menu-locale-container">
      <div id="menu">
        . . .

        <a href="<?php echo $this->url(array(), 'news'); ?>">
          <?php echo $this->translate('menu-news'); ?>
        </a>

      . . .         </div>
    </div>
. . .
</html>
```

NOTE
Remember that you'll need to add translation strings for the new menu item to the translation source files for each supported language, as discussed in Chapter 9. The code archive for this chapter, which can be downloaded from **http://www.zf-beginners-guide.com/**, has the necessary additions.

To see this in action, visit the URL **http://square.localhost/news** in your browser, and you should see something like Figure 10-4.

(continued)

Figure 10-4 Dynamically retrieving and integrating blog, news, and Twitter search results

Creating REST-Based Web Services

In addition to providing a comprehensive set of tools for accessing and integrating news feeds and Web services into a PHP application, the Zend Framework also makes it easy to expose application functionality by building your own REST-based Web services. This is usually accomplished through the Zend_Rest_Route and Zend_Rest_Controller components, discussed in the following section.

Understanding REST Routes

There are two key principles of REST-based architecture:

● An application is made up of multiple resources, each of which can be accessed with a unique URL.

● The method used to access a resource determines the action that is to be taken on that resource.

Request URL	Request Method	Description	Example
/api/items	GET	Get all items	GET /api/items
/api/items	POST	Add new item	POST /api/items
/api/items/:id	GET	Get item record	GET /api/items/25
/api/items/:id	PUT	Update item record	PUT /api/items/15
/api/items/:id	DELETE	Delete item record	DELETE /api/items/13

Table 10-2 Standard REST Routes

Table 10-2 illustrates the typical URL routes for a REST-based service.

It should be clear from Table 10-2 that, under the REST model, existing HTTP verbs, such as GET (get data), POST (create data), PUT (update data), and DELETE (remove data), indicate the action to be taken on the specified resource. Where required, a unique resource identifier is included with the request URL. Any additional arguments, particularly when creating new resources or updating existing ones, are passed within the body of the POST or PUT request.

The Zend Framework includes a Zend_Rest_Route component that can automatically enable these standard REST routes for the entire application, for a specific module, or for a specific controller. When matching URL requests, this component will automatically identify the request method, examine request arguments, and invoke one of the corresponding standard actions: indexAction(), getAction(), postAction(), putAction(), and deleteAction().

These five standard actions are defined as abstract methods of the Zend_Rest_Controller class. This controller, which itself extends the Zend_Controller_Action class, serves as the base for all REST-based controllers in the Zend Framework. Here's a controller skeleton that illustrates this more clearly:

```php
<?php
class Sandbox_RestController extends Zend_Rest_Controller
{
  public function indexAction()
  {
    // handle GET requests
  }

  public function getAction()
  {
    // handle GET requests
  }

  public function postAction()
  {
    // handle POST requests
  }
```

```
public function putAction()
{
  // handle PUT requests
}

public function deleteAction()
{
  // handle DELETE requests
}
}
```

Try This 10-2 Implementing REST-Based Web Services

From the preceding section, it should be clear that adopting REST architecture for an application, particularly with reference to the standard CRUD operations, involves two essential components:

1. A controller that extends Zend_Rest_Controller and implements actions corresponding to the standard HTTP methods;

2. A route that uses Zend_Rest_Route to match incoming URL requests with the aforementioned controller actions.

The best way to understand how this works is with an example. The following sections illustrate this by building a simple REST-based API for the SQUARE example application. This API will support GET and POST methods, and it will allow users to retrieve information on existing catalog items as well as post new items.

Creating a New Module

The first step is to create a new module—we'll call it "api"—to house the REST controller. To do this, change to *$APP_DIR/application/* and execute the following commands:

```
shell> mkdir modules/api
shell> mkdir modules/api/controllers
shell> mkdir modules/api/views
shell> mkdir modules/api/views/scripts
```

Defining the Controller

The next step is to define the API controller, which will handle all REST requests. As discussed previously, this controller should extend the abstract Zend_Rest_Controller, and implement all its abstract methods. Here's what it looks like:

```php
<?php
class Api_CatalogController extends Zend_Rest_Controller
{
  // disable layouts and rendering
  public function init()
  {
    $this->apiBaseUrl = 'http://square.localhost/api/catalog';
    $this->_helper->layout->disableLayout();
    $this->getHelper('viewRenderer')->setNoRender(true);
  }

  public function indexAction()
  {
    // handle GET requests
  }

  public function getAction()
  {
    // handle GET requests
  }

  public function postAction()
  {
    // handle POST requests
  }

  public function putAction()
  {
    // handle PUT requests
  }

  public function deleteAction()
  {
    // handle DELETE requests
  }
}
```

Notice the controller's init() method, which disables all layouts and view script rendering. This is because a REST API will typically return responses in XML, JSON, or (in some cases) ASCII text. This output can be generated from within the controller itself and sent directly to the requesting client.

Save this controller as *$APP_DIR/application/modules/api/controllers/CatalogController .php*.

(continued)

Defining the GET Actions

Next, let's define the `Api_CatalogController::indexAction`. You'll remember that this action is automatically dispatched when the router encounters a GET request without the "id" request variable, and it should return a list of all matching resources. Here's the code:

```php
<?php
class Api_CatalogController extends Zend_Rest_Controller
{
  public function indexAction()
  {
    // get records from database
    $q = Doctrine_Query::create()
         ->from('Square_Model_Item i')
         ->leftJoin('i.Square_Model_Country c')
         ->leftJoin('i.Square_Model_Grade g')
         ->leftJoin('i.Square_Model_Type t')
         ->addWhere('i.DisplayStatus = 1');
    $result = $q->fetchArray();

    // set feed elements
    $output = array(
      'title'   => 'Catalog records',
      'link'    => $this->apiBaseUrl,
      'author'  => 'Square API/1.0',
      'charset' => 'UTF-8',
      'entries' => array()
    );

    // set entry elements
    foreach ($result as $r) {
      $output['entries'][] = array(
        'title' => $r['Title'] . ' - ' . $r['Year'],
        'link'  => $this->apiBaseUrl . '/' . $r['RecordID'],
        'description' => $r['Description'],
        'lastUpdate' => strtotime($r['RecordDate']),
        'square:title' => $r['Title']
      );
    }

    // import array into atom feed
    // send to client
    $feed = Zend_Feed::importArray($output, 'atom');
    $feed->send();
    exit;
  }
}
```

```
// forward to indexAction
public function listAction() {
  return $this->_forward('index');
}
}
```

The `Api_CatalogController::indexAction` begins by executing a Doctrine query to obtain a list of all active catalog items. It then iterates over the result set, converting it into a nested array suitable for conversion into an Atom feed with `Zend_Feed::importArray`. This Atom feed is then returned to the client using the feed object's `send()` method.

CAUTION

The Zend Framework v1.9.2 and earlier included a bug that resulted in the router attempting to delegate REST requests for the `indexAction()` to a `listAction()` instead. The previous listing illustrates a simple workaround for this bug: Simply forward `listAction()` requests, if any, to the `indexAction()` using the `_forward()` controller method.

The `Api_CatalogController::getAction` is automatically dispatched when the router encounters a GET request with the "id" request variable, indicating a request for a particular resource. In this case, the action must retrieve the specified catalog record from the database and return detailed information about it to the requesting client. Here's the code:

```
<?php
class Api_CatalogController extends Zend_Rest_Controller
{
  public function getAction()
  {
    // get entry record from database
    $id = $this->_getParam('id');
    $q = Doctrine_Query::create()
          ->from('Square_Model_Item i')
          ->leftJoin('i.Square_Model_Country c')
          ->leftJoin('i.Square_Model_Grade g')
          ->leftJoin('i.Square_Model_Type t')
          ->where('i.RecordID = ?', $id)
          ->addWhere('i.DisplayStatus = 1');
    $result = $q->fetchArray();

    // if record available
    // set entry elements
    if (count($result) == 1) {
      // set feed elements
      $output = array(
        'title'  => 'Catalog record for item ID: ' . $id,
        'link'   => $this->apiBaseUrl . '/' . $id,
        'author' => 'Square App/1.0',
```

(continued)

```
      'charset' => 'UTF-8',
      'entries' => array()
    );

    $output['entries'][0] = array(
      'title' => $result[0]['Title'] . ' - ' . $result[0]['Year'],
      'link'  => $this->apiBaseUrl . '/' . $id,
      'description' => $result[0]['Description'],
      'lastUpdate' => strtotime($result[0]['RecordDate'])
    );

    // import array into atom feed
    $feed = Zend_Feed::importArray($output, 'atom');
    Zend_Feed::registerNamespace('square', 'http://square.localhost');

    // set custom namespaced elements
    $feed->rewind();
    $entry = $feed->current();
    if ($entry) {
      $entry->{'square:id'} = $result[0]['RecordID'];
      $entry->{'square:title'} = $result[0]['Title'];
      $entry->{'square:year'} = $result[0]['Year'];
      $entry->{'square:grade'} =
        $result[0]['Square_Model_Grade']['GradeName'];
      $entry->{'square:description'} = $result[0]['Description'];
      $entry->{'square:country'} =
        $result[0]['Square_Model_Country']['CountryName'];
      $entry->{'square:price'} = null;
      $entry->{'square:price'}->{'square:min'}= $result[0]['SalePriceMin'];
      $entry->{'square:price'}->{'square:max'} = $result[0]['SalePriceMax'];
    }

    // output to client
    $feed->send();
    exit;
  } else {
    $this->getResponse()->setHttpResponseCode(404);
    echo 'Invalid record identifier';
    exit;
  }
  }
}
```

This is very similar to the previous listing, except that in this case, the Atom feed contains additional elements (in a custom namespace) that hold details on the item type, grade, price, location, and description. Notice that, if the supplied resource ID cannot be matched to a record in the database, the feed creation process is skipped and the client is directly sent a 404 (page not found) error. This is an example of how REST architecture cleverly leverages existing standards—in this case, HTTP server error codes—to provide information on the status of a request.

Defining the POST Action

The `Api_CatalogController::postAction` is automatically dispatched when the router encounters a POST request. As per REST conventions, such a request should result in the creation of a new resource, with the body of the POST request containing the raw data required for resource creation. Here's the code:

```php
<?php
class Api_CatalogController extends Zend_Rest_Controller
{
  public function postAction()
  {
    // read POST parameters and save to database
    $item = new Square_Model_Item;
    $item->fromArray($this->getRequest()->getPost());
    $item->RecordDate = date('Y-m-d', mktime());
    $item->DisplayStatus = 0;
    $item->DisplayUntil = null;
    $item->save();
    $id = $item->RecordID;

    // set response code to 201
    // send ID of newly-created record
    $this->getResponse()->setHttpResponseCode(201);
    $this->getResponse()->setHeader('Location', $this->apiBaseUrl.'/'.$id);
    echo $this->apiBaseUrl.'/'.$id;
    exit;
  }
}
```

Notice that once the resource record has been created and saved to the database, the client is sent a 201 (created) response code, together with the URL to the newly created resource.

Ask the Expert

Q: **Why does your REST API return results as Atom feeds?**

A: While REST-based APIs can return data in any format, it's quite common for them to return Atom or RSS feeds. This is because most modern HTTP clients come with built-in support for these feeds, and most programming languages, too, include built-in or readily available parsers for these formats.

(continued)

Initializing the REST Routes

The final step is to initialize the REST API route. To do this, open the application bootstrapper and add the following method to it:

```php
<?php
class Bootstrap extends Zend_Application_Bootstrap_Bootstrap
{
  protected function _initRoutes()
  {
    $front = Zend_Controller_Front::getInstance();
    $router = $front->getRouter();
    $restRoute = new Zend_Rest_Route($front, array(), array('api'));
    $router->addRoute('api', $restRoute);
  }
}
```

```
Source of: http://square.localhost/api/catalog/ - Mozilla Firefox          _ □ ×
File  Edit  View  Help

<?xml version="1.0" encoding="UTF-8"?>
<feed xmlns="http://www.w3.org/2005/Atom">
  <id>http://square.localhost/api/catalog</id>
  <title><![CDATA[Catalog records]]></title>
  <author>
    <name>Square API/1.0</name>
  </author>
  <updated>2010-01-26T12:46:34+00:00</updated>
  <link rel="self" href="http://square.localhost/api/catalog"/>
  <generator>Zend_Feed</generator>
  <entry>
    <id>http://square.localhost/api/catalog/1</id>
    <title><![CDATA[Himalayas - Silver Jubilee  - 1958]]></title>
    <updated>2009-12-06T00:00:00+00:00</updated>
    <link rel="alternate" href="http://square.localhost/api/catalog/1"/>
    <summary><![CDATA[Silver jubilee issue. Aerial view of snow-capped
Himalayan mountains. Horizontal orange stripe across
top margin. Excellent condition, no marks.]]></summary>
  </entry>
  <entry>
    <id>http://square.localhost/api/catalog/2</id>
    <title><![CDATA[Britain - WWII Fighter - 1966]]></title>
    <updated>2009-10-05T00:00:00+00:00</updated>
    <link rel="alternate" href="http://square.localhost/api/catalog/2"/>
    <summary><![CDATA[WWII Fighter Plane overlaid on blue sky. Cancelled]]></summary>
  </entry>
  <entry>
    <id>http://square.localhost/api/catalog/4</id>
    <title><![CDATA[Singapore - Chinese Junks - 1966]]></title>
    <updated>2009-10-05T00:00:00+00:00</updated>
    <link rel="alternate" href="http://square.localhost/api/catalog/4"/>
    <summary><![CDATA[Chinese Junks on the Singapore River. Mint condition.]]>
</summary>
  </entry>
```

Figure 10-5   The API response to a GET request for all records

This _initRoutes() method takes care of initializing a new Zend_Rest_Route instance, and mapping it to the new "api" module created in the first step. The third argument to the Zend_Rest_Route constructor specifies an array of module and/or controller names for which REST support should be enabled.

At this point, your REST API is up and running. You can test it by requesting the URL **http://square.localhost/api/catalog** in your Web browser, which should produce an Atom feed of active listings from the stamp catalog database. Figure 10-5 illustrates what the output looks like.

In a similar vein, accessing the same URL with an additional item identifier, such as **http://square.localhost/api/catalog/1**, generates an Atom feed with details of the requested item. Figure 10-6 illustrates what this feed might look like.

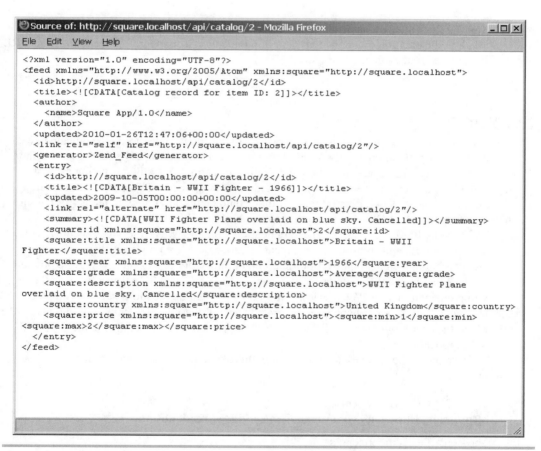

Figure 10-6   The API response to a GET request for a specific record

(continued)

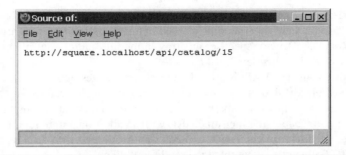

Figure 10-7 The API response to a POST request

And finally, POST-ing an array of data to the URL **http://square.localhost/api/catalog** will result in the creation of a new item record in the database, and a reference to the item URL will be returned to the client (see Figure 10-7).

Summary

Most weblogs and news sites include RSS or Atom feeds that can be used to syndicate new content to third-party applications. Writing parsers to consume these news feeds is a common application development task, and the Zend Framework simplifies it by providing a set of predefined components to generate, modify, and parse news feeds. This chapter discussed these components in detail, illustrating how they could be used to integrate feeds from online news sources into the SQUARE example application.

By allowing third-party access to an application's functions, Web services enable a new range of "mashups" and spin-off products that integrate data from multiple disparate sources while encouraging technical innovation. The Zend Framework makes it easy to jump on the Web service bandwagon: It includes generic clients for REST and SOAP access, as well as ready implementations for Web services exposed by popular applications such as Google, Amazon, and Twitter. This chapter demonstrated some of these implementations, and also illustrated the basics of creating a REST-based Web service from scratch using the SQUARE example application.

To learn more about the topics discussed in this chapter, consider visiting the following links:

- The Zend_Feed_Reader component, at
  http://framework.zend.com/manual/en/zend.feed.reader.html

- The Zend_Feed component, at
  http://framework.zend.com/manual/en/zend.feed.html

- The Zend_Rest_Client component, at
  http://framework.zend.com/manual/en/zend.rest.client.html

- The Zend_Soap_Client component, at
  http://framework.zend.com/manual/en/zend.soap.client.html

- The Zend_Service component, at
  http://framework.zend.com/manual/en/zend.service.html

- The Zend_Gdata component, at
  http://framework.zend.com/manual/en/zend.gdata.html

- The Atom Syndication Format 1.0 specification, at
  http://tools.ietf.org/html/rfc4287

- Wikipedia's discussion of the RSS format, at
  http://en.wikipedia.org/wiki/RSS

- Wikipedia's discussion of SOAP and REST architecture, at
  http://en.wikipedia.org/wiki/Web_service

- A discussion of REST versus SOAP Web services (Amit Asaravala), at
  http://www.devx.com/DevX/Article/8155

- A discussion of building REST-based interfaces with the Zend Framework (Matthew Weier O'Phinney), at
  http://weierophinney.net/matthew/archives/228-Building-RESTful-Services-with-Zend-Framework.html

- A screencast of writing a REST-based Web service and client (Jon Lebensold), at
  http://www.zendcasts.com/writing-a-restful-web-service-and-client-with-zend_controller-and-zend_httpclient/2009/04/

- A (non-framework) approach to building a REST API (Ian Selby), at
  http://www.gen-x-design.com/archives/create-a-rest-api-with-php/

- Some examples of HTTP response codes and how they can be used with a REST-based Zend Framework application (Sudheer Satyanarayana), at
  http://techchorus.net/create-restful-applications-using-zend-framework-part-ii-using-http-response-code

Chapter 11

Working with User Interface Elements

Key Tools & Concepts

- Improve site navigation with menus, sitemaps, and breadcrumb trails
- Learn about the Zend Framework's Dojo integration
- Create an AJAX-enabled autocomplete form input
- Use YUI Library widgets with the Zend Framework
- Understand how to create and use action helpers

Distilling the essence of a Web application into clear, consistent navigation is one of those things that sound easy in theory but are actually fairly hard to get right in practice. It often takes many hours of thought and experimentation to build a usable and consistent navigation map for a Web application. However, the effort is invariably worth it: Navigation is one of the key elements of Web site usability, and getting it right helps users locate information efficiently, making them happy and promoting repeat visits.

In addition to good navigation, it's also possible to improve application usability through the judicious use of client-side programming techniques. The rich client API in most modern browsers, together with the ready availability of client-side programming toolkits like jQuery, mooTools, and Dojo, make it possible to quickly add new behaviors and functions to a Web application, improving responsiveness, reducing wait time, and (again) making users happy.

What does this have to do with the Zend Framework, you wonder? Well, the Zend Framework includes a couple of components that are directly relevant to the goal of improving application usability. In particular, there's the Zend_Navigation component, which provides a flexible, sophisticated API for managing and implementing different types of site navigation structures; and the Zend_Dojo component, which makes it possible to directly integrate DHTML and AJAX widgets from the Dojo Toolkit with a Web application. This chapter discusses both these components, and also demonstrates how easy it is to integrate a third-party JavaScript toolkit, the Yahoo! User Interface (YUI) Library, with a Zend Framework application.

Working with Navigation Structures

Zend_Navigation provides an object-oriented approach to managing navigation links on a Web site or application. It provides a mechanism to express the relationships between the different pages of a Web application, and to render these relationships as menus, sitemaps, or breadcrumb trails. Links and link relationships may be expressed as nested PHP arrays, XML documents, or INI files.

Understanding Pages and Containers

The most basic navigational unit under the Zend_Navigation approach is a *page*, usually expressed as an instance of the Zend_Navigation_Page class. Every page has, at minimum, a label and either a URL or a module/controller/action combination; it may also include other optional information such as visibility, sort order, access privileges, and forward and reverse relationships. Pages are further organized into *navigation containers*, which are simply hierarchical collections of pages.

To better understand this, consider the following PHP listing, which illustrates the relationship between pages and containers:

```php
<?php
class Sandbox_ExampleController extends Zend_Controller_Action
{
  function navAction()
  {
      // initialize pages
      $config = array(
        Zend_Navigation_Page::factory(array(
          'label'    => 'Foreword',
          'uri'      => '/foreword',
        )),

        Zend_Navigation_Page::factory(array(
          'label'    => 'Chapter 1: Introducing the Zend Framework',
          'uri'      => '/chapter-01',
          'pages'    => array(
            Zend_Navigation_Page::factory(array(
              'label'    => 'Overview',
              'uri'      => '/chapter-01/overview',
            )),
            Zend_Navigation_Page::factory(array(
              'label'    => 'Features',
              'uri'      => '/chapter-01/features',
            ))
          )
        )),

        Zend_Navigation_Page::factory(array(
          'label'    => 'Index',
          'uri'      => '/index',
        ))
      );

      // initialize navigation container
      $container = new Zend_Navigation($config);
  }
}
```

The previous listing sets up an example navigation container for a book. The container itself is represented as a Zend_Navigation object and passed an array of Zend_Navigation_Page objects. Each top-level Zend_Navigation_Page object in the container represents a page at the top level of the navigational hierarchy, and each page has a title and URL. Each page may itself contain further child pages; these too are expressed as Zend_Navigation_Page objects and attached to their parent as a nested array. This hierarchical structure can easily be extended to cover the entire surface area of a Web site.

Page objects are themselves created as instances of either the Zend_Navigation_Page_Mvc class or the Zend_Navigation_Page_Uri class, both of which extend the abstract Zend_Navigation_Page class. The difference between the two arises from the manner in which the page link is defined: The former piggybacks on the Zend Framework's router by specifying each page's module, action, and controller, while the latter directly specifies the page link as a URL. The following example illustrates the difference:

```php
<?php
class Sandbox_ExampleController extends Zend_Controller_Action
{
  function pageAction()
  {
    // define MVC page
    $page = Zend_Navigation_Page::factory(array(
       'label'        => 'Contact Us',
       'module'       => 'default',
       'controller'   => 'contact',
       'action'       => 'index',
    ));

    // define URI page
    $page = Zend_Navigation_Page::factory(array(
       'label'     => 'Contact Us',
       'uri'       => '/contact',
    ));
  }
}
```

Each page object exposes a number of "getter" and "setter" methods, which can be used to set page properties. For example, the label, forward relationships, reverse relationships, and visibility can all be set with the page object's setLabel(), setRel(), setRev(), and setVisibility() methods, respectively, and they can be retrieved with the corresponding getLabel(), getRel(), getRev(), and getVisibility() methods. There's also the isActive() method, which returns a Boolean value indicating whether or not the page matches the current request.

TIP

In most cases, it is preferable to specify page objects as Zend_Navigation_Page_Uri instances. Not only are the corresponding URLs somewhat easier to read and understand, but the flexible nature of these objects means that they can also be used to create links to external or third-party resources. Zend_Navigation_Page_Mvc objects, on the other hand, must be mapped by the Zend Framework router and so can only be used to create links to internal application resources.

The Zend_Navigation container can be initialized, as shown previously, with an array of Zend_Navigation_Page objects. For long or complex navigational structures, however, this method can be somewhat unwieldy, so a Zend_Navigation container can also be initialized with a Zend_Config object, with the navigation configuration expressed as either an XML document or an INI file. Consider the following example, which illustrates one such XML document:

```xml
<?xml version="1.0" encoding="UTF-8"?>
<config>
  <home>
    <label>Home</label>
    <uri>/home</uri>
  </home>

  <products>
    <label>Products</label>
    <uri>/products</uri>
    <pages>
      <men>
        <label>Men</label>
        <uri>/products/men</uri>
        <pages>
          <item_1>
            <label>Dress Shirts</label>
            <uri>/products/men/16339</uri>
          </item_1>
          <item_2>
            <label>Trousers</label>
            <uri>/products/men/85940</uri>
          </item_2>
          <item_3>
            <label>Shoes</label>
            <uri>/products/men/75393</uri>
          </item_3>
        </pages>
      </men>
      <women>
        <label>Women</label>
        <uri>/products/women</uri>
        <pages>
          <item_1>
            <label>Skirts and Dresses</label>
            <uri>/products/women/75849</uri>
          </item_1>
          <item_2>
            <label>Bags</label>
            <uri>/products/women/64830</uri>
```

```xml
            </item_2>
            <item_3>
              <label>Shoes</label>
              <uri>/products/women/58303</uri>
            </item_3>
          </pages>
        </women>
      </pages>
    </products>

    <about>
      <label>About Us</label>
      <uri>/about</uri>
      <pages>
        <history>
          <label>Company History</label>
          <uri>/about/history</uri>
        </history>
        <team>
          <label>Management Team</label>
          <uri>/about/team</uri>
        </team>
        <awards>
          <label>Awards</label>
          <uri>/about/awards</uri>
        </awards>
      </pages>
    </about>

    <feedback>
      <label>Feedback</label>
      <uri>/feedback</uri>
    </feedback>
</config>
```

This XML document can be read into a Zend_Navigation container using Zend_Config, as follows:

```php
<?php
class Sandbox_ExampleController extends Zend_Controller_Action
{
  function navAction()
  {
    // initialize navigation container from XML file
    $config = new Zend_Config_Xml(APPLICATION_PATH . '/configs/site.xml');
    $container = new Zend_Navigation($config);
  }
}
```

TIP

Zend_Navigation is fully locale-aware, and will automatically translate labels into local-language equivalents, given a correctly configured Zend_Translate object. You can read more about Zend_Translate in Chapter 9.

It's easy to iterate over a Zend_Navigation container with the RecursiveIteratorIterator, retrieving the contents of individual Zend_Navigation_Page objects. Here's an example:

```php
<?php
class Sandbox_ExampleController extends Zend_Controller_Action
{
  function navAction()
  {
    // initialize navigation container
    $config = new Zend_Config_Xml(APPLICATION_PATH . '/configs/site.xml');
    $container = new Zend_Navigation($config);

    // iterate over container
    // display page information
    foreach (new RecursiveIteratorIterator(
      $container, RecursiveIteratorIterator::CHILD_FIRST) as $page) {
        echo $page->getLabel();
    }
  }
}
```

The Zend_Navigation container also exposes various methods for interacting with the pages contained within it. In particular, it exposes the findBy() search method, which can be used to retrieve all pages matching specific criteria. Consider the following example, which illustrates this:

```php
<?php
class Sandbox_ExampleController extends Zend_Controller_Action
{
  function navAction()
  {
    // initialize navigation container
    $config = new Zend_Config_Xml(APPLICATION_PATH . '/configs/site.xml');
    $container = new Zend_Navigation($config);

    // find all pages with matching URLs
    $container->findBy('uri', '/about');
  }
}
```

Rendering Navigational Elements

Of course, defining a site's navigation structure is only part of the problem; you still need to use it in some way. Typically, the Zend_Navigation container is initialized in the application bootstrapper and made persistent through the application registry. Here's an example that illustrates how the container can be set up:

```php
<?php
class Bootstrap extends Zend_Application_Bootstrap_Bootstrap
{
    protected function _initNavigation()
    {
      $config = new Zend_Config_Xml(APPLICATION_PATH . '/configs/site.xml');
      $container = new Zend_Navigation($config);
      $registry = Zend_Registry::getInstance();
      $registry->set('Zend_Navigation', $container);
    }
}
```

Once this is done, the Zend_Navigation view helpers can automatically access the registered navigation container from within a view script and turn it into menus, sitemaps, or breadcrumb trails suitable for use on a Web page. The following sections discuss these aspects in detail.

Menus

The Zend_Navigation Menu helper can automatically turn navigation data into a hierarchical set of unordered list items. Here's an example of how to use it in a view script:

```php
<?php echo $this->navigation()->menu(); ?>
```

The output of this code is a nested, unordered list of links, as shown in Figure 11-1.

It's also possible to customize this default output by specifying whether only the active menu branch should be displayed and by defining the depth of the menu tree that is rendered. These options are passed to the view helper's `renderMenu()` method as an associative array. Here's a revision of the previous example that illustrates this:

```php
<?php
echo $this->navigation()
        ->menu()
        ->renderMenu(null, array(
          'minDepth' => null,
          'maxDepth' => 1,
          'ulClass'  => 'nav',
          'onlyActiveBranch' => true
));
?>
```

Figure 11-2 illustrates the resulting output.

TIP

If you'd like the menu to be rendered using custom markup instead of the default unordered list, you can specify a custom view script for the Menu view helper with the `setPartial()` method.

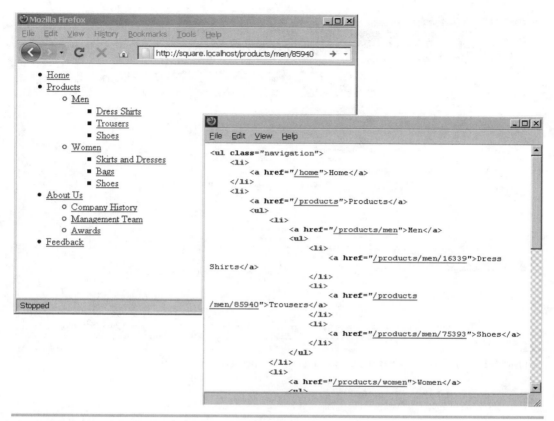

Figure 11-1 An autogenerated site menu

Breadcrumb Trails

There's also a Breadcrumbs navigation helper, which automatically creates breadcrumb trails based on the currently requested URL. In this case too, it's possible to customize the appearance of the breadcrumbs, including the separator, the indentation, and whether or not the last breadcrumb should be rendered as a link. Here's an example of how to use this helper in a view script:

```php
<?php
echo $this->navigation()
        ->breadcrumbs()
        ->setLinkLast(true)
        ->setSeparator(' / ');
?>
```

Figure 11-3 illustrates the output.

Figure 11-2 An autogenerated site menu with only the active branch visible

Links

The Links helper generates a set of `<link>` elements that express the relationship of a particular page to other pages in the document collection, as well as provide additional information to search engines. These `<link>` elements can express both forward and reverse relationships, and always appear within the `<head>` of an HTML document.

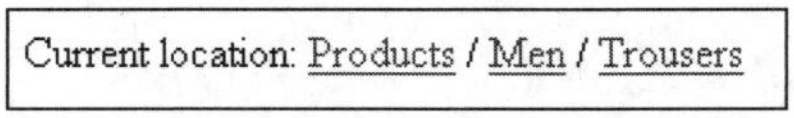

Current location: Products / Men / Trousers

Figure 11-3 An autogenerated breadcrumbs trail

Here's an example of how to use this helper in a view script:

```php
<?php echo $this->navigation()->links(); ?>
```

Figure 11-4 illustrates an example of the output.

Sitemaps

The Sitemap helper makes it possible to automatically generate an XML sitemap from the data in the navigation container. This sitemap is compliant with the Sitemap protocol that has been

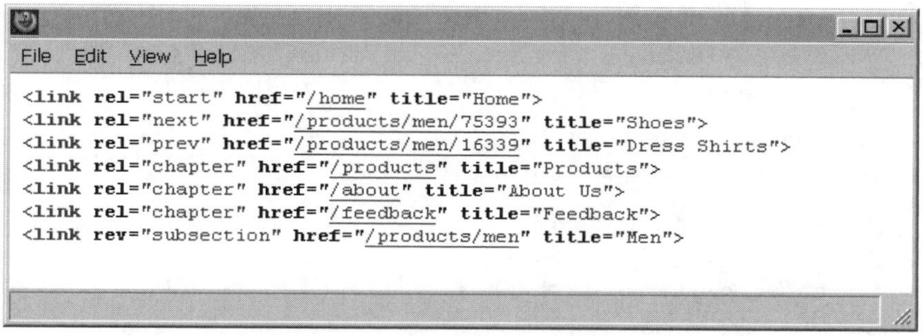

Figure 11-4   Autogenerated header links

adopted by Google, Yahoo!, and Microsoft, and you'll find links to more information about this protocol at the end of this chapter.

Here's an example of how to use this helper in a view script:

```php
<?php
echo $this->navigation()
        ->sitemap()
        ->setFormatOutput(true)
        ->setMaxDepth(1);
?>
```

Figure 11-5 has an example of the output.

Try This 11-1   Adding a Navigation Menu

Now that you know a little bit about how Zend_Navigation works, let's use it in the context of the SQUARE example application. Given that the application only has a single-tier main menu, this doesn't pose much of a challenge; however, it still provides a good illustration of how you might typically use Zend_Navigation in a practical context.

Defining Navigation Pages and Containers

The first step is to define the navigation container, and attach pages to it. As discussed in previous sections, one of the easiest ways to express this information is with an XML file. So, create a new file in your text editor and fill it with the following data:

```xml
<?xml version="1.0" encoding="UTF-8"?>
<config>
  <home>
```

(continued)

```
      <label>menu-home</label>
      <uri>/home</uri>
   </home>
   <services>
      <label>menu-services</label>
      <uri>/content/services</uri>
   </services>
   <catalog>
      <label>menu-catalog</label>
      <uri>/catalog/item/search</uri>
   </catalog>
   <news>
      <label>menu-news</label>
      <uri>/news</uri>
   </news>
   <contact>
      <label>menu-contact</label>
      <uri>/contact</uri>
   </contact>
</config>
```

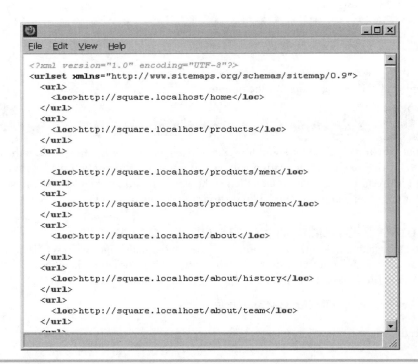

Figure 11-5 An autogenerated XML Sitemap

Save this file as *$APP_DIR/application/configs/navigation.xml*. Notice that this XML definition uses string identifiers for each menu label; these will be automatically localized to the currently selected language via Zend_Navigation's built-in compatibility with Zend_Locale.

Registering the Navigation Object

The next step is to update the application bootstrapper and configure and register an instance of the Zend_Navigation object. This instance will then become available in all application controllers and views, enabling the use of the various navigation view helpers.

To do this, update the application bootstrapper, at *$APP_DIR/application/Bootstrap.php*, and add the following method to it:

```php
<?php
class Bootstrap extends Zend_Application_Bootstrap_Bootstrap
{
    protected function _initNavigation()
    {
      // read navigation XML and initialize container
      $config = new Zend_Config_Xml(
        APPLICATION_PATH . '/configs/navigation.xml');
      $container = new Zend_Navigation($config);

      // register navigation container
      $registry = Zend_Registry::getInstance();
      $registry->set('Zend_Navigation', $container);

      // add action helper
      Zend_Controller_Action_HelperBroker::addHelper(
        new Square_Controller_Action_Helper_Navigation()
      );
    }
}
```

Notice that the last line of the _initNavigation() method references a Navigation action helper. This is a custom action helper that is called on every request and takes care of setting the active page in the main menu. This is discussed in detail in the next section.

CAUTION

Reading an external file to load the navigation container on every request, as shown in the previous section, can significantly degrade performance in high-traffic applications. An alternative in such cases, especially for simple navigation containers, is to use the navigation resource plug-in and define the container in the application configuration file itself. This eliminates the extra file read and helps keeps things speedy.

(continued)

Creating the Navigation Action Helper

Zend Framework action helpers are generally perceived as complex and hard to understand. In reality, though, this couldn't be further from the truth. *Action helpers* exist as a substitute for base controllers; they provide a way for developers to program common functionality into "helper objects" that can then be loaded and used at run time from any action controller.

Action helpers are typically registered using a *helper broker*, which exposes `addHelper()` and `removeHelper()` methods to immediately load and unload helpers from the helper stack. This is particularly important for helpers that are referenced in `preDispatch()` or `postDispatch()` methods. An alternative is to use the helper broker's `addPath()` or `addPrefix()` method to map the helper path; this information can then be used to load the helper on demand.

Once they've been loaded or mapped, helpers can be retrieved using the helper broker's `getHelper()` method, which returns the helper object. This helper broker is available for use in all action controllers via the controller object's `_helper` property, making it possible to load helpers on demand either within the application bootstrapper or as needed within specific controllers.

TIP

You might not have known it at the time, but you've already seen and used some of the Zend Framework's built-in action helpers in previous chapters. The ContextSwitch helper in Chapter 6 and the FlashMessenger helper in Chapter 3 are both examples of built-in action helpers, accessed from within controllers using the helper broker's `getHelper()` method.

Table 11-1 provides a complete list of the action helpers that are included in the Zend Framework.

With that background information out of the way, let's return to the task at hand: creating a custom action helper that will automatically check the current request URL, match it against the navigation container, and flag the current active page. To do this, create a new action helper at *$APP_DIR/library/Square/Controller/Action/Helper/Navigation.php*, and fill it with the following code:

Action Helper	Description
ActionStack	Queues multiple actions for execution
ContextSwitch	Enables output in different formats
FlashMessenger	Stores messages for retrieval on next request
Autocomplete	Formats and sends JSON/HTML arrays of data for autocomplete inputs
JSON	Enables output in JSON format
Redirector	Handles client redirection
ViewRenderer	Registers view scripts and handles view script rendering

Table 11-1 Action Helpers Included with the Zend Framework

```php
<?php
// code credited to Ryan Mauger, technical editor
class Square_Controller_Action_Helper_Navigation extends
Zend_Controller_Action_Helper_Abstract
{
  protected $_container;

  // constructor, set navigation container
  public function __construct(Zend_Navigation $container = null)
  {
    if (null !== $container) {
        $this->_container = $container;
    }
  }

  // check current request and set active page
  public function preDispatch()
  {
    $this->getContainer()
        ->findBy('uri', $this->getRequest()->getRequestUri())
        ->active = true;
  }

  // retrieve navigation container
  public function getContainer()
  {
    if (null === $this->_container) {
        $this->_container = Zend_Registry::get('Zend_Navigation');
    }
    if (null === $this->_container) {
        throw new RuntimeException ('Navigation container unavailable');
    }
    return $this->_container;
  }
}
```

This definition sets up a new action helper, which retrieves the Zend_Navigation container from the application registry and uses the container's findBy() method to check the current request URL against the page links in the container. If a match is found, the corresponding page is marked active. This task is performed on every request, by virtue of being placed in the helper's preDispatch() method.

Using the Menu View Helper

Why do we need to identify the active page at all? The information is useful to the Menu view helper, which will attach an "active" CSS class to the corresponding main menu branch at

(continued)

render time. This makes it possible to visually (and automatically) highlight the active menu item at any given time.

To see this in action, update the master layout to use the Menu view helper and dynamically generate the main menu, by updating the master layout file at *$APP_DIR/application/layouts/master.phtml* with the changes highlighted in bold:

```
<!DOCTYPE html PUBLIC "-//W3C//DTD XHTML 1.0 Strict//EN"
"http://www.w3.org/TR/xhtml1/DTD/xhtml1-strict.dtd">
<html xmlns="http://www.w3.org/1999/xhtml" xml:lang="en" lang="en">
...


        <div id="menu">
         <?php echo $this->navigation()->menu(); ?>
        </div>

...
</html>
```

Note that you'll also need to update the master layout stylesheet and add stylesheet rules for the dynamically generated menu and active menu item. You'll find the corresponding stylesheet rules in the code archive for this chapter, which can be downloaded from this book's companion Web site at **http://www.zf-beginners-guide.com/**.

When you now visit the application home page and select a particular main menu item—say, the contact form at **http://square.localhost/contact**—you'll notice that the corresponding main menu item is now automatically highlighted. Then, look behind the scenes and notice that Zend_Navigation's Menu view helper has dynamically generated the main menu for you.

Figure 11-6 illustrates the rendered output.

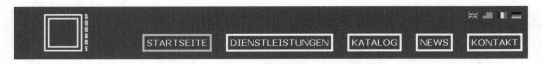

SQUARE
STARTSEITE
DIENSTLEISTUNGEN
KATALOG
NEWS
KONTAKT
Welcome!
Welcome to SQUARE, our cutting-edge Web search application for rare stamps.
We have a wide collection of stamps in our catalog for your browsing pleasure, and we also list hundreds of thousands of stamps from individual collectors across the country. If you find something you like, drop us a line and we'll do our best to obtain it for you. Needless to say, all stamps purchased through us come with a certificate of authenticity, and our unique 60-day money-back guarantee.
The SQUARE application is designed to be as user-friendly as possible. Use the links in the menu above to navigate and begin searching.

Figure 11-6 The automatically generated and highlighted navigation menu

Working with the Dojo Toolkit

The Dojo Toolkit is a cross-browser JavaScript library that includes both a data access layer for AJAX requests and responses (Dojo Data) and a set of predefined user interface components (Dijit). These components include layout and menu elements, data grids, dialog boxes, form controls such as autocomplete inputs, and date selectors, themes, and various animated page effects. The project is supported by some of the Web's biggest companies, including Google, IBM, AOL, and Sun Microsystems.

The Zend Framework makes it easy to get started with the Dojo Toolkit. The full version of the Zend Framework comes with a complete distribution of Dojo and Dijit interface components, and the framework also includes a Zend_Dojo component that simplifies the task of activating and using the Dojo Toolkit in a Web application. This Zend_Dojo component includes a data layer implementation, a view helper that assists in setting up the Dojo environment, and a set of form and layout extensions that can be used to add Dojo/Dijit functionality to view scripts. The following sections discuss these in detail.

Handling Dojo Data

The Dojo Toolkit defines a uniform format for client-server data exchange, and provides two basic datastores, `dojo.data.ItemFileReadStore` and `dojo.data.ItemFileWriteStore`, for interacting with this data. In its simplest form, this data is represented as a structured JSON object and looks something like this:

```
{
  "identifier":"name",
  "items": [
    {"name":"Agatha Christie"},
    {"name":"J. K. Rowling"},
    {"name":"Dan Brown"},
    {"name":"William Shakespeare"},
    {"name":"Dennis Lehane"}
  ]
}
```

The Zend_Dojo_Data component provides an object-oriented API for constructing this JSON representation, adding items to it, iterating over it, and querying it for matches. To illustrate, consider the following listing, which produces output equivalent to the previous code listing:

```php
<?php
class Sandbox_ExampleController extends Zend_Controller_Action
{
  public function dojoAction()
  {
    // define data items
    $authors = array(
      'Agatha Christie', 'J. K. Rowling', 'Dan Brown',
```

```
      'William Shakespeare', 'Dennis Lehane'
  );
  foreach ($authors as $a) {
    $items[] = array('name' => $a);
  }

  // initialize object and pass it data items
  $data = new Zend_Dojo_Data('name', $items);

  // output as structured JSON
  echo $data->toJson();
  }
}
```

As illustrated in this example, the object is initialized simply by passing the object constructor the name of the unique identifier field (in this case, `'name'`) and an array of data items. These data items must be expressed as associative arrays (or objects implementing the `toArray()` method), and must include the specified identifier as one of the array keys. Once initialized, the object may be exported either as a PHP array or a JSON string, via the `toArray()` or `toJson()` method.

TIP
The Zend_Dojo_Data component comes in particularly handy when implementing endpoints for Dojo/Dijit AJAX requests. You'll see an example of this further along in this chapter.

Using the Dojo View Helpers

Typically, enabling Dojo and Dijit components in a Web page involves loading the Dojo library files, initializing the Dojo parser, and enabling the required components, passing along configuration options as necessary. While this can certainly be done manually within your view scripts, the Zend Framework provides an easier way: the Dojo view helper, which can "Dojo-ify" a view by automatically generating all the necessary client-side initialization code inline.

Here's an example of using the Dojo view helper in a view script:

```
<?php
Zend_Dojo::enableView($this);
$this->dojo()->setLocalPath('/js/dojo/dojo.js')
             ->addStyleSheetModule('dijit.themes.tundra')
             ->setDjConfigOption('parseOnLoad', true)
             ->setDjConfigOption('locale', 'en-US')
             ->setDjConfigOption('isDebug', true);
echo $this->dojo();
?>
```

Figure 11-7 illustrates the markup generated by the helper from the previous listing.

```
<style type="text/css">
<!--
    @import "/js/dijit/themes/tundra/tundra.css";
-->
</style>
<script type="text/javascript">
//<![CDATA[
    var djConfig = {"parseOnLoad":true,"locale":"en-US","isDebug":true};
//]]>
</script>
<script type="text/javascript" src="/js/dojo/dojo.js"></script>
```

Figure 11-7   Autogenerated markup from the Dojo view helper

CAUTION

Note the call to Zend_Dojo::enableView in the previous listing. This method adds the Dojo view helper path to the Zend_View object; omitting it will usually result in an exception because Zend_View will be unable to find and load the required helper(s).

If you'd prefer to load Dojo Toolkit libraries from an external location, such as a Content Delivery Network (CDN), you can use the setCdnBase() method, as follows:

```
<?php
Zend_Dojo::enableView($this);
$this->dojo()->setCdnBase(Zend_Dojo::CDN_BASE_AOL)
            ->addStyleSheetModule('dijit.themes.tundra')
            ->setDjConfigOption('parseOnLoad', true)
            ->setDjConfigOption('locale', 'en-US')
            ->setDjConfigOption('isDebug', true);
echo $this->dojo();
?>
```

CAUTION

If you don't specify a local path to the Dojo libraries with setLocalPath(), the Dojo view helper will automatically assume that you wish to use the Google CDN.

In addition to the Dojo view helper, the Zend Framework also ships with a number of other view helpers that can be used to directly render Dojo and Dijit layout containers and form elements within a view script. Table 11-2 gives an abridged list of these helpers.

It's worth noting that the Dojo view helper will automatically detect your use of these helpers in a view script and generate the necessary client-side code to initialize them. Here's an example:

```
<html>
  <head>
  <?php
  Zend_Dojo::enableView($this);
```

```
$element = $this->NumberSpinner('temp', 25, array(
  'min' => 12,
  'max' => 41,
  'places' => 2
  )
);
$this->dojo()->setCdnBase(Zend_Dojo::CDN_BASE_AOL)
            ->addStyleSheetModule('dijit.themes.tundra');
echo $this->dojo();
?>
</head>
<body class="tundra">
  <?php echo $element; ?>
</body>
</html>
```

This example uses the NumberSpinner view helper to generate a Dijit number spinner form control. Figure 11-8 illustrates the resulting markup generated by the Dojo view helper.

Dojo View Helper	Description
Button	Button
CheckBox	Check box
ComboBox	Combined selection/text input
ContentPane	Content container
CurrencyTextBox	Currency input
DateTextBox	Date selector
Editor	Rich text editor
FilteringSelect	Selection control with filter
HorizontalSlider	Horizontal slider
NumberSpinner	Number input with increment controls
StackContainer	Stacked content container
TabContainer	Tabbed content container
Textarea	Text input
TextBox	Text input
TimeTextBox	Time selector
ValidationTextBox	Text input with validator
VerticalSlider	Vertical slider

Table 11-2 Dojo View Helpers Included with the Zend Framework (Nonexhaustive List)

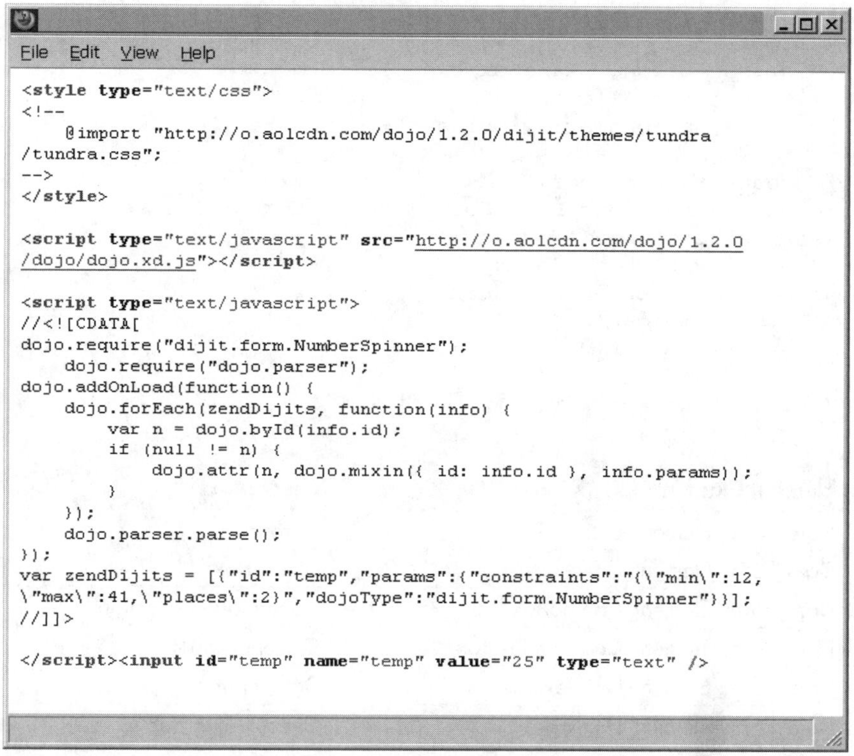

```
<style type="text/css">
<!--
    @import "http://o.aolcdn.com/dojo/1.2.0/dijit/themes/tundra
/tundra.css";
-->
</style>

<script type="text/javascript" src="http://o.aolcdn.com/dojo/1.2.0
/dojo/dojo.xd.js"></script>

<script type="text/javascript">
//<![CDATA[
dojo.require("dijit.form.NumberSpinner");
    dojo.require("dojo.parser");
dojo.addOnLoad(function() {
    dojo.forEach(zendDijits, function(info) {
        var n = dojo.byId(info.id);
        if (null != n) {
            dojo.attr(n, dojo.mixin({ id: info.id }, info.params));
        }
    });
    dojo.parser.parse();
});
var zendDijits = [{"id":"temp","params":{"constraints":"{\"min\":12,
\"max\":41,\"places\":2}","dojoType":"dijit.form.NumberSpinner"}}];
//]]>
</script><input id="temp" name="temp" value="25" type="text" />
```

Figure 11-8 Autogenerated markup from the Dojo view helper

Using Dojo Form Elements

The Dojo Toolkit includes a number of ready-made form widgets that can be used to quickly add common functionality to Web forms: a color picker, a WYSIWYG text editor, a number spinner, an autocomplete text input, a horizontal slider control, and so on. Zend_Dojo extends Zend_Form to support these additional elements, allowing them to be used in the same way as regular Zend_Form_Element instances.

Table 11-3 provides a list of Dojo-specific form widgets included with the Zend Framework.

To use these elements inside a form, update the Zend_Form instance to extend Zend_Dojo_Form instead of Zend_Form, and then attach Zend_Dojo_Form_Element elements to it in the usual manner. Here's an example, which illustrates by creating a Web form with a date picker, rich text editor, and vertical slider:

```php
<?php
class Form_Example extends Zend_Dojo_Form
{
```

```
public function init()
{
  $this->setAction('/sandbox/example/form')
      ->setMethod('post')
      ->setOptions(array('class' => 'tundra'));

  // create rich editor
  $message = new Zend_Dojo_Form_Element_Editor('message');
  $message->setLabel('Message:')
          ->setOptions(array(
            'width'  => '150px',
            'height' => '100px',
          ));

  // create date picker
```

Form Element Class	Description
Zend_Dojo_Form_Element_Button	Button
Zend_Dojo_Form_Element_CheckBox	Check box
Zend_Dojo_Form_Element_ComboBox	Combination selection/input
Zend_Dojo_Form_Element_CurrencyTextBox	Currency input
Zend_Dojo_Form_Element_DateTextBox	Date input
Zend_Dojo_Form_Element_DijitMulti	Check box group
Zend_Dojo_Form_Element_Editor	Rich text input field
Zend_Dojo_Form_Element_FilteringSelect	Selection control with filter
Zend_Dojo_Form_Element_HorizontalSlider	Horizontal slider
Zend_Dojo_Form_Element_NumberSpinner	Number input with increment controls
Zend_Dojo_Form_Element_NumberTextBox	Number input
Zend_Dojo_Form_Element_PasswordTextBox	Password input
Zend_Dojo_Form_Element_RadioButton	Radio button
Zend_Dojo_Form_Element_SimpleTextarea	Text input field
Zend_Dojo_Form_Element_SubmitButton	Submit button
Zend_Dojo_Form_Element_Textarea	Text input
Zend_Dojo_Form_Element_TextBox	Text input
Zend_Dojo_Form_Element_TimeTextBox	Time input
Zend_Dojo_Form_Element_ValidationTextBox	Text input with validator
Zend_Dojo_Form_Element_VerticalSlider	Vertical slider

Table 11-3 Dojo Form Element Classes Included with the Zend Framework

```
$dob = new Zend_Dojo_Form_Element_DateTextBox('dob');
$dob->setLabel('Date of birth:');

// create slider
$volume = new Zend_Dojo_Form_Element_VerticalSlider('volume');
$volume->setLabel('Volume level:')
        ->setOptions(array(
            'minimum'   => '100',
            'maximum'   => '0',
            'discreteValues' => '10',
            'style' => 'height: 100px'
        ));

// create submit button
$submit = new Zend_Dojo_Form_Element_SubmitButton('submit');
$submit->setLabel('Submit');

$this->addElement($message)
     ->addElement($dob)
     ->addElement($volume)
     ->addElement($submit);
    }
}
```

Figure 11-9 illustrates what the output looks like.

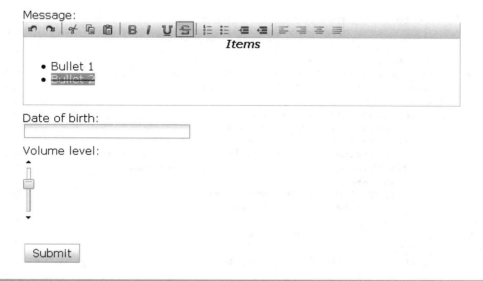

Figure 11-9 A form with Dojo/Dijit form elements

Try This 11-2 Adding a Dojo Autocomplete Widget

Now that you know what the Zend_Dojo component can do, let's try using it for something
practical: adding an autocomplete input to a Zend_Form instance. This is a reasonably
common requirement, and the following sections will walk you through the process.

Updating the Contact Form

For this example, assume that the autocomplete input is to be attached to the application's
contact form, which will "suggest" a list of countries based on the user's input. The first step,
therefore, is to update the Square_Form_Contact object to extend Zend_Dojo_Form instead of
Zend_Form, as discussed in the previous section, and to add a Dijit ComboBox element to it.
Here's the code:

```php
<?php
class Square_Form_Contact extends Zend_Dojo_Form
{
  public function init()
  {
    // initialize form
    $this->setAction('/contact')
        ->setMethod('post');


    // create text input for name
    ...


    // create text input for email address
    ...


    // create autocomplete input for country
    $country = new Zend_Dojo_Form_Element_ComboBox('country');
    $country->setLabel('contact-country');
    $country->setOptions(array(
        'autocomplete' => false,
        'storeId'    => 'countryStore',
        'storeType' => 'dojo.data.ItemFileReadStore',
        'storeParams' => array('url' => "/default/contact/autocomplete"),
        'dijitParams' => array('searchAttr' => 'name')))
          ->setRequired(true)
          ->addValidator('NotEmpty', true)
          ->addFilter('HTMLEntities')
          ->addFilter('StringToLower')
          ->addFilter('StringTrim');

    // create text input for message body
    ...
```

```
    // create captcha
    ...


    // create submit button
    ...


    // attach elements to form
    $this->addElement($name)
        ->addElement($email)
        ->addElement($country)
        ->addElement($message)
        ->addElement($captcha)
        ->addElement($submit);
    }
}
```

This revised definition adds a new Dijit ComboBox element to the contact form, and specifies the use of a remote Dojo datastore for autocomplete suggestions. The endpoint for the datastore is also specified, as */default/contact/autocomplete*. Save the revised object definition to *$APP_DIR/ library/Square/Form/Contact.php* and keep reading to see how this endpoint is defined.

Initializing the Dojo View Helper

The next step is to initialize the Dojo view helper. If your application doesn't use layouts, you can perform this initialization directly in the relevant view script. However, since the SQUARE example application does make use of layouts, this initialization must be performed within the layout itself.

This brings up an interesting point. As a general rule, it's important to minimize the total number of remote HTTP requests generated by a Web page, because each request adds overhead and increases the amount of time a user must wait for the page to load completely. With this in mind, it is obviously not very efficient to initialize the Dojo view helper in the layout script, as it will result in the Dojo libraries being requested and loaded even in cases when they are not needed.

A better approach in this case is to configure the Dojo helper in the application bootstrapper, but explicitly disable it such that it is not loaded by default in every view script. It can then be dynamically enabled, as needed, in those view scripts that require it.

To do this, first update the application configuration file to enable the view resource plug-in, by adding the following line to it:

```
resources.view = ""
```

Then, update the application bootstrapper at *$APP_DIR/application/Bootstrap.php* with the following method:

```
<?php
class Bootstrap extends Zend_Application_Bootstrap_Bootstrap
```

(continued)

```
{
    protected function _initDojo()
    {
        // get view resource
        $this->bootstrap('view');
        $view = $this->getResource('view');

        // add helper path to view
        Zend_Dojo::enableView($view);

        // configure Dojo view helper, disable
        $view->dojo()->setCdnBase(Zend_Dojo::CDN_BASE_AOL)
                    ->addStyleSheetModule('dijit.themes.tundra')
                    ->disable();
    }
}
```

This method grabs the Zend_View instance from the view resource plug-in and uses the
Zend_Dojo::enableView method to enable the Dojo view helper for the view. It then
configures the Dojo environment, setting up the CDN URL and stylesheet, and finally
explicitly disables the helper with its disable() method. The end result of this is that the
Dojo view helper is configured for use, but the Dojo Toolkit libraries will not be loaded
in view scripts unless explicitly asked to do so via a call to the view helper's enable()
method.

Updating the Master Layout

The next step is to update the master layout to check if the Dojo view helper is enabled and, if
yes, to load the Dojo environment. This is not very difficult to do, as the following additions to
the <head> of the *$APP_DIR/application/layouts/master.phtml* layout illustrate:

```
<!DOCTYPE html PUBLIC "-//W3C//DTD XHTML 1.0 Strict//EN"
"http://www.w3.org/TR/xhtml1/DTD/xhtml1-strict.dtd">
<html xmlns="http://www.w3.org/1999/xhtml" xml:lang="en" lang="en">
  <head>
    <meta http-equiv="Content-Type" content="text/html; charset=utf-8"/>
    <base href="/" />
    <link rel="stylesheet" type="text/css" href="/css/master.css" />
    <?php if ($this->dojo()->isEnabled()):
        echo $this->dojo();
      endif;
    ?>
  </head>
  <body class="tundra">
  ...
  </body>
</html>
```

Updating the Controller

The final step is to update the ContactController and define the endpoint for the autocomplete input. Here's the code, which should be added to *$APP_DIR/application/modules/default/ controllers/ContactController.php*:

```php
<?php
class ContactController extends Zend_Controller_Action
{
  public function autocompleteAction()
  {
    // disable layout and view rendering
    $this->_helper->layout->disableLayout();
    $this->getHelper('viewRenderer')->setNoRender(true);

    // get country list from Zend_Locale
    $territories = Zend_Locale::getTranslationList('territory', null, 2);
    $items = array();
    foreach ($territories as $t) {
      $items[] = array('name' => $t);
    }

    // generate and return JSON string compliant with dojo.data structure
    $data = new Zend_Dojo_Data('name', $items);
    header('Content-Type: application/json');
    echo $data->toJson();
  }
}
```

This method converts an array containing a list of countries into the JSON format expected by Dojo using the Zend_Dojo_Data component discussed earlier, and returns it to the requesting client.

To see it in action, visit the SQUARE application's contact form, by browsing to **http:// square.localhost/contact**, and you should see a new text input field for country name. Enter a few characters in this field, and watch as Dojo requests and presents a list of matching suggestions from the `ContactController::autocom pleteAction` defined in the previous section. Figure 11-10 illustrates an example of what you might see.

Figure 11-10 The Dojo ComboBox in action

Try This 11-3 Adding a YUI Calendar Widget

In the previous section, you saw how easy it is to add Dojo widgets to a Zend Framework application. However, Dojo isn't the only game in town, and it's also quite easy to integrate widgets and libraries from other client-side programming toolkits as well. This next section illustrates the process by adding a pop-up calendar widget from the Yahoo! User Interface Library (YUI) to a Zend_Form instance.

The target form, in this case, is the ItemUpdate form that was first defined in Chapter 5, and that allows application administrators to adjust catalog item properties and set display status. In this example, we'll update the form to use YUI's graphical calendar widget for single-click date input, instead of displaying separate selection lists for day, month, and year input.

For purposes of this example, assume that all the necessary YUI files are hosted remotely and loaded from the Yahoo! Content Delivery Network (CDN).

Updating the Form

The first step is to update the form object, creating a new element that will contain the calendar widget and removing the previous date selection lists. Here's the revised form definition, which should be saved to *$APP_DIR/library/Square/Form/ItemUpdate.php*:

```php
<?php
class Square_Form_ItemUpdate extends Square_Form_ItemCreate
{
  public function init()
  {
    // get parent form
```

Ask the Expert

Q: What is the Yahoo! User Interface Library?

A: To quote its official Web site, the Yahoo! User Interface Library, aka YUI, is "a set of utilities and controls, written with JavaScript and CSS, for building richly interactive web applications." It provides a huge number of ready-made widgets that developers can integrate into a Web application with minimal fuss, and it works on all modern browsers. Some of the widgets in this library include an image carousel, a color picker, a drag-and-drop interface, an upload progress monitor, tabbed and tree menu systems, a calendar widget, and an input autocompleter.

Among these widgets is a calendar widget, which displays a monthly calendar and provides navigation controls for the user to move back and forth between months and years. The user can select a particular date by clicking it; the widget will automatically convert the selected date into a standard date string and attach it to a specified form element.

```php
    parent::init();

    // set form action (set to false for current URL)
    $this->setAction('/admin/catalog/item/update');

    // remove unwanted elements
    $this->removeElement('Captcha');
    $this->removeDisplayGroup('verification');
    $this->removeElement('images');
    $this->removeDisplayGroup('files');

    // create hidden input for item ID
    $id = new Zend_Form_Element_Hidden('RecordID');
    $id->addValidator('Int')
       ->addFilter('HtmlEntities')
       ->addFilter('StringTrim');

    // create select input for item display status
    $display = new Zend_Form_Element_Select('DisplayStatus',
      array('onChange' =>
        "javascript:handleInputDisplayOnSelect('DisplayStatus',
          'divDisplayUntil', new Array('1')); cal.hide();"));
    $display->setLabel('Display status:')
            ->setRequired(true)
            ->addValidator('Int')
            ->addFilter('HtmlEntities')
            ->addFilter('StringTrim');
    $display->addMultiOptions(array(
      0 => 'Hidden',
      1 => 'Visible'
    ));

    // create input for item display date
    $displayUntil = new Zend_Form_Element_Text('DisplayUntil');
    $displayUntil->setLabel('Display until (yyyy-mm-dd):')
                 ->addValidator('Date', false, array('format' =>
'yyyy-MM-dd'))
                 ->addFilter('HtmlEntities')
                 ->addFilter('StringTrim')
                 ->addDecorators(array(
                     array('HTMLTag', array('tag' => 'div', 'id' =>
'divDisplayUntil')),
                   ));

    // create container for YUI calendar widget
```

(continued)

```
$calendar = new Zend_Form_Element_Text('Calendar');
$calendar->setDecorators(array(
                array('Label', array('tag' => 'dt')),
                array('HTMLTag', array('tag' => 'div', 'id' =>
'divCalendar', 'class' => 'yui-skin-sam yui-calcontainer', 'style' =>
'display:none;')),
                ));

    // attach element to form
    $this->addElement($id)
        ->addElement($display)
        ->addElement($calendar)
        ->addElement($displayUntil);

    // create display group for status
    $this->addDisplayGroup(
      array('DisplayStatus', 'DisplayUntil', 'Calendar'),
      'display');
    $this->getDisplayGroup('display')
        ->setOrder(25)
        ->setLegend('Display Information');
    }
}
?>
```

Updating the Master Layout

The Zend Framework's HeadScript and HeadLink view helpers offer an easy way to specify external resources on a per-action basis. These helpers allow developers to specify the JavaScript and CSS files for each action and view script at design time, and they automatically generate the necessary <link> and <script> markup at run time.

To use these helpers, update the <head> of the administrative layout at *$APP_DIR/ application/layouts/admin.phtml* with the changes highlighted in bold:

```
<!DOCTYPE html PUBLIC "-//W3C//DTD XHTML 1.0 Strict//EN"
"http://www.w3.org/TR/xhtml1/DTD/xhtml1-strict.dtd">
<html xmlns="http://www.w3.org/1999/xhtml" xml:lang="en" lang="en">
  <head>
    <meta http-equiv="Content-Type" content="text/html; charset=utf-8"/>
    <base href="/" />
    <link rel="stylesheet" type="text/css" href="/css/master.css" />
    <link rel="stylesheet" type="text/css" href="/css/admin.css" />
    <?php echo $this->headLink(); ?>
    <?php echo $this->headScript(); ?>
  </head>
  <body>
```

```
   . . .
   </body>
</html>
```

Updating the Controller

The next step is to update the `Catalog_AdminItemController::updateAction` with the following two changes:

● Specify the source JavaScript and CSS files for the YUI calendar widget using the HeadLink and HeadScript view helpers.

● Adjust the code to use the date string provided by the calendar widget instead of the three separate values (month, date, and year) provided by the current selection lists.

Here's the revised code:

```php
<?php
class Catalog_AdminItemController extends Zend_Controller_Action
{
  // action to modify an individual catalog item
  public function updateAction()
  {
    // load JavaScript and CSS files
    $this->view->headLink()->appendStylesheet(
     'http://yui.yahooapis.com/combo?2.8.0r4/build/calendar/
      assets/skins/sam/calendar.css'
    );
    $this->view->headScript()->appendFile('/js/form.js');
    $this->view->headScript()->appendFile(
      'http://yui.yahooapis.com/combo?2.8.0r4/build/yahoo-dom-event/
       yahoo-dom-event.js&2.8.0r4/build/calendar/calendar-min.js'
    );

    // generate input form
    $form = new Square_Form_ItemUpdate;
    $this->view->form = $form;

    if ($this->getRequest()->isPost()) {
      // if POST request
      // test if input is valid
      // retrieve current record
      // update values and replace in database
      $postData = $this->getRequest()->getPost();

      // comment date adjustment
      //$postData['DisplayUntil'] = sprintf('%04d-%02d-%02d',
      //   $this->getRequest()->getParam('DisplayUntil_year'),
```

(continued)

```
//   $this->getRequest()->getParam('DisplayUntil_month'),
//   $this->getRequest()->getParam('DisplayUntil_day')
//);

        if ($form->isValid($postData)) {
          $input = $form->getValues();
          $item = Doctrine::getTable('Square_Model_Item')
                  ->find($input['RecordID']);
          $item->fromArray($input);
          $item->DisplayUntil = ($item->DisplayStatus == 0) ?
            null : $item->DisplayUntil;
          $item->save();
          $this->_helper->getHelper('FlashMessenger')
            ->addMessage('The record was successfully updated.');
          $this->_redirect('/admin/catalog/item/success');
        }
      } else {
        // if GET request
        // set filters and validators for GET input
        // test if input is valid
        // retrieve requested record
        // pre-populate form
        $filters = array(
          'id' => array('HtmlEntities', 'StripTags', 'StringTrim')
        );
        $validators = array(
          'id' => array('NotEmpty', 'Int')
        );
        $input = new Zend_Filter_Input($filters, $validators);
        $input->setData($this->getRequest()->getParams());
        if ($input->isValid()) {
          $q = Doctrine_Query::create()
                ->from('Square_Model_Item i')
                ->leftJoin('i.Square_Model_Country c')
                ->leftJoin('i.Square_Model_Grade g')
                ->leftJoin('i.Square_Model_Type t')
                ->where('i.RecordID = ?', $input->id);
          $result = $q->fetchArray();
          if (count($result) == 1) {
            // comment date adjustment
            //$date = $result[0]['DisplayUntil'];
            //$result[0]['DisplayUntil_day'] = date('d', strtotime($date));
            //$result[0]['DisplayUntil_month'] = date('m', strtotime($date));
            //$result[0]['DisplayUntil_year'] = date('Y', strtotime($date));
            $this->view->form->populate($result[0]);
          } else {
            throw new Zend_Controller_Action_Exception('Page not found', 404);
          }
        } else {
```

```
            throw new Zend_Controller_Action_Exception('Invalid input');
        }
    }
    }
}
```

Updating the View

Finally, there's a little bit of JavaScript needed to initialize the widget in the view script, which is located at *$APP_DIR/application/modules/admin/views/scripts/admin-item/update.phtml*:

```
<h2>Update Item</h2>
<?php echo $this->form; ?>

<script type="text/javascript">
handleInputDisplayOnSelect('DisplayStatus', 'divDisplayUntil', new Array('1'));

cal = new YAHOO.widget.Calendar('cal', 'divCalendar', {close:true});
cal.render();
YAHOO.util.Event.addListener('DisplayUntil', 'click', cal.show, cal, true);
cal.selectEvent.subscribe(handleSelect, cal, true);

function handleSelect(type,args,obj) {
    var dates = args[0];
    var date = dates[0];
    var year = date[0];
    var month = date[1];
    var day = date[2];
```

Ask the Expert

Q: Why don't you simply specify "hard" links to the YUI JavaScript and CSS files in the master layout, instead of using the `headScript()` and `headLink()` view helpers?

A: The YUI files are only needed for certain view scripts. Since these files are read from a remote host over HTTP, it's suboptimal to create "hard" links to them in the master layout, because it would result in these files being requested on every page load. This adds unnecessary overhead and increases the number of seconds a user has to wait before the page is completely loaded. Using the view helpers makes it possible to load these files only when needed, producing a better user experience and improving performance.

(continued)

Figure 11-11 The YUI calendar widget in action

```
    var input = document.getElementById('DisplayUntil');
    input.value = year + '-' + padZero(month, 2) + '-' + padZero(day, 2);
}
</script>
```

Save these changes, and then navigate your way to the administration panel and select a catalog item for update. You should be presented with a form with fields for updating the various item properties. Select the "Display until" field, and you should be presented with a pop-up calendar for date selection. Figure 11-11 illustrates what this might look like.

Summary

This chapter focused on user interface elements, and the Zend Framework components that can create a better experience for application users. First, this chapter discussed the Zend_Navigation component, illustrating how to structure pages into containers and then generate sitemaps, menus, and breadcrumb trails from these containers. Next, it examined the Zend Framework's Dojo integration and illustrated how the Zend_Dojo component could be used to quickly integrate an autocomplete input into a Zend_Form instance. Finally, it looked at the process of using third-party JavaScript widgets in a Zend Framework application, with an example of integrating a YUI date picker into a Zend_Form instance.

To learn more about the topics discussed in this chapter, consider visiting the following links:

- The Zend_Navigation component, at
  http://framework.zend.com/manual/en/zend.navigation.html

- The Zend_Dojo component, at
  http://framework.zend.com/manual/en/zend.dojo.html

- Zend Framework action helpers, at
  http://framework.zend.com/manual/en/zend.controller.actionhelpers.html

- Zend Framework resource plug-ins, at
  http://framework.zend.com/manual/en/zend.application.available-resources.html

- The Yahoo! User Interface Library, at
  http://developer.yahoo.com/yui/

- The Dojo Toolkit, at
  http://www.dojotoolkit.org/

- The Sitemaps protocol, at
  http://www.sitemaps.org/

- A discussion of creating custom resource plug-ins (Stefan Schmalhaus), at
  http://blog.log2e.com/2009/06/01/creating-a-custom-resource-plugin-in-zend-framework-18/

Chapter 12

Optimizing Performance

Key Skills & Concepts

- Become familiar with application benchmarking and profiling tools
- Understand the benefits and types of caching
- Find out how to cache Web service responses and RSS feeds
- Learn various techniques for optimizing database query performance

Over the last few years, Web applications have become increasingly sophisticated, sporting a number of bells and whistles—AJAX user interfaces, streaming media, dynamically generated content—in an attempt to attract and retain visitors. But as applications become more complex, as their reliance on dynamic data sources increases, and as more and more requests need to be served per second, the first casualty is usually application performance.

However, there are a number of common techniques you can use to identify and work around performance bottlenecks in application code. Techniques like code profiling, caching, refactoring, and lazy loading can reduce server load and improve application response times. The Zend Framework comes with a number of tools that you can use for this task, and this chapter discusses some of them.

Analyzing Performance

Before you can get started with fine-tuning a Web application, you need detailed information on which parts of an application are suffering from degraded performance. A number of tools exist for benchmarking and profiling, and the following sections discuss them in some detail.

Benchmarking

ApacheBench, or *ab*, is a tool to benchmark Web server response times. It does this by sending multiple simultaneous requests to a server URL, timing the response, and generating detailed statistics of response times under varying load conditions. ApacheBench is part of the Apache Web server distribution and is available for both Windows and *NIX platforms. Although part of the Apache distribution, it can also be used to benchmark any other HTTP-compliant Web server.

Here's an example of using ApacheBench to benchmark a Web application, simulating 1000 requests for the same resource, sent 10 at a time:

```
shell> ab -n 1000 -c 10 http://server/request/url
```

Figure 12-1 illustrates an example of the output report generated by ApacheBench.

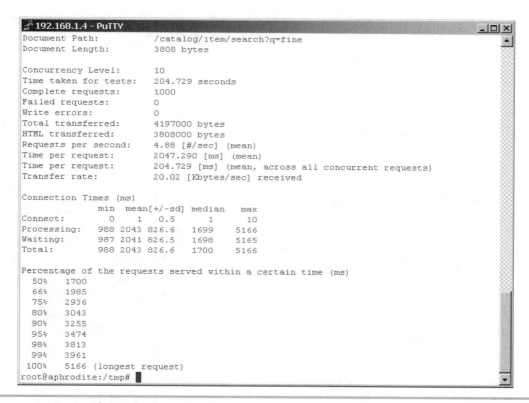

```
192.168.1.4 - PuTTY                                                     _ □ ×
Document Path:           /catalog/item/search?q=fine
Document Length:         3808 bytes

Concurrency Level:       10
Time taken for tests:    204.729 seconds
Complete requests:       1000
Failed requests:         0
Write errors:            0
Total transferred:       4197000 bytes
HTML transferred:        3808000 bytes
Requests per second:     4.88 [#/sec] (mean)
Time per request:        2047.290 [ms] (mean)
Time per request:        204.729 [ms] (mean, across all concurrent requests)
Transfer rate:           20.02 [Kbytes/sec] received

Connection Times (ms)
              min  mean[+/-sd] median   max
Connect:        0    1   0.5      1      10
Processing:   988 2043 826.6    1699    5166
Waiting:      987 2041 826.5    1698    5165
Total:        988 2043 826.6    1700    5166

Percentage of the requests served within a certain time (ms)
   50%    1700
   66%    1985
   75%    2936
   80%    3043
   90%    3255
   95%    3474
   98%    3813
   99%    3961
  100%    5166 (longest request)
root@aphrodite:/tmp#
```

Figure 12-1   ApacheBench summary statistics

As Figure 12-1 illustrates, this report provides useful information on the average number of seconds needed by the server to respond to a particular URL request. Running a similar test on other application routes builds up an accurate picture of which parts of an application are "slow" and could benefit from optimization.

An alternative to ApacheBench is the Microsoft Web Capacity Analysis Tool (WCAT). Like ApacheBench, this tool too simulates load on a Web server, returning data on measured throughput and response times. Although only available for the Windows platform, it does have a couple of interesting features: It can be used from multiple client systems simultaneously, and it can benchmark multiple-request "transactions" that must be executed in a specific sequence.

Here's an example of using WCAT to benchmark a Web application:

```
shell> wcat.wsf -terminate -run -clients localhost -t scenario.ubr -f
settings.ubr -s server -singleip -extended
```

Figure 12-2 illustrates an example WCAT output report.

Web Capacity Analysis Tool

computer: 192.168.1.2
build:
collected: 2/15/2010 23:46:18
title:

Contents	Summary	
• **Warnings**	**Transactions/sec**	
	8.90	
• **Overall Statistics**	**Pathlength/Transaction**	
o Network Statistics		
o Time Analysis	**Context Switches/Transaction**	
o Response Time Analysis	0.00	
o Request/Response Statistics		
o HTTP Status Codes	**Requests/sec**	
o Transaction Statistics	8.90	
o Errors		
	Pathlength/Request	
• **Per Client Statistics**		
o Time Analysis	**Context Switches/Request**	
o Response Time Analysis (Time to First Byte)	0.00	
o Response Time Analysis (Time to Last Byte)		
o Network Statistics	**% Processor Time**	
o Request/Response Statistics	0.00	
o HTTP Status Codes		
o Errors	**MBits/sec**	
	0.08	
• **General Information**		
o Server Information	**Total Errors**	
o Test Settings	0	

Figure 12-2 A WCAT benchmark report

Code Profiling

Once you've got some broad benchmarking figures and have identified areas for improvement, the next step is to profile the relevant controllers and actions, and understand where the bottlenecks are. One of the most popular tools for this task is PHP's Xdebug extension, available for both Windows and *NIX flavors of PHP.

The Xdebug profiler generates detailed statistics on the amount of time spent per function call in a script and the total time spent on script compilation, processing, and execution. These statistics make it possible to see which function calls are responsible for the maximum processing overhead, and thus identify areas for potential optimization. The Xdebug extension also overrides PHP's default exception-handling routines, providing more detailed debugging output and stack traces for both fatal and non-fatal errors.

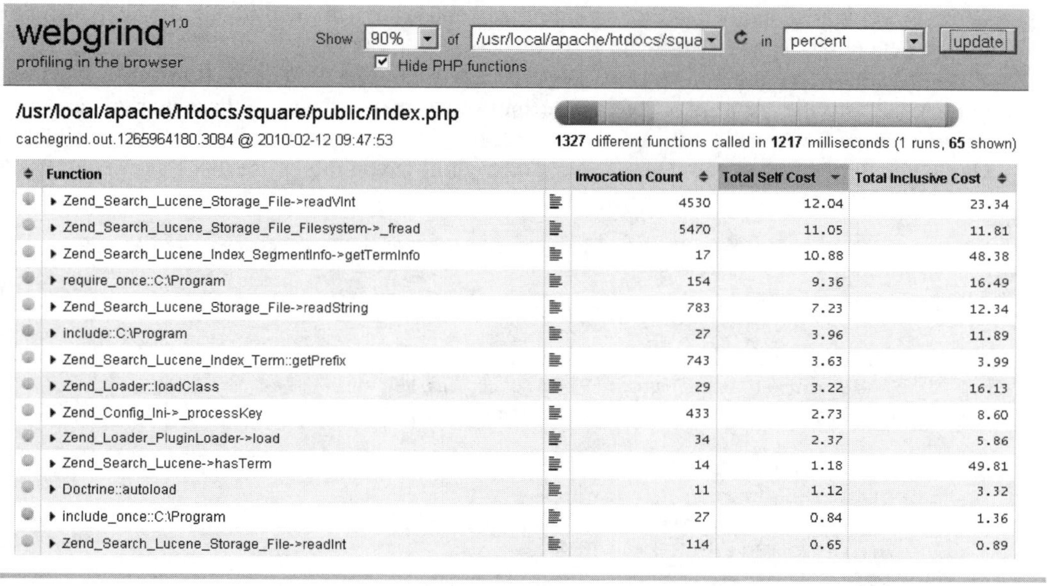

Figure 12-3   An Xdebug profile of a Zend Framework request, as viewed in Webgrind

Once configured, Xdebug will automatically profile every script executed through the PHP interpreter. Profile reports are formatted as *cachegrind files*, which may be viewed with a number of open-source tools, such as WinCacheGrind (Windows desktop), KCacheGrind (*NIX desktop), or Webgrind (PHP Web application). Profiles are stored in the output directory specified in the *xdebug.profiler_output_dir* variable in PHP's *php.ini* configuration file.

Figure 12-3 illustrates what such a profile might look like.

This type of profiling information is very useful to understand, for example, which method calls or framework components are taking up the majority of processing time and therefore are reasonable targets for optimization or substitution by other, lighter libraries.

NOTE

PHP's Xdebug extension is installed in the usual way, in PHP's *ext/* directory, and is activated by adding the `zend_extension_ts = /path/to/xdebug/ext` directive to the php.ini configuration file. You must also specify the `xdebug.profiler_enable`, `xdebug.profiler_output_dir`, and `xdebug.trace_output_dir` variables in the configuration file. For detailed installation instructions, see the Xdebug Web site link at the end of this chapter.

An alternative to Xdebug is the PEAR Benchmark class, which provides an API to benchmark PHP function calls. In this case, the benchmarking tool is embedded within specific actions, wrapping action code within calls to its `start()` and `stop()` methods. These methods are typically called at the beginning and end of an action, although they can also be used to benchmark specific subsections of an action.

Within these two method calls, it's a good idea to set user-defined section "markers" to identify the activities or transactions the script is undertaking; because these markers are included in the final report, they can help in identifying which transactions are responsible for what percentage of overhead. Here's an example of how you might use this class:

```php
<?php
class Sandbox_ExampleController extends Zend_Controller_Action
{
  public function queryAction()
  {
    // include profiler
    include_once('Benchmark/Profiler.php');
    $profiler = new Benchmark_Profiler();

    // start profiler
    $profiler->start();

    // profile filter/validator setup
    $profiler->enterSection("Setup");
    $filters = array(
      'q' => array('HtmlEntities', 'StripTags', 'StringTrim'),
    );
    $validators = array(
      'q' => array('Alpha'),
    );
    $input = new Zend_Filter_Input($filters, $validators);
    $input->setData($this->getRequest()->getParams());
    $profiler->leaveSection("Setup");

    // profile validation
    $profiler->enterSection("Validate");
    $check = $input->isValid();
    $profiler->leaveSection("Validate");

    // profile database query
    if ($check) {
      $profiler->enterSection("Query");
      $db = $this->getInvokeArg('bootstrap')->getResource('database');

      $sql = "SELECT * FROM city AS ci,
              country AS co,
              countrylanguage AS cl
              WHERE
                ci.CountryCode = co.Code AND
                cl.CountryCode = co.Code AND
                cl.Language = 'English' AND
```

```
                    cl.IsOfficial = 'T' AND
                    co.Continent LIKE '%$input->q%'";
        $result = $db->fetchAll($sql);
        $this->view->records = $result;
        $profiler->leaveSection("Query");
    }
    $profiler->stop();

    $this->view->profile = $profiler->_getOutput('html');
  }
}
```

Figure 12-4 has an example of the profiling data generated by PEAR Benchmark.

TIP

The PEAR Benchmark class, like other PEAR classes, doesn't work with the Zend Framework autoloader out of the box. To make it compatible with the Zend Framework autoloader, install it with the PEAR installer, check that your PEAR directory is part of the PHP include path, and then add the line `autoloaderNamespaces[] = 'Benchmark'` to the *application.ini* file.

Query Profiling

Xdebug and PEAR Benchmark are extremely useful for profiling PHP code, but they don't offer any information on what is often the biggest performance bottleneck in a Web application: the interaction between the application and the database server. As part of any profiling exercise, it is also necessary to profile the application's database queries and understand where they can be optimized. If you're using Zend_Db for your database queries, you can profile them with the Zend_Db_Profiler component, which makes it possible to inspect application queries and obtain a report of the elapsed time per query.

	total ex. time	netto ex. time	#calls	%	calls	callers
Setup	0.00324702262878	0.00324702262878	1	7.01%		Global (1)
Validate	0.00511384010315	0.00511384010315	1	11.03%		Global (1)
Query	0.0377938747406	0.0377938747406	1	81.54%		Global (1)
Global	0.0463509559631	0.000196218490601	1	100.00%	Setup (1), Validate (1), Query (1)	

Figure 12-4   A PEAR Benchmark profile of a Zend Framework request

The easiest way to use Zend_Db_Profiler is to attach it to the Zend_Db instance in the application bootstrapper, as follows:

```php
<?php
class Bootstrap extends Zend_Application_Bootstrap_Bootstrap
{
  protected function _initDatabase()
  {
    $db = new Zend_Db_Adapter_Pdo_Mysql(array(
        'host'      => '127.0.0.1',
        'username'  => 'user',
        'password'  => 'pass',
        'dbname'    => 'world'
    ));
    $profiler = new Zend_Db_Profiler();
    $profiler->setEnabled(true);
    $db->setProfiler($profiler);
    return $db;
  }
}
```

The query profiles captured by the profiler can be retrieved with the Zend_Db_Profiler object's getQueryProfiles() method. This method returns an array of Zend_Db_Profiler_Query objects, each of which exposes getQuery() and getElapsedSecs() methods to retrieve the query string and query execution time, respectively. Here's an example of retrieving profile data from the profiler using these methods:

```php
<?php
class Sandbox_ExampleController extends Zend_Controller_Action
{
  public function queryAction()
  {
    // get database adapter
    $db = $this->getInvokeArg('bootstrap')->getResource('database');

    // run query
    $sql = "SELECT * FROM city AS ci,
              country AS co,
              countrylanguage AS cl
              WHERE
                ci.CountryCode = co.Code AND
                cl.CountryCode = co.Code AND
                cl.Language = 'English' AND
                cl.IsOfficial = 'T' AND
                co.Continent LIKE '%$input->q%'";
    $result = $db->fetchAll($sql);
    $this->view->records = $result;
```

```
    $this->view->profiles = array();

    // get query profile data
    foreach ($db->getProfiler()->getQueryProfiles() as $profile) {
      $this->view->profiles[] = array(
        'sql'   =>  $profile->getQuery(),
        'time'  =>  $profile->getElapsedSecs(),
      );
    }
  }
}
```

Figure 12-5 illustrates an example of the profile data generated by the previous listing.

There's also a specialized Zend_Db_Profiler_Firebug extension that can send query profiling data directly to the Firebug console. To use this, update the application bootstrapper to use this extension, as follows:

```php
<?php
class Bootstrap extends Zend_Application_Bootstrap_Bootstrap
{
  protected function _initDatabase()
  {
    $db = new Zend_Db_Adapter_Pdo_Mysql(array(
        'host'     => '127.0.0.1',
        'username' => 'user',
        'password' => 'pass',
```

```
            Array
            (
                [0] => Array
                    (
                        [sql] => connect
                        [time] => 0.010577917099
                    )

                [1] => Array
                    (
                        [sql] => SELECT * FROM city AS ci,
                            country AS co,
                            countrylanguage AS cl
                            WHERE
                                ci.CountryCode = co.Code AND
                                cl.CountryCode = co.Code AND
                                cl.Language = 'English' AND
                                cl.IsOfficial = 'T' AND
                                co.Continent LIKE '%amer%'
                        [time] => 0.010577917099
                    )

            )
```

Figure 12-5   Query profile output generated by Zend_Db_Profiler

```
        'dbname'   => 'world'
    ));
    $profiler = new Zend_Db_Profiler_Firebug('Query log');
    $profiler->setEnabled(true);
    $db->setProfiler($profiler);
    return $db;
  }
}
```

Figure 12-6 illustrates an example of the Firebug console output generated by the Zend_ Db profiler.

The Zend Framework doesn't include a built-in profiler for Doctrine-based database queries, but it's quite easy to add this with a third-party component from the Imind project. This project includes a number of Doctrine-specific extensions for the Zend Framework, one of which is the Imind_Profiler_Doctrine_Firebug component. This component logs Doctrine queries to the Firebug (the Firefox browser debugger) console, making it possible to measure query performance in real time.

To profile Doctrine queries with the Imind Doctrine profiler, attach the profile to the Doctrine connection manager in the application bootstrapper, as follows:

```
<?php
class Bootstrap extends Zend_Application_Bootstrap_Bootstrap
{
    protected function _initDoctrine()
    {
        require_once 'Doctrine/Doctrine.php';
```

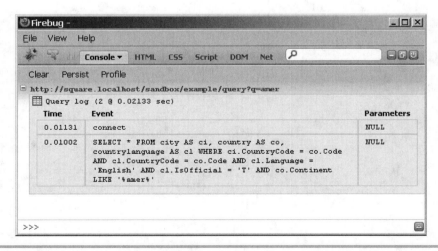

Figure 2-6   Query profile output generated by Zend_Db_Profiler, as seen in the Firebug console

```
        $this->getApplication()->getAutoloader()
            ->pushAutoloader(array('Doctrine', 'autoload'), 'Doctrine');
        $manager = Doctrine_Manager::getInstance();
        $manager->setAttribute(
            Doctrine::ATTR_MODEL_LOADING,
            Doctrine::MODEL_LOADING_CONSERVATIVE
        );

        $config = $this->getOption('doctrine');
        $conn = Doctrine_Manager::connection($config['dsn'], 'doctrine');

        $profiler = new Imind_Profiler_Doctrine_Firebug();
        $conn->setListener($profiler);
        return $conn;
    }
}
```

As a result of the previous addition, all Doctrine queries will now be automatically profiled and the results displayed in the Firebug console. Figure 12-7 illustrates an example of the Firebug console output generated by the Imind Doctrine profiler.

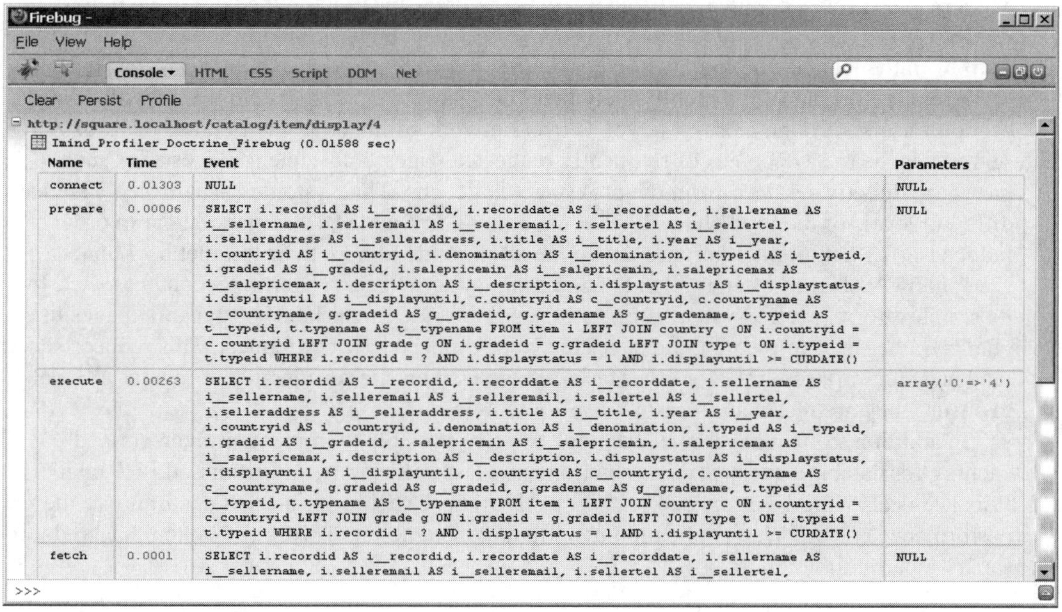

Figure 12-7 Query profile output generated by the Imind Doctrine profiler, as seen in the Firebug console

NOTE
Once you have a list of queries and some data on how long they're taking to execute, the next step is usually to analyze them and try to get them to run faster. If you're using MySQL, attaching the EXPLAIN keyword to the beginning of each SELECT query returns a chart describing how the query will be processed. Included within this chart is information on which tables the query will access and the number of rows the query is expected to return. This information comes in handy to see which tables should be indexed to speed up performance and to analyze where the bottlenecks are. Take a look at the section entitled "Query Tuning" later in this chapter for some common techniques you can use to make your queries run faster.

Caching Data

One of the quickest ways to ease performance bottlenecks in a Web application is by using a cache.

What's that, you ask? Very simply, a *cache* is an intermediate location containing copies of frequently requested pieces of information. Whenever a request for one of these information fragments comes in, the system will pull out and return the cached copy, which is invariably faster than generating the information anew from the original data source.

Caches can be maintained at various levels depending on the requirements of the user. Unknown to many, the most commonly used caching mechanism is the Web browser itself. Modern Web browsers download content to a temporary location on the hard drive before rendering it to the user. And usually, if you visit the same page again, the browser will just pick it up from the local cache (unless you configured it differently).

At your workplace, it's highly likely that you share your Internet connection with a large group of users, through a proxy server. Clever network administrators often use the proxy server's cache to save copies of frequently requested pages. Subsequent requests for such pages are directly serviced from the proxy server's cache. This system is usually replicated at different levels of the food chain; it's not uncommon to find ISPs caching content in order to reduce traffic that might otherwise eat up precious bandwidth on their Internet backbone.

Finally, Web sites often implement a caching system to serve their own content faster. In its simplest form, such a system consists of sending static "snapshots" of dynamic pages to clients, rather than re-creating the pages anew in response to every request. This reduces server load and frees up resources for other tasks. The snapshots are regenerated at regular intervals to ensure they are reasonably fresh.

In addition to such page-level caching, it is also possible to implement finer-grained caching for database query results, function and class definitions, and compiled PHP code (this last is also known as *opcode caching*). All of these caching strategies can improve the performance of your Web application by reducing the amount of work the system has to do to satisfy a particular request.

Understanding Cache Operations

The Zend Framework includes a Zend_Cache component, which provides a comprehensive API to store and retrieve data from a cache. This data may include database result collections, function or method return values, objects, static files, or rendered page output. The cache itself may be implemented either as an on-disk store or an in-memory store; Zend_Cache supports a number of different stores, including flat file, SQLite database, memcached server, or APC opcode cache.

Every cache entry has two key attributes: a *lifetime* and a *unique identifier*.

●   The lifetime value, usually specified in seconds, indicates the period for which a cache entry should be considered "valid" or "fresh." Once this time period has elapsed, the cache entry becomes "stale" and must be regenerated from the original data source.

●   Since a single cache can hold multiple entries, every entry must be given a unique identifier. This identifier serves as a marker for the cache entry and is used to retrieve the cached data.

To better illustrate how this works, consider the following example:

```php
<?php
class Sandbox_ExampleController extends Zend_Controller_Action
{
  public function cacheAction()
  {
    // define cache configuration
    $front = array(
      'lifetime' => 600,
      'automatic_serialization' => true
    );
    $back = array(
      'cache_dir' => APPLICATION_PATH . '/../tmp/cache'
    );

    // initialize cache
    $cache = Zend_Cache::factory('Core', 'File', $front, $back);

    // use cache if available
    if(!($this->view->records = $cache->load('cities'))) {
      // set query
      $sql = "SELECT * FROM city AS ci,
              country AS co,
              countrylanguage AS cl
              WHERE
                ci.CountryCode = co.Code AND
                cl.CountryCode = co.Code AND
                cl.Language = 'English' AND
                cl.IsOfficial = 'T'";

      // get database adapter
      $db = $this->getInvokeArg('bootstrap')->getResource('database');
```

```
        // execute query and save results to cache
        $result = $db->fetchAll($sql);
        $cache->save($result, 'cities');
        $this->view->records = $result;
    }
  }
}
```

This listing begins by initializing a new Zend_Cache instance using the `Zend_Cache::factory()` method. This method accepts the name of the cache frontend and backend, together with an array of configuration options for each. The previous example uses the Core frontend, which is the simplest available Zend_Cache frontend, together with the File backend, which stores cache entries as disk files. Configuration options for each of these, such as the number of seconds each cache entry is valid for and the location of the directory for cache files, are specified as associative arrays. The return value of the `Zend_Cache::factory()` method is a correctly configured Zend_Cache instance.

The basic logic of cache utilization is quite simple, and is depicted in the flow chart in Figure 12-8. This business logic is illustrated in the previous code listing, which caches the result of a database query. The code first checks if the required result is present in the cache. If it is, it is directly assigned to the view, without the database server coming into the picture

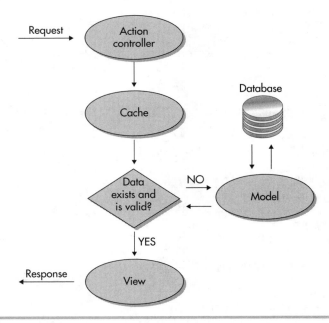

Figure 12-8 Flow chart of cache operation

at all. If it is not, a query is executed on the database server to obtain the required data, and a copy of the result is saved to the cache. This cached data is then used to serve subsequent requests, until it expires and needs to be regenerated.

Checking whether the data exists in the cache is accomplished with the `load()` method, while writing data to the cache is done with the `save()` method. Notice that both methods require the unique cache entry identifier, which, in the previous listing, is the string `'cities'`. The `save()` method additionally lets you specify the entry lifetime, in seconds, as an optional third argument; if present, this value will override the default value specified in the frontend configuration options.

TIP
Many Zend Framework components, including Zend_Translate, Zend_Db, and Zend_Feed_Reader, can be passed a configured Zend_Cache instance, and they will then automatically use this cache to store relevant metadata or lookup information. You'll see an example of this later in the chapter.

Understanding Cache Frontends and Backends
As discussed in the previous section, Zend_Cache offers a number of different cache frontends and backends, each designed for a different purpose. Tables 12-1 and 12-2 provide a list.

A few examples are useful to illustrate how these can be used in an MVC application. Consider, for example, the Class and Function frontends, which make it possible to cache computationally expensive procedures so as to reduce server load. Here's an example of the Class frontend in action:

```php
<?php
class Sandbox_ExampleController extends Zend_Controller_Action
{
  public function cacheAction()
  {
    // define cache configuration
```

Cache Frontend	Description
Core	All-purpose base cache implementation
Class	Caches method return values
Function	Caches function return values
File	Caches disk files
Capture	Caches rendered page output or output blocks
Page	Caches rendered page output

Table 12-1   Cache Frontends Included with the Zend Framework

Cache Backend	Description
Apc	Stores cache entries to the APC opcode cache
File	Stores cache entries as disk files
Memcached	Stores cache entries to a memcached server
Sqlite	Stores cache entries in an SQLite database
Static	Stores cache entries as static HTML files
Two_Levels	Stores cache entries in two locations
XCache	Stores cache entries using an XCache cache
ZendServer	Stores cache entries using the Zend Server cache
Blackhole	Stub implementation that caches entries to the system bitbucket (only useful for testing)
Test	Test implementation with predefined cache entries (only useful for debugging)

Table 12-2 Cache Backends Included with the Zend Framework

```
$front = array(
  'lifetime' => 600,
  'automatic_serialization' => true,
  'cached_entity' => new Order
);
$back = array(
    'servers' => array(
      array(
        'host' => 'localhost',
        'port' => 11211,
        'timeout' => 5,
        'retry_interval' => 15,
      )
    )
  );

// initialize cache
$cache = Zend_Cache::factory('Class', 'Memcached', $front, $back);

// use cached object to perform method calls
$this->view->result =
  $cache->findCheapestShippingProvider(100, 33.6, 1, 'NY');
  }
}
```

In this example, the findCheapestShippingProvider() method accepts a set of inputs, such as total weight, number of items, delivery speed, and destination, and then internally consults and ranks various options to identify the cheapest shipping provider for those inputs.

In most cases, this would be a time-consuming process involving a few database queries and calls to Web service endpoints. It therefore makes sense to cache the output of this method call so that repeat queries with the same input "fingerprint" can be directly retrieved from the cache. Cached data is stored in a memcached server, instead of a disk file, for faster retrieval.

Here's another example, this one using the File frontend with the APC backend:

```php
<?php
class Sandbox_ExampleController extends Zend_Controller_Action
{
  public function cacheAction()
  {
    // define master file
    $localConfigFile = APPLICATION_PATH . '/configs/my.ini';

    // define cache configuration
    $front = array(
      'lifetime' => 600,
      'automatic_serialization' => true,
      'master_files' => array($localConfigFile)
    );
    $back = array();

    // initialize cache
    // load master file from cache
    $cache = Zend_Cache::factory('File', 'Apc', $front, $back);
    if (!($config = $cache->load('localconfig'))) {
      if (file_exists($localConfigFile)) {
        $config = new Zend_Config_Ini($localConfigFile);
        $cache->save($config, 'localconfig');
      }
    }
  }
}
```

This example automatically caches the specified master file in the APC shared memory cache and uses this for subsequent requests. The key thing to note here is that the File frontend will automatically detect any change to the master file and, when such a change occurs, invalidate the cached version and re-create it on the next request.

NOTE
The Static backend is interesting, because it saves rendered pages as static HTML files on disk. These files can then be served up in response to requests, bypassing PHP altogether and producing a dramatic increase in performance. Using this backend requires some alteration to the server's URL rewriting rules, but the result is often worth the effort, especially for high-traffic URLs. The Zend Framework manual has a detailed example of how to use this backend, together with example rewriting rules that you can extend for different scenarios.

Using the Cache Manager

In most cases, the cache will be configured and initialized in the application bootstrapper and "exported" across the application using Zend_Registry, so that it can be used within different actions. However, in many cases, there is a need to use different cache configurations depending on the type of data being cached. For example, you might want to cache RSS and Web service feeds in disk files while storing frequently executed query results in a memory-based cache, because retrieving data from disk files usually takes longer than pulling it out of memory.

Striking the correct balance between the different cache types is therefore of critical importance in achieving an optimal mix of speed and efficiency. This task is made somewhat easier with the Zend Framework's Zend_Cache_Manager component and resource plug-in, which makes it possible to configure multiple cache types in the application configuration file. This reduces the amount of configuration needed in the application bootstrapper, and makes it possible to use different caching styles for different actions (or even within the same action).

Here's an example of one such cache configuration:

```
resources.cachemanager.mycache.frontend.name = Core
resources.cachemanager.mycache.frontend.options.lifetime = 600
resources.cachemanager.mycache.frontend.options.automatic_serialization = true
resources.cachemanager.mycache.backend.name = Apc
```

It is now possible to directly utilize this cache instance within an action, as follows:

```php
<?php
class Sandbox_ExampleController extends Zend_Controller_Action
{
  public function cacheAction()
  {
    // get cache
    $cache = $this->getInvokeArg('bootstrap')
                  ->getResource('cachemanager')
                  ->getCache('mycache');

    // use cache if available
    if(!($this->view->records = $cache->load('cities'))) {
      // run query
      $sql = "SELECT * FROM city AS ci,
                  country AS co,
                  countrylanguage AS cl
              WHERE
                  ci.CountryCode = co.Code AND
                  cl.CountryCode = co.Code AND
                  cl.Language = 'English' AND
                  cl.IsOfficial = 'T'";

      // get and use database adapter
      $db = $this->getInvokeArg('bootstrap')->getResource('database');
```

```
      $result = $db->fetchAll($sql);
      $cache->save($result, 'cities');
      $this->view->records = $result;
    }
  }
}
```

NOTE

It's important to note that configuring a cache in the application configuration file does *not* automatically initialize it. For performance reasons, Zend_Cache_Manager will only initialize a Zend_Cache instance when it is invoked by name with the getCache() method, and not before.

Caching Doctrine Queries

While Zend_Cache can certainly be used to cache the results of database queries, as demonstrated in the very first example in this section, it's also possible to use Doctrine's own caching mechanism for this purpose. Doctrine comes with two different caching systems, one for queries and one for query results, and both are reasonably easy to activate and use, with minimal code refactoring needed.

The Doctrine query cache holds parsed representations of Doctrine_Query objects, allowing repeat queries to be directly sent on the server without first needing to be parsed. The Doctrine result cache does everything the Doctrine query cache does, but also stores serialized representations of the query results and returns this wherever possible, thereby taking the database

Ask the Expert

Q: Is a memory cache always preferable to a disk cache?

A: A disk cache is generally considered "slower" than a memory cache, because retrieving data from disk files usually takes longer than pulling it out of a memory-based cache like memcached or APC. With this in mind, it often makes sense to cache frequently accessed data in a memory cache rather than in a disk cache, such that it can be retrieved and served up faster.

However, it is incorrect to conclude from this that application performance can be maximized simply by storing all data in a memory-based cache, because one must also consider the size of the data being cached. In most cases, memory is a far scarcer resource than disk space, so it usually makes more sense to use a disk cache when the data to be cached is large in size. Storing everything, including the kitchen sink, in a memory-based cache will usually end up hurting, rather than helping, performance as the system will quickly run out of memory for other critical tasks.

server out of the loop and significantly improving performance. Cached data can be stored in a memcached server, an APC shared memory cache, or any other Doctrine-supported database.

Activating the Doctrine query cache is quite simple: Initialize the Doctrine driver for the corresponding cache backend, and pass this to the Doctrine_Manager instance using the `Doctrine::ATTR_QUERY_CACHE` attribute. Here's an example:

```php
<?php
// set up cache driver
$servers = array(
  'host' => 'localhost',
  'port' => 11211,
  'persistent' => false
);
$cache = new Doctrine_Cache_Memcache(array(
    'servers' => $servers,
    'compression' => false
  )
);

// attach cache to Doctrine manager
$manager = Doctrine_Manager::getInstance();
$manager->setAttribute(Doctrine::ATTR_QUERY_CACHE, $cache);
?>
```

Once initialized in this manner, the Doctrine query cache is automatically active for all queries executed through Doctrine.

A similar approach is to be followed for the Doctrine result cache, as follows:

```php
<?php
// set up cache driver
$servers = array(
  'host' => 'localhost',
  'port' => 11211,
  'persistent' => false
);
$cache = new Doctrine_Cache_Memcache(array(
    'servers' => $servers,
    'compression' => false
  )
);

// attach cache to Doctrine manager
$manager = Doctrine_Manager::getInstance();
$manager->setAttribute(Doctrine::ATTR_RESULT_CACHE, $cache);
?>
```

It's important to note, though, that the Doctrine result cache is not automatically active for all queries executed through Doctrine; Doctrine must be explicitly told to use this cache on a

per-query basis, by adding the `useResultCache()` method to the corresponding Doctrine_
Query object. Here's an example of how to do this:

```php
<?php
class Sandbox_ExampleController extends Zend_Controller_Action
{
  public function cacheAction()
  {
    $id = $this->_getParam('id');
    $q = Doctrine_Query::create()
          ->from('Square_Model_Item i')
          ->leftJoin('i.Square_Model_Country c')
          ->leftJoin('i.Square_Model_Grade g')
          ->leftJoin('i.Square_Model_Type t')
          ->where('i.RecordID = ?', $id)
          ->addWhere('i.DisplayStatus = 1')
          ->useResultCache(true);
    $this->view->result = $q->fetchArray();
  }
}
```

NOTE
If you're using MySQL as your database, you should know that MySQL comes with its
own query cache, which is enabled by default. This query cache stores the result set of
SELECT queries and, on the next request for the same query, retrieves the results from
the cache instead of running the query again. Be aware, however, that only queries that
are textually exact will match what's in the query cache; any difference will be treated
as a new query. For example, 'SELECT * FROM airport' won't return the result from
'select * FROM airport' in the cache.

Optimizing Application Code

While caching can certainly produce significant performance improvements in a Web
application, it's not the only tool available to clever application developers. The following
sections examine some other common optimization strategies:

Query Tuning

There are a number of techniques you can use to optimize the performance of your database
queries and ensure that they're working as efficiently as possible. The following sections
discuss some of these techniques, with special reference to MySQL, by far the most commonly
used database server in modern Web application development.

Use Joins Instead of Subqueries

MySQL is better at optimizing joins than subqueries, so if you find the load averages on
your MySQL server hitting unacceptably high levels, examine your application code and try

rewriting your subqueries as joins or sequences of joins. For example, the following subquery is certainly legal:

```
SELECT id, name FROM movie WHERE directorid IN
  (SELECT id FROM director
   WHERE name = 'Alfred Hitchcock');
```

But the following equivalent join would run faster due to MySQL's optimization algorithms:

```
SELECT m.id, m.name FROM movie AS m, director AS d
  WHERE d.id = m.directorid AND d.name = 'Alfred Hitchcock';
```

You can also turn inefficient queries into more efficient ones through creative use of MySQL's `ORDER BY` and `LIMIT` clauses. Consider the following subquery:

```
SELECT id, duration FROM movie
  WHERE duration =
  (SELECT MAX(duration) FROM movie);
```

This works better as the following query, which is simpler to read and also runs much faster:

```
SELECT id, duration FROM movie
  ORDER BY duration DESC
  LIMIT 0,1;
```

Use Temporary Tables for Transient Data or Calculations

MySQL also lets you create temporary tables with the `CREATE TEMPORARY TABLE` command. These tables are so-called because they remain in existence only for the duration of a single MySQL session and are automatically deleted when the client that instantiates them closes its connection with the MySQL server. These tables come in handy for transient, session-based data or calculations, or for the temporary storage of data. And because they're session-dependent, two different sessions can use the same table name without conflicting.

Since temporary tables are stored in memory, they are significantly faster than disk-based tables. Consequently, they can be effectively used as intermediate storage areas, to speed up query execution by helping to break up complex queries into simpler components, or as a substitute for subquery and join support.

MySQL's `INSERT...SELECT` syntax, together with its `IGNORE` keyword and its support for temporary tables, provides numerous opportunities for creative rewriting of `SELECT` queries to have them execute faster. For example, say you have a complex query that involves selecting a set of distinct values from a particular field, and the MySQL engine is unable to optimize your query because of its complexity. Creative SQL programmers can improve performance by breaking down the single complex query into numerous simple queries (which lend themselves better to optimization) and then using the `INSERT IGNORE...SELECT` command to save the results generated to a temporary table, after first creating the temporary table with a UNIQUE key on the appropriate field. The result is a set of distinct values for that field and possibly faster query execution.

Explicitly Specify Required Fields
It's common to see queries like these:

```
SELECT (*) FROM airport;
SELECT COUNT(*) FROM airport;
```

These queries use the asterisk (*) wildcard for convenience. However, this convenience comes at a price: The * wildcard forces MySQL to read every field or record in the table, adding to the overall query processing time. To avoid this, explicitly name the output fields you wish to see in the result set, as shown in this example:

```
SELECT id, name FROM airport;
SELECT COUNT(id) FROM airport;
```

Index Join Fields
Fields that are accessed frequently should be indexed. As a general rule, if you have a field involved in searching, grouping, or sorting, indexing it will likely result in a performance gain. Indexing should include fields that are part of join operations or fields that appear with clauses such as WHERE, GROUP BY, or ORDER BY. In addition, joining tables on integer fields, rather than on character fields, will produce better performance.

Use Small Transactions
Clichéd though it might be, the KISS (Keep It Simple, Stupid!) principle is particularly applicable in the complex world of transactions. This is because MySQL uses a row-level locking mechanism to prevent simultaneous transactions from editing the same record in the database and possibly corrupting it. The row-level locking mechanism prevents more than one transaction from accessing a row at the same time—this safeguards the data, but has the disadvantage of causing other transactions to wait until the transaction initiating the locks has completed its work. So long as the transaction is small, this wait time is not very noticeable. When you are dealing with a large database and many complex transactions, however, the long wait time while the various transactions wait for each other to release locks can significantly affect performance.

For this reason, it is generally considered a good idea to keep the size of your transactions small and to have them make their changes quickly and exit so that other transactions queued behind them do not get unduly delayed. At the application level, two common strategies exist for accomplishing this.

● Ensure that all user input required for the transaction is available before issuing a START TRANSACTION command. Often, novice application designers initiate a transaction before the complete set of values needed by it is available. Other transactions initiated at the same time now have to wait while the user inputs the required data and the application processes it, and then asks for more data, and so on. In a single-user environment, these delays will not matter as much because no other transactions will be trying to access the database. In a multiuser scenario, however, a delay caused by a single transaction can have a ripple effect on all other transactions queued in the system, resulting in severe performance degradation.

● Try breaking down large transactions into smaller subtransactions and executing them independently. This will ensure that each subtransaction executes quickly, freeing up valuable system resources that would otherwise be used to maintain the state of the system.

Optimize Table Design and Server Configuration

The techniques discussed in this section are all suggestions for application-layer optimization. However, for further performance improvements, you should also consider various techniques for optimizing performance at the database layer, such as:

● Using indexes to speed up searching, grouping, or sorting

● Selecting an appropriate table engine

● Specifying table join fields to be of the same data type and length

● Increasing the available memory for various server-side buffers, such as the read buffer, the sort buffer, and the thread cache.

You'll find more information on these techniques in the manual for your database server.

Lazy Loading

Both the Zend Framework and Doctrine include autoloaders that can automatically find and load class definition files "on demand." This technique, commonly known as *lazy loading*, can significantly improve performance by reducing the number of file reads performed by a PHP script.

To activate the Zend Framework autoloader, the Zend Framework manual suggests adding the following lines of code to the application's *index.php* script:

```
<?php
require_once 'Zend/Loader/Autoloader.php';
Zend_Loader_Autoloader::getInstance();
?>
```

To fully benefit from the autoloader, it is also necessary to strip out all the `require_once()` and `include_once()` function calls from your Zend Framework installation. The Zend Framework manual provides an example of a simple command-line script that can do this for you automatically. You'll find a link to the relevant manual page at the end of this chapter.

It's also a good idea to rearrange your PHP include path such that the Zend Framework directory is at or near the top of the list. This is because when attempting to `require()` or `include()` a file, PHP will look in each directory on the include path, and this can end up being a time-consuming operation when the target directory is at the end of the include path. Moving the Zend Framework directory ahead of others helps reduce the time taken to find and load included files.

Try This 12-1 Improving Application Performance

Let's now look at utilizing some of the techniques discussed in the preceding sections to improve the performance of the SQUARE example application.

NOTE
The following section includes a discussion of how to cache application data in memcached, the distributed memory caching system. It assumes that you have a working installation of the memcached server, together with the PHP memcached extension. In case you don't already have these components, you can download them from the Web using the links at the end of the chapter. If memcached is not available for your platform, or if you're unable to get it working correctly with PHP, you can still try out the following example simply by switching the second cache to use a file backend instead of a memory backend in the example configuration.

Configuring the Application Cache

This example will make use of two caches: a disk cache and a memcached memory cache. To keep things simple, this example assumes that the memcached server is running on the local host, using default parameters, and requires no special configuration. So, the first step is to define a location for the file cache, and then configure cache parameters using the Zend_Cache_Manager component.

To begin, create the directory for the file cache, as follows:

```
shell> cd /usr/local/apache/htdocs/square/data
shell> mkdir cache
```

Then, update the application configuration file at *$APP_DIR/application/configs/application.ini* and add the following directive to it:

```
resources.cachemanager.news.frontend.name = Core
resources.cachemanager.news.frontend.options.lifetime = 600
resources.cachemanager.news.frontend.options.automatic_serialization = true
resources.cachemanager.news.backend.name = File
resources.cachemanager.news.backend.options.cache_dir =
APPLICATION_PATH "/../data/cache"

resources.cachemanager.memory.frontend.name = Core
resources.cachemanager.memory.frontend.options.lifetime = 300
```

(continued)

```
resources.cachemanager.memory.frontend.options.automatic_serialization = true
resources.cachemanager.memory.backend.name = Memcached
resources.cachemanager.memory.backend.options.servers.host = localhost
resources.cachemanager.memory.backend.options.servers.port = 11211
resources.cachemanager.memory.backend.options.servers.timeout = 5
resources.cachemanager.memory.backend.options.servers.retry_interval = 10
```

With all the configuration out of the way, let's start caching!

Caching Translation Strings

Both Zend_Translate and Zend_Locale can use a preconfigured Zend_Cache instance to store locale data and translation strings for fast lookup. It's quite easy to set up caching for these components: Simply pass their static `setCache()` methods a correctly configured Zend_Cache instance, and they'll take care of the rest.

To enable caching for these two components, update the application bootstrapper with a new `_initCache()` method, as follows:

```php
<?php
class Bootstrap extends Zend_Application_Bootstrap_Bootstrap
{
  protected function _initCache()
  {
    $this->bootstrap('cachemanager');
    $manager = $this->getResource('cachemanager');
    $memoryCache = $manager->getCache('memory');
    Zend_Locale::setCache($memoryCache);
    Zend_Translate::setCache($memoryCache);
  }
}
```

Caching Query Results

If you take a look at the `Catalog_ItemController::displayAction` and the `Catalog_AdminItemController::displayAction`, you'll see that both actions use the same Doctrine query, with one minor difference: The former contains an additional check to ensure that the catalog item has been approved for display to the public. Since this is essentially the same code repeated twice over, it is an ideal candidate for refactoring into a model method.

To do this, add the following method to the Square_Model_Item model class, at *$APP_DIR/library/Square/Model/Item.php*:

```php
<?php
class Square_Model_Item extends Square_Model_BaseItem
{
  public function getItem($id, $active = true)
  {
    $q = Doctrine_Query::create()
         ->from('Square_Model_Item i')
```

```
            ->leftJoin('i.Square_Model_Country c')
            ->leftJoin('i.Square_Model_Grade g')
            ->leftJoin('i.Square_Model_Type t')
            ->where('i.RecordID = ?', $id);
    if ($active) {
      $q->addWhere('i.DisplayStatus = 1')
        ->addWhere('i.DisplayUntil >= CURDATE()');
    }
    return $q->fetchArray();
  }
}
```

Then, update the `Catalog_ItemController::displayAction` method to reference the `getItem()` method defined in the model, instead of formulating the Doctrine query directly. While you're at it, go ahead and cache the results of the method using the memory cache defined earlier. Here's what the revised `Catalog_ItemController::displayAction` method will look like:

```php
<?php
class Catalog_ItemController extends Zend_Controller_Action
{
  // action to display a catalog item
  public function displayAction()
  {
    // set filters and validators for GET input
    $filters = array(
      'id' => array('HtmlEntities', 'StripTags', 'StringTrim')
    );
    $validators = array(
      'id' => array('NotEmpty', 'Int')
    );
    $input = new Zend_Filter_Input($filters, $validators);
    $input->setData($this->getRequest()->getParams());

    // test if input is valid
    // retrieve requested record from cache or database
    // attach to view
    if ($input->isValid()) {
      $memoryCache = $this->getInvokeArg('bootstrap')
                          ->getResource('cachemanager')
                          ->getCache('memory');
      if (!($result = $memoryCache->load('public_item_'.$input->id))) {
        $item = new Square_Model_Item;
        $result = $item->getItem($input->id, true);
        $memoryCache->save($result, 'public_item_'.$input->id);
      }
      if (count($result) == 1) {
        $this->view->item = $result[0];
```

(continued)

```
                $this->view->images = array();
                $config = $this->getInvokeArg('bootstrap')->getOption('uploads');
                foreach (glob("{$config['uploadPath']}/
                  {$this->view->item['RecordID']}_*") as $file) {
                  $this->view->images[] = basename($file);
                }
                $configs = $this->getInvokeArg('bootstrap')->getOption('configs');
                $localConfig = new Zend_Config_Ini($configs['localConfigPath']);
                $this->view->seller = $localConfig->user->displaySellerInfo;
                $registry = Zend_Registry::getInstance();
                $this->view->locale = $registry->get('Zend_Locale');
                $this->view->recordDate = new Zend_Date($result[0]['RecordDate']);
              } else {
                throw new Zend_Controller_Action_Exception('Page not found', 404);
              }
            } else {
              throw new Zend_Controller_Action_Exception('Invalid input');
            }
          }
        }
    }
```

A similar approach can be followed with the `Catalog_AdminItemController::dis playAction`. Look in the code archive for this chapter, which you can download from **http:// www.zf-beginners-guide.com/**, for the revised code.

Ask the Expert

Q: How does refactoring model methods help in improving performance?

A: Chapter 4 discussed the "fat model, skinny controller" approach, which proposes that business logic should be located within models, rather than controllers, wherever possible. In addition to various other benefits, following this approach can improve performance when it is used in combination with caching. As shown earlier in the section "Caching Query Results," you can use caching to block the method calls on the model altogether if cached result data already exists, thereby reducing the number of lines of code that need to be executed. And fewer lines of code automatically translates to faster script parsing and execution.

Caching Twitter and Blog Feeds

In its current incarnation, the `NewsController::indexAction` retrieves a fresh set of Twitter search results and the most current news and blog feeds on every request. This data is accessed over HTTP and is expensive to retrieve; at the same time, it is also non-critical, low-impact information. This makes it an ideal target for caching.

Consider the following revision of the `NewsController::indexAction`, which uses the File frontend to cache Twitter search results and blog/news feeds in order to improve response times:

```php
<?php
class NewsController extends Zend_Controller_Action
{
  public function indexAction()
  {
    // get Twitter search feed
    $q = 'philately';
    $this->view->q = $q;

    // get cache
    $fileCache = $this->getInvokeArg('bootstrap')
                      ->getResource('cachemanager')
                      ->getCache('news');

    $id = 'twitter';
    if(!($this->view->tweets = $fileCache->load($id))) {
      $twitter = new Zend_Service_Twitter_Search();
      $this->view->tweets = $twitter->search($q,
        array('lang' => 'en', 'rpp' => 8, 'show_user' => true));
      $fileCache->save($this->view->tweets, $id);
    }

    Zend_Feed_Reader::setCache($fileCache);
    $this->view->feeds = array();
    // get Google News Atom feed
    $gnewsFeed = "http://news.google.com/news?hl=en&q=$q&output=atom";
    $this->view->feeds[0] = Zend_Feed_Reader::import($gnewsFeed);

    // get BPMA RSS feed
    $bpmaFeed = "http://www.postalheritage.org.uk/news/RSS";
    $this->view->feeds[1] = Zend_Feed_Reader::import($bpmaFeed);
  }
}
```

Notice from the previous listing that Zend_Feed_Reader caching is enabled with a simple call to the static `Zend_Feed_Reader::setCache()`, passing it an instance of a configured Zend_Cache object.

If you were to measure application performance before and after making the above changes, you'd notice a distinct improvement in performance. To illustrate, consider Table 12-3, which displays sample "before" and "after" statistics using ApacheBench on a test deployment of the SQUARE application. The report was generated for 100 total requests, with a concurrency level of 10.

URL	Without Caching		With Caching		Improvement with Caching (percent)
	Number of requests served per second	Mean time per request (ms)	Number of requests served per second	Mean time per request (ms)	
http://square.localhost/news	0.45	2242.00	2.07	483.91	Approximately 360 percent
http://square.localhost/catalog/item/1	3.32	301.563	9.52	105.00	Approximately 187 percent

Table 12-3   ApacheBench Benchmarks for the Example Application, Pre- and Post-Cache Implementation

Ask the Expert

Q: Why aren't you using the Doctrine result cache to cache query results?

A: While it is certainly possible to use the Doctrine result cache for query results, doing so invariably requires one to load the Doctrine model(s). The approach used in this example bypasses this step, such that the Doctrine model is not invoked at all. This reduces the amount of code executed even further and only helps to increase overall performance.

Summary

This chapter, the last in this book, explored the important topic of Zend Framework performance optimization, discussing some of the techniques and options available to help you squeeze a little more speed out of your application. In addition to providing a quick overview of the tools available for performance analysis and code profiling, the chapter examined various strategies for performance optimization, including query and output caching, lazy loading, SQL query tuning, and code refactoring.

Application optimization is almost a science unto itself, and it is impossible to cover in the limited space available in this chapter. However, adopting these techniques will help you build more efficient applications, and they should be a part of your standard development process.

To learn more about performance optimization, and to download some of the tools mentioned in this chapter, consider visiting the following links:

- The Zend_Cache component, at
  http://framework.zend.com/manual/en/zend.cache.html

- The Zend_Db_Profiler component, at
  http://framework.zend.com/manual/en/zend.db.profiler.html

- Information on Doctrine caching, at
  http://www.doctrine-project.org/documentation/manual/1_1/en/caching

- Information on MySQL performance optimization, at
  http://dev.mysql.com/doc/refman/5.1/en/optimization.html

- Strategies for Zend Framework performance optimization, at
  http://framework.zend.com/manual/en/performance.html

- ApacheBench documentation, at
  http://httpd.apache.org/docs/2.0/programs/ab.html

- WCAT, at **http://www.iis.net/downloads/default.aspx?tabid=34&i=1466&g=6**

- Xdebug, at **http://xdebug.org/**

- Webgrind, at **http://code.google.com/p/webgrind/**

- Wincachegrind, at **http://sourceforge.net/projects/wincachegrind/**

- Kcachegrind, at **http://kcachegrind.sourceforge.net/**

- The PEAR Benchmark package, at
  http://pear.php.net/package/Benchmark

- Memcached, at **http://memcached.org/**

- The PHP memcached extension, at
  http://pecl.php.net/package/memcache

- The Imind Doctrine profiler, at
  http://code.google.com/p/imind-php/wiki/Imind_Profiler_Doctrine_Firebug

- A discussion of profiling PHP scripts with Xdebug and Webgrind (Anant Garg), at
  http://anantgarg.com/2009/03/10/php-xdebug-webgrind-installation/

Although you've reached the end of this book, it should be clear that your Zend Framework odyssey is far from over… if anything, it's only just beginning! The preceding chapters have given you the grounding necessary to begin creating your own high-quality Zend Framework applications. The rest is up to you and your imagination. Good luck, and happy coding!

Appendix

Installing and Configuring Required Software

Key Skills & Concepts

- Learn to obtain and install MySQL, PHP, and Apache software from the Internet
- Perform basic testing to ensure that the applications are working correctly
- Find out how to automatically activate all required components on system startup
- Take basic steps to safeguard the security of your MySQL installation

In this book, you learned about the Zend Framework and how it can be used to build sophisticated Web applications. The examples in this book assumed that you have a correctly configured Apache/MySQL/PHP development environment. In case you don't, this appendix will show you how to install and configure these components and create a development environment that can be used to run the code examples in this book.

CAUTION

This appendix is intended to provide an overview and general guide to the process of installing and configuring MySQL, PHP, and Apache on UNIX and Windows. It is *not* intended as a replacement for the installation documentation that ships with each software package. If you encounter difficulties installing the various programs described here, visit the respective program's Web site or search the Web for detailed troubleshooting information and advice (some links are provided at the end of this appendix).

Obtaining the Software

There are a couple of different ways you can get an Apache/MySQL/PHP development environment running on your Windows or *NIX system:

1. You can download an all-in-one, integrated stack that contains all the necessary pieces and dependencies, preconfigured to work together.
2. You can download the different pieces separately and configure them yourself.

The first approach is recommended if you're new to PHP, or to open-source development in general, as it will get you up and running with minimal heartache. Here are two popular stacks you should consider:

- Zend Server Community Edition is an integrated, robust stack provided by Zend Technologies. In addition to the standard Apache/MySQL/PHP components, it also includes a number of debugging and optimization tools, plus (as a bonus) the latest version of the Zend Framework. It is available for Microsoft Windows, Mac OS X, and Linux operating systems, and it can be freely downloaded from **http://www.zend.com/**.

- XAMPP is a community-supported distribution that includes the latest versions of Apache, PHP, MySQL, and Perl. It is fully configured for out-of-the-box use, and is extremely popular for quickly setting up a PHP-based development environment. It also includes additional tools, namely, an FTP server and a Web-based MySQL management tool. It is available for Microsoft Windows, Mac OS X, Linux, and Solaris, and can be freely downloaded from **http://www.apachefriends.org/en/index.html**.

The downside of using an integrated stack is that you'll learn significantly less than if you use the second, do-it-yourself approach, since all the components come preconfigured for you. If you have the inclination and interest, configuring the individual pieces separately is a great learning experience; it is discussed in depth in the rest of this appendix.

The first step is to make sure that you have all the software you need. Here's a list:

- **PHP** PHP provides an application development framework for both Web and console applications. It can be downloaded from **http://www.php.net/**. Here too, both source and binary versions are available for Windows, UNIX, and Mac OS X platforms. UNIX users should download the latest source archive, while Windows users should download the latest binary release. At the time this book goes to press, the most current version of PHP is PHP v5.3.1.

- **Apache** Apache is a feature-rich Web server that works well with PHP. It can be downloaded free of charge from **http://httpd.apache.org/** in both source and binary form, for a variety of platforms. UNIX users should download the latest source archive, while Windows users should download a binary installer appropriate for their version of Windows. At the time this book goes to press, the most current version of the Apache server is Apache v2.2.14.

- **MySQL** The MySQL database server provides robust and scalable data storage/retrieval. It is available in both source and binary versions from **http://www.mysql.com/**. Binary distributions are available for Linux, Solaris, FreeBSD, Mac OS X, Windows, HP-UX, IBM AIX, SCO OpenUNIX, and SGI Irix, and source distributions are available for both Windows and UNIX platforms. The binary version is recommended, for two reasons: It is easier to install, and is optimized for use on different platforms by the MySQL development team. At the time this book goes to press, the most current version of the MySQL database server is MySQL v5.1.43.

In addition to these four basic components, UNIX users may also require some supporting libraries. Here's a list:

- The *libxml2* library, available from **http://www.xmlsoft.org/**

- The *zlib* library, available from **http://www.gzip.org/zlib/**

- The *gd* library, available from **http://www.boutell.com/gd/**

Finally, users on both platforms will need a decompression tool capable of dealing with TAR (Tape Archive) and GZ (GNU Zip) files. On UNIX, the *tar* and *gzip* utilities are they are usually included with the operating system. On Windows, a good decompression tool is WinZip, available from **http://www.winzip.com/**.

NOTE
The examples in this book have been developed and tested on MySQL v5.1.30, with Apache v2.2.14, PHP v5.3.1, and Zend Framework v1.9 and v1.10.

Installing and Configuring the Software

Once the required software has been obtained, the next step is to install the various pieces and get them talking to each other. The following sections outline the steps for both Windows and UNIX platforms.

NOTE
If you use an Apple workstation, you can find instructions for installing PHP on Mac OS X in the PHP manual, at **http://www.php.net/manual/en/install.macosx.php**.

Installing on UNIX

The installation process for UNIX involves a number of distinct steps: installing MySQL from a binary distribution; compiling and installing PHP from a source distribution; and compiling and configuring Apache to properly handle requests for PHP Web pages. These steps are described in greater detail in the following subsections.

Installing MySQL
To install MySQL from a binary distribution, use the following steps:

1. Ensure that you are logged in as the system's root user.

   ```
   [user@host]# su - root
   ```

2. Extract the content of the MySQL binary archive to an appropriate directory on your system—for example, */usr/local/*.

   ```
   [root@host]# cd /usr/local
   [root@host]# tar -xzvf /tmp/mysql-5.1.30-linux-i686-glibc23.tar.gz
   ```

   The MySQL files should be extracted into a directory named according to the format *mysql-version-os-architecture*—for example, *mysql-5.1.30-linux-i686-glibc23*.

3. For ease of use, set a shorter name for the directory created in Step 2 by creating a soft link named *mysql* pointing to this directory in the same location.

   ```
   [root@host]# ln -s mysql-5.1.30-linux-i686-glibc23 mysql
   ```

4. For security reasons, the MySQL database server process should never run as the system superuser. Therefore, it is necessary to create a special mysql user and group for this purpose.

Do this with the `groupadd` and `useradd` commands, and then change the ownership of the MySQL installation directory to this user and group:

```
[root@host]# groupadd mysql
[root@host]# useradd -g mysql mysql
[root@host]# chown -R mysql /usr/local/mysql
[root@host]# chgrp -R mysql /usr/local/mysql
```

5. Initialize the MySQL tables with the *mysql_install_db* initialization script included in the distribution.

```
[root@host]# /usr/local/mysql/scripts/mysql_install_db --user=mysql
```

Figure A-1 demonstrates what you should see when you do this.

As the output in Figure A-1 suggests, this initialization script prepares and installs the various MySQL base tables, and also sets up default access permissions for MySQL.

6. Alter the ownership of the MySQL binaries so that they are owned by `root`.

```
[root@host]# chown -R root /usr/local/mysql
```

Ensure that the `mysql` user created in Step 4 has read/write privileges to the MySQL data directory.

```
[root@host]# chown -R mysql /usr/local/mysql/data
```

7. Start the MySQL server by manually running the *mysqld_safe* script.

```
[root@host]# /usr/local/mysql/bin/mysqld_safe --user=mysql &
```

MySQL should now start up normally.

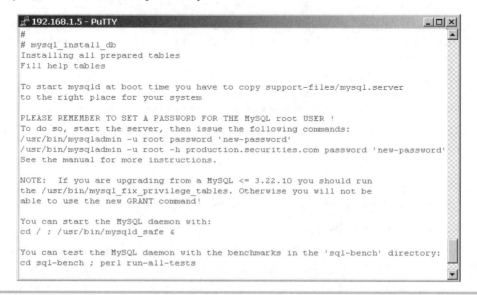

Figure A-1   The output of the mysql_install_db script

Once installation has been successfully completed and the server has started up, skip down to the section entitled "Testing MySQL" to verify that it is functioning as it should.

Installing Apache and PHP

PHP can be integrated with the Apache Web server in one of two ways: as a dynamic module that is loaded into the Web server at run time, or as a static module that is integrated into the Apache source tree at build time. Each alternative has advantages and disadvantages:

● Installing PHP as a dynamic module makes it easier to upgrade your PHP build at a later date, as you only need to recompile the PHP module and not the rest of the Apache Web server. On the flip side, with a dynamically loaded module, performance tends to be lower than with a static module, which is more closely integrated with the server.

● Installing PHP as a static module improves performance, because the module is compiled directly into the Apache source tree. However, this close integration has an important drawback: If you ever decide to upgrade your PHP build, you will need to reintegrate the newer PHP module into the Apache source tree and recompile the Apache Web server.

This section shows you how to compile PHP as a dynamic module that is loaded into the Apache server at run time.

1. Ensure that you are logged in as the system's root user.

```
[user@host]# su - root
```

2. Extract the contents of the Apache source archive to your system's temporary directory.

```
[root@host]# cd /tmp
[root@host]# tar -xzvf /tmp/httpd-2.2.14.tar.gz
```

3. To enable PHP to be loaded dynamically, the Apache server must be compiled with Dynamic Shared Object (DSO) support. This support is enabled by passing the *--enable-module=so* option to the Apache *configure* script, as follows:

```
[root@host]# cd /tmp/httpd-2.2.14
[root@host]# ./configure --prefix=/usr/local/apache
               --enable-module=so --enable-rewrite
```

4. Now, compile the server using the make command, and install it to the system using make install.

```
[root@host]# make
[root@host]# make install
```

Figure A-2 illustrates what you might see during the compilation process.

Apache should now have been installed to */usr/local/apache/*.

5. Next, proceed to compile and install PHP. Begin by extracting the contents of the PHP source archive to your system's temporary directory.

```
[root@host]# cd /tmp
[root@host]# tar -xzvf /tmp/php-5.3.1.tar.gz
```

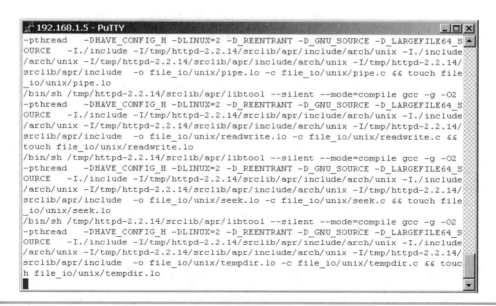

```
192.168.1.5 - PuTTY
-pthread    -DHAVE_CONFIG_H -DLINUX=2 -D_REENTRANT -D_GNU_SOURCE -D_LARGEFILE64_S
OURCE    -I./include -I/tmp/httpd-2.2.14/srclib/apr/include/arch/unix -I./include
/arch/unix -I/tmp/httpd-2.2.14/srclib/apr/include/arch/unix -I/tmp/httpd-2.2.14/
srclib/apr/include    -o file_io/unix/pipe.lo -c file_io/unix/pipe.c && touch file
_io/unix/pipe.lo
/bin/sh /tmp/httpd-2.2.14/srclib/apr/libtool --silent --mode=compile gcc -g -O2
-pthread    -DHAVE_CONFIG_H -DLINUX=2 -D_REENTRANT -D_GNU_SOURCE -D_LARGEFILE64_S
OURCE    -I./include -I/tmp/httpd-2.2.14/srclib/apr/include/arch/unix -I./include
/arch/unix -I/tmp/httpd-2.2.14/srclib/apr/include/arch/unix -I/tmp/httpd-2.2.14/
srclib/apr/include    -o file_io/unix/readwrite.lo -c file_io/unix/readwrite.c &&
touch file_io/unix/readwrite.lo
/bin/sh /tmp/httpd-2.2.14/srclib/apr/libtool --silent --mode=compile gcc -g -O2
-pthread    -DHAVE_CONFIG_H -DLINUX=2 -D_REENTRANT -D_GNU_SOURCE -D_LARGEFILE64_S
OURCE    -I./include -I/tmp/httpd-2.2.14/srclib/apr/include/arch/unix -I./include
/arch/unix -I/tmp/httpd-2.2.14/srclib/apr/include/arch/unix -I/tmp/httpd-2.2.14/
srclib/apr/include    -o file_io/unix/seek.lo -c file_io/unix/seek.c && touch file
_io/unix/seek.lo
/bin/sh /tmp/httpd-2.2.14/srclib/apr/libtool --silent --mode=compile gcc -g -O2
-pthread    -DHAVE_CONFIG_H -DLINUX=2 -D_REENTRANT -D_GNU_SOURCE -D_LARGEFILE64_S
OURCE    -I./include -I/tmp/httpd-2.2.14/srclib/apr/include/arch/unix -I./include
/arch/unix -I/tmp/httpd-2.2.14/srclib/apr/include/arch/unix -I/tmp/httpd-2.2.14/
srclib/apr/include    -o file_io/unix/tempdir.lo -c file_io/unix/tempdir.c && touc
h file_io/unix/tempdir.lo
```

Figure A-2   Compiling Apache

6. This step is the most important in the PHP installation process. It involves sending arguments to the PHP *configure* script to configure the PHP module. These command-line parameters specify which PHP extensions should be activated, and they also tell PHP where to find the supporting libraries needed by those extensions.

```
[root@host]# cd /tmp/php-5.3.1
[root@host]# ./configure --prefix=/usr/local/php
            --with-apxs2=/usr/local/apache/bin/apxs
            --with-zlib --with-gd --with-mysqli=mysqlnd
            --with-pdo-mysql=mysqlnd
```

Here is a brief explanation of what each of these arguments does:

- The *--with-apxs2* argument tells PHP where to find Apache's APXS (APache eXtenSion) script. This script simplifies the task of building and installing loadable modules for Apache.

- The *--with-zlib* argument tells PHP to activate compression (zip) features, which are used by different PHP services.

- The *--with-gd* argument tells PHP to activate image-processing features.

- The *--with-mysqli* argument activates PHP's MySQLi extension and tells PHP to use the new MySQL native driver (mysqlnd) as the MySQL client library.

- The *--with-pdo-mysql* argument activates PHP's MySQL PDO driver and tells PHP to use the MySQL native driver as the MySQL client library.

7. Next, compile and install PHP using make and make install.

```
[root@host]# make
[root@host]# make install
```

You can also run make test at this point to run the unit tests for PHP and review any failures. If all goes well, PHP should now have been installed to */usr/local/php/*.

8. The final step in the installation process consists of configuring Apache to correctly recognize requests for PHP pages. This is accomplished by opening the Apache configuration file, *httpd.conf* (which be found in the *conf/* subdirectory of the Apache installation directory), in a text editor and adding the following line to it:

```
AddType application/x-httpd-php .php
```

Save the changes to the file. Also, check to make sure that the following line appears somewhere in the file:

```
LoadModule php5_module          modules/libphp5.so
```

9. Start the Apache server by manually running the *apachectl* script.

```
[root@host]# /usr/local/apache/bin/apachectl start
```

Apache should start up normally.

Once installation has been successfully completed and the server has successfully started, skip down to the section entitled "Testing PHP" to verify that all is functioning as it should.

Installing on Windows

Compiling applications on Windows is a challenging process, especially for novice developers. With this in mind, it is advisable for Windows users to focus instead on installing and configuring prebuilt binary releases of MySQL, SQLite, PHP, and Apache, instead of attempting to compile them from source code. These releases can be downloaded from the Web sites listed earlier, in the section "Obtaining the Software," and are to be installed one after another, as outlined in the following subsections.

Installing MySQL

MySQL is available in both source and binary forms for both 32-bit and 64-bit versions of Microsoft Windows. Most often, you will want to use either the "Essentials" or "Complete" binary distributions, which include an automated installer to get MySQL up and running in just a few minutes.

To install MySQL from a binary distribution, use the following steps:

1. Log in as an administrator (if you're using Windows XP/Vista/7).

2. Double-click the *mysql-*.msi* file to begin the installation process. You should see a welcome screen. (see Figure A-3).

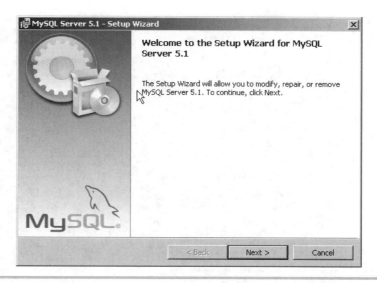

Figure A-3 Beginning MySQL installation on Windows

3. Select the type of installation required.

Most often, a Typical installation will do; however, if you're the kind who likes tweaking default settings, or if you're just short of disk space, select the Custom installation option, and decide which components of the package should be installed.

4. MySQL should now begin installing to your system.

5. Once installation is complete, you should see a success notification. At this point, you will have the option to launch the MySQL Server Instance Configuration Wizard, to complete configuration of the software. Select this option, and you should see the corresponding welcome screen.

6. Select the type of configuration. In most cases, the Standard Configuration will suffice.

7. Install MySQL as a Windows service, such that it starts and stops automatically with Windows (see Figure A-4).

8. Enter a password for the MySQL administrator (`root`) account (see Figure A-5).

The server will now be configured with your specified settings, and automatically started. You will be presented with a success notification once all required tasks are complete.

You can now proceed to test the server as described in the section "Testing MySQL," to ensure that everything is working as it should.

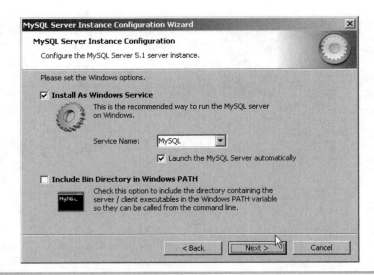

Figure A-4 Setting up the MySQL service

Installing Apache
Once MySQL is installed, the next step is to install the Apache Web server. On Windows, this is a point-and-click process, similar to that used when installing MySQL.

1. Begin by double-clicking the Apache installer to begin the installation process. You should see a welcome screen (see Figure A-6).

2. Read the license agreement, and accept the terms to proceed.

Figure A-5 Setting the administrator password

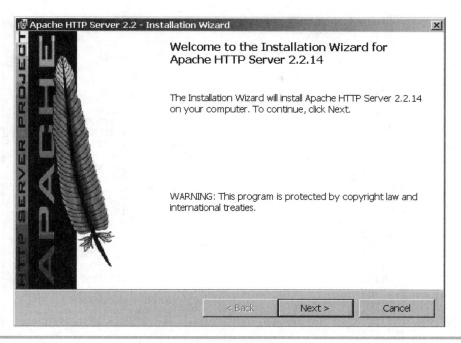

Figure A-6 Beginning Apache installation on Windows

3. Read the descriptive information, and then proceed to enter basic server information and the e-mail address to be displayed on error pages.

4. Select the type of installation required. You can select the Custom installation option if you want to decide which components of the package should be installed.

5. Select the location to which Apache should be installed—for example, *C:\Program Files\ Apache*.

6. Apache should now begin installing to the specified location. The installation process takes a few minutes to complete, so this is a good time to get yourself a cup of coffee.

7. Once installation is complete, the Apache installer will display a success notification and also start the Apache Web server.

Installing PHP

There are two versions of the PHP binary release for Windows—a ZIP archive, which contains all the bundled PHP extensions and requires manual installation, and an automated Windows Installer version, which contains only the basic PHP binary with no extra extensions. This section outlines the installation process for the PHP ZIP archive.

1. Log in as an administrator (if you're using Windows XP/Vista/7) and unzip the distribution archive to a directory on your system—for example, *C:\php*. After extraction, this directory should look something like Figure A-7.

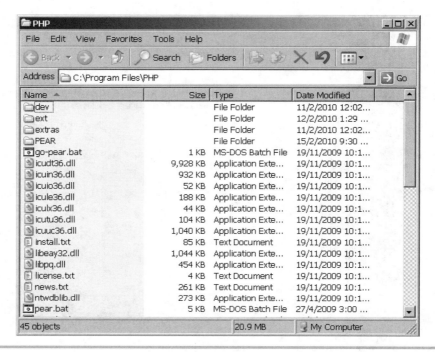

Figure A-7 The directory structure created on unpackaging a PHP binary distribution for Windows

2. Next, rename the file *php.ini-recommended* in your PHP installation directory to *php.ini*. This file contains configuration settings for PHP, which can be used to alter the way it works. Read the comments within the file to learn more about the available settings.

3. Within the *php.ini* file, locate the following line:

```
extension_dir = "./"
```

Alter it to read

```
extension_dir = "c:\php\ext\"
```

This tells PHP where to locate the extensions supplied with the package. Remember to replace the path "*c:\php*" with the actual location of your PHP installation.

4. Next, look for the following lines and remove the semicolon at the beginning (if present) so that they read as follows:

```
extension=php_mysqli.dll
extension=php_pdo_sqlite.dll
extension=php_pdo_mysql.dll
extension=php_zip.dll
extension=php_gd2.dll
```

This takes care of activating PHP's MySQL, GD, Zip, and PDO extensions.

5. Open the Apache configuration file, *httpd.conf* (which can be found in the *conf/* subdirectory of the Apache installation directory) in a text editor, and add the following lines to it:

```
AddType application/x-httpd-php .php
LoadModule php5_module        modules/libphp5.so
```

These lines tell Apache how to deal with PHP scripts and where to find the *php.ini* configuration file.

6. When the Apache server is installed, it adds itself to the Start menu. Use this Start menu group to stop and restart the server, as shown in Figure A-8.

PHP is now installed and configured to work with Apache. To test it, skip down to the section entitled "Testing PHP."

Adding memcached Support to PHP Chapter 12 of this book makes use of the memcached memory caching engine. To add support for this engine to PHP, there are a few additional steps to be performed. Very briefly, they are as follows:

1. Download, compile, and install the memcached and libevent libraries from **http://tangent .org/552/libmemcached.html** and **http://www.monkey.org/~provos/libevent/** (*NIX only).

2. Install the memcached server from **http://memcached.org/** (*NIX source) or **http://code .jellycan.com/memcached/** (Windows binary).

3. Install the memcache PHP extension from PECL at **http://pecl.php.net/package/ memcache** (*NIX source) or **http://downloads.php.net/pierre/** (Windows binary).

4. Activate the memcache PHP extension in the PHP configuration file and restart the Web server for the changes to take effect.

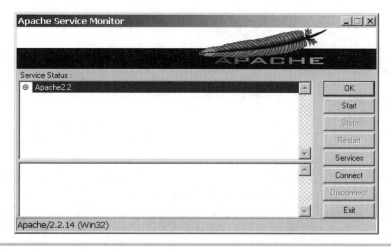

Figure A-8 Apache server controls on Windows

Testing the Software

Once all the software components have been installed, use the following sections to test that they are all correctly configured and active.

Testing MySQL

Once MySQL has been successfully installed, the base tables have been initialized, and the server has been started, you can verify that all is working as it should via some simple tests.

First, start up the MySQL command-line client by changing to the *bin/* subdirectory of your MySQL installation directory and typing the following command:

```
prompt# mysql -u root
```

You should be rewarded with a prompt, as follows:

```
Welcome to the MySQL monitor.  Commands end with ; or \g.
Your MySQL connection id is 26288
Server version: 5.1.30-community MySQL Community Edition (GPL)
Type 'help;' or '\h' for help. Type '\c' to clear the buffer.
mysql>
```

At this point, you are connected to the MySQL server and can begin executing SQL commands or queries to test whether the server is working as it should. Here are a few examples, with their output:

```
mysql> SHOW DATABASES;
+-----------+
| Database  |
+-----------+
| mysql     |
| test      |
+-----------+
2 rows in set (0.13 sec)

mysql> SELECT COUNT(*) FROM mysql.user;
+-----------+
| count(*)  |
+-----------+
|        1  |
+-----------+
1 row in set (0.00 sec)
```

If you see output similar to this example, your MySQL installation is working as it should. Exit the command-line client by typing the command **exit** and you'll be returned to your command prompt.

Testing PHP

Once you've successfully installed PHP as an Apache module, you should test it to ensure that the Web server can recognize PHP scripts and handle them correctly.

To perform this test, create a PHP script in any text editor containing the following lines:

```
<?php
phpinfo();
?>
```

Save this file as *test.php* in your Web server document root (the *htdocs/* subdirectory of your Apache installation directory), and point your browser to *http://localhost/test.php*. You should see a page containing information on the PHP build, as shown in Figure A-9.

Eyeball the list of extensions to make sure that the MySQL, GD, SimpleXML, Zip, and memcached (optional) extensions are active. If they aren't, review the installation procedure, as well as the installation documents that shipped with the software, to see what went wrong.

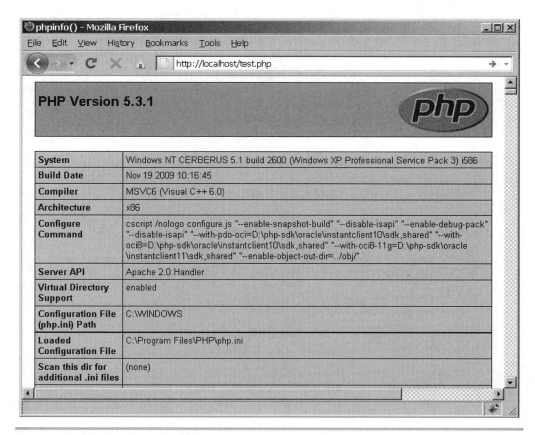

Figure A-9 Viewing the output of the `phpinfo()` command

Setting the MySQL Super-User Password

When MySQL is first installed, access to the database server is restricted to the MySQL administrator, aka 'root'. By default, this user is initialized with a blank password, which is generally considered a Bad Thing. You should therefore rectify this as soon as possible by setting a password for this user via the included *mysqladmin* utility, using the following syntax in UNIX:

```
[root@host]# /usr/local/mysql/bin/mysqladmin -u root password 'new-password'
```

In Windows, you can use the MySQL Server Instance Configuration Wizard, which allows you to set or reset the MySQL administrator password (see the section entitled "Installing on Windows" for more details).

This password change goes into effect immediately, with no requirement to restart the server.

Summary

As popular open-source applications, MySQL, Apache, and PHP are available for a wide variety of platforms and architectures, in both binary and source forms. This appendix demonstrated the process of installing and configuring these software components to create a PHP development environment on the two most common platforms, UNIX and Windows. It also showed you how to configure your system to launch these components automatically every time the system starts up, and it offered some tips on basic MySQL security.

To read more about the installation processes outlined in this appendix, or for detailed troubleshooting advice and assistance, consider visiting the following pages:

- MySQL installation notes, at
  http://dev.mysql.com/doc/refman/5.1/en/installing-binary.html

- General guidelines for compiling Apache on UNIX, at
  http://httpd.apache.org/docs/2.2/install.html

- Windows-specific notes for Apache binary installations, at
  http://httpd.apache.org/docs/2.2/platform/windows.html

- Installation instructions for PHP on Windows, at
  http://www.php.net/manual/en/install.windows.php

- Installation instructions for PHP on UNIX, at
  http://www.php.net/manual/en/install.unix.php

- Installation instructions for PHP on Mac OS X, at
  http://www.php.net/manual/en/install.macosx.php

Index

A

ab (ApacheBench) tool, 382–383
action attribute, 37
action helpers for navigation, 358–359
Action Message Format (AMF), 3, 7
actions overview
    methods, 24
    naming conventions, 34
ActionStack helper, 358
ActiveRecord pattern, 105, 107
adapters
    authentication, 162–164
    translation files, 289–291
addActionContext() method, 193–194
addContext() method, 193–194
addDecorators() method, 96
addDisplayGroup() method, 93
addDocument() method, 183
addElement() method, 53, 93, 150
addField() method, 183
addFilter() method, 70–72, 75
addFilters() method, 72
addHelper() method, 358
adding records, 120–121
addMessage() method, 87

addMultiOption() method, 136
addPath() method, 358
addPrefix() method, 358
addslashes() function, 70
addTranslation() method, 290
addValidator() method, 74, 79, 81, 91–92
addWhere() method, 119
addWriter() method, 255
/admin prefix, 141
adminDeleteAction() method, 142
administrative actions, 140
    controllers, 141
    layout, 142–144
    protecting, 167–168
    routing, 141–142
    structure, 140–141
ALERT log level, 257
Alnum filter, 73
Alnum validator, 77
Alpha filter, 73
Alpha validator, 77, 84
alphabetic and alphanumeric strings, testing for, 74
Amazon Web service, 324–325
amazonAction() method, 324
AMF (Action Message Format), 3, 7
Apache configuration files, 13

429